RUSSIAN THEATER

FROM THE EMPIRE TO THE SOVIETS

BOOKS BY MARC SLONIM

THE EPIC OF RUSSIAN LITERATURE FROM
ITS ORIGINS THROUGH TOLSTOY

MODERN RUSSIAN LITERATURE FROM
CHEKHOV TO THE PRESENT

THREE LOVES OF DOSTOEVSKY

AN OUTLINE OF RUSSIAN LITERATURE

Anthologies

SOVIET LITERATURE
(EDITED WITH GEORGE REAVEY)

MODERN ITALIAN SHORT STORIES

THIS THING CALLED LOVE
(EDITED WITH HARVEY BREIT)

RUSSIAN THEATER

FROM THE EMPIRE TO THE SOVIETS

by MARC SLONIM

THE WORLD PUBLISHING COMPANY

CLEVELAND AND NEW YORK

PUBLISHED BY The World Publishing Company
2231 West 110th Street, Cleveland 2, Ohio

PUBLISHED SIMULTANEOUSLY IN CANADA BY
NELSON, FOSTER & SCOTT LTD.

Library of Congress Catalog Card Number: 61-15304

FIRST EDITION

HC961

CONTENTS

(Illustrations will be found following pages 100 and 260.)

8. THE FIRST YEARS OF THE REVOLUTION 228

The situation of the theaters 228. The Proletcult and the *avant-garde* groups 231. The new mass audience and the socialization of the theater 239. Meyerhold and his activities between 1920 and 1928 243.

9. FROM INNOVATORS TO CONSERVATIVES 257

Tairov and his experiments 259. Vakhtangov's role in the Russian theater 263. M. Chekhov and the workshops 271. The classic repertory 282. The Moscow Art Theater and Academic Theaters during the Revolutionary era 284. Opera and movies of the twenties 288.

10. TWO DECADES OF SOCIALIST REALISM 293

The emergence of Soviet repertory 293. The offensive of RAPP 302. The doctrine and practice of socialist realism 306. The theater in the thirties and forties 308. The liquidation of the *avant-garde* 316. The war interlude 330. The problems of the Soviet theater under Stalin and Zhdanov 335. The "thaw" and the perspectives of the future 339.

AUTHOR'S NOTE

THE AUTHOR of this book did not intend to write a comprehensive history of the Russian theater, which would require several volumes. His purpose was less ambitious: to offer an introduction to a vast and fascinating subject and to provide those who are interested in drama and scenic arts, as well as students of Russian culture, with an outline of main trends in the development of the Russian theater, chiefly in repertory and staging, at the end of the nineteenth and the first half of the twentieth century. In selecting and presenting the material, the author has tried to show the struggle between tradition and innovation which made the theatrical life in Russia so exciting and rich in creative spirit. The necessity to contain the book within a certain size compelled the author to make substantial cuts in the text and did not permit him to deal adequately with ballet and operatic arts or to explore such post-Revolutionary occurrences as the children's theater. He hopes, however, that despite such omissions, his work will be useful as a guide and as an incitement to further study. During the four years it took the author to complete this book, he received assistance from various quarters, and he would like to extend his special thanks to the Slavonic Division of the New York Public Library, and to Mrs. Helen McMaster, a friend and colleague, who read the manuscript and made valuable editorial comments.

MARC SLONIM

Bronxville, N. Y.
1961

RUSSIAN THEATER

FROM THE EMPIRE TO THE SOVIETS

1

The Origins of the Russian Theater

THE FORMAL HISTORY of the Russian theater begins on that memorable day of October 17, 1672, when comedians, directed by a few Germans, gave their first performance at the court of Moscow. But the manifestations of Russian natural theatrical instinct can be traced back, many centuries before this event. In fact, the pagan ceremonies of the ancient Slavs, such as the expulsion of winter and the welcome of spring, and the later Christian festivals of Christmas and Easter, or the mixed rituals of the Carnival, analogous to the Greek Dionysian rites, were true theatrical performances. What remains of them in Russia from the eighteenth, nineteenth, and even twentieth centuries, and has been collected and studied by ethnographers and folklorists, shows a strong drive for self-expression in various ways which definitely stem from prehistoric times and, in any case, from the pre-Christian epoch. In modern Russian the current expression for marriage is "to perform a wedding," and in ancient times the wedding was actually divided in scenes or acts: proposal, engagement, and marriage. Each act had its own subdivisions: sometimes the rape of the bride, the flight and the fight, the reconciliation, the ransom, the religious blessing, the union of the newlyweds, and the traditional proof of the bride's virginity. The wedding lasted two or three days and had solo numbers and choral ensembles. Similarly, professional mourners were invited to a funeral; they were often the same persons who had taken part in the wedding.

17

Reciters of epic ballads also followed a dramatic pattern and accompanied their chants with musical instruments and acting. Choral dancing included a large group of performers; it followed a centuries-old pattern of step and song. Various ceremonies linked with agricultural life, such as the Conjuration of Spring, games connected with cattle breeding, hunting, and weaving, often developed into mass actions of purely theatrical character. In the Ritual of the Goat, similar to that of the Greek drama, a group of disguised peasants, one of them masked to represent the goat, danced and sang to the sounds of a drum and stringed instruments; they came to their master's house before the New Year, during the Christmas holidays, and acted as a chorus, intermingling religious and erotic verses. The Carnival's Funeral was also a well-known popular rite (it inspired the prologue of *The Snow Maiden* by N. Rimsky-Korsakov); next came the "Sending Off the Mermaid." When Greek Orthodox Christianity was introduced into Russia in the tenth century, the external side of the liturgy and the theatrical magnificence of the Mass captured the imagination of princes and of commoners. Later, in the Middle Ages, pagan and Christian influences merged in mixed rituals, such as the lenten carnival with its "burning or seeing off the Butter Week," and with masquerading as animals, mostly goats and foxes.

A coarse substitute for laic theatrical performances was offered by the games or *ludi* of mummers and merrymen, called *skomorokhi* (literally from the Byzantine *skom-archos,* "main entertainer"); in the Middle Ages it corresponded to the German *Spielmann.* Their dancing and gamboling figures with flutes (resembling Attic fauns) can be seen on the ancient murals of Saint Sophia Cathedral in Kiev. Various measures taken by princes and tsars, as well as by the Church, against the skomorokhi between the tenth and sixteenth centuries, show the position they occupied in Russian life. Chroniclers mention various kinds of these "pagans who did the devil's job and spread temptation among the faithful" by playing cymbals and a kind of guitar (*gusli*) and by singing immodest songs. In the sixteenth century the Church complained that groups of vagrant skomorokhi were roaming from one village to another, sometimes in groups of sixty or a hundred persons. Very often they wandered with tamed animals, mostly bears. In general, the exhibition of bears, usually accompanied by a goat (or a buffoon disguised as a goat), a couple of showmen, and trained dogs, was one of the most popular entertainments in Muscovy. The "bear merriment" was so highly appreciated that rich boyards usually kept several bears for the amusement of their family and guests. Princes and tsars and their wives and daughters also took great pleasure in comic acts performed by bears—imitations of how boys steal berries or girls go bathing or fools overeat and overdrink. Court jesters and buffoons borrowed most liberally from the pranks of the skomorokhi and their trained animals. Olearius, who visited Russia in 1630, described wandering musicians singing "shameless" songs, comedians directing puppet shows in which the audiences mostly enjoyed the story of a gypsy selling a horse to the naive Petrushka, and merrymen performing all sorts of obscene frolics. A great deal of this was social satire about boyards and governors, who were shown as being stupid, greedy, and ridiculous.

Between the tenth and sixteenth centuries (and even later) the puppet show was one of the beloved forms of theatrical entertainment. In the nineteenth and even in the twentieth century before the 1917 revolution, in almost every country fair or big market of Central Russia and the Ukraine, large crowds watched with delight the escapades of Petrushka, this Russian Harlequin or Pierrot. In ancient times the puppet show was an addition to the dances, songs, and sketches of the skomorokhi. Undoubtedly their jokes were coarse, their actions crude, and their whole performance probably had strong phallic significance. A higher type of puppet theater came to southern Russia from Poland in the sixteenth century. It became connected with the dramatics of the Kievan Theological Academy where various episodes from the Bible were then enacted. On many occasions the performance was divided into two parts, and after a religious representation there were coarse scenes from current life.

The Greek Orthodox Church did introduce some morality plays in Russia, but unlike those in Catholic countries of Western Europe, they were limited in scope and in number. Since the Mass was celebrated not in Latin but in the native Slavonic tongue, the Russian Clergy did not need the help of morality plays for the enlightenment of its preaching. In fact, the few

morality plays performed in Russia were closely connected with
the liturgy and were usually performed not in the streets but
inside the church itself. The most popular among them were
"Jesus on the Donkey," a dramatic procession which took place
on Palm Sunday, often with the participation of Church dignitaries, the roots of which can be traced back to the first centuries
of Christendom: "The Last Judgment," with frequent emphasis
on horror scenes, and the beloved "Drama of the Burning Furnace." The latter—a story of Anany, Azary, and Misail, the three
adolescents who refused to adore the Golden Calf, were about
to be thrown into the burning cauldron, but were rescued by
angels at the last moment—was usually shown on the last Saturday before Christmas. The furnace, in the form of a pulpit, surrounded by lighted candles, was placed in the middle of the
church. It formed part of the divine service as early as the sixteenth century and remained for some three hundred years the
richest and most diversified religious dramatic performance.

Of all other theatrical shows of later periods, only the academic
or school drama of Catholic origin, brought to the Ukraine from
Poland at the beginning of the seventeenth century, had a literary text and was acted by specially trained companies. Usually
based on some Biblical or evangelical subject, it had a prologue
(often in verse), three or five or even more acts, and was presented first in Latin and then in Russian. Its aim was to popular-
ize religious and moral ideas in allegorical form. In the Kievan
Theological Academy, established in 1615, it was considered an
educational supplement to the study of rhetoric and poetics. The
text was either written by a teacher or chosen from the existing
Polish or Russian repertory; the members of the class enacted
it on holidays or for occasional school festivals. The stage had
two stories: earth and heaven. Unlike the Western stage, the
Russian one had no hell: this, however, is questioned by some
historians. Allegorical figures followed the pattern found in the
book of symbols by the German Jesuit Mazepa: in general, the
school drama was transplanted from Jesuit colleges and preserved
their imprint for a great length of time. The best early drama,
mostly written by St. Dimitry of Rostov (he died in 1709), were
Christ's Passion, Esther and Ahasuerus, and *The Repentant Sinner.* During summer vacation, the students took their plays on

the road and often performed them in the houses of landowners and rich peasants, who paid the actors in food, drink, and clothing.

II

The development of Muscovy under the Tsar Alexey in the second half of the seventeenth century brought about a new spirit at the court. The morality and the pious academic play were too abstract, and the traditional bear entertainment and merrymen dance and song seemed too crude and primitive. The Tsar's chief adviser, Artamon Matveyev, who was married to a Scotswoman (Hamilton) and had lived abroad, told him marvelous stories about the French theater. Alexey also heard a great deal about performances held in his capital in the houses of foreigners. Charles Howard, Earl of Carlisle, the English Ambassador, had offered a comedy to his guests in 1664. Eager to know more about the Western theater, Alexey sent Colonel Nicholas von Staden abroad with the mission of finding and bringing to Russia a company of actors and musicians. And while von Staden was negotiating in Riga and in German lands with comedians who were reluctant to undertake a voyage into unknown and frightening Muscovy, Alexey asked Johann Gottfried Gregory, the minister of the Lutheran Church in Moscow and an amateur poet, to stage at the court the Biblical story of Esther (also called "Artaxerxes' Play"). With the assistance of two Germans, a translator, and a stage director, and one Russian, Gregory gathered sixty-four people, mostly sons of foreigners, and in a few months rehearsed and made ready the performance. A special theater was built in the Tsar's residence, the village of Preobrazhenskoye (Transfiguration). It was lighted by tallow candles in wooden candelabra, the walls decorated with bright raspberry and green cloth, the benches and the Tsar's seat upholstered in red velvet, and the curtain slid along a thick iron rod to which it was attached by sixty brass rings. The stage, decorated by fir trees on both sides, had a red carpet and a bright blue background which represented the sky. Costumes were sprinkled with gold; Esther wore a magnificent white dress with golden stripes, the warriors had real swords, and Haman was hanged on a real gallows. Music was played between the scenes. The day of the first performance, October 17, 1672, the Tsar came alone, without his family, and was first stunned and then so enchanted that he stayed in the theater for ten consecutive hours. The succeeding performances were public: Alexey invited his boyards and high officials who came from the capital in a long procession; those who showed little desire to attend "foreigners' tricks," were summoned by the Tsar's messengers. The new entertainment had great success, and the Tsar's whole family was allowed to enjoy it from a special box endowed with sliding gratings and curtains. Later, the performances were transferred to Moscow. They included a comedy about David and Goliath, and interludes, such as *Orpheus* and *Bacchus and Venus,* as well as the comedies *Judith, Bayazet, and Tamerlan.*

Johann Gregory, born in Marburg and sent to Russia in 1662 by the *Kurfuerst* of Saxony, was well educated and intelligent. He probably knew little about theater before being commissioned by Alexey. We can assume, however, that as a German student he must have participated in academic performances. In any case, he was so elated by the success of his venture that the following year, in 1673, he started a theatrical school with twenty-six pupils, all his expenses being paid from the Tsar's treasury. Gregory's dramatic productions had a deep symbolic and historical meaning: the formal theater in Russia had been by the Tsar's order; from its start it was attached to the court and subsidized by the state; it was directed by the Germans; it immediately assumed political overtones and aimed at serving the monarchy—in *Esther* the praise of the wise sovereign was obviously inserted to please Alexey; it became the subject of a political struggle, i.e., the "Westernizers," the supporters of progressive reforms, backed it, the "conservatives" damned it.

The repertory of Gregory's theater, which continued for several years, was mostly borrowed fom the Kievan Academy. It later added the comedy or parable of *The Prodigal Son* by Simeon Polotsky (1629-1680), a monk, a tutor to the Tsar's children, a poet, and an important playwright, who wrote a new version of *The Burning Furnace* and praised the Tsar in prologues couched in heavy syllabic verse. His comedy *The Prodigal Son* had a strong antiforeign tendency and evinced elements of realistic satire. Apparently Gregory also presented a lachrymose

Comedy of Adam and Eve and plays inspired by English dramatic material. The Moscow public welcomed with enthusiasm this entertainment and found it exciting. The death of Alexey in 1676 suspended official performances; however the unofficial ones continued in the Tsar's palace: his daughter Sophia wrote plays and acted with a group of amateurs from her own court.

III

Pyotr I, whose grandiose reforms tended to a quick Europeanization of Russia, welcomed the import of actors from the West and brought to Moscow an itinerant German company led by Johann Kunst. Like Gregory, Kunst spent a great deal of time training future Russian actors.

Pyotr saw immediately the importance of the theater for spreading his ideas, and moved the stage from the Tsar's palace into a state theater on Red Square, constructed in 1702. Being an anti-clerical and wishing to break away from the Byzantine tradition which he thought the cause of Russia's backwardness, Pyotr called for plays from contemporary European repertory, and Kunst fulfilled his wishes. The German director produced a version of *Jodelet the Prince* by Corneille and of *Don Pedro and Don Juan,* an old Italian play previously staged in Paris, and three times a week presented dramas and farces. He even made an unsuccessful attempt to interest the Muscovites in an opera.

After the death of Kunst in 1703, his place was taken by a former jeweler, Otto Furst, also a German. The pupils of Kunst and Furst formed the cast of Russian theatrical companies which offered performances in 1709 when the Imperial theater was moved from Moscow to St. Petersburg, the new capital on the Neva River. Pyotr's youngest sister Natalia was a passionate lover of theater and herself a playwright. She built a wooden pavilion for a court theater and staged there thirteen plays.

All we know of theatrical repertory under Pyotr shows the utilitarian and political character the Tsar tried to instill into the new entertainment. Pursuing his general objective of political reform and the education of the nobility, he considered theater a most important means of carrying out his plans. He found help in the newly established Slavonic Greek and Latin

Academy of Moscow, which produced a series of long-winded performances hailing Pyotr's military victories and reforms. These were dramatized on the stage in archaic forms of religious and scholarly allegories. The plays with this patriotic content were often written by the heavy hand of Feofan Prokopovich (1687-1736), who also composed a few historical dramas, and by some of Pyotr's intimate collaborators. The Tsar also used the theater for the justification of his personal life: when he got rid of his Greek Orthodox wife and married Catherine, a Lutheran of German origin, a change was made in the play of *Esther*—the Biblical king was shown leaving his nasty stuttering spouse in order to wed a good and virtuous foreigner.

After Pyotr's death in 1725 and a few years of relative apathy, theatrical life was resumed in 1730. The Empress Anna (1730-1740), Pyotr's niece, added brilliance to the Russian Court and patronized balls and masquerades, but in her private apartments she returned to old Muscovy amusements and revived the antics of jesters, dwarfs, and buffoons. On stage she preferred German plays with comic peasants and coarse scenes at the end of which actors wrangled and beat each other with sticks. Germans were at that time masters of the Russian theater, and a whole Teutonic company was imported into Russia from Leipzig. But an important event marked the first year of Anna's reign: a group of Italian actors, singers, and mimes, under the direction of the talented Neapolitan composer, Francesco Araia, made its appearance in St. Petersburg—and this was the beginning of the Italian influence. The Italians brought with them, among other things, the *commedia dell'arte* with its improvisations and masks; they impressed the spectators with their elaborate sets, machines, and various technical tools. They greatly enhanced the stagecraft in Russia, and their Giovanni Buon, an architect from Bologna, was acclaimed as the master of his trade. From 1735 to 1759, Araia was a prominent figure in Russian theater and music. He introduced the opera in St. Petersburg: among his works which were *Bellerophon* and especially *Semiramis,* the latter presented every week. In the court theater (where a special sergeant was appointed in 1739 "to dust the benches") as well as in a hall built in the Summer Garden, dramas and comedies alternated with operas. At the same time, a new form of theatrical was introduced by another Italian: Antonio Fusano and his beautiful wife Giulia organized ballet performances. They were soon replaced by Jean Baptiste Landet, a Frenchman, who is usually considered the father of Russian ballet. He established a school of dance, formed a *corps de ballet,* and trained boys and girls for the stage. His school, recognized and supported by the Empress, supplied dancers of both sexes to all foreign choreographers who later came to Russia.

It is interesting that from its very beginnings the Russian ballet found itself under the conflicting influences of two schools: the Italians, who stressed their acrobatic techniques—Noverre speaks of the jumps introduced by Fusano; and the French, who paid more attention to plastic elegance and grace, such as Landet showed in his highly acclaimed ballets of flowers, *Cupid and Psyche* and *The Judgment of Paris,* performed in the true Versailles manner.

Important changes occurred in the Russian theater during the reign of Yelisaveta, Pyotr's daughter. Her gay disposition and love of pleasure created most favorable conditions for all kinds of theatrical presentations. Her court became resplendent with luxury and tried to imitate Versailles. Her ladies-in-waiting and gentlemen-of-the-chamber produced various shows at the Winter Palace. One of them, *Rose Without Thorns,* an old Russian tale, was accompanied by song and dance; a few years later the amateurs staged a musical comedy by Arkady Kolychev, a native composer. In 1750, Yelisaveta signed an ukase which authorized theatrical performances in private houses. A number of foreign companies and single actors, attracted by rumors of Imperial generosity, were now coming to St. Petersburg. The Germans, however, were being replaced by the French: led by Serigny, French actors gave excellent performances of tragedies by Racine and Corneille and comedies by Molière. In an attempt to counteract the growing French influence, the Italians staged in 1742, for the festivities of Yelisaveta's coronation in Moscow, the opera *La Clemenza di Tito,* accompanied by a spectacular prologue with dances, music, and recitation, all under the title *Russia, Afflicted and Consoled* which attracted thousands of spectators. The whole show was an artistic apotheosis of the Empress.

Despite the success of foreign companies, the main event of

the period was the birth of the national theater. In 1749, the tragedy *Khorev*, written by the Russian poet Alexander Sumarokov, was produced by the cadets of the Academy for the Nobility, a mixed military and liberal arts institution, from which the author himself had graduated. In this institution the love of the theater was strong, and the cadets formed a large group of amateurs which staged *Zaïre* by Voltaire. They were very eager to act in the plays by Sumarokov, whom they considered a great writer. The success of these new productions was such that its echo reached the Empress. She wanted to see them, and the next year *Khorev* was presented at the court and met with unanimous acclaim. This was the beginning of a whole series of performances devoted to Sumarokov's works (*Hamlet* "adapted from Shakespeare,"* *Sineus and Truvor, Aristona*, etc.) .

By a strange coincidence, another, almost simultaneous venture marked the beginnings of the Russian national theater. Fyodor Volkov, a merchant's son, who had spent two years in St. Petersburg and was passionately interested in the theater, came home to Yaroslavl, a small provincial town, with the firm decision to become an actor. He taught the art of acting to his brothers and friends, fixed up a barn (and later a house) as a theater, arranged sets and properties, and soon astonished and captivated his townsmen with his amateur performances. Enthusiastic audiences helped him to build a real theater seating one thousand, and the news of Volkov's enterprise soon reached the capital. Yelisaveta summoned Volkov to St. Petersburg, and the Yaroslavl company performed *The Repentance of A Sinner* at the court. This old morality play represented the sinner in a suit covered with black patches, each bearing the mark of his daily transgressions. Behind him, his guardian angel fought with demons, and the sinner wavered between hell and heaven. Finally he was won over to the sides of the angels, his black patches falling one by one. In the last scene, the sinner, in a white tunic, was dying happily and rendering his soul to God.

The show made such an impression that Yelisaveta sent some of Volkov's actors to the Academy for the Nobility for further education. By that time, in the early 1750s, quite a number of

---

* Sumarokov remembered Voltaire calling Shakespeare, "a drunken savage" and, accordingly, attempted to make the English poet "tamed and orderly."

Russians became playwrights, while native talents also came to the fore in opera and ballet. In 1755 *Cefal and Procris,* book by Sumarokov, music by Araia, was performed by Russian singers and dancers; later it was called the "grandmother" of Russian musicals. All this activity convinced the Empress that a formal step was needed for the establishment of a national theater. On August 30, 1756, the Senate received an Imperial decree by which a Russian theater for comedies and tragedies was instituted in a stone house on Vassily Island of St. Petersburg, with a yearly budget paid by the Treasury. Sumarokov, appointed its director, was granted the right to fix the monthly salaries of the actors and theatrical help. The subsidies for the Russian company, however, were low; in 1756, it received 5,000 rubles, while the French got 20,000 and the Italians 30,000. The German theater was definitely declining and it gradually became a semiprivate institution, mainly for the middle class. The aristocracy preferred the French. Still, Russian actors were given brocade, velvet, and precious stones for their costumes, for the public loved rich and even luxurious externals. At the same time Yelisaveta ordered the poet Tredyakovsky and the great scholar Lomonossoy to write tragedies.

The newly born enterprise, open to the public and hardly a rival to the court theater, which continued to function as before, was served mostly by Volkov and his company. Some former cadets, in whom love of the stage proved greater than the attraction of an army career, joined the cast. The plays shown on Vassily Island were mostly translations from the French. *Tartuffe, L'Avare, École des maris* and other comedies by Molière were great favorites. The cast in *Le Bourgeois gentilhomme,* given in 1788 was so large ("singers, musicians, dancers, cooks, tailors, apprentices, and other people engaged in interludes and ballets and in making rich settings") that the entrance fee was doubled.

After Yekaterina's dramatic ascension to the throne (1762), Volkov and his brother Gregory, who took part in the coup d'état, were knighted. The next year, together with Sumarokov, an eager stage director, they organized a magnificent popular festival in Moscow under the title *Minerva's Triumph* (Minerva being, of course, the new and young Empress). The show lasted two weeks; performances given on huge chariots, each driven by twelve to twenty-four oxen, presented Mars, Pallas, Bacchus,

satyrs, nymphs, and fauns, and alternated mythological scenes
with comic sketches. This sort of carnival cost Volkov his life.
He caught cold while supervising the procession in icy weather
and died at the age of thirty-four.

Under Yekaterina II, the theater flourished in Russia. The
Empress loved all theatrical arts and was herself a playwright:
she composed (not without the help and advice of some of her
friends) three lyrical dramas, eleven comedies—among them an
imitation of *The Merry Wives of Windsor*—and five popular
operas. One of her pseudohistorical plays, *The Early Reign of
Oleg*, produced in 1794, two years before her death, was a huge
panoramic show with six hundred supers. Most of her plays were
performed in the Court Theater she built in the Winter Palace.
Courtiers and members of the imperial family acted in amateur
companies and even appeared in ballets. One evening Prince
Pavel, the heir apparent, complained that the applause of the
court audience spoiled his choreographic effects.

In 1773 Yekaterina ordered the construction of a theater building later called the Bolshoy (Large) Theater, and in 1779 the
Imperial Theatrical School for the training of actors, singers,
and dancers was founded. Four years later a special Administration
of Theaters was established by imperial order. The text of
Yekaterina's decree specified the sums the Russian Treasury had
to pay to: 1) Italian singers for court concerts and grand opera;
2) Russian theater; 3) French theater; 4) German theater; 5)
comic and Italian opera; 6) ballet; 7) orchestras for the court
and all other performances. The State spent large sums of money
for the theater, but controlled it completely and administered it
according to the will of the sovereign. While the Hermitage
Theater was reserved for court performances, theaters outside the
capital were taxed one fourth of all their gross profits, the money
going to the orphanages. Later, and throughout the whole nineteenth century, all taxes collected from theaters were used for
educational and charitable purposes.

Thus from its very beginning, Russian theatrical life was dependent on the throne and was made an affair of state. On one
hand, it opened great material possibilities and protected actors,
musicians, and dancers from uncertainties and financial distress;
on the other hand, it made them government employees—with

all the disadvantages coming from such a position. St. Petersburg and Moscow theaters were entirely subject to the Imperial Administration. Provincial theaters which had begun growing by the end of the eighteenth century were actually directed and administered by local imperial authorities and in many cases, without enjoying the privilege of state financial support, depended in fact on the Central Administration. The farther they were from the capital, however, the more independence they seemed to possess. We know, for instance, that the Kharkov Theater (capacity four hundred), with its orchestra seats built by subscription and its six o'clock shows on Tuesdays and Fridays, enjoyed for a long time an idyllic kind of freedom, enhanced by close relationship between the actors and the local governor.

Private theaters owned by rich noblemen and landowners were outside of the State Administration's jurisdiction, and their number and importance grew constantly. In the second half of the eighteenth century there were fifteen such home theaters in Moscow alone. Complete companies were then recruited from serfs. Many noblemen, impressed and delighted by court performances, decided to imitate them on their estates, and turned their slaves into actors, singers, and dancers. "By the beginning of the nineteenth century," says a contemporary, "in each wealthy aristocratic manor orchestras played, choruses sang, and stages were built on which peasant artists served the gods of all arts." The new entertainment became so fashionable that guests were treated to theater as they were to food and drink. On some smaller estates, musicians also performed as actors. This was the case of Mikhail Matinsky, a serf and one of the first Russian composers, whose opera *Pasha of Tunis* became very popular.

Some of the "serf theaters" assumed unequaled range and magnificence. Prince Yusupov, who owned 21,000 serfs, had a whole *corps de ballet* on his estate besides dramatic and opera companies, all drafted from his serfs. Count Kamensky spent 30,000 rubles for one performance of the *Khalif of Baghdad,* casting several hundred of his serfs. Prince V. Shakhovskoy, Prince V. Shcherbatov, Prince M. Volkonsky, the nobleman Rzhevsky, and many others owned large companies and built magnificent theater halls.

While some masters used their actresses and dancers as concubines, others looked upon them as mere pieces of property and treated them accordingly. Young men and women were trained in theatrical arts with the help of the whip and the birch. Corporal punishment was largely used for maintaining discipline. In some instances dancers who did not satisfy their masters were spanked or whipped in the presence of guests, immediately after the official performance. One actress was flogged after a performance for "not having shown enough dignity in her role of a French noblewoman." And often an actress or a ballerina after a particularly brilliant appearance would be summoned to her master's bedchamber.

There were, however, other theatrical ventures where the atmosphere was more humane and the customs much milder. Among them, the most important belonged to Count Peter Sheremetyev, owner of three theaters. His main theater in Kuskovo was built from the plans of the Italian architect Valli, while the stage and the interior decorations were done by the famous Pietro Gonzago (1751-1831), a great painter, architect, and decorator. Sheremetyev's serf actors were well trained and well treated. His main company counted 230 members, and they produced dozens of dramas, comedies, and operas. The quality of the performances was so high that the French Count de Ségur, astonished by the acting and by the lavishness of staging, called them "simply magnificent" in his Memoirs. Sheremetyev had a special agent in Paris who sent him all theatrical novelties. His performances were attended by the upper crust of Russian aristocracy, members of the imperial family, and all foreign dignitaries and princes who happened to travel in Russia. They reached their peak after 1787 when one of his actresses, Parasha Zhemchugova, became the star of the company and charmed all the spectators, among them the heir apparent Pavel, the Austrian Emperor Joseph II, and the Polish King Stanislas Poniatovsky. Her own master fell deeply in love with this brilliant comedienne and beautiful woman, and married her by special authorization of the Tsar. After she died in childbirth in 1803, Sheremetyev was inconsolable, lost his interest in the theater, and this marked the decline of the Kuskovo venture.

Since serf actors were the property of their masters, they were often exchanged or given as gifts. Bankrupt noblemen would sell their entire theatrical companies—wholesale or retail. The

State Administration of Imperial Theaters watched carefully for occasions to acquire good actors, especially dancers, at low prices. Some of the actors and dancers, once the property of the state, were then set free or had to buy their emancipation.

Serf actors often found themselves in tragic situations and suffered from the discrepancy between their legal status and their artistic or personal aspirations. Despite their sad destiny, which was often depicted in Russian literature (particularly in A. Herzen's *The Magpie,* N. Leskov's *Artist of the Toupée,* and S. Shmelyov's *The Inexhaustible Cup*), these men and women, pushed on to the stage by their masters, made an important contribution to the Russian theater; and many talented actors in the nineteenth century who came from the darkness of serfdom owed their training to the estate theaters.

I V

The *Dramatic Lexicon,* which contains the list of plays given in the Russian language in Moscow and St. Petersburg up to 1787, mentions ten comedies by Molière, two tragedies by Racine, *Richard III* and *Julius Caesar* by Shakespeare. *The Barber of Seville* and *The Marriage of Figaro* by Beaumarchais, *Clavigo* by Goethe, four plays by Holberg, various pieces by Voltaire, tragedies by Corneille, and comedies by Destouches. In general, translations from French, German, and Italian (Goldoni) predominated, and contemporary Western playwrights supplied most of the current repertory. But the second half of the eighteenth century saw, next to the establishment of the national stage and a growing number of nationally trained actors, an emergence of original plays, operas, and scenarios for ballet produced by the Russians. Count Sheremetyev's library had, by the end of the eighteenth century, 250 Russian plays, printed or in manuscript, of which 105 were comedies.

The Russian playwright had but a very limited amount of popular art from which to draw his subjects, as was the case in various other European countries, and this explains why he naturally reverted to foreign sources. Only a few morality plays from the "school drama" survived in the eighteenth century, and an even smaller number of popular shows (including Punch and

Judy themes) were adapted to the new stage from old versions. Besides, the court and the aristocratic theater looked down their noses at the coarse, often primitive, creations derived from popular folklore. One example of the popular drama that had enough vigor to affirm itself throughout all historical vicissitudes is the well-known *Comedy of the Tsar Maximilian and His Son Adolphe*. Its initial Latin text, probably of Byzantine origin, was strongly Russified and changed in the sixteenth century by all sorts of allegorical or topical episodes. It remained for centuries a favorite with the peasants and the lower classes, and when Alexey Remizov, an outstanding modern novelist, revived it in 1911, he based his text on nineteen variants. The story was divided into two parts. In the first part, Maximilian falls in love with a pagan witch and changes his faith. His son Adolphe refuses to become an apostate and is executed. His death is followed by a comic interlude involving a gravedigger, his deaf wife, a bogus doctor, and a tailor. In the second part, the Tsar sends his other son, Anika the Warrior, to fight his enemies. Great victories turn Anika's head; he boasts that he can conquer death, whereupon he is killed—and again the gravedigger and his companions make jokes and sing couplets about "time which runs like a river stream, and man's life which is like a candle: it is put out by a whiff."

The school of classicism or pseudo classicism found several imitators in Russia. Alexander Sumarokov (1718-1777), the creator of Russian classicist repertory, was completely dependent on the French literary theory and translated Boileau's letter on poetic art into Russian. He believed in the representation of ideal life in tragedies, subject to the three unities of space, time, and action, and of "low" reality in comedies. Faithfully following the accepted esthetic canons, he wrote nine tragedies in which noble characters, mostly princes, kings, and war lords, struggled between love and duty or passion and loyalty. It is true that he referred to Russian history and often tackled patriotic themes, but his heroes, despite their Slavic names, were the same virtuous men in disguise one could find in Racine or Corneille. Dramatic situations were treated in generic abstract form, and sublime emotions were expressed in rhetorical speeches. The public reacted very favorably to the works of the "Russian Racine" as Sumarokov was called by his numerous admirers. They loved not only the novelty of references to national traits and events, but also the idealization of their own way of life. Basically the tragedies exalted and beautified the monarchy established on nobility and aristocracy, and hailed an ideal relationship between the sovereign and his loyal courtiers.

The enlightened absolutism embodied in the court and the persons of Russian empresses, particularly that of Yekaterina II, justly sought artistic support in these tragedies. At the same time, *Khorev, Sineus and Truvor,* and *Dimitry the Pretender* (1747-1771) were fulfilling an important role of raising the Russian theater and its national repertory to the contemporary level of Western literature. Sumarokov transplanted French models on Moscow soil and Russified them. Yakov Kniazhnin (1742-1791), Sumarokov's son-in-law, continued in the same vein, his *Didones* and *Sofonizbas* bearing Slav names and being stirred by patriotic feelings. Other tragedies (including the earlier pieces by Lomonossov and Trediakovsky) did not leave any profound trace. Mikhail Kheraskov (1733-1807), author of a pompous epic *Rossiada*, wrote heavy and imitative tragedies. Later, at the beginning of the nineteenth century, tragedies by Ozerov won a tremendous success for political reasons.

In general, the Russian branch of French tragedy never produced any lasting work. It is highly significant that the Russians proved to be much more at home with the realistic comedy. Even the champions of tragedy, such as Sumarokov and Kniazhnin, did much better in the "low" genre of comedy. It is true that the satrical tendency was most popular under Yekaterina II, who believed in the possibility of *ridendo castigare mores.* A great number of comedies were written and produced between 1760 and the end of the century, and the public, especially outside of court theaters, received them with enthusiasm. From 1780 to 1805, 44 per cent of the Russian repertory in Moscow theaters consisted of comedies (32 per cent were operas and interludes—pantomimes and ballets). Comedies varied from the sentimental type represented by V. Lukin with his *The Spendthrift Reformed by Love* (1765) to the satrical exposés by Kniazhnin, whose *The Braggart* and *Queer Fellow* ridiculed the aristocratic seekers of titles and fortune. Sumarokov's didactic comedies, as well as those by Knia-

zhnin and others, sinned, however, by their schematic compositions and the sharp division of characters into black and white.
The comic spirit pervaded also the opera and its lasting favorites:
Aniuta (1772), by M. Popov which depicted the life of peasants,
The Gostinny Dvor in St. Petersburg by M. Matinsky, and particularly *The Miller* (1779) by A. Ablesimov,* which had hundreds of performances and remained a box office attraction
throughout the nineteenth century.

But only with Dimitry Fonvizin (1743-1792) a truly national
comedy was created: his *The Minor* (1781) actually marks the
birth of Russian theatrical repertory. It had a triumphant career
for almost two hundred years and is today as fresh as the day
when it was produced for the first time on a private stage in
1782 by the actors of the St. Petersburg Imperial Theater. Previously in his first comedy, *The Brigadier,* Fonvizin depicted the
life of the provincial gentry. But only in *The Minor* did he
reach the fullness of realistic detail and the sharpness of portraiture. The main character, Prostakova, a coarse and shifty
noblewoman, rules her household, including her nincompoop of
a husband, with an iron hand and is generous only in distributing
slaps and raps. Her son, the Minor, is ignorant and stupid: like
his mother, he despises the studies he is compelled to take in
order to obtain a commission in the army or a civil service rank.
The mother tries to marry him to Sophia, her ward, whose
money she had appropriated, but her own brother, a middle-aged
vulgar and bestial landowner enters in competition with his
young nephew. Finally, Sophia is liberated from Prostakova's
tyranny and can be united with an officer she loves. But this
denouement, as well as the conventional figures of two positive
"men of virtue" who secure the "punishment of vice," do not
spoil the vigor of the dramatic conflict and the bold presentation
of a whole social scene. The play, with its sustained action, excellent images of secondary characters such as grotesque teachers
or mistreated serfs, its brisk, amusing dialogues, its humor, and
its racy popular language, was acclaimed a genuine masterpiece,
both as drama and as literature. It opened the road to the glorious

---

* The full title was: *The Miller, the Witchdoctor, the Cheater and the Matchmaker.*

series of Russian comedies, from Griboyedov and Gogol to Ostrovsky and Chekhov.

V

Several types of theaters existed in Russia by the end of the eighteenth century: the Hermitage Court Theater, the Imperial Theaters in St. Petersburg and Moscow (antecedents of the Bolshoy and the Maly) where presentations were given of dramas, comedies, operas, and ballets by Russian and foreign companies; theaters for the people, organized by the government; provincial theaters belonging to towns or local administrations; and, finally, private theaters, mostly owned by landowners and rich aristocrats. By the end of the century, the latter became a serious menace to any other private initiative: it is known that M. Medox, who built a beautiful theater in Moscow and got a concession from the government, was so handicapped by the competition of serfs' companies of the region that by 1806 he had to renounce his projects and hand over his enterprise (which had fifteen male and eight female actors) to the Imperial Administration.

In the same way as the national repertory, native actors successfully competed with foreign rivals. Some amateurs became professionals, like Volkov, and many actors received good training in theatrical schools subsidized by the government, while others emerged from the serfs' companies.

Fyodor Volkov (1729-1763), whom Belinsky, the great Russian critic, called "the father of Russian theater," was an actor of tragic as well as comic roles, a teacher, a stage director, a translator, and even a man of action who took part in politics. He started acting in a very conventional court manner which paid most attention to "nobility of gait and gestures" but gradually acquired more finesse and facial expression. Of course, he recited his parts in the sing-song kind of speech which was introduced by the French, and in climactic scenes shouted with pathos. In general, his manner was highly emotional.

More accomplished were the artistic gifts of Ivan Dmitrevsky (1734-1821), whose influence was greatly felt by the Russian stage for many decades. Actor, pedagogue, stage director, translator, art historian, and friend of the great writers of his time, he belongs to the history of Russian culture as much as he does to that of the theater. After Volkov's death he became the leading Russian actor and was acclaimed by the court and the public as a magnificent interpreter of tragedies. A poet made him say:

> For you, Russia's sons,
> I made Racine's art shine.

Handsome, dignified and poised, endowed with a vibrant voice, he resembled a courtier and had the polite and cautious manner of a diplomat. His acting was rather cold, intellectual, and well prepared, aiming at calculated effects which never failed to impress the spectators. He went abroad to perfect his art, got acquainted in Paris with the great French actor Talma, and came home more convinced than ever that success in acting was mainly due to rational study rather than temperament and intuition. In the tradition of Russian actors who did not follow the French strict division into *emploi,* or parts, he acted in tragedies of Sumarokov and Kniazhnin, in comedies by Molière, Beaumarchais, and Lukin, and contributed to the production of Fonvizin's *The Minor* by acting the role of the old *raisonneur* Starodum. He concluded his acting career in 1787, from which time onward he was active as a teacher and director in the theaters of St. Petersburg and Moscow where he actually formed generations of actors. In 1802, Dmitrevsky, whose schooling was limited to a small provincial seminary, was elected a member of the Imperial Academy. This was the crowning of his constant efforts to raise the status of the actor and to assure himself of a dignified position in society.

At the beginning of his road, Dmitrevsky, like Volkov, played feminine as well as masculine parts: later the increasing number of female actresses made such substitution unnecessary and this practice was abandoned by mid-century. In 1758, Dmitrevsky married Agrafena Musina-Pushkina, one of the pioneer actresses and first ladies in Volkov's company; she was an excellent *soubrette* in French comedies but left the stage because of family duties (she gave Dmitrevsky six sons and four daughters). Another important actress was Tatiana Troepolskaya, who played Ophelia, Juliet, and various tragic parts; she died suddenly in her dressing room in 1774. Yekaterina Semenova, whose parents had been a present to a nobleman, started as a serf actress but was free later and acclaimed as a brilliant performer.

Peter Plavilshchikov (1760-1812), whose articles demanded a national repertory reflecting Russian life, and who acted successfully in Sheridan's *The School For Scandal*, and in *The Minor*, V. Pomerantsev, who evinced strong realistic tendencies, J. Shusherin, A. Krutitsky, an excellent interpreter of comic parts, and many other talented men and women helped raise the level of acting in Moscow and St. Petersburg to such heights that by the turn of the century the Russian theater appeared a distinct national unit with its own traditions, plays, actors, and stage-craft—and this despite the large number of foreign technicians, directors, and teachers. By the beginning of the nineteenth century, the Russians had outgrown the early phase of theatrical imitation and apprenticeship and were entering a new period of independent and glorious development.

2

FROM ROMANTIC DRAMA TO GOGOL

BY THE TURN of the century, the Russian theater with native actors and a mixed repertory was firmly established and thoroughly organized. Since its administration was directly responsible to the Emperor, general direction and even details of theatrical life often depended on the moods and whims of the monarch. During the short reign of Pavel I, who was subject to fits of madness and was called the "sentimental tiger" by his contemporaries, actors and playwrights were often confronted with the most contradictory orders, and the existence of the Imperial Theatrical Administration itself was often precarious. Stability in the theater improved, however, after Pavel's death in 1801, and his reactionary policy was replaced by the benign and liberal atmosphere promoted by Alexander I, his son and successor.

The fluctuations of Alexander's political sympathies, the war against Napoleon, and the struggle between the conservative and the progressive forces of Russian nobility were reflected in the life of the theater during the first quarter of the century. It was an era when national consciousness developed rapidly, making repeated demands for national repertory. The controversy between classicists and the growing Romantic Movement added a great deal to the heated discussions of plays and methods of acting. A sharpening of social distinctions also played its role in preferences of the public. The court and the high aristocracy were, of course, the most influential patrons of the performing

38

arts. They favored foreign actors and companies, and plays in French or German, as well as the ballet and, particularly, the opera. In Imperial Theaters under Alexander I, 135 operas were presented and only 45 were Russian. The music and librettos for the latter, however, were seldom Russian. We know, for instance, that Caterino Cavos, an Italian composer who came to Russia in 1797 and stayed there forty-two years, wrote music for thirty-two Russian and six translated operas.

The nobility, the aristocratic youth, the provincial landowners, the newly formed intelligentsia, and the rising middle class, as well as the liberal bureaucrats, preferred the drama and showed more and more interest in national repertory. They constituted the new public which filled the halls of the Bolshoy Theater in Moscow and Alexandrinsky Theater in St. Petersburg and supported passionately their favorite plays and actors. Theater devotees had their reserved seats: the "left" aisle was reserved for those steady customers who took performances very seriously and whose approval or opposition could often determine the rise or fall of plays and actresses.

Alexander I gave the Imperial Theaters more money and independence, and also raised considerably the status of the actor: a contributing factor was the number of aristocratic amateurs and the example of numerous nobles who became professional actors. The Emperor hardly ever interfered personally in the daily life of "his theaters," and the role of the heads of the administration consequently rose in proportion. The directors of the Imperial Theatrical Administration, Alexander Naryshkin (until 1812), Prince Tufyakin (until 1822), and their successors A. Maikov, Count Miloradovich (killed during the Decembrists' uprising in 1825), Prince Dolgorukov, and, after 1829, Prince S. Gagarin, all belonged to the Tsar's intimate circles and held a great deal of power but usually limited themselves to administrative functions or, like Prince Tufyakin, to amorous exploits with ballerinas and leading actresses. They usually entrusted the artistic direction, the repertory, and the training of actors to their more enlightened friends. In the early twenties, a special post was established: Director of the Moscow Imperial Theaters. In 1801, Prince Alexander Shakhovskoy (1771-1846) was appointed director of the repertory section of the Imperial Theaters. This fat, short, and clumsy man, with a bald head and a big nose, looked like an eccentric, but was a deeply devoted "Knight of Melpomene," as he used to say in his slightly pompous manner. Poet and dramatist, he wrote some twenty plays, of which the polemical five-act comedy in verse, *Lesson to Coquettes* or *Lipetsky Spa* (1815), ridiculing the romantics and the liberal youth, was greatly talked about, while his other work, *The Bigamous Wife,* relating the adventures of a merchant's wife who became mistress of a bandit chief, enjoyed popular success until the late seventies. It was Shakhovskoy who worked out rules and regulations for the Imperial Theaters which, after their approval by the Tsar in 1825, remained practically intact until the 1917 Revolution. He studied theatrical techniques in Paris and was passionately interested in training actors. Despite his faulty pronunciation and very peculiar teaching methods, he succeeded in conveying to his pupils his love of dramatic literature and his striving for artistic perfection. His method was to demonstrate how the part should be acted and have his pupils imitate him: in certain passages, he insisted that the artist had to scream or whisper, to swing the left foot or raise the right hand. His competitors in actor training were Nikolay Gnedich, the learned and famous translator of the *Iliad* and *Odyssey,* and the critic Katenin. Gnedich coached the actress Yekaterina Semenova, daughter of a landowner and one of his women serfs, and made annotations on the manuscript of her parts, indicating how separate sentences ought to be recited: such as "with contempt," "gently," "beating the chest," "raising the head." The great test for Semenova came after the guest appearance of Mlle. George, the famous French tragic actress whose double attraction as Paris's leading lady and Napoleon's mistress made all of St. Petersburg rush to her performances. George impressed her spectators by the amplitude of her recitation: she went from great loudness to a perfectly audible whisper, and from a slow majestic pace to a feverishly rapid tempo. Semenova, an actress who excelled in tragic roles, became George's rival. By 1811 there were two camps in Moscow —Georgists and Semenovists. The latter, after the representation of *Tancred,* offered their idol a diamond diadem worth 100,000 rubles. Although the press often called her "the Russian George," Semenova's manner was distinctly different. A pupil of Dmitrev-

sky and of Gnedich, she displayed a beautiful grandeur of gestures and that "free, lucid way of acting with frequent bursts
of genuine inspiration" which delighted Pushkin, who said that
"speaking of Russian tragedy one mentions Semenova and perhaps
her alone." When tragedy gave way to the Romantic drama,
Semenova made the mistake of playing parts which did not suit
her. She finally married Prince S. Gagarin and abandoned the
stage.

Russian tragic actors took from the French the declamatory
sing-song manner of reciting. But unlike the French members
of a company, they had to act in a wide range of roles, including
the comic ones. Some of them, however, shone only in tragic
roles. Alexey Yakovlev (1773-1817), for example, was applauded
as Agamemnon, Othello, Hamlet, Orestes, Oedipus, and particularly, as an interpreter of Pozharsky and Dimitry Donskoy in
Ozerov's tragedies.

The staging and directing of tragedies hardly differed from the
typical French models and historical accuracy was completely
sacrificed to other considerations. Count de Monfaucon tells that
he saw Mlle. Duclos enact Electra in a dress with paniers and a
long train and a hair-do three stories high, powdered, and crowned
with flowers.

The last representative of the eighteenth century classical
tragedy, Vladislav Ozerov (1770-1816) attained enormous success because his plays appealed to the strong nationalistic feeling
of Russian society, enhanced by the war against Napoleon. His
Dimitry Donskoy, performed during the Napoleonic invasion of
1812, depicted the times when Russian princes tried to repel the
Tartars, and the public applauded every word which reminded
them of ancient glory and recurrent national crisis. The audience,
who needed a reflection of their present emotions, acclaimed
Ozerov regardless of his literary merits: overtaken by a national
resurgence in the midst of war, they didn't mind his pathos, his
long monologues, his lack of action—always reported by messengers—and his high-pitched style. The need for the heroic and
"elevated" assured the triumph of his *Oedipus in Athens* (which
he borrowed from Ducis) or his sentimental love story *Fingal
and Polyxena;* all Russian actors of the period loved acting in
Ozerov's plays, and when the old Dmitrevsky made his last ap-

pearance in *Dimitry Donskoy* on the St. Petersburg stage at the moment when Napoleon's troops were occupying Moscow, he provoked a delirium among the spectators. But fifteen years later, Ozerov was completely forgotten and his plays striken from the repertory.

The approach of new times was felt in various ways. One of the signs was the prevalence of comedies. The link between the past and the present was assured by Ivan Krylov (1768-1844), the greatest Russian satirist, whose fables expressed the popular wisdom and formed the first example of literature for the masses. His comedies riduculed gallomania, sentimentality, and other social foibles. *A Lesson to Daughters, The Pastry, The Fashion Shop,* and the opera *Ilya Bogatyr,* all written in simple direct style and based on common sense and realistic observation, formed a singular counterpart to the artificial and stilted abstractions of the classicists. His realism was shared by a group of secondary dramatists who appealed to the public, despite their lack of real literary merit, because they offered something simple and familiar. Such was the case of Nikolay Khmelnitsky (1789-1840), who wrote *The Prattler* and two dozen other plays, or of Alexander Pisarev (1803-1828), author of comedies and vaudeville sketches taken from the French. At one point August von Kotzebue (1761-1819), a prolific author of German extraction provided a series of sentimental plays about average people which had a certain vogue and were favored by the authorities because of their reactionary spirit. The same political reasons contributed to the rise in 1834 of Nestor Kukolnik (1809-1868), author of declamatory, verbose, and monotonous plays with static characters glorifying absolute monarchy and official nationalism. He reached his summit in the historical drama, *The Almighty's Hand the Fatherland Has Saved*—an awkward title—which depicted the election of Mikhail Romanov, the head of the dynasty, to the throne of Russia in 1613. Its production cost 40,000 rubles and provoked the enthusiasm of Tsar Nikolay I. The only magazine which dared criticize Kukolnik was suppressed. Kukolnik wrote some fifteen plays using the cheapest and most vulgar theatrical effects, but the Imperial Theater had to stage them. The liberals invariably made Kukolnik the target of their most poisonous criticism.

A strange fate befell one of the best comedies of the eighteenth century, *Chicane* or *The Slanderer* by Vassily Kapnist. Written in 1798, it was directed against bribery and portrayed with vigor and satirical realism a gang of characters who firmly believed that the Almighty had provided them with hands "just to grab what they could." The Emperor Pavel ordered the author sent to Siberia. The evening of the day that the unfortunate dramatist started on his road to exile, Pavel I saw a performance of *The Slanderer* at the court theater—as the sole spectator—liked it, immediately revoked his previous order against Kapnist, and gave him the rank of State Councilor. The comedy, however, was not put on the stage until 1805, was banned again, and did not see the footlights until half a century later when it was finally produced in 1853.

The satirical comedy culminated in the great work of Alexander Griboyedov, his *Wit Works Woe* or *It Is Folly To Be Wise*, written about 1823. This play reflected the mentality of young noblemen who had brought home liberal and even revolutionary ideas from the campaigns they had fought in Europe against Napoleon. The discontented youth began criticizing the conservatism and backwardness of their society, and demanded reforms and progressive measures. From this state of mind was born the political movement which led in 1825 to the Decembrists' revolt. Griboyedov portrayed in his comedy in verse the conflict between the two generations and the outburst of new ideas and emotions. His hero, Chatsky, a passionate and intelligent young nobleman, returns to Moscow after three years of travels abroad and rushes to see Sophia, the girl he loves. She is the daughter of Famusov, a rich, gossipy, and fussy high functionary, blindly devoted to the conventions and standards of wealthy nobility. To Chatsky's surprise Sophia is cool and distant, and it takes him some time to discover that she is infatuated with Molchalin, her father's secretary. This "yes man" is making his way in the world by fawning before not only his superiors but even their dogs, and is firmly convinced that young folk "should not dare to hold their own opinions." Chatsky is disgusted by the servility of Molchalin, whom he tries to expose to Sophia. Frustrated in his love, he blames Moscow society for having changed Sophia into such a blind and frivolous creature. One of his targets is Colonel Skalozub, who sees the source of all evil in books and thinks they ought to be burned; "a corporal," says Skalozub, "would be a much better teacher for young people than that fellow Voltaire." At a ball given by Famusov, Chatsky is horrified when the other guests turn out to be a gallery of hypocritical prigs, greedy old women, rich and stupid dowagers, poisonous "lionesses," feather-brained maidens in search of husbands, and pretentious fops and dandies. Chatsky makes vehement speeches insulting all these representatives of a reactionary world, and Sophia, hurt by his denigration of Molchalin, maliciously spreads the rumor that the young man is out of his mind. Desperate and revolted, Chatsky leaves Famusov's house to resume his wanderings. He has but one small satisfaction: Molchalin, who plans to marry Sophia to advance his career but prefers to have fun with her chambermaid Liza, is caught and exposed by his fiancée. This is the only moral justification offered by Griboyedov in his pessimistic and biting satire. Its effect, however, is, toned down by the last appearance of Famusov, who cares only about one thing—"What will the Princess Maria Alexeyevna say?"

Griboyedov summed up his work in these words: "In my comedy there are twenty-five fools to one reasonable man, and this man, of course, stands in conflict with the society surrounding him." Chatsky is unable to change the environment he despises and criticizes, he limits himself to verbal protest, and he finally chooses to resume his travels. Thus he personifies the new type of the Russian intellectual whose brains and idealism are wasted and serve no practical purpose, and he indicates the long series of "superfluous men"—later described by Turgenev, Goncharov, Leskov, and Chekhov.

Belinsky, the great critic of the epoch, writes of the impression Griboyedov's comedy made on its readers: "What a lethal power of sarcasm, what biting irony, what an analysis of characters and society, and what language, what verse—energetic, compressed, lightning-like and so very Russian." The dramatic conflict between the progressive intellectual and his retrograde environment were not the only merits of Griboyedov's comedy—even though it represented one of the most exciting problems of Russian life and challenged those whom the author dubbed "eminent scoundrels." What made it a live work of art was its realism. It was topical—its full-blooded characters were taken from life, they were familiar figures in the two capitals of the 1820s, and they talked of well-known incidents and events. But they were also types, thoroughly Russian ones, and Griboyedov's brio and irony also had national traits. One can easily say that the author of *Wit Works Woe* had been influenced by Molière's *Le Misanthrope,* that French comedies he translated and adapted in his youth left their imprint on him. As a matter of fact, Griboyedov, a friend of Shakhovskoy, followed the structure of the then reigning comic form and obeyed the rules of the three unities (although in four instead of five acts). But the simplicity of plot structure of his comedy, its sharp epigrammatic verse, which became proverbial and was incorporated into Russian colloquial speech, and its truly Russian spirit, made Griboyedov's work unique and determined its place. The author did not live long enough to see it produced. Completed in 1823 and read in 1824 at various literary gatherings, *Wit Works Woe* was circulated throughout the country in manuscript before appearing in print. Its production was banned until 1831, by which time Griboyedov, who had served as a diplomat as well as being a poet and dramatist, was already dead. As Russian envoy in Teheran, he was killed in 1829 at the age of 34, by a mysteriously incited Persian mob. From 1831 to 1863 the play was performed (with large cuts) in the two capitals, but banned in the provinces (although recited occasionally in semiclandestine performances). The unabridged version of the comedy did not come to the stage until 1869.

Wit Works Woe is one of the leading pieces of national repertory. In fact, it has been called the first great Russian comedy— and every important actor of the ninteenth and twentieth centuries sought to excel in it. The part of Chatsky, this "ardent dreamer in the land of eternal snow," attracted artists from Karatyghin and Lensky to Stanislavsky and Kachalov. Others impersonated successfully the grotesque characters of Molchalin, Famusov, Skalozub and others. But it took almost half a century before the interpretation of the comedy rendered adequately the truly realistic spirit of the work. In any case, *Wit Works Woe* marks a substantial change in the Russian theater. As an achievement of the realistic national repertory, it follows—but on a higher level—Fonvizin's *The Minor*.

It is significant that romanticism did not produce important works by the Russians and that from 1830 to 1850, only foreign plays represented the new school. Alexander Pushkin, the greatest Russian poet and a lover of the theater, composed romantic scenes in verse (*Mozart and Salieri, The Stone Guest, The Feast During the Plague*), but his miniature tragedies, written in 1830, made only infrequent appearances on the stage. *Mozart and Salieri* was recited one evening in 1832 and had two performances between 1832 and 1854; *The Avaricious Knight* had its first performance in 1852, *The Stone Guest* in 1847, and again in 1862. Only at the beginning of the twentieth century did the Moscow Art Theater attempt to revive Pushkin's dramatic scenes. It is quite clear that their influence could only be literary. Almost the same thing happened with *Boris Godunov*—this remarkable popular tragedy written by Pushkin in 1825 under the influence of Shakespeare. It portrays Boris Godunov, an enlightened ruler and statesman, who committed murder in his struggle for the throne by sending assassins to stab Prince Dimitry, an obstacle and a threat to Godunov's ambition. His conscience tormented him while times of trouble started for Russia: an escaped novice Grishka Otrepiev, posing as a miraculously saved Dimitry and as a pretender to the Russian crown, gained the support of the Poles and moved against Moscow. These historical events enabled Pushkin to depict sharp human conflicts and distinct, simple or complex characters, among them Godunov himself, his children, his cunning rival Shuisky, the flighty false Dimitry, the majestic chronicler Pimen, in whom the friar, Nestor, author of a twelfth century historical narrative, was beautifully portrayed, and a score of minor but thoroughly Russian figures.

The freedom and variety of scenes, the deep national significance of the protagonists, the sweeping and deep interpretation of Russian history, the sense of destiny and magnitude which pervaded the play, and its poetic strength and majesty—all made it a literary sensation, a landmark of the new movement, and a victory over the obsolete patterns of the French pseudo-classic tragedy. This was a model of a work which combined historical exactitude with the romantic intensity of human conflict. But this great drama with its strong impact on Russian literature was banned by the theatrical censors. In fact, it was only in September 1870 that the tragedy's first performance took place in Mariinsky Theater in St. Petersburg. Three years later it started its triumphal career—but as a book for the famous Mussorgsky opera which was destined to open a new chapter in Russian and European music.

Thus Pushkin's dramatic writings were not incorporated into the contemporary repertory and therefore could not exert an influence on the development of Russian theatrical life. The same can be said about Mikhail Lermontov, the Russian Byron whose work represented the most genuine substance of national romanticism. He wrote a few dramas (*The Spaniards, Men and Passions, The Strange Man*) in a highly romantic vein, representing the dark hero and sharp conflict of passions, but his most important theatrical work is *Masquerade* (1835) written when he was twenty-one. He tried hard to put it on the stage, and revised it three times but could not break the resistance of censors, who banned it in 1836. Permission to present *Masquerade* was not given until 1862, but then it failed to arouse the audience. By a strange irony of destiny, it was not played again until the last days of the tsarist regime in 1917 and did not become a theatrical success until 1933 and 1938 when it was a century old.

The hero of Lermontov's drama, Arbenin, suspects Nina, his beautiful wife, of betrayal and finally murders her in a fit of jealousy—although in reality she is innocent. This plot serves as a vehicle for a study of character: Arbenin (closely related to Pechorin, the protagonist of Lermontov's well-known novel *A Hero of Our Time*) is a man of strong will-power, passionate, bitter and lonely. He despises the aristocratic society to which he belongs and criticizes its vices and hypocrisy with sharp intelligence—but he is unable to detach himself from its ties; he is capable only of sterile negation—until he falls victim to his own social environment. Although Arbenin is much more violent and desperate than Chatsky, there is a link between the two. But where Griboyedov used irony and humor, Lermontov resorted to sarcasm and violence, and the mood of his play is dark and vehement.

Romantic tendencies took hold of the Russian stage during

the reign of Nikolay I (1825-1855) immediately after the unsuccessful revolt of the Decembrists, who obviously were political romantics. The Tsar, himself a theater fan, went often to plays, spent a great deal of money for his Imperial Theater and did not spare expense in inviting foreign stars to Russia. It was under Nikolay that the bureaucracy of the theatrical administration took a definite shape. The statutes for the theater drawn up by Stepan Gedeonov, the head of Imperial Theater Administration, were completed in 1837 and approved two years later. These fixed all regulations about parts, rehearsals, costumes, deportment, fines, and punishments for the transgressors, turning actors into state functionaries. From 1803 until 1882, all actors and actresses were divided into "leading," "understudies," "second parts," "utilities" and "accessories." Parts were classified as in the French theater: the leading lady, first lover, ingénue, noble father, etc. Socially, the status of actors was gradually improving. In 1839, members of Imperial Theaters were graded according to three ranks, and those of the first category were granted the status of "honorary hereditary citizens" (a privileged group of urban population). Their prestige was also growing as attested by the number of poems prominent authors dedicated to actors and actresses.

Nikolay I liked what Turgenev later called "pseudo-magnificent" or "pseudo-grand" drama with an emphasis on outward brilliancy, and since his favorites were historical pieces which hailed tsars and monarchy, he indirectly promoted the romantics, but of a very special kind. Russian romanticism in the theater began with historical plays of a strong nationalistic tendency. When the new Alexandrinsky Theater designed by Carlo Rossi opened its doors in 1832, it offered to the first-night audience *Pozharsky* by V. Kriukovsky, a patriotic concoction about a prince who came to the rescue of monarchy in days of stress and danger of the seventeenth century. This choice forecast the future repertory which included inflated dramas by V. Kukolnik, and later plays by Nikolay Polevoy, critic and journalist, who combined romanticism with devotion to the throne and wrote such patriotic and rather insipid plays as *The Grandfather of The Russian Fleet*. His *Parasha the Siberian Girl*, taken from X. de Maistre's novel, moved spectators for decades by the sentimental story of a "simple-hearted" young woman who comes to the

capital to straighten out the injustice done to her father. Polevoy, like Kukolnik (who wrote verbose dramas on Tasso, San-
nazzaro, and Il Domenichino), reverted to Italian history, and
his *Ugolino* had for many years been a great success. It tells the
story of the cruel Pisan tyrant thrown into prison with his
children and dying from hunger (Dante made him gnaw at the
skull of his henchman). But the greatest feat of Polevoy was his
translation and adaptation of *Hamlet*. Produced on January 22,
1837, in Moscow with Mochalov in the title role, it became an
event of tremendous importance, a highlight of theatrical history.
Belinsky devoted a long article to it and the performance marked
a turning point in the romantic drama. In general, Shakespeare's
tragedies (which had been often given before) now became an
organic part of repertory in the two capitals and in the provinces,
and the parts of Hamlet or King Lear or Othello were cardinal
tests for any tragic actor. This meant that classic tragedy was being replaced by the romantic drama of which Shakespeare was
considered the summit.

Polevoy was a self-taught merchant's son, his dramas reflected
some traits of petty bourgeois mentality and therefore they contained romantic passion with elements of the "lachrymose, sobbing drama"—but this attracted nonaristocratic spectators of the
middle class. In general, the romantic theater was greatly supported by audiences which did not belong to the ruling classes.
They also determined the success of the trends which became
predominant in the thirties and the forties: the lachrymose or
sobbing play, the melodrama, and vaudeville. The sobbing play
(and the melodrama) mixed moving episodes with comic interludes; it usually dealt with people of humble extraction. It had
already made its appearance in translations and imitations in the
eighteenth century when Sumarokov called it obnoxious and
disgusting, because it lacked any elevated feelings and grandeur
of characters or action. But government clerks, merchants, tradesmen, and university students, as well as impoverished landlords,
loved it, and this explains the success of Kotzebue's plays in the
nineteenth century: his *Hatred of Men and Repentance, Hussites
at Naumburg,* and others, were sobbing plays.

The melodrama differed from the sobbing play by its crude
devices, gaudy colors, the impetus of its action and the surprise

of its denouement, and by its use of black and white in characterization. It stressed emotions and sharp contrasts in a direct,
primitive way. Instead of the rationalized and aristocratic art
of the classic tragedy, with its royal heroes, here was a world of
intrigue, murder, and violence presented in a more democratic
and often trivial environment, with more sensuality and individualism, in an atmosphere more complex (as to plot) but more
familiar (as to people). Such plays as *Two Orphans, Thirty
Years of A Gambler's Life* with their *deus ex machina* solutions
were extremely popular until the middle of the century. Some
of the melodramas resembled tragedies in a convex mirror: their
sequence of murders, shots, villains who commit suicide in fits
of repentance, and noble heroes without fear or reproach, reflected the traits of tragedy—without its depth, grandeur, or
solemnity.

Toward the end of the thirties, the division of genres into
drama, ballet and opera had definitely taken place, and each of
them began an independent existence. It did not, however, prevent the blending of songs and choreography in vaudeville,
which invaded and conquered the Russian stage in big cities as
well as in the provinces. Vaudeville came from the light opera
or *opera buffa* of the eighteenth century, but its name had a more
remote origin: it could be traced to Olivier Basselin, born in
Vau de Vire, Normandy, in the fifteenth century; his drinking
and satirical songs became famous under the name of his native
village, and their appellation was corrupted later from Vau-
devire into vaudeville. Starting in the eighteenth century, *vaux
de vire* or vaudevilles were interpolated into French comedies.
After the decline of the comedy with couplets (Desaugiers,
Scribe, Labiche), vaudeville gave its name to the light comedy
with songs and, occasionally, dances. In Russia, it was usually
a one-act play with topical couplets; it blossomed and expanded
in the 1830s and reigned supreme for some twenty years. During
the sixties it abandoned its songs to the operetta, its erotic pranks
to the "French-style farce," and the rest to various forms of light
comedy. But in the first half of the nineteenth century, vaudeville
delighted huge audiences with its topical songs and farcical
situations. There was anecdotal vaudeville written by Fyodor Koni
(1809-1879), by Peter Karatyghin (1805-1879), brother of the

tragedian, and by Dimitry Lensky-Vorobyev (1805-1860), an excellent comic actor and the author of some seventy plays, of
which *Lev Gurych Sinichkin* remained a hit for over a hundred
years. It portrays the life and mores in a provincial theater whose
manager is completely dependent on aristocratic patrons; the
latter regard actresses as their harem, and try to seduce a young
woman who makes her debut. Various familial, theatrical, amorous, and other incidents and errors in which the father of the
actress plays a prominent part form the structure of this amusing
vaudeville. Despite its naïveté and, at times, coarse humor, it
offered a magnificent opportunity to comic actors, and even in
the twentieth century, such artists as Davydov or Varlamov didn't
disdain to appear in it. Critics and serious writers waged a losing
battle against vaudeville. Belinsky and Gogol pointed out its
artificiality, clumsiness, and shallowness, but it resisted all attacks until taste changed and new forms of entertainment gained
popularity. Among them were, of course, the ballet and the
opera.

A new impulse to the ballet was given at the beginning of
the century by Charles Didelot. Contemporaries describe him as
a thin, big-nosed man with a red wig and a laurel wreath on his
head, resembling a caricature of Apollo. But he was an excellent
dancer and choreographer. Under his influence (he worked in
St. Petersburg in 1801-1811, and in 1816-1829), the pantomime
and the dance steps of his Italian predecessors became more
animated and colorful. Besides all technical improvements, he
taught his pupils that upward movement of the Romantics,
that very tearing off from the earth into the sky which necessita-
ted leaps and the toe dance. Didelot was also the first to introduce
flying scenes in which a complicated system of wires and pulleys
carried the dancers through the air as by a supernatural force.
Foreign stars influenced the Russian ballet considerably—particularly Marie Taglioni during her performances in 1837-1842,
when this eerie, delicate, and ethereal artist charmed the spectators in *Les Sylphides* and other romantic ballets. The fiery Fanny
Elssler and a more poetic Grisi also provoked great enthusiasm
and had pupils and imitators.

The music and choreography of most ballets were of foreign
origin, but the Russian dancers were growing in skill and talent

to such an extent that in the forties and fifties many of them went abroad and were acclaimed in Paris, Vienna, London, Milan, and Berlin. This was the case with Yelena Andreyanova (1819-1857) and Nadezhda Bogdanova (1836-1897), who competed with Elssler and Grisi and made Europe talk about the extraordinary flowering of St. Petersburg ballet. The West did not see other Russian favorites: the beautiful Evgenia Kolossova (1782-1869), who was superb in native character dances, or Avdotia Istomina (1799-1848), whom Pushkin immortalized in enthusiastic verse. Taglioni found Istomina heavy ("more force than grace") but the Russian audiences did not share this opinion. Together with a host of talented ballerinas, such as Danilova, who died at the age of seventeen, the Russian ballet affirmed itself magnificently. Of course it remained almost exclusively the art of the upper classes, and ballet performances were always social occasions often enhanced by the presence of the emperor and the court.

The opera was also patronized by the nobility, and aristocratic audiences went mad for Bellini, Rossini, Donizetti, and Meyerbeer. But in the late thirties, two great changes occurred: the opera started attracting larger groups of listeners, losing its exclusive character and becoming a more democratic entertainment, and the Russian national opera affirmed itself successfully. After the attempts of the eighteenth century even foreign composers living in Russia, such as Cavos, tried to use Russian folklore motifs; and the works of some Russian musicians, such as Alexey Verstovsky, the author of the popular historical romantic opera *Askold's Grave* (1835), had a strong native flavor. But only Mikhail Glinka (1804-1857) with his *Life for the Tsar* (Ivan Sussanin) offered an original and thoroughly Russian work equal to the highest achievement of Western operatic art. It is significant that it saw the light the same year (1836) that Gogol's *The Inspector General* was performed for the first time. Both marked a new era in the history of the Russian theater and music. *Life for the Tsar* told of the peasant Ivan Sussanin, who at the time of troubles and war at the beginning of the seventeenth century, misled Polish invaders in search of Mikhail Romanov, the future tsar, and perished as a loyal and patriotic hero. The subject matter of the opera and the magnificence of its production brought the Tsar and his family to the first night, but the aristo-

cracy dismissed Glinka's national music as "made for coachmen."
To punish officers of the Imperial Guard, Grand Duke Mikhail
used to send them to Glinka's "boring misfit." Glinka's second
opera, *Ruslan and Liudmila,* performed in 1842, magnificently
contrasted oriental motifs and Russian tunes, and like *Life for
the Tsar* expressed the very essence of national genious. "Glinka
leans directly on the people," said the critic Stassov, "but he
speaks in forms of contemporary European music." Thus Glinka
initiated the Russian operatic school—and his successors, Dargomyzhsky, Balakirev, Mussorgsky, Rimsky-Korsakov, and Tchaikovsky brought it to a glorious development in the next half
century.

The serious opera hardly encouraged good acting; the latter
was more easily found in the comic opera where artists had to
provoke the mirth of the audience. The romantic opera was
more static, arias slowed down the action, and the singer limited
his acting to monotonous gestures of the right hand. Contemporaries did not expect acting from opera singers; they paid attention
only to their voices. Décors and costumes of operas and ballets
were conventional. They did not take into consideration any
national or historical specifications of the book and were generally
either lavish or shabby "frames" for the performers. The frame
often had nothing to do with the content and spirit of the opera
or the ballet.

But while the romantic tendency prevailed in opera, ballet,
and melodrama, realistic trends reached great heights in the
works of individual playwrights. Griboyedov's comedy ended a
period which originated in the satirical play of the eighteenth
century, but the trend it represented was taken up, and very
vigorously, by Gogol's social comedy and Turgenev's drawing-
room comedy.

Nikolay Gogol (1809-1852) was greatly interested in theater.
His father wrote plays and acted as an amateur in performances
given at the estates of his wealthy Ukrainian neighbors. The
young Gogol had been very active in school theatricals, and when
he went to St. Petersburg in 1828, he made an attempt to become
a professional actor, but failed his audition. Later he wrote articles
on the theater, fought against vaudeville, and expressed very
interesting opinions on the role of the stage director: "He

should," said Gogol, "hear the inner life contained in a play
and try to harmonize all its parts, as in an orchestra; a part
should be studied on the stage together with other actors and not
at home, and the director should watch rehearsals from the front
row."

But even more important than those remarks, which were
remembered more than fifty years later by the initiators of the
Moscow Art Theater, was Gogol's claim for "truth in representation of life." "O great Molière," he wrote, "he who developed
his characters so fully and widely and watched so profoundly all
their nuances, and you, stern and cautious Lessing, and you
noble and fiery Schiller, who showed man's dignity in such a
poetic glow, look what is happening after you on our stage, what
a strange monster under the guise of melodrama, sneaked in
among us! And where is our life, ourselves with our own idio-
syncrasies and traits? The melodrama is lying most impudently.
Isn't it incomprehensible? Only a great, deep rare genius can
catch what surrounds us daily, what always accompanies us, what
is ordinary—while mediocrity grabs with both hands all that is
out of rule, what happens but seldom and catches the eye by
its ugliness and disharmony. . . . The strange has become the
subject matter of our drama. The whole point is to tell a new,
strange, unheard-of accident: murder, fire, wild passions, hench-
men, poisons, effects, eternal effects."

In 1832 Gogol was writing a comedy *The Decoration of Wladimir of the Third Category* of which we have but fragments in
other plays, and was saying in letters to friends: "I am crazy about
writing a comedy." Between 1832 and 1837 he actually composed
several plays, *The Gamblers, The Morning of a Business Man,
The Servants' Hall,* and *The Law Suit* (both deriving from
Wladimir), and *The Marriage,* a farcical play. None of them was
presented before 1842, when they were published in a revised
text. His next theatrical attempt was, however, his last—and
the most famous: in 1836 *The Inspector General* was produced
in the Alexandrinsky Theater in the presence of the Emperor and
his family. Six weeks later, Gogol, unable to sustain the stress
of polemics provoked by his comedy, left Russia. He wrote all
sorts of afterpieces to *The Inspector General,* trying to justify
himself and his good intentions. All of these writings are most

revealing for the student of Gogol's psychology but they do not add anything to the work itself. Its significance lies in the fact that the public and the critics—and the actors—took it for a thoroughly realistic play.

The plot of the comedy, suggested to Gogol by Pushkin, was treated by the playwright as a typical "comedy of errors." Its action takes place in a small provincial town ruled by a coarse and harsh mayor, Skvoznik-Dmukhanovsky, and by a gang of ignorant, corrupt, and stupid officials, each a perfect knave in his own way. This little world is roused by the rumor that an Inspector General from the capital has arrived incognito in order to investigate the town's administration. When told that a stranger by the name of Khlestakov has put up at the inn and is behaving in a most perplexing manner, the mayor and his acolytes believe that this is the Inspector General traveling incognito. The mayor gives Khlestakov a splendid reception and is ready to throw his own daughter into the arms of the important guest. Khlestakov, a flirtatious boaster, tells tall tales to the officials, who all offer him bribes, and then departs, his pockets filled with money and gifts in the midst of happy confusion caused by his engagement to the Mayor's daughter. At this very moment the prying Postmaster rushes in with a letter he has just opened. It is written by Khlestakov and describes his extraordinary adventure to a friend in St. Petersburg, laughing at the dupes who had mistaken him for an Inspector General. The Mayor and his assistants scarcely have any time to express their shame and anger: the arrival of the real Inspector General is officially announced to the petrified group of city fathers.

This grotesque stunned the audience when first presented in April 1836, and only the presence of the Emperor, who liked the play saved it from the clutches of censorship—even though some cuts had to be made for further performances. The play seemed so extraordinary that on the morrow of the first night the whole of St. Petersburg society was in an uproar. The conservatives found it a calumny and dangerous propaganda, while the liberals argued that its was true to life, and Belinsky saw it as an example of the "natural school" which aimed at the realistic rendering of life. Moreover, he felt that the portrayal of characters transformed this masterpiece from a simple representation of a contemporary scene into a moral judgment of Russian reality, a triumph of "critical realism."

Gogol was taken aback by the violence of public reaction and tried to minimize the social impact of his own work. It is true that in his own words his aim in writing *The Inspector General* was "to pile up all the vile things in Russia and to laugh at them." The comedy had a folk saying for its epigraph: "Don't blame the mirror if it is your own mug that's crooked." Gogol was terribly upset when everyone recognized his own image in the mirror and damned the author. As usual, this extraordinary and most complex writer was hardly aware of what he was doing and he tried to justify himself and to soften the blow he had unconsciously dealt to the bureaucratic order of the Russian State. He claimed that his main and perfectly honest hero of the comedy was laughter itself, that the idea of the Inspector General, or the Supreme Judge, had religious implications. He could never get over the fact his comedy had become a banner of triumph for one part of Russian society and a symbol of subversion for the other.

Regardless of Gogol's intentions, opinions and attempts at repentance, *The Inspector General* entered the Russian theater not so much as a grotesque (which it is) but as the first truly realistic comedy opposed to the current melodrama, farces, and vaudeville. Belinsky was the first to see that the trivial anecdote of the plot grew into a vast social satire enhanced by psychological and dramatic unity. The conduct and speech of each character in the play necessarily stemmed from his personality, and therefore actions and words seem convincingly real. The events follow a closely-knit sequence, without side issues and sub-plots, and each person appearing on the stage is directly or indirectly involved in the devolopment of the main action. The sparkling and funny dialogue, the comic incidents, the rendering of moral defects and speech peculiarities of each character, the extraordinary portrayal of Khlestakov, the flighty and shallow representative of St. Peterburg's lower bureaucracy—all contributed to making memorable each performance of the comedy. Firmly established in the Russian repertory, it became one of the most important landmarks in the history of Russian dramatic literature and one of the crucial stage tests for actors. It also provided a vast field for original interpretations. As we will see later, each new school of acting made a try at *The Inspector General;* for a century, realists, symbolists, experimentalists staged Gogol's immortal work in their own peculiar manner.

Second in importance in Gogol's dramatic work is *The Marriage* (written in 1833). This delightful story concerns Podkolesin, a bachelor whom an eager matchmaker lures into the house of the bride-to-be, where he finds several other matrimonial "candidates" and becomes so appalled by the prospects of married life that he escapes by jumping from the window. *The Marriage* did not appeal to the writer's contemporaries—and this, despite excellent acting by Sosnitsky and Shchepkin (in 1842). Until 1916, there was no significant performance of this comedy which contains a gallery of marvelous and extremely funny characters. There is no doubt that this play (which has autobiographical as well as symbolic significance) influenced the early one-act comedies by Chekhov.

A native realistic comedy appeared at the moment when realistic tendencies were gaining also among the actors in their acting methods and techniques. Even during his lifetime, Gogol had the satisfaction of seeing his comedy acted by the best and most enlightened scions of dramatic art. The first night, in 1836, Ivan Sosnitsky portrayed the Mayor as a cold swindler, sweet as a snake and bitter as gall, a tall shifty, foxy man, with elongated features and measured gestures. Shchepkin, in Moscow, gave another interpretation: his Mayor was a carnivorous cunning rascal, ignorant and impulsive, a short, thick, broad man of coarse instincts. Both were memorable images. Gogol had less luck with Khlestakov: the first night Dur interpreted the young man in an almost farcical vein; later Samarin made him too dandyish and sedate, and Maximov too insignificant. He gained in stature and color with Shumsky, who caught the emptiness and triviality of the impersonator.

The difference in interpretation corresponded to the rivalry between two Imperial centers, the dramatic school of the Alexandrinsky Theater in St. Petersburg and that of the Maly Theater in Moscow.

In 1832, the company of the Alexandrinsky Theater was installed in the new building constructed from the designs of Carlo

Rossi in magnificent neo-classical style. It attracted all sorts of
public—more democratic than other Imperial theaters of the
capital, where ballet and opera were given in the Mariinsky*
Theater and performances in French or German in the Mikhailovsky (established in 1833). According to Belinsky, Alexandrinsky's audience, however, was uniform and mainly consisted
of government employees, civil servants of various ranks, and of
university students. The repertory was motley, including romantic dramas, classical tragedies, vaudeville, and a host of historical
plays—from patriotic Russian ones to translations of Shakespeare
and Schiller or minor European writers. Some contemporaries
in the forties complained of the sentimental and trivial effects
of "monstrous German dramas" and "false situations in the
second-rate French sobbing comedies and vaudevilles" or home-
spun comic ineptitudes. Some adaptations from foreign languages were done in most ridiculous ways: in a play located in
Naples, actors drove around the stage in sleighs and wore sheepskin coats. The Alexandrinsky company, nevertheless, had good
actors, among them Dmitrevsky's pupil, Ivan Sosnitsky (1794-
1871), an intelligent, skillful comedian and a good teacher in
his own right. But the king of Alexandrinsky was the great
tragedian Vassily Karatyghin (1802-1853). Tall and handsome,
he had an excellent appearance and a sonorous, expressive voice.
He paid great attention to his make-up and costumes, knew how
to use effects—particularly in tragedies and melodramas in which
he acted a great deal—but never exaggerated or abused those
effects. He had a talent for walking, speaking, making the appropriate gestures, and doing the right thing at the right moment,
but according to his biographers, he did not put his whole heart
into his acting; he knew how to restrain his own feelings and,
as a result, he did not provoke strong emotions among his spectators. The audiences admired him and were greatly thrilled by
the skillful, masterful way he projected his parts. His innate gift
was sustained by continuous self-control, analysis and profound
knowledge of the stage. The polish and perfection of his acting
satisfied the most refined and exigent taste. A marvelous technician, he could act in most diverse roles: from Hamlet to Louis

* It got this name in 1860 after the construction of what previously was called
Bolshoy (Big) theater of St. Petersburg.

XI, from Leicester in *Mary Stuart* to Coriolanus, and from Don Carlos to Karl Moore in Schiller's *The Robbers*. Belinsky and Herzen reproached him for the effects by which he built up tension in his heroic roles, and even discerned in it some melodramatic tendency. He loved to use contrasts in his acting—jumping from the low register to high. He would say very quickly those parts of his speech he did not consider interesting, as if he wanted to get rid of them—then suddenly with a shout he would start to recite distinctly and loudly. He incessantly moved his hands, accompanying the modulations of his voice. His influence on Russian actors was such that at the end of the century, Stanislavsky found Karatyghin's methods still being used by the majority of Russian actors.

As a young man, Karatyghin had feuds with the administration and was sent to jail in 1822 because he remained seated when A. Maikov, the Director of Imperial Theaters, came on the stage. Later, however, he became a favorite of the court and of Gedeonov, the new Director. When he went abroad in 1845, after twenty-five years of a professional career, he was particularly recommended and carried letters to all Russian ambassadors in Europe. When he died, the Emperor sent condolences to his wife, Alexandra Kolosova, a good actress in her own right.

An important place on the Alexandrinsky stage was held by the Samoilov family—a true theatrical dynasty. Vassily Samoilov (1812-1887), son of a popular opera singer, had a gift for imitation and was superb in the role of a French tutor speaking a broken Russian. He was also very good in portraying flayed aristocrats and impoverished but boastful noblemen. One of his best roles was his portrayal of Krechinsky in the famous comedy by Sukhovo Kobylin. He also excelled in vaudeville and comedy. When working on a part, Samoilov usually made a sort of a graph, marking all the climaxes and carefully designing all the upward and downward movements and degrees of tension of the play. He also followed Karatyghin in the careful preparation and rational control of his acting. He himself usually made the sketches for his costumes.

His three sisters were all excellent actresses: Maria became well known after her brilliant interpretation of Mirandolina in *Locandiera* by Goldoni, but abandoned the stage in 1837 to marry a rich merchant; Vera (1824-1880) played society women or melancholy characters and was at her best in parts which required a fine psychological design; and Nadezhda (1818-1899) was a born comic actress, long remembered in *The Mischievous Girl* by N. Kulikov, a playwright and one of Alexandrinsky's stage directors. She portrayed a girl from a small provincial town who went on a visit to St. Petersburg and, back home, gave an account of the capital's theaters and acted out what she had seen —including the performances by two French actresses, Plessy and Volnay, and dances by Fanny Elssler.

But while Karatyghin's tradition reigned supreme on the Alexandrinsky stage, different artistic methods flourished in Moscow.

The Moscow Maly (or "small") Theater, erected to replace the Petrovsky Theater and opened to the public in 1808, got its final quarters in 1824 and from that moment on became one of the most important centers of Russian theatrical art. Ballet and opera performances continued in the Bolshoy (or "Big") Theater* and the Maly Theater became the home of drama and comedy. It attracted large audiences, among them university students, literati, and intellectuals from various strata of society. For more than a decade a gifted tragedian, Pavel Mochalov, held spellbound this motley crowd of spectators. His father Stepan had also been an actor, and Muscovites loved his old-fashioned manner in melodramas and his cheap effects in *The Marriage of Figaro*. Mochalov (1880-1848), born as a serf, stunned Belinsky by his interpretation of Hamlet and was proclaimed the greatest Russian artist of the century. A man of strong impulses, he acted by inspiration. Unable to control himself, he was at his worst when trying to do his best. From his debut at the age of seventeen, he displayed an uneven and highly emotional genius. An uneducated man, shy to the extreme when not in his usual company of actors, he did not know how to work, had hardly any skill or craft, acted blindly, and simply expressed himself on the stage. As a lyrical and romantic figure (at one time he had been under the influence of Byronism), he symbolized art as a mysterious divine force. Whenever inspiration descended upon him, he was irresible in his flow of passionate words and the sweep of his nervous, com-

*With a seating capacity of two thousand, built in 1824 by Bove, according to designs by Mikhailov; it burned in 1853, was restored by A. Kavos in 1856, and renovated under the Soviets.

pelling gestures. But inspiration was capricious, and often he would be dull for the most part of the performance and then suddenly flare up and rise to a true artistic height in a few passages. The audience, who forgave their idol his bad acting, eagerly awaited those sublime instants of ecstasy. Mochalov had bad manners and a rather poor appearance (a round back), but he could transform himself and become whomever he was embodying, and he was stunning as Othello, Richard the Lion-Hearted, Romeo, Don Carlos, or the heroes of Polevoy or Kukolnik. The explanation of this miracle lay in his personality. He possessed an indomitable spirit of protest, a fire, a romantic yearning. "He brought on the stage," said one of his contemporaries, "the torments of his great soul, his anxieties, his feelings of doom." In the years of social and political reaction after the defeat of the Decembrists, he represented the agony of a whole generation which acclaimed in him their dreams, their tensions, their defeats, and their inner strivings. The university youth determined his success and supported his high reputation. All the followers of the new Romantic Movement glorified him as a Russian Keane. The critic Apollon Grigoriev compared him to a forest, and Karatyghin to a well-kept garden. When he came upon the stage shouting monologues as if he were persecuted by the Furies, the spectators felt the revolt against fate and oppression and applauded so enthusiastically that the authorities worried about the dangerous impact of the emotions Mochalov aroused. His "instinctive" manner was greatly admired and imitated by provincial actors, often degenerating into shallow and loud exaggeration. But, of course, Mochalov could not be held responsible for these distortions; he also had more intelligent followers, such as Kornily Poltavtsev (1833-1865) and Nikolay Rybakov (1811-1876), though the latter shifted from tragic and romantic parts to realistic impersonations of Ostrovsky's characters. The young Varvara Asenkova (1817-1841) also belonged to Mochalov's school; from vaudeville she moved toward the temperamental incarnation of Ophelia, Cordelia, and other heroines.

Mochalov's reliance on temperament and inspiration was opposed by Mikhail Shchepkin (1788-1863), whose following became larger than that of the romantic actor and continued to grow in the fifties and sixties. Shchepkin's father was a butler on Count Volkenstein's estate, and Mikhail was born a serf. He acted as an amateur in the Count's rural theater, was authorized to go on the road, and after 1808 became a professional actor. He married a "free" girl who consented to become a serf through her marriage. The Count, proud of Shchepkin's successes, refused to part with him, and the young actor did not become a free man until 1821 when a special performance was organized in Poltava to raise the sum set as the price of his liberty. To the honor of local nobility, it must be mentioned that they did not hesitate to pay from 200 to 700 rubles a seat and collected 10,000 rubles on the side. By 1823, Shchepkin became a member of the Moscow Imperial Theater, and thus began his triumphant career. He had diversified and wide range of impersonations, and contemporaries called him Proteus: he went from acting in the kind of melodrama in which a noble lover rescues his happy rival and abandons to him his beloved, to doing a parody of that very melodrama; and he was as excellent in Molière's comedy as in Russian vaudeville. Basically, he was a comedian but he knew how to make his audience cry with the same mastery that made them laugh. Next to memorable impersonations of Famusov in *Wit Works Woe* or of the Mayor in *The Inspector General,* he created a pathetic figure of the poor old Kuzovkin in Turgenev's *The Parasite.* His delivery stemmed from his "inner laboratory" and was the fruit of sustained work. A first-rate technician known for his assiduity (he never missed a rehearsal), he began his acting in the usual manner of the era: he whispered and shouted, mumbled indistinctly in dialogues and made his monologues in a pompous recitation, emphasizing the "most significant sentences." In 1810, at the age of 22, he was startled by an amateur actor, Prince Meshchersky, who moved and talked in a quiet unobstrusive fashion. Shchepkin tried to imitate him and found it extremely difficult; breaking away from conventional ways was not so easy and naturalness—which became his sole aim—could be reached only at the price of constant effort and hard training. Gradually Shchepkin developed his own method. He strove toward a full impersonation of a character by giving him the complete semblance of reality; he polished every "life detail," and he used intonation, change of voice register, gait, gestures, and make-up and costumes to create a live image. Simplicity and intelligence were the basis of his acting, and behind the ease of his appearance there was always a long and careful preparation. It was through him that the tradition of painstaking labor, seriousness, and a high level of craftsmanship was established in the Maly Theater. He also initiated the preliminary reading of plays to the whole company before the casting of parts and insisted on giving the performance a spirit of unity and harmony. No wonder that his ideas of "warm naïveté," "natural style" and "ensemble" puzzled the veterans of the stage who firmly believed in consecrated gestures. Shchepkin himself tells of one such conservative who, after having finished his tirade, forgot to raise his hand at the end and started to leave the stage; then—half-way off—corrected his error by stopping and "raising that darned hand."

The natural school promoted by Shchepkin brought up a whole generation of actors who excelled in "character parts," particularly in comedies by Gogol, Turgenev, Griboyedov, and Ostrovsky (Shchepkin himself was less successful in Ostrovsky's works). Close to Shchepkin was Sosnitsky, and later such great artists as Varlamov, Davydov, Sadovsky, Yakovlev, and Fedotova all recognized their indebtedness to the father of Russian realistic acting. Stanislavsky said that Shchepkin established the basis for Russian genuine dramatic art.

A kind and affable man with wide interests, Shchepkin was on friendly terms with the great writers of his era—particularly Gogol, Pushkin (who rated him so highly that he wrote the beginning of his *Memoirs*), Aksakov, Belinsky, Herzen, and others. The Maly Theater acquired the surname of "Second Moscow University" because of the strong personal ties between the theater and the academic world: several professors, such as A. Storozhenko and A. Vesselovsky, were members of the theater's Literary Committee while many actors belonged to the "Society of Friends of Russian Literature." Students went to the Maly Theater as if it were home. And Shchepkin did everything to enhance this reputation and stress the dignity of an actor's job: "to the actor," he said, "the theater is a temple, it is his sanctuary." He strongly believed in the high educational impact of good plays, and always strove for the reflection on the stage of all the artistic and intellectual tendencies of his time.

In this he got, of course, the support of the progressive press. All the prominent writers of the thirties and forties contributed largely to the theatrical criticism. Belinsky, the leading Russian critic, wrote about Mochalov and Shchepkin: Pushkin, Prince Viazemsky, Herzen, Gogol, Aksakov, and others devoted pages and pages to reviews of plays and to appraisal of actors. Dailies, weeklies, and monthlies continually published articles on the theater. And partisans of romanticism or of realism fought for or against diverse schools of acting in the same manner they did about literary trends. The theater in Russia was indeed becoming an important and serious thing.

3

The second half of the nineteenth century

THE LATE FIFTIES and the early sixties brought about a great change in Russia; it began with the abolition of serfdom and the emancipation of the peasants, the judiciary, administrative, and educational reforms, the transformation of old ways of life, and the improvements in bureaucratic and military practices. This complete rebuilding of the structure of the State signed a death warrant for the old Russia of Nikolay. A new social and economic order gradually renovated the Empire, and for half a century, until 1905, the country remained within this framework. It was, of course, an order based upon class privileges and autocratic rule, despite its monolithic facade. It was often shattered by clashes of interests between the governing minority and the discontented majority, and undermined by the alternation of progress and reaction which has always been the constant rhythm of Russian history; yet all the trends and aspirations of modern Russia came to life in many areas and were developed precisely during this epoch of stir and innovation. Literature and art, music and theater, science and technology, expanded more than ever before, and, in the sixties a new and different spirit took hold of the Russian intellectuals and artists.

One of the most significant changes concerned the readers, listeners, and spectators. The increase of the urban population and the emergence of educated men and women from the lower and middle classes infused new blood into audiences, and enhanced realistic tendencies in all the arts. The "natural school" found allies in the ever-increasing nonaristocratic elements of Russian society, and the mentality of the intellectuals in the sixties proved to be strictly antiromantic. The well-known movement of "nihilism" represented by Turgenev in *Fathers and Sons* was one of the manifestations of this spirit which fought against idealistic illusions and the estheticism of the forties, and attempted to replace the exaggerations and sublime flights of romanticism by a down-to-earth attitude and hard practical sense.

While in literature and poetry the works of Turgenev, Goncharov, young Tolstoy, and many other writers marked the triumph of the realistic school, their inroads upon theatrical repertory were far from being as decisive and as victorious. For many years, melodrama and vaudeville with strong romantic overtones, composed by second-rate playwrights, maintained their grip on the Russian stage, particularly in the provinces, and the partisans of realistic art had to wage a bitter fight against numerous foes before obtaining recognition. It is significant, for instance, that only a few playwrights dared to follow the Gogol tradition. In the early forties Turgenev said that Gogol's comedies were the isolated achievements of a genius, and that they were far from becoming a common heritage of the Russian stage. His only hope was that the seeds the author of *The Inspector General* had sown would bear fruit someday. By a strange paradox, it was Turgenev himself who tried to bring forth those fruits although his strength did not lie in the dramatic form and his art, with its sense of measure and balance, seemed far removed from Gogol's grotesque morbidity.

Turgenev's early theatrical experiments (he was then twenty-five) had a definite romantic flavor (*The Imprudence,* 1843, probably an imitation of Mérimée's pseudo-Spanish plays), but his next comedy *Penniless* portrayed a young nobleman who wastes his time and money in St. Petersburg and is as flighty and boastful as Khlestakov, while his old servant is obviously modeled after Khlestakov's man Ossip.

In 1847, Shchepkin asked Turgenev to write a comedy for him; he received *The Parasite* the next year. Then censors, however, were horrified by the play and banned it. Not until 1857 was it published, and then under another title; it was not performed until 1861. In 1849 Turgenev sent Shchepkin another comedy, *The Bachelor,* which was produced the same year (in St. Petersburg and in Moscow) with Shchepkin, Martynov, V. Samoilova, and was favorably received by the press and the public. *The Parasite* depicts an impoverished nobleman, Kuzovkin, who lives on the estate of his former benefactors, now long dead. Their daughter Olga after some years comes to visit the manor with her husband, Yeletsky, a stiff and egotistical St. Petersburg bureaucrat. Kuzovkin gets drunk, is trapped into playing the buffoon and, exasperated by alcohol and humiliation, confesses to being Olga's father. But a few hours later, in a fit of repentance and shame, he retracts the confession and is finally bought off by Yeletsky, who sends him away. Kuzovkin departs, leaving Olga in a state of confusion and puzzlement. This portrayal of a pathetic buffoon gives a strong sentimental and dramatic quality to the play and obviously stems from Gogol's "little man," later taken up by Dostoevsky. *The Bachelor* is written in a lighter vein but its humor is mixed with sentimentalism. Moshkin, the hero of the play, a kind and shy man of fifty who has adopted Masha, a young orphan, is closely related to Makar Devushkin (*Poor Folk* by Dostoevsky). Moshkin tries to marry off his ward to Vilitsky, a weak and egotistical young clerk, but the latter, influenced by his German friend von Fonk, decides that Masha is too simple for him and abandons her. In order to restore Masha's self-esteem and give her social status, Moshkin himself offers to marry her. Actually he yields to a genuine but hidden feeling of love. The comic indecisions of Vilitsky and the character portrayal of Moshkin and his provincial friend are inspired by Gogol's *The Marriage.*

The next dramatic works by Turgenev were more original. They are interesting in their own right—and also because they form a link with Chekhov. *The Lunch with the Marshal of Nobility* depicts a ridiculous scene of an abortive attempt to bring together brother and sister who simply cannot agree on the division of the common property they inherited from their parents. All the protagonists are treated as masks, the situations are grotesque and this one-act play (which has been brilliantly interpreted by Shchepkin, Karatyghin, Sosnitsky and other excellent actors) is truly hilarious. Its humor is very close to that of Chekhov's one-act "jokes."

An entirely different structure is presented by *A Month in the Country* (1850), probably the best of Turgenev's plays. It is a drawing room comedy with a simple plot but a rather complex psychological design. The heroine, Natalia Islayeva, married to a rich landowner who is too absorbed in his agricultural projects to pay enough attention to his young wife (she is in her late twenties), is being courted by Rakitin, a neighbor; she responds to his love but within the limits of a rather innocent "amorous friendship." Her dormant desires, however, are awakened by Belyaev, the tutor of Islayeva's ten-year-old son. The discovery of her own feelings toward Belyaev comes to Natalia together with another shocking revelation: the tutor seems to be interested in Verochka, Islayeva's seventeen-year-old ward. In order to eliminate her rival, Natalia uses all sorts of feminine tricks and is ready to marry Verochka off to Bolshintsov, an old, fat landowner. The process of growing jealousy in the older woman is parallel to the awakening of womanhood in Verochka, who becomes aware of what is going on and affirms her right to make her decisions. In the end, the confused tutoi and the offended Rakitin depart, leaving Natalia alone. The play has subtle twists of mood and strong undercurrents—just like Chekhov's comedies. To make the comparison more striking. *A Month in the Country* does not lack in secondary characters, such as a cynical doctor who reminds us of Chekhov's superfluous men. Some Russian critics pointed out the resemblance between several scenes in this comedy and those in Balzac's *The Stepmother*, which Turgenev undoubtedly had seen in Paris.

Then censors mutilated *A Month in the Country* to such an extent that its integral text did not appear until 1869, and its first performance took place only in 1872 in Moscow. It was received coolly but later, in 1882, Savina, the famous acrtess and Turgenev's last love, in the part of Verochka, made the play a great success. It continued to run for years in the Alexandrinsky Theater, and in the nineties the same Savina shifted to the role of Natalia, creating a memorable interpretation.

Of the two other Turgenev plays, *A Provincial Lady* (1851)

and *An Evening in Sorrento* (1852), a proverb-comedy in Musset style (like his previous trifle in the French manner—*Where
It Is Thin It Breaks*), only the first was produced successfully
by Shchepkin and Rykalova in Moscow the year of its publication, and then occasionally revived in the nineties.

Even more significant than Turgenev's comedies is *A Hard
Lot*, a "popular tragedy" by Alexey Pisemsky, author of *A Thousand Souls*, one of the most striking and realistic descriptions of
pre-reform Russia. He wrote many other novels and stories in the
"down to earth," close-to-the-soil manner. *A Hard Lot* was the
first drama portraying the life of the peasants and bringing forth
protagonists from the lower classes. It told the story of Yelizaveta,
a peasant woman who, in the absence of her husband Anany, becomes the mistress of their noble master and begets a child by
him. Upon his return Anany learns of his dishonor, mistreats
the unfaithful wife, and finally kills her child. He escapes and
hides for a week, but remorse and the wish for self-punishment
force him to surrender. In the last scene, during his interrogation
by the police, Anany reveals his sense of justice and his desire
for expiation. Before being shipped to prison, he takes leave
of everybody with a truly Christian feeling of humility and repentance. When performed for the first time in the Alexandrinsky
Theater (in 1863) with Pelageia Strepetova as Elizaveta, this
grim story held the audience on the edge of their seats: its in-
exorable development, its strong characters, its stark realism, its
tragic spirit, were a novelty for Russian spectators of the time.
It represented a bold and unusual triumph of realistic portraiture on the stage.

Pisemsky wrote his drama in 1859; two years earlier Saltykov-
Shchedrin, the great satirist, the "Russian Swift," wrote his
comedy *Death of Pazukhin*, which is unique in its bitter laughter
and frightening exploration of low passions. It concerns Pazukhin, an old millionaire who is dying but refuses to write his last
will and keeps his money in a chest under his bed. The plump
Zhivoyedova, his housekeeper and mistress whom he bought from
her parents when she was fifteen; his son Prokofy, whom he repudiated because of the latter's attachment to old religious
rituals; his stupid daughter Nastasia married to Furnachev, a
cunning official; his old friend Lobastov, a retired general; and a

few others persons, including his servant Bayev, engage in all kinds of intrigue in order to get his money should he die intestate. Finally Prokofy, the housekeeper, and the general reach some kind of underhanded agreement and outwit Furnachev, who enters Pazukhin's room as soon as the old man expires and helps himself to a pocketful of bills. The whole struggle for money around the deathbed, with its ridiculous and grotesque incidents, is presented as an exposure of greed and hypocrisy, done in a rather crude manner very akin to Saltykov's novel *The Golovlyov's Family*. After the first performance of the play in 1859 censors banned it for more than thirty years. Saltykov died in 1889 and *The Death of Pazukhin* was first revived in the Alexandrinsky with Varlamov in 1893. The Moscow Art Theater took it up in 1914 and then after the revolution (1924, 1939). Other theatrical companies also produced this sharp and engrossing play in the first half of this century.

I I

Turgenev, Pisemsky, and Saltykov were novelists, not playwrights, and their contribution to the theater was secondary. The central figure of the sixties and seventies is, of course, Ostrovsky, the creator of national repertory and a professional playwright. His personality and influence were so paramount in theatrical history that he overshadowed another important builder of plots and painter of characters—Alexander Sukhovo-Kobylin (1817-1903)—who is, perhaps, the most outstanding representative of the Gogolian school in Russian dramatic literature. Born into a wealthy and highly cultured aristocratic family, Sukhovo-Kobylin received an excellent and varied education and was a great admirer of Gogol, whom he knew personally. In 1850 he was accused, together with his servants, of the murder of his French mistress and for several years had to endure police persecutions and judicial investigations. He went through arrests, trials, court sentences, reversals of verdict, appeals and counter appeals, interventions of high administrative bodies—until the Emperor himself put an end to this nightmare. During the years he tried to prove his innocence, Sukhovo-Kobylin got acquainted with all sorts of illegal proceedings behind the scenes, and met

corrupted officials, false witnesses, scheming shysters, and pompous bureaucrats. He made use of this painful experience in his
plays.

Despite a certain ruthlessness in characterization, his first
comedy of manners, *Krechinsky's Wedding,* was conceived in
lighter vein than the two following ones. It portrayed with a rare
combination of irony and sharp humor two characters typical of
the disintegration of the nobility: Krechinsky, an adventurer,
rascal, and gambler, member of all fashionable clubs, who is
hiding under his charming manners of a true nobleman the
cynicism of a bird of prey, and Raspluyev, his adviser, equally
ready to do anything for money, a dangerous parasite, pitiful
in distress and sentimental in good fortune. Krechinsky has the
inventiveness and the temperament of a great crook; Raspluyev
is a failure, a knave who has been pushed around too much.
When in a tight corner, Krechinsky, with his usual genius for
bold solutions, gets engaged to Lidochka, the lovely but inex-
perienced daughter of Muromskoy, a naive and limited country
squire. To raise the money for the wedding, Krechinsky borrows
an expensive diamond pin from his fiancée and pawns it for a
substantial sum, replacing it at the last moment in the broker's
office with a worthless counterfeit. Caught redhanded a few hours
later, he finds an easy escape because Lidochka refuses to sue him.

This ending leads directly into the second part of the trilogy,
The Case, in which Lidochka and her father are shown as innocent victims of a police conspiracy: they are accused of being
Krechinsky's accomplices and bled white by dishonest investi-
gators and greedy officials. The special file of Muromskoy grows
and fattens—and so do the incomes of all those who help to
build "the case." The naive Muromskoy makes futile attempts
to fight against red tape and legalistic shenanigans, only to learn
that nobody cares for justice, and that the whole empire is an
enormous cobweb to catch the weak. He dies in the office of
Varravin, a Very Important Person and a cunning swindler.
Varravin's subordinate, the unsuccessful bureaucrat Tarelkin,
makes a speech at the end of the play complaining of his failure
in graft and chicanery. Here again, the ending leads into the
opening scenes of the third part of the trilogy, *Tarelkin's Death.*
It deals with Tarelkin, who steals intimate papers from Varravin

and, with a view of future blackmail, stages his own death and assumes a disguise. Varravin, however, smells the fraud and makes Raspluyev, who in the meantime has become a police officer, arrest Tarelkin and accuse him of being a vampire and an incubus. Raspluyev enthusiastically begins to build an absurd case against Tarelkin, gathering witnesses and torturing his victims in order to get their confessions. At the end, Tarelkin recognizes his defeat, gives back Varravin's papers, and is set free—to start a new round of dirty tricks and fishy schemes.

Krechinsky's Wedding, written in 1854, was produced in the Moscow Maly Theater the next year, with Shumsky as Krechinsky, Shchepkin as Muromskoy, and Prov Sadovsky as Raspluyev. In 1856, Samoilov staged it in St. Petersburg, himself playing the title role in the Alexandrinsky Theater. The play soon became one of the most popular items of Russian repertory and is still considered a classic. Next to brilliant characterization of all the protagonists, it has that swift tempo, that rhythm which the French call "brio" or "entrain" and without which no comedy can succeed; it also possesses a most captivating verbal sharpness, a pitiless realistic touch, typical of Sukhovo-Kobylin's craft. The action is condensed into three acts, the scenes are drawn with precision and dynamism, and, despite its complexity, the plot moves with an irresistible inner logic.

The Case is of a more serious and bitter mood. A social satire, it contains one of the most complete and devastating indictments of Russia's red tape, graft, hypocrisy, and the dishonesty of the ruling class, and it has a kind of dramatic conflict and comic spirit different from the others in the trilogy. Here the individual (called "the nothing") is pitted against the blind power of the State (called "the forces") and is crushed in the unequal struggle. The irrational and irresistible nature of "forces" reminds us of Kafka's *The Trial.* This perfectly realistic play written by somebody who knew all the ins and outs of Russian police stations, courts, and prisons had strong symbolic undertones. No wonder that this "atrocious exposé," as the old Imperial censors called it, could not come before the footlights until 1882, twenty-one years after it had been written. Even then it was "revised" and badly cut. Its unabridged text was not available to theatrical audiences until the 1917 Revolution.

The third part of the trilogy assumes macabre, almost surrealistic overtones, and the scenes of Raspluyev's interrogation at
the police station is a grotesque nightmare in which the protagonists appear as masks and ghosts. The fantastic quality of
situation and dialogue, coupled with a scrupulous accuracy of
detail, make *Tarelkin's Death* a unique play in Russian and,
perhaps, in European repertory (it is akin again to Kafka and,
partly, to Pirandello). Of course, it was banned by the censors
and produced only after the Revolution (the production of the
revised play in 1900 by amateurs does not count). But even in
our times, it has proved too difficult for large audiences and has
never become a favorite.

Despite all the differences of the three plays, they all belong to
the genre of realistic exposés—psychological in the *Krechinsky
Wedding,* social in the satirical *The Case,* and broadly symbolic
and philosophical in *Tarelkin's Death.* Their main characters,
Krechinsky and Raspluyev, will live next to the figures created
by Gogol, Ostrovsky, and Chekhov, and the trilogy is a masterpiece of Russian literature. It is easy to predict that soon the time
will come for a "rediscovery" of Sukhovo-Kobylin in Russia and
abroad (the production of *Krechinsky's Wedding* in Paris a few
years ago had what is usually called a *succès d'estime*). In the
meantime, these three plays occupy a place of honor in the history of the national theater. One can object that except for
Krechinsky's Wedding their actual impact has been reduced because of censorship—but this is a common occurence in the sixties
and seventies, and many of Russia's most popular dramatic works
have been produced with a considerable delay because of political
conditions.

III

The natural or realistic school won universal recognition in
literature long before it was accepted in the theater. Its victory
on stage did not come until Ostrovsky's work became an integral
part of national repertory—in the two capitals as well as in the
provinces.

It is difficult to describe Ostrovsky's role in the history of the
Russian theater without being suspected of bias and exaggeration.

His plays in translation do not irradiate any special attraction for a foreign reader and, with the exception of *The Storm,* are hardly suitable for the European or American stage. From a purely literary standpoint, they are lacking in psychological depth and seem one-dimensional. The plots are simple, the characterizations static, the development of action seldom holds any major surprise for the spectator, and some of the devices employed to enchance suspense appear on the borderline of naïveté.

Yet these unsophisticated comedies and dramas are constructed with such a consummate craft, they reveal such an infallible sense of stage effects and techniques, they create such an atmosphere of reality and truth, and their protagonists appear so believable and alive, that they never fail to grip audiences, from the most primitive to the most refined.

Among the many factors that determined Ostrovsky's success in the past and assured him such a prominent place in today's Russia (his plays are still box-office hits throughout the Soviet Union) are his art, the strong national flavor of his writing, and its vigorous, life-affirming spirit. Unlike his predecessors, Ostrovsky was a born playwright and an expert and specialist of the stage. Not only was all his life devoted to the theater and closely associated with actors, but all his thought and observation inevitably took the form of scenic images expressed in dramatic form. While working on a play, he would read aloud each part, and he knew exactly how every word would sound on the boards. He read his plays in public with wonderful mastery. Some critics called him "the virtuoso of aural perception," opposing him to Gogol's emphasis on visual perception. Such a statement is certainly arbitrary in regard to such a master of the word as Gogol, but it is true that the main virtue of Ostrovsky's plays lies in their verbal richness and variety: his racy dialogue renders all the flavor of the popular speech, seasoned with proverbs, jingles, and assonances; it offers all the nuances of colloquial expressions coined by different social groups, while each protagonist is mainly characterized by his highly individualized way of talking and verbal peculiarities. Since the great majority of Ostrovsky's plays dealt with common people, he marked the end of the aristocratic comedy and began the democratization of the Russian stage. Those very members of the middle and lower classes who proved to be staunch supporters of the natural school, found a familiar environment in Ostrovsky's plays. His dramas and comedies were typically Russian in form, spirit, and language, and they had a definite "flavor of the soil." The Russian comedy, partly inspired by foreign models in the eighteenth century, swiftly moved from Fonvizin and Griboyedov, who represented the nobility, to the strange anecdotes of Gogol's *Marriage* and the social satire of *The Inspector General* or to the exposés by Sukhovo-Kobylin. But only in Ostrovsky it became concerned with the life of the lower orders. His comedies, based on humorous observations, do not report any extraordinary event or spectacular climax; they lack unusual incidents, grotesque exaggerations, or stark colors; they tell almost trivial stories about ordinary people, and portray provincial landowners, petty officials, little merchants, gossipy burghers, and small artisans. This is true Russia—those obscure millions who lived and toiled behind the splendid façade of a decaying nobility. This character of Ostrovsky's work, which makes him a much more significant painter of national reality than many of his contemporaries, is enhanced by his attitude toward life—concrete, down-to-earth, imbued with a basic thirst for justice, a healthy sense of humor, and an optimistic outlook; his vitality, wit, and wisdom are those of the Russian masses—and Tolstoy noticed this genuine national essence of Ostrovsky's plays. Whoever wants to get a true feeling of Russia should study them.

Alexander Ostrovsky (1823-1886) was born in Moscow into the family of a civil servant who obtained the rank of nobility through incessant labor. Alexander studied law but could not get his degree because of financial difficulties, and abandoned the university for various jobs, mostly as a court clerk. His occupations gave him vast insights into the lives of merchants, business men, pettifoggers, matchmakers, and the like. His first play, initially called *The Bankrupt* and later *It's a Family Affair*, depicted Bolshov, a rich and smug merchant ruined by cunning rascals who play on his blind obstinacy and willfulness. Read in manuscript, *The Bankrupt* was enthusiastically received in prominent Moscow literary circles and established Ostrovsky as a member of the artistic and intellectual élite. But the censors found it dangerously subversive; Ostrovsky lost his government job and was put on the list of persons "of doubtful loyalty." A few years later, however, the ban on *The Bankrupt* was lifted, and the play, under another title, was presented to the public. By that time Ostrovsky's comedy *Poverty Is No Disgrace* had already been performed and acclaimed as a masterpiece. It presented a family conflict. Tortsov, a wealthy little tyrant, decides to marry his daughter Liubochka to Korshunov, an old, perverted merchant, but Liubochka is in love with Mitia, a poor working lad in the employ of Tortsov. Mitia loves his boss' daughter passionately, but nobody dares oppose her father's whim. The marriage with Korshunov is about to take place when Tortsov's brother, Liubim, a drunkard and the family black sheep, tells the truth about the old Korshunov in an outburst of indignation and makes Tortsov change his mind: he is going to give Liubochka to Mitia, not because they love each other, but because he wants to show that he can do whatever he pleases with his daughter and with his subordinates. The Slavophiles with whom Ostrovsky associated at the time hailed the true national traits of the drunken Liubim and saw in his speeches the expression of the "Russian soul." They also loved the scenes in which Ostrovsky depicted national songs and customs preserved in Tortsov's house and were inclined to minimize the evil effects of his despotism. The playwright, however, refused to take this attitude and in his later works strengthened his critical and satirical position. Between 1855 and his death in 1886 he produced some eighty plays (without counting his translations of Molière, Dumas, Shakespeare's *Anthony and Cleopatra,* etc., which served him as literary training in his youth). He traveled widely throughout the country, particularly in the Volga region which inspired several of his comedies, including those on the decaying nobility, and a whole series of historical dramas (*Kozma Minin, Vassilissa Melentyeva,* etc.). He also wrote poetic folklore fantasies of which the popular *The Snow Maiden* became the book for the well-known Rimsky-Korsakov opera, while *The Dream on the Banks of Volga* inspired Tchaikovsky, Arensky, and other composers. But the great majority of his plays were devoted to those little people and their boastful bosses whom he knew so well from first-hand experience.

Ostrovsky depicted small government clerks who finally became corrupted by old grafters and demanding wives (*A Profitable Job,* 1857), noble wastrels and beautiful gold diggers (*Wild*

Money, 1859) , scheming fortune seekers, upper class parasites, and idlers (*Wolves and Sheep,* 1872) , heartless aristocrats (*Without Dowry,* 1863) , victims of serfdom (*The Ward,* 1859) and of poverty (*Poor Bride,* 1852) , or gave memorable portrayals of provincial actors (*The Forest,* 1870, *Talents and Suitors,* 1882) . Most of his comedies dealt with a very special section of Russian society— the old-fashioned merchants and tradesmen who recently had detached themselves from their rural and patriarchal background, moved to cities and towns, made money, and formed the core of a backward and conservative middle class. They maintained in their mansions on the other side of the Moskva river or on the banks of the Volga, the exclusive mores and rituals of olden days, and Ostrovsky revealed what was happening in this secluded little world, protected from indiscreet glances by high walls, closed shutters, watchdogs, and fierce guards. In these strongholds of paternal authority, the father reigned supreme like God in heaven or tsar on earth, and the imposed rules of behavior, including the prearranged marriages of daughters and sons, were enforced by ruthless beating and financial pressure. Dobroliubov, the critic of the sixties, hailed Ostrovsky's plays as an important public service because they depicted "the realm of darkness," in which petty tyrants, bred on superstition, ignorance, and cruelty, victimized their families at home and their employees in the store or at the office. Ostrovsky's most successful portrayals were those of *samodurs* (willful, absurdly despotic, intellectually and morally limited egotists) who did as they pleased and trampled on human dignity and freedom.

In general, following the literary tradition, Ostrovsky opposed the predatory type to the meek "simple heart," the despot to the victims, the wolves to the sheep. While his *samodurs* such as Tortsov or Bolshov or Kabanikha abuse their power, their daughters, wives, sons, and employees suffer in silence without even daring to rebel against the yoke. In *The Storm,* considered his masterpiece, Ostrovsky portrayed Katerina, a sensitive and poetic young woman, married to Tikhon, the obedient son of Kabanikha, one of the cruelest and harshest specimens of a "samodur." Pushed to desperation by her oppressive family environment, Katerina, during her husband's absence, has a short love affair with Boris, a handsome and gay fellow. But after having "sinned" she is tormented by repentance, and during a storm on the Volga, her nerves on edge, Katerina makes a public confession, and thus seals her doom. Kabanikha and Tikhon make her life a misery, and she finally commits suicide by throwing herself into the river. No other play by Ostrovsky renders so vividly the gloom of the despotic family pattern and the backwardness of a Russian provincial town. But the critics, led and misled by Dobroliubov, saw in *The Storm* a "ray of light in the realm of darkness," interpreting Katerina's "fault" and even her suicide as a protest against oppressive conditions. Considering that the drama ends with the death of the heroine while her lover is shipped to China and her husband is completely subdued by his rigid mother, one is hardly inclined to accept such an optimistic view.

The character of Katerina, with her dreams and religious yearnings, transcends the narrow limits of a social phenomenon; and her dramatic conflict with her environment, enhanced by mystical forebodings and the eerie atmosphere of storm, lightning, and thunder, is symbolic of the inevitable clash between the "pure soul" and crude reality. As an image of womanhood, endowed with national characteristics and a complex personality, Katerina is one of the most successful figures of Russian repertory, and hundreds of actresses rose or fell trying to find her right scenic embodiment.

When we study the totality of Ostrovsky's work, we see clearly that despite their "realistic objectivity," claimed by the author and his critics, they had important political implications: the oppresson, rudeness, and despotism which Ostrovsky depicted in family life was but a reflection of the whole system on which the police state of Imperial Russia was established.

The censors did not miss the meaning of Ostrovsky's hidden message even though the author never drew any conclusions and never departed from his manner of straight realistic representation. All his life Ostrovsky had to fight censorship and officialdom. At the beginning of Ostrovsky's career, the director of Imperial Theaters snubbed his plays as being too crude, vulgar, and "smelling of barns and grocery shops." Yet the general recognition of Ostrovsky's genius and the tremendous success of his plays wherever they were produced, broke the barriers and opened to the playwright the doors of Maly and Alexandrinsky Theaters. Between 1854 and 1872, more than thirty plays by Ostrovsky had some 766 performances in Russian theaters. Toward the end of his life, he was appointed director of the artistic department of the Moscow Imperial Theaters and this was the first time that such a job was entrusted to a professional. Ostrovsky, who spent all his life in the theater, was also the founder of dramatic schools and himself a teacher of actors. A steady advocate of assiduous work and constant study of technique, he never failed to stress above everything naturalness in acting and to repeat Dobroliubov's maxim, "the principal virtue of an artistic production is its living truth." Like many of his contemporaries, he paid but small attention to the *mise en scène*. When the famous Meiningen company came to Russia with their magnificent décors and performed *Julius Caesar*, Ostrovsky complained: "I saw neither Caesar nor Shakespeare, I saw an excellent, disciplined company of mediocre actors and disgustingly wailing actresses." He greatly appreciated, however, the acting of the crowd.

Convinced that the role of the stage director or of the painter and architect was quite secondary in comparison with that of the interpreter, Ostrovsky devoted much time and energy to raising the status of the actor; he initiated the Actor's Guild and founded various institutions of financial and medical assistance to old or infirm actors.

Ostrovsky's repertory created a whole school of acting. The impersonation of *samodurs* and other types of the "realm of darkness" required a special kind of "national realism," as some critics used to call it. Of course, Shchepkin and his followers hailed Ostrovsky's comedies and were happy to interpret them. Yet a new type of actor, more pervaded with the "spirit of the soil," was needed for Ostrovsky's plays. One of such actors was Prov Sadovsky (1818-1872), the head of a whole theatrical dynasty. His son Mikhail (1847-1910) with his wife Olga (1850-1919), and their daughter Elizaveta (1870-1934) and son Prov (1874-1947), continued their tradition right into the Soviet era. All of them served in the Moscow Maly Theater. Shchepkin discovered Prov Sadovsky in 1839, rescued him from the "quagmire of provincial stage" and made him a regular member of the Maly Theater as "third category actor." After his success in Molière and Gogol (*The Gamblers*), he emerged as a first-rate artist, more concrete and less versatile than Shchepkin but searching for the same ease and naturalness as his great protector. He reached his zenith in the part of Rusakov, in Ostrovsky's *Don't Sit in the Wrong Sledge*. His great comic talent, his intimate knowledge of the middle class into which he himself was born, united to an assiduous polishing of gestures and intonations, and his physique of a typical "great Russian" made him an ideal interpreter of Ostrovsky. He was equaled later by I. F. Gorbunov (1831-1895), who shifted, however, from Ostrovsky's plays to his own comic skits in which he displayed an extraordinary sense of linguistic nuance and verbal humor. He made quite a hit by creating the figure of General Ditiatin, a retired military man eager to express his often absurd opinions on all matters.

The Maly Theater became "Ostrovsky's House," and all senior members of the company not only made their debuts in his plays but continued to interpret them, shifting from one part to another. Firmly established in the Russian repertory with his numerous plays, Ostrovsky became by the eighties an organic and very important part of the national stage. Today he still reigns supreme on the boards of all the theaters in the Soviet Union.

IV

The two writers whose plays stand independently in the repertory of the eighties and the nineties, both bear, by a strange coincidence, the name of Tolstoy: *The Power of Darkness*, the second great play about Russian peasantry, the comedy *Fruits of Enlightenment* and the drama *The Living Corpse* are the most important dramatic works by Leo Tolstoy, while Count Alexey Tolstoy, the noble and delicate patrician poet, is the author of a historical trilogy in blank verse which includes *The Death of Ivan the Terrible, Tsar Fyodor Ivanovich,* and *Tsar Boris* (1865-1870).

Leo Tolstoy, the great master of epic narrative, made various attempts at writing for the stage, particularly the "people's" theater, for which he supplied didactic, moralistic adapatations of his own stories such as *The First Distiller* or *Peter, The Baker*. He did not produce a true drama until 1886—the year he finished

The Power of Darkness. It concerns a well-to-do peasant, Peter, whose second wife, Anisia, has an affair with Nikita, their farm hand. Pushed by Matriona, his greedy and scheming mother, Nikita helps his mistress to poison her husband and, after the latter is out of the way, marries the young widow. But the marriage does not bring them happiness. Nikita becomes a drunkard, runs after other women, and seduces Akulina, Peter's daughter and Anisia's stepdaughter. When Akulina gives birth to a child, Anisya and Matriona, determined to hide her "fault" and marry her to a suitable peasant, compel Nikita to kill and bury the baby. Tormented by his sense of guilt Nikita, on the verge of suicide, finally confesses his crimes in the midst of Akulina's engagement party. Among the strongly individualized protagonists of the drama, such as sensual and hard-driving Anisia, completely blinded by her passion, or Matriona, Nikita's devilish mother, or the naive Akulina, the most extraordinary character is that of old Akim, a stuttering and ignorant human wreck, utterly unable to express himself and make an articulate speech, but actually representing the only voice of moral conscience in a world of violence, crime, and callousness. As a realistic play, *The Power of Darkness* belonged to the main stream of the period, but it had the directness and the psychological completeness of characterization and that very "illusion of life" which readers all over the world admire in Tolstoy's great novels. The censors, however, found this picture of Russian peasants as backward murderers and villains too gloomy and even dangerous. So it was presented in Paris and Berlin but not in Russia. Not until 1895 could Suvorin produce the play in his theater in St. Petersburg. It was then taken up by the Alexandrinsky Theater where it became a steady item of the repertory with Savina playing Anisia's or Akulina's role. It is worth while mentioning that the first performance of *The Power of Darkness* took place at Antoine's Théâtre Libre, in Paris (in French, of course). The Moscow Art Theater produced it in 1902.

The Fruits of Enlightenment, a light comedy exposing the idle nobility which spends its time in spiritualistic seances and is more superstitious than the supposedly ignorant servants, was written by Tolstoy for some holiday entertainment for his own family. Stanislavsky obtained it for a private performance at the

Hunter's Club in Moscow in 1891, and later it was included in the national repertory.

The Living Corpse, written in 1900, contains twelve episodes out of the fifteen initially planned by the author, but it has an artistic unity and a fully developed plot. Published in 1911, after Tolstoy's death, it became the most popular of all his plays. The Moscow Art Theater presented it in the fall of 1911, and it ran for over fifty performances. Between January and October 1912, it was shown in 243 theaters throughout the country, the Moscow Art Theater production serving as model for most of them, and it had some nine thousand performances. It became an important item of national repertory before and after the Revolution.

In Fedya Protassov, the hero of the drama. Tolstoy portrays a weak but sensitive man dissatisfied with the life of the upper classes and his own idle and superfluous existence. He leaves his wife, although he loves her, and decides to simulate a suicide to make her free to marry an honest and adoring suitor. Protassov disappears into the anonymous crowd of bums and drunkards but his scheme is denounced, his wife and her new husband are accused of bigamy, and all three are threatened by the soulless machine of the State and what is hypocritically called justice. This is too much for Protassov, and he kills himself in the courtroom.

Two other plays by Tolstoy, *Light Shining in the Darkness,* with strong autobiographical allusions, and the popular *All Comes From Her,* remained unfinished and were hardly ever presented on the stage.

The other Tolstoy, Alexey, a defender of "pure esthetics," was opposed to the current realistic trend. His historical plays are romantic dramas with psychological conflicts and the alternation of light and shade. While strictly observing historical truth, the author made all his characters colorful and unusual, and placed emphasis on the picturesque and on the clashes of strong personalities or, as in his second tragedy, on the contrast between the dreamy, weak character of Fyodor and his willful, ambitious courtiers. Since the reign of Ivan the Terrible and his successor was filled with wars, conspiracies, murders, executions, and attemps at coups d'etat, Tolstoy easily found what he considered "material fitting for a Shakespeare," whom he admired greatly.

But that same material was considered disrespectful of royalty, and Tolstoy, despite his high position at the court and personal friendship with the Tsar, had great difficulties having his trilogy performed. As we will see later, the success of his second tragedy was due mainly to the Moscow Art Theater. But this did not happen before the close of the century.

In the seventies and nineties, next to the classical repertory, which included on one side Fonvizin, Griboyedov, and Gogol, and on the other, Shakespeare, Molière, Hugo, and Schiller as great favorites, the Imperial Theaters had to accept Ostrovsky, but their daily fare was made partly of translations (Dumas, Scribe, Feydeau, etc.) and partly of plays produced by a special group of dramatists. Those were "our own playwrights," as the administrators of the Maly and particularly of the Alexandrinsky used to say. The reputation of those writers, however, was greatly inflated, the best of them even such as Alexander Potekhin (1829-1908), whose mildly populist tendencies seemed to tickle the progressive youth, or Dmitry Averkiev (1836-1905), whose historical play *The Olden Days of Kashirsk* (1872) was repeatedly on the billboards, lacked solid literary qualities. Others, such as Ippolit Shpazhinsky, Victor Krylov (who wrote 115 plays), Pyotr Nevelzhin, Victor Ryzhkov, and others, were authors of spiritless concoctions made to please this or that actor and especially the high officials of the Imperial Theatrical Administration. Plays were judged by stage directors (some of them with no qualifications for their posts other than being former officers of the Guard) according to the parts they could offer to the stars. But even the latter often refused to appear in those half-baked dramas and comedies: Ermolova declined to act in *Earthly Paradise,* by Karpov, and Yuzhin resigned in protest against some trash by Shpazhinsky. While some of those "dramatists in residence" had a certain dexterity in presenting stereotyped stage effects and situations, all of them were so alien to "great literature" that their plays did not appear in print and were turned down by periodicals and publishers. Only a few of them, such as Sumbatov and Nemirovich Danchenko, were exceptions.

At the beginning of the nineties, this situation provoked a true yearning for a "literary theater," and the conservatism and the low level of contemporary plays produced in most theaters could no longer satisfy the audience. A crisis in the repertory was imminent, and the need for renovation was acutely felt throughout the country.

V

The monopoly of the Imperial Theaters created a peculiar situation in the second half of the nineteenth century: the whole style and repertory of the Russian stage depended on what was going on in Moscow and St. Petersburg. Private theatrical enterprises did exist legally in the provinces, but in the two capitals they could come to life only under disguise or in very devious ways paved by huge bribes. Usually amateurs, or even professionals, performed in clubs and at so-called family reunions. Some performances were given under the auspices of the Circle of Lovers of Dramatic Art, established in Moscow in 1861. In St. Petersburg, many plays were produced at "dramatic evenings" at the Nobility Assembly (which possessed a good stage) and at the Painters or Merchants Clubs. Summer stock theaters and operettas had no difficulty in obtaining special licenses. In any case, by the middle of the seventies there were some twenty-five theatrical ventures (not including the Imperial Theaters) functioning fairly regularly in Moscow and St. Petersburg. This meant that the monopoly lost its political justification—especially in the light of the huge development of theaters in the provinces and the number of companies on the road which often included prominent artists. Under the pressure of public opinion and a few enlightened men of the theatrical administration, among them Ostrovsky, the government decided to legalize the existing conditions and to abolish the monopoly. From 1882, private theatrical enterprises were allowed in the whole territory of the Empire, including the capitals. This, of course, contributed greatly to the expansion of theatrical arts in Russia; it also influenced the increase in the number of theatrical schools and the improvement of their programs. The main reforms were introduced already in the sixties when the Russian Musical Society opened a Conservatory in St. Petersburg (1862) and in Moscow (1866). Both of them trained singers, actors, and dancers. Threatened by these powerful competitors, the Imperial schools pressed by E. Voronov of the Alexandrinsky Theater, a staunch defender of liberal education, changed their structure and curriculum in 1866: opera training was separated from drama classes and the ballet, and the graduates were not automatically enrolled in the Imperial companies. In 1884, the ballet school became independent and grew in size and importance. A decade earlier, various private dramatic, ballet, and musical schools sprang up throughout the country, and large cities opened their own conservatories. When, in 1897, the first Theatrical Convention took place in St. Petersburg under the leadership of Lensky and Yuzhin, it paid a great deal of attention to problems of artistic training and education.

The effects of the abolition of monopoly were not felt until the early nineties. Until that time, the Imperial Theaters continued to lead the whole theatrical life of the country. The most important among them in the second half of the century was, of course, the Maly Theater. Its traditional ties with the academic world, its reputation for humanist liberalism, its early acceptance of realism, and its serious classical repertory (offered every week) made it a kind of Russian Academy similar to the Parisian Comedie Française. It was called "Moscow's second university" and students claimed to learn as much from its performance as from lectures of their professors. In his memoirs, Stanislavsky tells how his young friends in the eighties "prepared" for an evening at the Maly: they read the play and the critical articles about it, met to discuss it, and sometimes even invited a lecturer to make a speech and supervise the debate.

The Maly was called "the house of the actor," and in fact the training of its company, which included such a large number of outstanding actors and actresses, explained its lasting appeal. The audience was so absorbed by the acting that they forgot or forgave the shabbiness of the *mise en scène*, and that the artists did not pay much attention to the externals. "We did not think," writes one of them, "of the poor settings, the historical untruth of the costumes and makeup, the stiffness of the supers and the immobility of the crowd which sometimes consisted of soldiers drafted from various regiments by military command (different ones for each performance!)."

The Maly Theater was considered the citadel of realism; Shchepkin's method and spirit prevailed in the training of its artists, and for decades its company seemed perfectly homogeneous—which never failed to impress provincial actors and provoke imitation—thus contributing to the Theater's national impact. This does not mean, however, that the realistic way of acting was fully applied to the interpretation of classics, particularly the foreign ones. Shakespeare, Hugo, Schiller, and many others were shown in a traditional romantic manner, a doubtful and dated French tradition with shouts and whispers, broad gestures, and conventional postures. When Ostrovsky was asked once about the customary performance of Schiller's *Mary Stuart,* he said slowly: "How all this undermines the Russian actor." Only great talents had the courage and the ability to break away from such a pseudo-romantic routine.

One of them was Maria Yermolova (1853-1928), the leading lady of the company for many decades, called by Stanislavsky, "the heroic symphony of the Russian Theater." She shifted to the drama from the ballet and became the idol of the progressive youth after her debut in *Fuente Ovejuna* by Lope de Vega, in which she played the part of Laurencia, an ordinary girl who emerges as the leader of a popular uprising. She created such a believable and passionate image of the young woman that the whole house was stunned. The performance turned into a political demonstration and the play was banned, but Yermolova's fame was assured. After that memorable evening, she gave admirable impersonations of Mary Stuart and Joan of Arc in Schiller's tragedies, of Imogene in *Cymbeline,* of Lady Macbeth and Cordelia, and of many other highly dramatic or tragic parts. A timid, kind, and extremely modest woman in private life, easily embarrassed by compliments and hardly aware of her own genius, she revealed on stage an extraordinary sensitivity, an insight into all the nuances of emotions, and a passionate temperament. One could say that she belonged to those artists who always project themselves into their roles and therefore never cease to act the same part. But Yermolova knew how to express herself in such different ways, in so many disguises, that she appeared as a new woman every evening. She possessed many assets: a handsome, mobile face with sparkling eyes, a beautiful figure, a warm, low voice, a combination of strength and femininity, of inspiration and self-control. Her manner of acting was very dynamic, her gestures often violent, her monologues passionate, and her whole manner intense and rather sharp. But even in her most extreme flights and outbursts there was a plastic harmony, a rhythm, a balance of movements, due perhaps to her physical perfection that set the whole into an esthetic equilibrium. At the same time, her acting seemed very simple and natural, and in that she was a true pupil of Shchepkin's school. She stirred her audiences so deeply, and her magnetic power over them was so engrossing, that they accepted whatever she did or said on the stage as the supreme truth. In a play by one of the usual scribblers, she had to die after having taken a poisoned drink, and she acted so realistically that her own colleagues in the wings and Chernevsky, the stage director, got quite worried and wondered what kind of liquid she had drunk, while several spectators rushed to the foyer to call a doctor: they all were convinced that she was actually dying. Her art, however, was not limited to dramatic effects and emotional overtones. She knew how to draw a fine and subtle psychological design. She was a wonderful Negina in Ostrovsky's *Talents and Suitors*: she played the part of an actress compelled to become the mistress of the rich Dudukin in order to continue her stage career. The scene in which she yielded to Meluzov, a humble and poor teacher—while knowing very well that the next day she would be sold and lost forever—remained one of the most memorable achievements of her craft: sensuality, sensitivity, regret, fear, and cunning—all wrapped in feminine charm and human pity—were shown in a succession of nuances of such variety and intensity that spectators could never forget this extraordinary performance. Each of her appearances was an event that packed the house. She united romantic color with artistic truth, and there was such a spiritual beauty in the images she created that her art acquired a starlike luminosity and fascination. She was the first actress to receive the honorary title of the People's Artist in the Soviet Union and today one of Moscow's theaters bears her name.

A different trend was represented by Glikeria Fedotova (1846-1925), who entered the Maly Theater at the age of sixteen and soon became one of the leading ladies of the company. The range of her impersonations was very wide, and the public applauded her in plays by Shakespeare or Schiller and in light comedies by lesser playwrights. But she was at her best in character roles, particularly in Ostrovsky's, in which she could display all the humor and precision of her skillful, articulate, down-to-earth interpretation. One of the mainstays of the realistic school, she brought into her impersonations such a breath, such a pulsation of blood, that they appeared "truer than reality," as one of her reviewers remarked after her interpretation of Kabanikha in *The Storm*. Her portrayals had a sculptural, multidimensional quality, and they were so complete and natural that her acting appeared perfectly spontaneous. Only in her old age, when she had left the stage and her small drawing room had become one of Moscow's artistic centers, did she discuss all the work, all the pain, all the devices and techniques which she had put into her craft. Nadezhda Nikulina, particularly brilliant in Ostrovsky parts (1843-1923), Yelena Leshkovskaya (1869-1925), Nadezhda Medvedeva, who possessed an unusual capacity for observation and mimickry, and Sofia Akimova, continued and expanded Fedotova's tradition in the Maly Theater. In a way Fedotova was a feminine counterpart of Prov Sadovsky and Serghei Shumsky. The latter was considered the most important follower of Shchepkin; he never left anything to improvisation, studied his parts thoroughly, prepared them in a systematic, rational manner, polishing every detail and displaying on the boards an aristocratic elegance of gestures, an excellent diction, and a well-controlled and restrained naturalness. He was at his best as Krechinsky and in Ostrovsky's comedies. Next to him, Ivan Samarin (1817-1885) made himself a name in foreign repertory and also as an excellent Khlestakov. In the latter years of his career, he made an ideal Famusov and Falstaff. Samarin hid a strong temperament under the externals of a refined and graceful old gentleman whose inclination toward stoutness did not impair his good manners and elegant looks.

Toward the end of the century, the influence of two other actors was strongly felt in the Maly company: that of Lensky and of Yuzhin. Alexander Lensky (1847-1908), son of Prince Gagarin and an Italian woman, was not only an excellent "first lover" who gave wonderful interpretations of Chatsky, Hamlet, Petruccio, Don Juan, and Romeo, but also was a great teacher and well-educated man, a painter and sculptor in his spare time. He attached great importance to outward appearances and fussed about make-up and costumes. A very handsome man with big blue eyes, fine expressive hands, an elegant gait, and a caressing voice, his impeccable diction reflected his sensitivity for words and intonations and his love of poetry. Since 1889, he had been active as producer and stage director, and he made everybody realize the seriousness of artistic endeavor and the necessity of discipline and steady training. He did his best to improve the repertory and to promote reforms. In this task he was fully supported by his influential colleague, Prince Sumbatov, known as Alexander Yuzhin (1857-1927), a highly talented interpreter of romantic-heroic parts. His acting went hand in hand with his playwriting. Sumbatov was the author of fourteen plays, some of which (such as the mordant comedy *The Gentlemen,* or the dramas, *The Old Tempering, The Casting Net,* and *Hawks and Ravens*) were very successful. He broke the monotonous routine of dramatic trash contributed by the "resident playwrights." Later (in 1909) he became director of the company and a staunch defender of realism and the classical repertory. Alexandra Yablochkina, herself a distinguished member of the Maly Theater, praised him in her *Memoirs* (1955) for not having let a "single mystical, decadent, or symbolist play on the stage of our theater." It is quite possible that this sentence was dictated by political considerations: she wanted to make Yuzhin a precursor of socialist realism.

Among other and very numerous members of the Maly Theater, mention should be made of Vassily Zhivokini (1808-1874), a vaudeville performer so loved by the public that he would address the audience in an impromptu speech before the beginning of a performance. An exceptional comic, full of fun and mirth, a buffoon and a skilled actor, who knew how to provoke laughter by a sheer twist of his hands or by merely turning his eyes, he enjoyed a tremendous popularity, and many comic actors in the seventies and eighties tried to imitate the ways of this "charming little monster."

The theatrical life in Moscow was centered around the Maly for the drama and Bolshoy for opera and ballet. St. Petersburg presented more variety. The Alexandrinsky Theater, main competitor of the Maly, attracted middle-class audiences and a part of the intelligentsia. The aristocrats considered it "the theater for the people"; they patronized Mariinsky (Marie Theater), where faithful subscribers applauded a series of ballets and operas, and the Mikhailovsky (Michael's Theater), the host to a permanent French company. Among private enterprises, the leading theaters were those established by Korsh (these gave light comedies and eventually turned toward more substantial plays) and by Alexey Suvorin, a big publisher, journalist, and dramatist. His political position as defender of autocracy and his high connections allowed Suvorin to produce plays previously banned or frowned upon by censorship. In the early nineties he staged *Tsar Fydor* by Alexey Tolstoy, *The Willful Ones* by Pisemsky, and *The Power of Darkness* by Leo Tolstoy. He had good actors in his company, among them Bravich and Orlenev.

The repertory of the Alexandrinsky Theater was similar to that of the Maly, only with an emphasis on adaptations from the French and less frequent productions of Ostrovsky. On the whole, it was more conservative, more bureaucratic, and more sensitive to the Parisian *théâtre du boulevard* than its Moscow twin. But it was quite successful in attracting a good many actors and actresses of national reputation.

One of the greatest actors of the Alexandrinsky was Vladimir Davydov. He was born in 1849 as Ivan Gorelov, a nobleman; and since his father, a naval officer, did not approve of his infatuation with the stage, he acted under the pseudonym of Davydov. Very much impressed with what he saw of the Maly Theater and by Ira Aldridge, the American Negro actor, whom he saw give a masterful interpretation of Othello in a Russian provincial town, Davydov joined a second-rate road company. Between 1867 and 1880, he developed his acting, working incessantly and learning a great deal from the actress Alexandra Schubert, a friend of Dostoevsky. He was excellent in light repertory, especially vaudeville and operettas, and danced and sang very well. At the Alexandrinsky Theater, he created a memorable Molchalin and made a hit in various Ostrovsky comedies. In 1886 he went to the Korsh Theater, acting superbly in *The Inspector General* and as Famusov. Back at the Alexandrinsky in 1886, he became the idol of the university

youth, and his matinees attracted crowds of students. Forced to
act in trivial farces and comedies, he often resorted to easy comic
effects, but whenever he had a good part in the classical repertory
he made an extraordinary characterization. By the end of the
century, he started gaining weight, and soon became quite heavy,
but he knew how to use this disadvantage and chose suitable
parts. In 1922, on his seventy-third birthday celebration, he still
gave a wonderful interpretation of Famusov, and this performance
showed his popularity: more than two hundred delegations came
to congratulate the old actor, he received a huge ovation at the
Maly Theater in Moscow, and five hundred telegrams brought
him greetings from all over Russia.

The French director Antoine said in 1915 that he and Lucien
Guitry considered Davydov their master and admired the way he
merged realistic truth with lavish theatricality. Davydov had a
benign comic genius. His mayor in *The Inspector General* was
a rascal, ignorant, sly but not vicious, basically weak and, at the
end, slightly pitiful. He portrayed Raspluyev in the same vein.
He was an exceedingly good Falstaff in *The Merry Wives of
Windsor*. His art enabled him to portray a living person, without
effects or tricks. He followed the tradition of Alexander Martynov, (1816-1860) who taught how to discover "the human element" in each, most humble part, and to show it in acting. (Later
Stanislavsky, in his training years, came to the formula: find out
and show the good in the villain and the bad in the virtuous
man. But Martynov characterized human failure and stuck to
the "humiliated and the wronged" in the pathetic Gogolian manner.) Davydov had a powerful streak of the paternal and the
patriarchal, he loved ease and prosperity, he was jovial and calm,
his humor was outspoken, healthy, and natural, without any
malice or sting to it; and while Martynov was a "sad comedian,"
Davydov was a gay, positive one, he never provoked repulsion,
he was definitely pleased with this world, and his laughter sounded mild and kind. He always tried to tone down any realistic
crudity. His tremendous vitality was doubled by skill: the foundations of his art were analytical, he studied every gesture, every
posture, and his slogan "to live on the stage, reflecting life"
suggested thorough technical preparation.

The leading lady of the Alexandrinsky, and its uncrowned queen, was Maria Savina.* The daughter of a provincial school teacher who became an actor, she went on the boards as a child, and at the beginning of her career had no faith in herself and no particular love of the stage. She was almost without education but she had a lively mind, strong temperament, good looks, and great charm of youth and vitality. Qualified trained actresses such as Irina Sandunova-Koni (1811-1891), or Alexandra Schubert (1827-1909), gave her good advice and helped her. Contemporaries say that in her twenties she was enchanting; her ingenuity and spontaneity set her apart because she overlooked clichés and routine. This was not an easy thing to do since the provincial theater in which Savina lived for many years stubbornly clung to sacrosanct devices: "emotion—walking quickly back and forth, opening a letter with trembling hands, clinking a glass, and bumping it against the jug or teeth; calm—yawning and stretching; death—clasping the chest, tearing the collar off the shirt; narrowing the eyes to express contempt and crumpling the handkerchief in restrained anger." The public, accustomed to these signs, learned them like a language, and seemed surprised (and, at times, delighted) when confronted with a new acting technique. When Savina was accepted by the Alexandrinsky in 1874, she was in full possession of her artistic personality, and it took her little time to win over the audience. She soon became identified with the Alexandrinsky Theater as its leading lady and held great power within it for many years. A friend of Turgenev, she created or re-created his *A Month in the Country,* and his *Provincial Lady*. She was at her best when embodying society woman. Here she could display her intuitive understanding of a character and her deep analytical qualities of impersonation, the refinement in precision of detail, and the brilliant craft by which she learned to master and channel her natural gifts. The outward gloss of her impersonation, to which she often added a slight touch of bohemianism, was best displayed in trivial plays, supplied by such inferior dramatists as Krylov and Shpazhinsky, who modeled their custom-made productions to suit all the as-

* Although some sources give 1854 as her birth date, Savina was probably born in 1850 and came to Alexandrinsky at the age of twenty-four and not at twenty as some biographers assert. She died in 1915.

pects of her talent. Some of her best parts, therefore, belonged to such plays as *The Scapegrace* and *Female Chitchat,* that have long been forgotten.

Other talented artists completed the Alexandrinsky company: the excellent comic actor Konstantin Varlamov (1848-1915), familiarly called the Fatty or Uncle Kostia, famous for reviving vaudeville and often a counterpart of Davydov; the somber and melodramatic Mamont Dalsky (1865-1918), whose Othello and Karl Moore made the public delirious; the elegant Vassily Dalmatov (1862-1912), the dandy of the Russian stage, or the subtle and intelligent Pavel Svobodin (1850-1892).

Provincial companies flourished in the eighties and nineties. In big cities permanent theaters were established for drama and opera. In Odessa the municipal theater had annual performances of Italian opera where renowned singers alternated with guest performances of Russian dramatic companies, and it had other theaters for comedies, operettas, and the like. One of the most enlightened provincial directors, Nikolay Solovtsov, himself a good actor (1875-1902), gave his name to an excellent permanent repertory theater he founded in Kiev. Kharkov, Rostov-on-Don, Nizhni Novgorod and other Volga towns, and many other regional centers got their permanent theaters or were served by road companies, among which were those directed by Nikolay Sinelnikob and Ivan Sibiriakov.

In the smaller towns and in lesser companies, however, the situation of the actor and the artistic level of performances were rather low. Financial insecurity, dependence on crooks and speculators who assumed the jobs of theater managers, the necessity of making the round of the homes of rich merchants and officials to sell tickets for "benefit performances," the cynical attitude of patrons toward young and pretty actresses (depicted by Ostrovsky and in *The Golovlyovs* by Saltykov) —all this, together with shabbiness of costumes and sets and the poor material conditions of houses, created a rather pitiable situation. Ostrovsky and the leading actors and directors of Moscow and St. Petersburg however, did a great deal at the beginning of the nineties to improve the financial and moral standards of the road companies and to raise their artistic quality.

VI

Toward the end of the century, particularly in the eighties and the beginning of the nineties, the best Russian theaters paid a great deal of attention to the actor but the *mise en scène* was poor and sometimes ridiculous. Baron Driesen tells in his memoirs: "Furniture was put on stage according to a pre-established order —contrary to that of any house: for instance, two arm chairs on one side of the stage, a table in between, and two chairs on the other side, a sofa in the background and a table next to a wall. No real pictures, decorations, ornaments or curtains were hung on the walls: they were all painted on sets. There was no period style. Court salons were always Gothic, a drawing room in a wealthy house had murals like those in a Venetian palace, and a poor man's room was as large as the stage. Costumes were classified as Italian, Spanish, and French, Louis XV or Henry IV—but the actors did marvels." Stanislavsky says that theater tailors knew only three kinds of period costumes: the "Faust," the "Huguenots" or "Mary Stuart," and for Russian historical plays "the boyard." In the provinces, Hamlet often appeared in modern dress or—in small towns—in a hussar uniform. Actresses were supposed to wear silk, muslin, and French coiffures in whatever play they appeared, and it was quite an event when an actress, Chitau, broke the tradition and came on stage in a cotton dress and with smooth hair. Sofia in *Wit Works Woe* was always wearing the latest Parisian low-necked dresses, while secondary characters wore black suits. Historical costumes were old and dirty but peasants always looked bright and clean. The same pictures on the wall (a waterfall and the repentant Magdalene) were seen three or four times a week in all plays, together with the same curtains and the same sets. In 1865 in the Alexandrinsky Theater, there were only two sets, and the director was simply afraid of accessories.

After the classic architectural forms of the famous Gonzago (1751-1831) and his monumental settings in stone, staging assumed a pastoral and idyllic character with Canoppi, whose "interior of an izba" of gigantic dimensions survived until the end of the century. By the sixties, the technique of the stage was pretty well fixed in a conventional way. The painted canvases of the background and sides were held by wooden bars on top and bottom; the sides were unframed. The paddock (ceiling) hung independently or was joined to the side drops so as to form an arch—usually there were several rows of such arches; the background, the drops, as well as the hangings, either had to be pulled up to the fly-house, which required a double height of stage, or rolled, which often resulted in their being crumpled. The framing of the canvases on four sides secured their preservation.

The king of staging in the nineteenth century was Andreas Roller (1805-1891), a German from Bavaria, who replaced the Italians and supplied all the Russian theaters with his pupils and followers. He worked a great deal for the opera and ballet and introduced everywhere a "general style" completely devoid of any national or period flavor. His Russian dwellings were exactly like Swiss chalets, and his sets for Kiev in *Ruslan and Liudmila* presented a German Gothic town with a medieval church and city hall. His feast halls were in a Romano-Gothic style, and all his sets, even though many of them were quite pleasant, were utterly conventional and completely devoid of historic accuracy. But his machines were excellent, and in ballet he could produce startling effects of light and movement.

In the seventies and eighties, however, the Russian painters Bocharov, Shishkov, and others, started a new trend—and this coincided with the growing role of archaeologists, historians, and architects sought more frequently by most advanced stage directors. In the eighties Shishkov organized a special class of theatrical decorative painting at the Art Academy, and by the beginning of the nineties, some private theatrical ventures secured the collaboration of prominent painters of the period, such as Polenov, Serov, and Vasnetsov. Yet all these attempts remained isolated until bold steps were taken by the Moscow Art Theater at the very end of the century.

In the ballet, the evolution of costumes from Taglioni to Legnani tended toward a greater freedom of body and movement. With the shortening of skirts and tunics, Didelot introduced tights and leotards. Then the long soft tunics and soft slipper were replaced by short dresses of heavier material and broad, solid shoes to permit triple turns and numerous fouettés.

After the romantic period, the appearance of Fanny Elssler

in 1848 marked a change in taste: her Gisèle was concrete, passionate, and down to earth. She displayed a richness of mimicry and gesture, a dramatic force so different from Taglioni's ethereal flights. The erotic, *terre à terre* Zucchi, the acrobatic Brianza, and Legnani, with her admirable fouettés, became the lawgivers of the Russian ballet which definitely moved toward technical perfection of *pointes,* or toe dancing. Ballet became more and more a show, a "grand spectacle" with huge painted canvases as backdrops, intricate systems of lighting, and lavish costumes. The spectator from the aristocracy and upper bourgeoisie who went to the Mariinsky Theater in St. Petersburg, and to the Bolshoy in Moscow, or applauded Imperial Ballet companies on tour in the provinces, wanted a whole evening of entertainment, a ballet in five or six acts with prologue, epilogue, and perhaps an apotheosis. This required a huge company, a large and highly disciplined *corps de ballet,* and lavishness and magnificence of staging. Marius Petipa, born in 1822 in Marseilles into a family of dancers, became the ballet dictator of Russia from 1870 to 1903 and attached his name to this period.

After a long series of distinguished choreographers, such as Duport and Didelot (who remained in Russia for twenty-five years), or Jules Perrot, the husband of Carlotta Grisi, or Saint Leon, the highly talented author of *Coppelia,* Petipa made his debut with *The Daughter of Pharaoh,* which he created for Carolina Rosati, taking T. Gautier's *The Romance of a Mummy* as his libretto. He did it while Saint Leon, the ballet master of the Mariinsky Theater, was in London. A few years later, in 1869, Saint Leon departed, and Petipa became the true king of the Russian Imperial Ballet. This old man, who had begun his career by dancing with Elssler and Grisi and ended it by directing Pavlova, was a living symbol of the art of dance, and his 74 main ballets and 30 "entertainments" (*divertissements*) show his creative power and inventiveness. Only in 1885 did he accept Leon Ivanov as his assistant, and in 1888 he hired the Italian, Cecchetti, who became the teacher of all the stars of Russian ballet. Otherwise he did everything himself, and he worked to his last day. Whatever one can say about the conventionality of his production, which was wrongly called classical ballet, he certainly gave his imprint to a half century of Russian choreographic art and shaped the form and style of most Russian dancers of the nineteenth and the beginning of the twentieth century. And since this is considered the great flourishing period of the national ballet, it is useless to deny his influence and his importance. It was under the leadership of this Russified Frenchman that the so-called Russian school of ballet reached its height and asserted itself as a national art. Russian male and female dancers formed whole companies, and foreign leading dancers came to St. Petersburg and Moscow only as guests. Thus the independence of Russian ballet had already become an accomplished fact in the eighties. When stage directors, about the same time, felt the necessity of inviting painters and architects to renovate the sets and to improve the *mise en scène,* ballet was one of the first theatrical forms to follow the new trend. Petipa, despite all the conservatism and conventionality of his taste, was well aware that ballet was a show, and in his own way tended toward a development of ballet staging.

The same thing occured in the opera. Of course, the Italians still reigned in the operatic art of the capitals and big provincial cities, and the *mise en scène* of a *Rigoletto* or of a *Traviata* was as conventional in the nineties as it had been thirty years earlier. But the end of the century witnessed a new fact: the emergence and the growing popularity of the national Russian opera written by Russian composers on familiar subjects taken from Russian history and literature. And the staging of these operas was entrusted to directors who called on Russian painters, archaeologists, and architects to give a new realistic flavor to sets and costumes.

The light opera and the operetta was, from the sixties on, the undisputed domain of the Austrians and the French, and Offenbach was as popular in St. Petersburg as in Paris.

But serious operatic works showed a tendency toward musical drama, and recitative was replacing the *cantilena,* or bel canto. *Russalka* by Dargomyzhsky, staged in 1856, surprised the public by its novelty in this regard. *The Guest of Stone* by the same composer, showed an even stronger spirit of musical dramatization.

With Glinka, Russian music went to popular sources and became pervaded with the national spirit—in rhythms and tunes. The mighty five, Balakirev, Borodin, Cui, Mussorgsky, and Rimsky-Korsakov, upheld Glinka's tradition of using Russian themes in solos and choruses while combining them with all the technical refinements of Western music and, particularly in the case of Mussorgsky, presenting new and bold innovations of tone, harmony, and expression which were destined to influence greatly the whole of European music. In the eighties and nineties, the Russian opera had a series of powerful works acclaimed by the audience. Most of their librettos were taken from romantic literature or folklore—*Boris Godunov* and *Khovanshchina* by Mussorgsky, *Prince Igor* by Borodin, *Pskovitianka* and *Sadko* by Rimsky-Korsakov, and many others. One can say that Russian opera with its expressionism, its new accents, and its realistic flavor, made gigantic steps in the second half of the century and almost outdistanced the dramatic art in its amazing flourishing.

This musical evolution necessarily brought to life a new generation of interpreters. The tradition of Italian opera originated an unequal distribution of the cast: the maximum of bel canto went to tenors and sopranos (including the coloratura); basso or alto were reserved for character parts, mostly comic or old. Very often the bassos were the best actors. Dramatic impersonation was subordinated to vocal qualities, and therefore its level usually remained low. Very few singers combined beautiful voices with sensitive acting; among them was Ossip Petrov (1806-1878), the great basso, who began his career in St. Petersburg in the thirties and became famous in the parts of Sussanin and Farlaf, in the *Life for the Tsar*, Varlam in *Boris Godunov*, and the Miller in *Russalka*. Petrov initiated what could be called realistic acting in opera with a slight idealization of all the parts he sang. Petrov and his wife (a contralto) were intimate friends of Mussorgsky.

Representative of a whole school of intelligent opera singers who strove toward a believable and realistic interpretation of operatic roles were Ivan Yershov and Fyodor Stravinsky. Yershov (1867-1943), tenor soloist with the Mariinsky starting in 1895, was excellent in Wagner's works and as Lensky in Tchaikovsky's *Eugene Oneghin*. The basso Fyodor Stravinsky (1843-1902), father of Igor Stravinsky, was also with the Mariinsky and well known for his roles in Serov's *The Fiend*, Verdi's *Falstaff*, and *Mephistopheles* by Boito. They, together with a small group of critics and sensitive listeners, felt that the staging of operas needed a drastic change.

Thus, by the end of the nineties, while all the theatrical arts in Russia reached a high degree of maturity and often originality, there was a general expectation of reform and improvement. The cultural atmosphere of the period bred new ideas and daring experiments—and the end of the century marked a turning point in the history of the national theater.

4

The Beginnings of
The Moscow Art Theater

A REMARKABLE PERIOD of stir and renovation swept over all the arts in Russia at the end of the nineties, and this movement, often called modernist because of its artistic tendencies and theories, later became known as the "silver age," as compared with the golden age of the classics. Young men and women of the intelligentsia of the nineties, enchanted by the Western symbolists and decadents, hailed estheticism and art for art's sake and looked for new modes of literary and artistic expression. In literature, the movement coincided with the return to neoromanticism. The emphasis on individualism, the devotion to fantasy, refined sensitivity, and sensualism, took diverse forms in different arts. In painting, for instance, the down-to-earth and often tendentious canvases of populist painters and their social messages were replaced by experiments in light and color, with strong leanings toward impressionism and various postimpressionistic schools. In music, the growth of national composers led to new harmonizations and a reform in the operatic art.

At the end of the century the impact of foreign influence was strongly felt in Russian culture: French symbolist poets, from Verlaine to Rimbaud, Scandinavian dramatists and novelists, from Ibsen to Hamsun, German philosophers and musicians, from Nietzsche to Wagner, were taken as models and passionately discussed among the young. What gave unity to the whole movement, despite the diversity of its manifestations in all fields of

Asenkova as Esmeralda
in the late 1830s.

Karatyghin as Hamlet
in the 1840s.

Shchepkin, the great realistic
actor of the 1840s.

Mochalov, the great tragedian
of the 1840s.

Kommissarzhevskaya a
Nina in *The Sea Gull,*
Alexandrinsky Theater
1896.

Yermolova, known as "the heroic
symphony of the Russian stage" of
the nineteenth century.

The Sea Gull, Act I, in the Moscow Art Theater, 1898; sets by Simov.

Nemirovich Danchenko in 1898.   Stanislavsky in 1898.

Three Sisters, Act III, at the Moscow Art Theater, 1901.

Three Sisters, the Moscow Art Theater, 1901. Left to right: Knipper as Masha, Savitskaya as Olga, and Litovtseva as Irina.

Stanislavsky as Vershinin in *Three Sisters*
at the Moscow Art Theater, 1901.

Kachalov as Tuzenbakh in *Three Sisters*
at the Moscow Art Theater, 1901.

Moskvin as Yepikhodov in *The Cherry
Orchard,* the Moscow Art Theater, 1904.

Ivanov, Act I, in the Moscow Art Theater, 1904; sets by Simov.

The Cherry Orchard, Act IV, The Moscow Art Theater, 1904; sets by Simov.

A scene from Gorky's *The Lower Depths* at the Moscow Art Theater, 1902.

A setting for *Sakuntala* at the Kamerny Theater, 1914.

Tairov, director of
the Kamerny Theater, 1914.

the arts, was a common rejection of the past and an adventurous spirit of search and discovery. This intense desire for innovation was in the air, and one of the leaders of the modernists in literature, jeered at by the older generation, had called the pioneers of the new art "the premature announcers of a delayed spring."

In the theater the discontent with conventional repertory and worn-out settings was accompanied by the feeling that production and acting were out-dated and had lost all creative force. New Western ventures such as Antoine's Théâtre Libre in Paris and the Meiningen Company provoked great interest and seemed to indicate the right direction. After the abolition of the Imperial Theaters' monopoly, a major freedom was felt in all the areas of theatrical arts, and the influx of young actors who graduated from the newly established schools between 1880 and 1890 intensified the general atmosphere of expectation.

While the influence of Antoine and the German director Brahm was limited to a few professionals, the Meiningen Company made a great impression on the general public in 1885 and 1890, and their guest performances in Russia were a sensation. The patron of the company, Duke George II of Saxen-Meiningen, a historian, designer, and lover of theater (late in life he married Ellen Franz, an actress), spent large sums of money to build a remarkable theatrical company. He placed it under the leadership of Ludwig Kronek (Chroneghk), a talented, intransigent, and stern director who imposed an iron rule on his fellow actors. The Meiningens became world-famous by combining a scrupulous presentation of historical repertory with the innovations they introduced into the composition of their group and the techniques of the stage. Kronek's basic assumption was that a play is an artistic whole and not a collection of parts: to give a feeling of unity, the performance must be directed by one person; a highly disciplined company must obey the director; parts must be treated as living characters; and the visual side of production must be given utmost attention. Still using drops and painted flats, Kronek designed them to look solid, and even took to three dimensional props (trees, pillars). He created illusion in stage lighting by the use of gaslight, not only from the front, but above and on both sides of the stage.

When the Meiningens at Moscow and St. Petersburg performed

Julius Caesar with the scenery of the Roman Forum transported, as it seemed, from Rome, or *Mary Stuart* with a perfect copy of the throne room, and when they filled the stage with live, gesticulating, highly individualized supers who produced marvelous mass scenes, the audience went wild with enthusiasm. The historical, almost ethnographical, naturalism of the Meiningens was a revelation. Specialists were greatly impressed by the centralization of the performance according to a thorough plan, but some critics claimed that the dictatorship of the director oppressed the actor, that the externals predominated at the expense of the insight and art of individuals (this despite the fact that the Meiningens had such excellent actors as Barnay and Teller). And some people felt that the old romantic plays did not suit the new lines of reform. However, during their two guest appearances, the Meiningens made a tremendous impression and brought about distinct changes in Russian theatrical production.

Another powerful factor was Mamontov's Opera. Savva Mamontov, a builder of railways and a millionaire, was a lover of theater and himself a designer, singer, and dramatist. Surrounded by gifted enlightened friends, he was also active in promoting handicraft and folklore research. His strong feeling for national art was devoid of any chauvinism. Later, in his opera enterprise, he produced nineteen foreign operas in addition to forty-three Russian ones. In 1882 he staged, in his huge Moscow mansion, *The Snow Maiden* by Rimsky-Korsakov with scenery settings made by the famous painter, Victor Vasnetsov. This was the beginning of a whole movement which later led to the public opera-theater being subsidized and actually directed by Mamontov. He paid great attention to settings and externals, gathered around his venture all the young and talented painters, mostly of the impressionist school, such as Korovin, Golovin, Vrubel, Vasnetsov, Polenov, and promoted such artists as Chaliapin and Zabello-Vrubel, the poetic interpreter of Princess Volkhova in *Sadko* by Rimsky-Korsakov. Fyodor Chaliapin, the famous basso, made sensational appearances as Boris in Mussorgsky's *Boris Godunov,* and as Mephistopheles in Gounod's *Faust.* Mamontov greatly favored the "mighty five" and all the achievements of the new trends in contemporary Russian music. At the beginning of the century he gave lavish performances of *Prince Igor, Boris*

Godunov, and a series of operas by his favorite composer, Rimsky-Korsakov. The impact of Mamontov's Opera, when it was reopened in 1896, was enormous. It proved that modern painters, architects, costume makers, and directors could produce a visually beautiful show which was at the same time a source of strong emotional and esthetic pleasure. The example was so convincing that even the Imperial Theaters learned their lesson and began to invite young painters to design opera and ballet scenery.

Mamontov's venture, however, did not get enough public support and, being too much of a financial liability, had to be discontinued after a few years. Its ways and traditions were resumed by Diaghilev in his Russian and European ballet companies, by Zimin in his Moscow opera house in which some hundred operas were produced between 1904 and 1917, and by the Theater of Musical Drama established in St. Petersburg by Lapitsky in 1911. Mamontov's experiments, moreover, made a lasting impression upon the founders of the Moscow Art Theater.

Mamontov's Opera was typical of the atmosphere which reigned in the nineties among wealthy Moscow merchants. Most of them were generous patrons of art; they did not limit themselves to offering money but often worked in the field they supported, and worked relentlessly, passionately. Pavel Tretiakov spent huge sums for beautiful canvases but it was his genuine love of art that made his collection (which he later donated to the city of Moscow) one of the best in tsarist Russia and now the pride of the Soviets. Serghei Shchukin, another merchant, patiently collected French impressionists and post-impressionists and of this period, his gallery is perhaps the best in the world. His brother Peter, interested in Russian antiques, built a large historical museum. Alexey Bakhrushin, lover of the theater, established the first Russian Theatrical Museum, and several rich merchants, among them Soldatenkov and Sabashnikov, became publishers of valuable books.

Most of these Maecenases were friends of Serghei Alexeyev, a rich industrialist and father of Konstantin, later known under the name of Stanislavsky. Konstantin's maternal grandmother was Marie Varley, a French actress who had married a Russian and settled in Moscow. Born in 1863, Konstantin received an excellent education; even as a child he was often taken to the opera, to guest performances of famous foreign actors, and to regular dramatic shows. Throughout his adolescence he took part in numerous amateur performances organized in his family's house where stage facilities were specially built by his father. Later he took lessons in singing, ballet, and drama. At one time his dream was to become an opera singer. Theater was his passion, and when he was called to help and later to succeed his father, he divided his time between business and the stage—strongly leaning toward the latter. Sent to Paris for commercial purposes, he registered at the Conservatory and went to the theater twice a day, never missing a matinée. While acting in amateur companies, he met Stanislavsky, a Polish actor about to retire, and took his name to acquire more freedom for his histrionic experiments. In 1888 he became chairman of the Society for Arts and Letters, which aimed at bringing together people active in various fields of art, and also intended to offer its members regular theatrical performances. Alexander Fedotov, husband of the famous actress, and Fyodor Kommissarzhevsky, a well-known singer, acted as consultants of the company directed by Stanislavsky. During the two years of its activity, Stanislavsky had the opportunity to try his hand at different plays such as *The Avaricious Knight* by Pushkin, *George Dandin* by Molière, and *The Hard Lot* by Pisemsky. Despite all the money Stanislavsky sank into the venture, it was a financial loss, and the Society had to rent its locale to the Hunters' Club. The latter asked Stanislavsky's company to continue their performances, provided they produce a new play every week.

After having learned a great deal from the Meiningens, Stanislavsky had by that time become an expert director and actor. He assembled an excellent company of amateurs and professionals, among them Samarova, Lilina (who became his wife), Luzhsky, Artem, Sanin, Alexandrov—all of whom later made great contributions to the Moscow Art Theater. At the end of the nineties, Stanislavsky began a series of innovations which made his performances at the Hunters' Club outstanding. The old house of the Hunters' Club had burned down and the newly built one had vast technical possibilities for the stage director. He used these in mass scenes in *Uriel Acosta* by Gutzkov, the play about a Jewish heretic in Holland engaged to a beautiful girl but excommunicated by the rabbis of the synagogue. In the second act, Stanislavsky staged a party in the garden of the rich Manassah, Uriel's future father-in-law; the magnificent feast was interrupted by a hollow sound of trumpet and piercing squeaks of pipes announcing a horrifying procession of rabbis in black cassocks. The scene in which the mob assails the heretic Uriel and almost kills him was put on with such veracity that Stanislavsky, in the part of Uriel, was terrified. The audiences were also startled by the staging of an hallucination scene in *The Polish Jew* by Erkmann-Chatrian, where a respectable Alsatian judge, who had killed a Jewish traveler, has a vision of being convicted by shadows and ghosts. This kind of symbolism was also used in the fantastic picture of heaven into which is risen Hannele, a poor girl in Hauptmann's play of the same title; the beggars, prostitutes, and thieves who surrounded her on earth are transformed into luminous figures after their deaths—a touching and highly allegoric scene designed by Stanislavsky in unearthly, faded colors. Not less remarkable was his scenery in *Othello*: he presented the island of Cyprus with historical accuracy, including its streets, palaces, and colorful oriental mobs. Later he reverted to symbolism in Hauptmann's *The Sunken Bell* in which he stunned the spectators by a beautifully arranged forest with an ingenious use of various levels. The performance of *The Hamlet Stepanchikov* (a comedy taken from Dostoevsky's novelette) and of Tolstoy's *The Fruits of Enlightenment* (a private show because of the censorship) were also highlights in Stanislavsky's career. Vera Kommissarzhevskaya, then a completely unknown young actress, was given a small part in Tolstoy's comedy.

The list of plays acted and directed by Stanislavsky between 1888 and 1896 shows not only the great range of his apprenticeship which goes from serious drama to light operetta, but is also a reflection of his basic duality: he was equally attracted by faithful representation of life in a scrupulous naturalistic manner, and by whimsical impressionism and symbolism. This ambivalence corresponded to his doubts and artistic uncertainties. In 1896 Stanislavsky reached his thirty-third year. He had a past of almost fifteen years of successful acting and ten years of directing, but he was still searching for new methods in both fields. At that time he was a tall, very handsome man with sparkling blue eyes under thick black eyebrows, a black mustache (which he didn't shave off until 1903 when playing the part of Brutus in *Julius Caesar*). Despite his age, his hair was already gray and this gave a peculiar character to his youthful appearance and light gait. His stature, his energetic bearing, and graceful movements seemed quite natural but actually were due to incessant work on his gestures and attitudes. His distinguished and well-controlled exterior and his air of self-assurance hid a passionate and complex nature. A very cultured, widely read and traveled man, he was constantly beset by all sorts of inner problems, by the search for artistic perfection, by a whirl of conflicting ideas, and by a burning desire for self-expression. He had tremendous physical and spiritual vitality and could work relentlessly for endless hours without noticing how exhausted all his co-workers were. He had charm, inspired trust, was gracious with people, spent all his money for others and for his beloved theatrical ventures, but in the moments of creative ecstasy which drove him blind and mad, he would have furious fits of temper if not obeyed immediately or if met with opposition or bad faith. The actors of the Hunters' Club called him "express director" because of his desire to do everything without any delay and because of the intense manner in which he worked on-stage. He had great resourcefulness and logic, and his love of objects, of things, married to his great inventiveness, served him well in his projects with scenery and props. He owed his realism to Fedotov and the Meiningens, but his bent toward poetic symbolism and psychological complexities came from his own emotional nature and from the period in which he lived: the three S's were the credo of the age—subjectivism, sensitivity, and symbolism. Yet Stanislavsky was not quite sure what direction to take, and was satisfied least of all with his own acting. Besides, he felt the necessity to expand his experiments at the Hunters' Club and try for a larger and better organized theatrical enterprise. Such an opportunity presented itself in 1897 when Nemirovich Danchenkov forcefully made his appearance.

Vladimir Nemirovich Danchenko (1858-1943), a nobleman, son of an impecunious lieutenant-colonel and a provincial lady of Caucasian origin, was a small landowner, related to Russian aristocracy through his wife, Baroness Korf. Formed in the intellectual atmosphere of Moscow University, he began in the eighties as a dramatist and a theatrical critic in newspapers and magazines, and later, in 1891, as a teacher in the Philharmonic Dramatic School into which he had been introduced by Sumbatov-Yuzhin. The friendship with the latter opened the doors of the Maly Theater to Nemirovich Danchenko. As a playwright he was very successful, and in 1896 his play about a double suicide, *The Worth of Life,* became the greatest hit of the season and was awarded the Griboyedov prize. He told the judges that they should have given it to *The Sea Gull* by Chekhov—at that moment the greatest failure of the season.

As a teacher Danchenko insisted upon thorough comprehension of all aspects of the play and fought a relentless war against conventionality and affectation. He had among his pupils Olga Knipper, later Chekhov's wife, Vsevolod Meyerhold, and Ivan Moskvin, all of whom played an important role in the history of the Russian theater. They all performed in the "examination play"—Ibsen's *A Doll's House*—and this first performance had the same dramatic impact as the opera *Eugene Oneghin* that Tchaikovsky produced a few years earlier as the graduating performance at the Conservatory. But Nemirovich Danchenko understood very well that even the most brilliant performance of graduating students could not change much in the routine of the Russian stage. He wrote a memorandum about the necessity of reforms in the Maly Theater which he addressed to the Imperial Administration. Not too confident of the results of such a daring step, he also decided to have a talk with Stanislavsky, whose work he knew and appreciated, and wrote him a letter asking for a meeting in the restaurant Slaviansky Bazaar. Nemirovich Danchenko's report and proposals were rejected by the Imperial Administration on that very June 21, 1898, when he met Stanislavsky for the first time. The "chat" in a private room of the restaurant started at two o'clock in the afternoon and ended at six o'clock the next morning. Thanks to their memoirs, we know what the two men discussed during those historical eighteen hours. Two theatrical visionaries, so different in background and temperament, discovered that working quite separately and under dissimilar circumstances they had come to the same conclusions and conceived the same hopes. They felt that despite all the virtues of individual actors, the situation in well-established theaters, and especially the Imperial Theaters, was quite desperate, and a reform of the stage could come only from a new theater. Both took great pleasure in attacking the old institutions, and an even greater one in agreeing on the necessity of establishing a new joint undertaking. They were confident of each other because their ideas on what should be done coincided so fully. They discussed in detail "the new laws for the theater [we] wanted to start." In the morning, they rode to Liubimovka, the Alexeyev family estate near Moscow (later Chekhov spent a summer there meditating on his *The Cherry Orchard*). Stanislavsky always liked "to put it down on paper" and, according to his custom, made a record of their general agreement; then they went over the list of Nemirovich Danchenko's pupils and Stanislavsky's company to make a final selection of whom they wanted with them in the projected venture. They also established a working plan, including plays, "each of which had to have its own particular scenery," and they talked about the necessity of educating the public and the actor, and stressed even the minute particulars such as the style of announcements and the curtain (which should be drawn to the sides rather than raised). They agreed on the way of producing a play—and dreamt of five or six dress rehearsals. And finally they divided the whole artistic realm into two parts: the literary, assigned to Nemirovich Danchenko, and the production-al, led by Stanislavsky. They agreed, however, that whenever Nemirovich wished to produce a play, he would assume full responsibility for its direction. They decided to hold equal rights, including that of veto: Stanislavsky on the form and Nemirovich on the content (they were not quite clear at that time of the true significance of these terms). The name of the theater was found later: Moscow Popular Art Theater, The word "popular" or "everybody's" was dropped in a couple of years.

II

To be able to open the theater in the fall of 1898, the two directors had to begin working immediately, and they started with the energy characteristic of them both. N. Arkhipov (later known as assistant stage director Arbatov) offered a barn on his estate near Pushkino, some thirty miles from Moscow, and all the future members of the company took lodgings in the nearby villages, living in groups under rather primitive conditions, and rehearsing every day from eleven to five and in the evening from eight to eleven in the barn transformed into a little theater with an improvised stage. They were all young, enthusiastic, and healthy people; they lived like a community, doing everything themselves (Stanislavsky swept the floor, and ruined a samovar when making tea—he put burning charcoal inside the pipe but forgot the water). But the same Stanislavsky was transformed into a severe leader at the rehearsals of the company and acted again as "an express director." It is difficult to imagine the high spirit of rebellion, idealism, and strenuous work which animated this group of men and women who were also tied together by friendship and love (a dozen marriages resulted from this common life within six months). "We were perfectly happy then; the future did not frighten us, we were united by warm friendship and in love with the idea of the new theater; it loomed in front of us as something vague but beautiful and gave us enthusiasm, strength, and fire. We worked and dreamt whole days and nights." In this description Stanislavsky omitted to say that the work and dreams were already determined by certain theatrical principles. The company presented an ideological and artistic unity because all its members shared a common aversion to the past, and common aspirations toward the reforms of acting and play production.

Later, Stanislavsky defined this attitude: "Our program was revolutionary; we rebelled against the old way of acting, against affectation, and false pathos, against declamation and bohemian exaggeration, against bad conventionality of production and sets, against the star system which ruined the ensemble, and against the whole spirit of performance and the insignificance of repertory."

During these summer rehearsals of *Tsar Fyodor,* chosen for the opening of the new theater, it became quite clear what were the main foundations of the new enterprise. Of course, the principles that emerged from these early experiences were later sharpened and developed—but from the beginning, Stanislavsky and Nemirovich Danchenko formulated and put into practice some basic requirements. The main innovation was, of course, the idea of an artistic ensemble, shaped by the organizing will of the director. All the elements of the performance were harmonized and nothing was left to whim or improvisation. Later, the enemies of the Moscow Art Theater remarked that it was too well organized. In any case their method led to a rational, conscious attitude toward acting. Since the play was conceived and produced as an artistic whole in which the pictorial, the musical, the verbal were merged, each actor had to find his place as a part of this whole. The abolition of the star system came as a logical conclusion to this conception. Stanislavsky challenged the usual routine of building a performance around a great actor or actress, be it such an outstanding figure as Savina of the Alexandrinsky or Yermolova of the Maly Theater. When he announced "there are no small parts, there are only small actors" and later began casting plays in a fashion the old hands called fantastic, he was only following his main idea and was giving his actors the opportunity to experience various artistic possibilities. "One must love art, and not oneself in art," was one of his favorite slogans. And his leading actor, after having interpreted Hamlet, might be moved to a small part of a supernumerary: "but even as a supernumerary he has to show he is an artist. . . . The poet, the actor, the painter, the dressmaker, the stagehand, serve one and the same goal expressed by the author in the very essence of his play. Laziness, caprice, hysterics, inaccuracy, lateness, bad character, ignorance of the part, are harmful to the whole and must be rooted out." These maxims revealed the twofold aims of the Stanislavsky–Nemirovich Danchenko company: from the beginning and more than twenty years later it was an educational institution; behind the wings it educated the actor and trained him in a very definite way. It also educated the spectator. Nemirovich Danchenko spoke of "discipline for the public" before the theater opened its doors—and both directors worked hard in giving a new dignity to their "house of art": they created sober and elegant surroundings, refused to admit customers after the curtain was raised, and the actors were not allowed to come out and bow, except after the last act. The public was trained to behave in the Moscow Art Theater as if they were in a temple—a unique atmosphere was being created in this Moscow sanctuary of the muses.

The discipline of the actor was in full conformity to the

principles of seriousness and rational organization. The new techniques (mainly introduced and supported by Nemirovich) consisted of shifting the preparatory work to the analysis of the play.
From the first rehearsals in the barn of a country estate, the
Moscow Theater set a firm tradition: before any casting, the
whole company had to attend the reading of the play and to
discuss it. Later, such discussions came after introductions made
by guest lecturers and literary critics. Unlike other directors,
Stanislavsky and Nemirovich Danchenko rejected the method of
individual coaching. Instead, scenes were rehearsed one at a time,
and general rehearsals of the whole play were held only when the
director was satisfied with each scene.

This piecemeal technique offered Stanislavsky and Nemirovich
Danchenko the opportunity for their educational activity: the
rehearsals often resembled courses in dramatics.

In training their company, both directors had to overcome
obstacles of stage tradition. In the forties, Shchepkin had waged
war against the clichés of Dmitrevsky, but by the end of the
nineteenth century there had grown an accumulation of devices
which went back to the same Shchepkin, and the public had
become used to certain patterns, such as a repetition of intonations and gestures and welcomed them as old, well-known friends,
deriving joy from their recognition—almost in the same fashion
as it enjoyed the familiar tricks and the trills of a coloratura. The
Moscow Art Theater began a ruthless fight against those trite intonations, those routine manifestations of grief or joy, against
shouting in dramatic scenes, against saccharine attitudes in love
dialogue, against the accepted body movements for expressing
the pathos of death. Instead of this well-known code or language,
they wanted gestures, attitudes, and intonations dictated by actors'
emotions in particular, unique situations, and the actors were
immediately stopped during rehearsals whenever they reverted to
nonmotivated gestures, routine inflections of voice, or repeated
traditional patterns of stage behavior. The incessant search of the
actor was to be for genuine and fresh, highly individualized, external manifestations or physical expressions of emotion.

The second requirement was that the actor was to act all the
time he was on stage, and not to stand with empty eyes waiting
for his cue. The third point concerned "learning from life": each

actor had to catch in life itself the characteristic features of his part—and this included costume, make-up, voice, gait, etc. The Moscow Art Theater stressed the importance of "artistic observation" as a source of successful stage expression—and this requirement was often considered (quite wrongly in this writer's opinion) the proof of Stanislavsky's and Nemirovich Danchenko's philosophy of realism.

This was linked to the "no star" principle, to the teamwork of the company. No actor had a fixed *emploi* and was obliged to assume different parts, provided they suited him. And since the same principle was applied to all members of the group, including supers, the Moscow Art Theater easily produced live and picturesque crowds, and its mass scenes could compete with, and, in some instance became superior to, those of the Meiningens. Because of the "no star" principle some secondary parts acted by the best artists of the company often stood out in such relief that the public would be absorbed by them—and this was a point many theater devotees considered a defect.

As far as the very techniques of acting, both Stanislavsky and Nemirovich Danchenko waged a relentless war against so-called temperament which, in the majority of cases and especially in the provinces, was a false pathos, an artificial pitch, and a purely external showing off of intensity. The public, accustomed to explosions of passion and forceful manifestations of wrath or despair, at first regretted the familiar "great style" and found the Moscow Art group pale or not sufficiently vigorous. It took a certain time to educate the spectators to this new manner based on the inner feelings of the protagonist and rendered in subdued fashion. The accent on understatement in the theory and practice of the Moscow Art Theater was probably one of the reasons for its merely moderate success in classical tragedy.

Both directors agreed on a very important point: the actor had to live on the stage, forgetting the public entirely. The actor should not be conscious of the public and subject his movements and words to the thought of the thousand-eyed monster watching him. He should rather have the impression that the spectators were eavesdropping and looking through a keyhole—while the actors behind that imaginary fourth wall spoke and moved according to the inward necessity of the play. Faithful to this conception, the actors broke the secular rules of the stage by turning their backs to the public, speaking to each other and not to the audience, and making all their movements stage-centered and not audience-directed. Of course one can interpret this method as realistic or naturalistic, and reproach the reformers for not regarding the performance as a show, as a spectacle. But both Stanislavsky and Nemirovich Danchenko were extremely conscious of the visual side of the theater, and at the beginning the public responded mostly to the innovations that struck the eye. In any case, the whole development of theatrical arts in the twentieth century moved in that direction. Stanislavsky and his companions understood that spectators come to see as well as to hear and that the "show" part of a play is as important as its text and its auditive rendering. It is true that one of the main efforts of the Moscow Art Theater concentrated on combining the verbal and the visual elements of performance, and the equilibrium they reached was not only a question of measure or theoretical distribution of different ingredients but an organic synthesis, a harmony which in itself was a feat of artistic creativity dependent on a sense of proportion as much as on rational planning. Yet, on the whole, Stanislavsvky paid great attention to the production of the play because he believed that settings, sounds, and objects supported the emotions the actor had to create. In other words, the visual side of the performance was, at the start of the Moscow Art Theater, but a means subordinated to other, higher purposes. This attitude later gave rise to passionate polemics and even to struggle among Stanislavsky's pupils: some of them, such as Meyerhold, made the production an objective in itself and sacrificed to it the text, or what Nemirovich Danchenko liked to call "the content" of the play—or at least its verbal integrity.

III

All these theoretical premises were not so plainly defined at the start of the Moscow Art Theater activities, but they gradually gained in precision and clarity. In the summer of 1898, however, the attention of both directors was absorbed by two tasks: the transformation of the old Hermitage Theater in Carriage Row that they had rented, and the preparation of the production of *Tsar Fyodor,* chosen for the opening night.

Nemirovich Danchenko assumed the financial and administrative leadership of the Company, which was constituted as a cooperative society. The Hermitage was old and dirty, it lacked technical equipment, and its heating system was so bad that in the winter costumes froze to the wall. Everything had to be repaired and modified at a racing pace if the performers wanted to offer the public a "hall with cultural atmosphere" as was their wish.

The production of the play presented other difficulties. It was a historical drama depicting the pathetic destiny of Fyodor, the son of Ivan the Terrible, a weak and delicate creature unable to reign and struggle against the intrigues of power-greedy boyards and the iron will of Boris Godunov, his first councilor. In order to re-create the Moscow of that period, actors, painters, and members of the staff organized expeditions to monasteries, local fairs, and old provincial towns, where they purchased wooden plates, cups, cloth, dresses, and objects of the sixteenth century. They worked in museums and even succeeded in borrowing from them genuine robes and jewels. There is no doubt that in this research they were inspired by the Meiningens, and one is tempted to say that they aimed at a naturalistic reproduction of historical surroundings. As a trend, this tendency was the most obvious one and, in a way, the most spectacular and comprehensible for the public, so that it seemed to be the main feature of the new theater. Unfortunately, it obscured for many critics and spectators, charmed by Stanislavsky's historical productions, the more important ideas of the company. It must be admitted, however, that those who saw the first performance of *Tsar Fyodor* on October 14, 1898, felt they were witnessing not only a historical drama but also a historical event: a new era had begun for the Russian theater. Of course, what greatly impressed the crowd on this memorable first night and provoked its enthusiasm was the production. The public was literally astonished when they saw on the stage the exact replica of the Archangel's Cathedral or the Tsar's quarters in the Kremlin reproduced with such exactitude that the actors had to bend down to pass through the low doors leading from the stage. In the first scene the covered terrace of huge wooden pillars going to the left behind the wings, the perspective of the roofs of Moscow to the right, and a sort of parapet or balustrade between the footlights and the artists seemed so authentic that the spectators could hardly believe they were in a theater. The author's remark "enter boyards" was interpreted by Stanislavsky as a procession of bearded dignitaries arranged in the order of their aristocratic priority; the noblemen walked in slowly, turned to cross themselves in front of icons, then bowed twice to the Tsar and the Tsarine, performing the venerable Moscow rites. Their robes, jewels, and weapons were all museum pieces, and the whole stage with its rare furniture, genuine sixteenth-century objects and costumes was like an animated color engraving of an old master. An earthly note in Flemish style was struck by the scene in which the discontented boyards were offered huge plates of goose, pork, beef, fruit, and vegetables, while barrels of wine and honey were rolled in, and a beautiful maid, Princess Mstislavskaya, went from one guest to another with the "honor drink." The naturalness of the conversation between the guests and the signing of a petition which gave tragic forebodings to the glitter of the feast, blended gestures, costumes, words, and settings in such a perfect manner that the illusion of life seemed complete. No less striking was the scene of a wooden bridge over the Yaouza river with barges passing under it, people of all sorts milling round on the bridge, and a blind beggar at its entrance singing a song of olden times (the music of which had been provided by Alexander Grechaninov, then a young composer).

Added to the accuracy of furnishings and objects was the historical truthfulness of intonation and diction (imitating the slow talking of the boyards) and the new natural make-up, constantly used by Stanislavsky and completely alien to the exaggerated masklike quality of the reigning routine. The acting was also unusually simple and true to life although the audience paid less attention to actors than to real wood frames and metallic handles of windows and doors, or to authentic furnishings and arms. And this was unjust because Ivan Moskvin gave a lively portraiture of Fyodor, and Olga Knipper, as Irina, his wife, and Vishnevsky in the part of Boris Godunov, were also excellent. The success of *Tsar Fyodor* was tremendous—and this despite some bilious reviews which called the new venture "a whim of the rich amateur Stanislavsky" or "a copy of Meiningens." The public reacted so enthusiastically that at once the Moscow Art Theater was firmly established. The opening of *Tsar Fyodor* remained a memorable date and a box office success: at its 100th performance, three years later, a scroll from 9,522 grateful spectators was presented to the actors and directors.

This archaeological-historical kind of realism, as we said before, formed one of the most important trends throughout the evolution of the theater. One is tempted to say that it remained its most conservative and, as far as the audience was concerned, most successful feature. Stanislavsky applied the same method of research and authenticity to all historical and period plays, whether it was *The Merchant of Venice* or *Julius Caesar*. For the latter, he went with his actors to Rome and reproduced on the Moscow stage the narrow streets, the Forum, and the picturesque southern crowd of Caesar's city. In the same way, the company made an expedition to the island of Cyprus in preparation for *Othello*. In order to make the public understand the seriousness of these efforts, productions of new plays were accompanied with matching exhibitions. The spectators of *Julius Caesar,* for instance, could see in the foyer stalls Russian translations of Shakespeare, as well as genuine objects of the period—coins, armor, and paintings and engravings.

The best results, of course, were obtained with national Russian plays. *Tsar Fyodor* was part of a trilogy by Alexey Tolstoy, and his other play, *The Death of Ivan the Terrible,* with its vaulted bed chamber of the expiring tyrant-tsar, was also produced with great success. In the same vein of historical accuracy were evocations of the Russian romantic forties in *A Month in the Country* by Turgenev, or of the twenties in *Wit Works Woe* by Griboyedov. The naturalistic detail, the faithfulness to life was also a guiding principle in the production of contemporary plays. This caused Stanislavsky and Nemirovich (particularly the latter as the promoter of Ibsen in Russia) to bring furniture from Norway for *Hedda Gabler* and *An Enemy of the People* or to present Chekhov's comedies in authentic settings of Russian provincial homes and estates. In some instances the realism of the theater was exaggerated: the critics quipped that when Stanislavsky reproduced night it was so dark on the stage that nobody could see anything, and if nightingales were singing in the forest, one could hardly hear the actors. The reproduction of the flophouse in Gorky's *The Lower Depths* was so accurate that actors wore real rags and dirty shoes. In a play by Ostrovsky, the director used a special trick in order to create the illusion of the fourth wall: the sun shone from the audience and in its light on the floor one could see the reflections of curtains, flower pots, and the tracing of windows of an imaginary wall. For years the whole Moscow Art Theater movement was identified with naturalistic faithfulness to life, and this trend was considered most revolutionary at the end of the nineteenth and the beginning of the twentieth centuries. Of course, underneath all this attachment to the realistic detail was the feeling of love, devotion, and romantic dedication. Stanislavsky and his friends were passionate men, and they did everything with the utmost sincerity and self-absorption. In order to make the chimes sound real in *Tsar Fyodor,* Stanislavsky studied bells and investigated their ringing in the forlorn churches and monasteries of northern Russia. There were no insignificant minutiae for him; every trifle was looked upon as an important part of a highly organized whole. The same attitude was extended from properties to acting: before interpreting Colonel Vershinin in Chekhov's *Three Sisters,* Stanislavsky wore for weeks the military uniform in which he had to appear on the stage. For the same purpose, the cast of *Julius Caesar* had to walk around for days in togas and tunics. All the sound effects which made the productions of the Moscow Art Theater so famous the world over—the rustling of leaves, the buzzing of insects, the echoes and strange noises in the forest, the familiar clattering of glasses or forks and knives, or some more subtle and at times mysterious resonances such as the distant banging of the wooden pail in a Chekhov play—were all expressions of a consistent artistic credo. On the whole, the Moscow Art Theater easily won its victory in this domain: realism on the stage was universally recognized in the Russian theater by the beginning of the twentieth century. The battle was also won by the realists in the Théâter Libre in Paris and other similar institutions on the continent and in England. If the impact of the Moscow Art Theater consisted simply in the affirmation of naturalistic detail in production and faithfulness to life in acting, its role would have been rather limited. Fortunately, its scope was much broader and its search for artistic renovation much deeper, while Stanislavsky's capacities revealed themselves as much more profound. The proof of this (which Soviet critics and historians of Stalin's era tried in vain to distort and diminish) was offered a few months after the opening of the Theater.

IV

Several factors contributed to the tremendous success of *Tsar Fyodor*: the public always showed interest in national-historical repertory and its curiosity was sharpened by the fact that the play, banned by censorship for thirty years, was now produced by a new venture. Rumors about the lavishness of Stanislavsky's settings and the revolutionary innovations of his company had created an atmosphere of expectation. A month later, however, the novelty was somewhat diminished, and the Theater met its first difficulties. *Antigone* by Sophocles and *The Merchant of Venice* (in which Shylock, to the disapproval of the audience, spoke with a Jewish accent) were not as spectacular as *Tsar Fyodor*, and the Shakespearean drama was not even well attended and did not make money. Stanislavsky wanted to present *Hannele* by Hauptmann, but the Church censors banned the performance —at the last moment. The financial affairs of the company were far from prosperous—until the production in December 1898 of Chekhov's *The Sea Gull*. This was not only a triumph for the author but also a vindication of Nemirovich Danchenko's flair and a new page in the annals of the theater. Without betraying its principle of "faithfulness to life," the Moscow Art Theater showed its originality and distinction from the Meiningens: it produced a modern play which used realistic detail for the purpose of creating a psychological mood. Now it had found its most important, most distinctive feature which, in the course of years, also proved to be the most successful: the rendering of emotions and psychological nuances through a special blending of significant detail with a new manner of acting, supported by teamwork, artistic settings, and thoroughly planned, meticulously organized production. While the Moscow Art Theater found in

Chekhov the author whose plays marvelously fitted its artistic aspirations and experiments, Chekhov met in its actors and directors the very people who could understand and realize his own theatrical aims. It was an "ideal marriage," as a later historian called this fateful alliance between the playwright and his interpreters.

By 1898, Anton Chekhov (1860-1904) achieved great popularity in Russia as the author of short stories—humorous at first but more serious as he advanced in years. This was the time of his literary maturity and his steady rise as a writer of the first magnitude. He was, however, less successful as a dramatist even though he had been always attracted by the theater. His early attempts to be a playwright dated from his youth. He was twenty when he wrote his first play—without a title: it represented great historical and biographical interest because it contained themes and figures of his subsequent works, but it was devoid of any real literary merit and conceived in an imitative, traditional manner. A few years later, at the age of twenty-four, Chekhov wrote a one-act play, *On the Road,* actually dramatizing his story *In Autumn.* It was followed by a series of one-act plays, either in the comic-pathetic style, or in the genre of vaudeville. In the first category was *The Swan Song,* a monologue of an old provincial actor who falls asleep in the empty theater, awakens, evokes all his unhappy existence, and exchanges a few words with the prompter. The monologue *On the Harm of Tobacco* (1886) is also in this almost Gogolian comic vein. Between 1888 and 1892 Chekhov wrote dramatized jokes—*The Bear, The Proposal, A Tragedian in Spite of Himself, The Wedding, The Jubilee*— all reflecting his genius for characterization and his exposé of human vanity and stupidity, enhanced by farcical situations.

His first unpublished play (it came to light only in 1923) represents his more serious dramatic experiment. It is related to *Ivanov.* In *The Wood Spirit* he made the first draft of what eight years later became *Uncle Vanya.*

One can say that *Ivanov* is Chekhov's first important contribution to the theater. It is true that this drama is traditional in structure and has melodramatic effects, that it does not show the originality and full mastery of Chekhov's art. But it does contain most of the elements that became, in his subsequent works, the

foundation of a new dramatic style and technique. The play revolves around one hero—but Ivanov is an unheroic protagonist,
a superfluous man, this well-known personage of Russian nineteenth-century literature. An idle landowner who has lost all
his money and can do nothing with his life, Ivanov still has intellectual aspirations and can strike the feminine imagination by
his idealistic attitudes and beautiful words—as he has done with
Anne, a Jewess who left her parents and changed her religion
in order to marry him. When she falls ill and is about to die, he
actually abandons her—to the disgust of Doctor Lvov, who calls
him an egoist and a parasite. Ivanov seeks new love with Sasha,
a young girl who believes in him and is ready to sacrifice herself
for the man she idealizes. After Anne's death, Ivanov wants to
marry Sasha but at the last moment lacks strength and courage
to begin a new life and prefers to escape by committing suicide.

There is no doubt that Chekhov's intention was to give a
psychological portrait of a man he considered typical of his epoch
and, in general, of the Russian intelligentsia. Ivanov is akin to
those spineless and unhappy creatures Chekhov depicted by the
dozen in his stories and novelettes. He even wanted to call him
Ivan Ivanovich Ivanov—based on the commonest of Russian
names—to emphasize his banality, and he spoke of *Ivanov* as a
drama without a hero in the usual romantic meaning of the
term. When the play was produced in 1887 in the Korsh Theater
in Moscow and two years later in the Alexandrinsky Theater in
St. Petersburg, critics saw in Ivanov a psycho-pathological individual and claimed that his defects were unusual. The spectators, however, and the author himself—and today we agree with
them—felt that this prematurely old, bored, and disillusioned
intellectual was a realistic portrait of his contemporaries, and as
such was also a social type. It is true that Chekhov did not speak
about the social causes of Ivanov's failure—Soviet criticism is
always intimating that the playwright had in mind the hidden
roots of a social-political situation which produced the Ivanovs.
Such a supposition may perhaps be legitimate, but nothing in
the play itself can validate this theory.

More interesting is the fact that in *Ivanov* Chekhov used various modern devices such as intervals, pauses, and significant
details instead of naturalistic descriptions, a lyrical tone of con-

versation, non-rational structure of dialogue, and situations presented as psychological revelations. But this was not made clear until the Moscow Art Theater took up the drama in 1904.

Although *Ivanov* had a certain success in Moscow and St. Petersburg, was later included in the repertory of provincial companies, and was well received throughout Russia, actors and directors failed to see the difference between Chekhov's dramatic style and their conventional plays. Nemirovich Danchenko realized it when *The Wood Spirit* was produced by M. Abramova's private theater in Moscow (1889), and he spoke of the lack of concordance between the lyrical conception and the scenic realization of the play as the main reason for its failure (it folded after the first night). *The Wood Spirit* had been previously rejected by the Imperial Theaters' literary committee with this explanatory remark: "It is a magnificently dramatized novelette but not a play." It is interesting to note that while the protagonist of this work, Mikhail Krushchev (later developed into Astrov in *Uncle Vanya*), is treated by the author in his usual manner of impressionistic portraiture, the whole play reveals a more obvious moralistic tendency than any other Chekhovian drama or comedy. In most of the plays, the inner meaning is hidden and the conclusions are left to the spectator. But in *The Wood Spirit* the author becomes obvious. The world goes to the dogs, says Chekhov, not because of bandits and thieves but because of hatred and animosity among good people. Small mean things corrode life, and the intelligentsia, filled with good intentions and noble ideas, is oblivious and complacent. The importance of unimportant things—this is Chekhov's credo, and in *The Wood Spirit* he wanted to show that behind the façade of banality there is the world of tragic conflicts. "Men dine, just dine," he wrote, "and in this moment their fate is decided and their lives are destroyed." He applied this conception to his next play *The Sea Gull*, and the main reason for its early failure was that Chekhov's artistic intention was not understood by the performers.

One of the protagonists of *The Sea Gull*, this drama without a central hero, the young playwright Treplev says that he refuses to follow the old literary patterns. Looking for new forms, he writes a symbolic drama about the end of the world. His mother,

Arkadina, an actress, and her lover Trigorin, a well-known novelist, laugh at his attempts. Treplev certainly sounds silly in his rhetoric and mannerisms copied from the poetic flights of the decadents, but he is perfectly sincere in his rejection of old conventions and his search for new means of dramatic expression. What he says about the necessity of renovation (in the last act) reflects Chekhov's own feelings. Treplev's ineffectuality derives not from faulty esthetic theory but from his weakness and incapacity to sustain a struggle against odds. He is also a superfluous man, and he loses Nina Zarechnaya, the girl he loves and to whom he has given the leading part in his abortive play, because he is not able to fight and conquer. Nina, seduced and abandoned by Trigorin, comes back to Treplev, but not as the same fresh, free, and happy creature—the sea gull. Frustrated in love and creation, Treplev commits suicide. The other protagonists of the play are also unhappy and unsuccessful—and even the famous Trigorin does not believe in his own talent and tries to conceal his inner disintegration. The whole atmosphere of the play is one of melancholy and defeat. The author seems to tell us that beauty, freedom, dreams, love, art—all are ruined and soiled by falsity, weakness, and meanness. Life is represented as a series of trivial gestures and trite conversations, ruled by deceit and pretense, and the only consolation left to the spectator is the nostalgic dream of beauty and emancipation, floating about like notes of a distant music.

This play has obvious symbols such as that of the Sea Gull, senselessly killed by a cruel hunter during her flight over a lake (representing Nina, stupidly ruined in her youthful rapture and joy of life), but it also contains more subtle and allusive meanings and images. It combines them with typically Chekhovian insistence on mere trivialities, minutiae of everyday rites and customs, and those conversations which actually are monologues by various protagonists, each of them following his own line of thought and hardly listening to others. Not only is the play based on hushed voices and understatements, but its surface is static and all its dramatic action takes place off-stage. The spectator, for instance, is not shown Nina's affair with Trigorin, her struggle, her decision to become an actress, and her humiliating experiences in small theaters; the climactic suicide of Treplev is merely related. One can say that such a device is not new and that the Greeks preferred to report battles, adventures, and death through messengers or wise old men, precursors of the *raisonneurs* of the French comedy and tragedy, but in Chekhov's case it was not simply a reluctance to make a display of clashes and violence. His whole drama was a psychological one, and he was interested not in capturing attention by dramatic effects but in conveying a sense of fatality, in communicating the feeling of human destiny—through moods and lyrical suggestion.

In 1896 *The Sea Gull* was accepted for production by the Alexandrinsky Theater (not without the help of A. Suvorin, Chekhov's friend and a very influential director of a daily paper and of a private theater, and a very good actress, Levkeyeva, who chose it for her benefit performance). Casting was difficult because the actors found their parts unsuitable and did not like the drama. Savina, the leading lady, did not participate in *The Sea Gull*. When Chekhov came to rehearsals, he saw that the actors were perturbed and could not find the right intonations; morever, they did not know their parts, considered the wording "too common," and were relying on their temperament and last-moment inspiration. The so-called secondary roles—those of Dr. Dorn, of Masha, who is actually his daughter and now suffers from unrequited love for Treplev, of Arkadina, the aging actress, and of other pathetic or comic figures—these were hastily prepared and entrusted to inferior actors. Not even Vera Kommissarzhevskaya, the charming young actress who interpreted Nina, truly understood the character she was to portray. The whole performance was a terrible failure: the actors presented the play in a dull conventional manner, and the public either laughed or yawned. The fiasco was so complete that the humiliated author fled from the theater and left the capital the next morning. As a contemporary put it, *The Sea Gull* fell with a crash, and the common joke was that Chekhov produced a dead duck instead of a sea gull. Now, the unhappy playwright remembered how Lensky, one of the leaders of Alexandrinsky had written to him: "Drop writing for the theater. This is not at all your line." Yet Lensky loved Chekhov and his literary work. Now Chekhov himself wrote to Nemirovich Danchenko: "Never again will I write plays or try to produce them, not if I live to be seven hundred years old." His correspondent, however, had an entirely different opinion. Nemirovich Danchenko admired *The Sea Gull,* and in 1898 when the Moscow Art Theater found itself at a crossroads, he insisted on including the drama in the repertory and on obtaining the author's permission to give it another try. The decision was reached after violent discussions with Stanislavsky, who at first had strong doubts about the merits of the play. It was much later that he recognized its imporance and added that its success was due to the concurrence of several factors: the contribution of Nemirovich Danchenko, who was at the same time a writer, a man of the theater, and a director free from stage conventionalities; also the highly talented designer of settings, the painter Simov.

Nemirovich understood that the weakest point of the new theater was its lack of modern repertory. He was looking for a literary work that would bring out all the new methods they had been experimenting with in historical drama. And with surprising critical intuition, he saw in the play that had been such a miserable failure, a source of new esthetic and psychological revelation.

The Sea Gull, required a tremendous preparatory effort (it had twenty-six rehearsals). At the beginning things went badly, but Nemirovich Danchenko insisted on continuing the search for the right creative line. He believed in his own intuition and tried to instill in the actors his own emotion and faith. According to his theory, the director had to convey to the cast the artistic intention of the author, the inner content of his images, and the subtlest nuances of his thought and feelings. Sometimes he simply explained or interpreted the text of the play which the actors had to memorize with the utmost precision, and at times he showed them how a part could be acted—making ample provisions for what he called "the law of inner justification." During the rehearsals he used precise definitions and discriminated between such different matters as the atmosphere of a scene, the physical characteristics of a part (gay, sad, ill, active, somnolent), the external characteristics of a role (a society woman, an army officer, a landowner), and the style of the entire setting (comic, pathetic, farcical). Later, in Stanislavsky techniques, there was a tendency to divide a scene into smaller units. In training actors

for *The Sea Gull,* the directors emphasized the necessity of subordinating gestures, diction, and make-up to the general mood
and central theme of the play—thus driving at a complete consistency of tone and design. The same idea became basic for the
scenery—in perfect agreement with the ultimate scenic aims.
Chekhov's emphasis on the significant detail found a responsive
echo in a company already trained in naturalistic accuracy. What
was effected during the rehearsals of the play was simply a
shifting of the center of gravity: a detail had to be truthful and
authentic, not in itself as an end, but as a means of communication. Later, when Stanislavsky wanted to get from Chekhov some
light on his interpretation of Trigorin, he heard, not without
amazement: "Yes, magnificent acting, but you need holes in your
shoes and checked trousers." This was the same kind of lesson
Stanislavsky himself, in a more direct way, tried to teach his
actors: an image, a character on the stage had to be so well
thought through that the slightest specifications of costume, make-
up or behavior had to fit into the wholeness of an artistic interpretation.

The first night of *The Sea Gull,* December 29, 1898, found
the whole company in a state of electric tension. They were
perfectly aware of the great risk the Theater was taking by producing a play that had been such a failure two years ago; it had
challenged the public and the critics. Only Vishnevsky was sure
of success. Stanislavsky sat in the orchestra, his back to the public, holding his nervously trembling legs with both hands. Nemirovich Danchenko did not even want to be among the audience
and spent the whole first act in the foyer. The actors took tran-
quilizing pills and made signs of the cross before their entries.
The house was not filled completely, even though quite a few
free tickets had been distributed among Chekhov's friends. It
was not as picturesque and dramatic as the first performance of
Hugo's *Hernani* in 1830 when the romantics were ready to harm
the bourgeois bodily, but under the quiet respectibility of the
Moscow Art Theater there was the same excitement of a great
night.

The main difficulty was in finding new inflections, new diction,
a new rhythm of performance—briefly, a new theatrical language.
But even after the second act, it became evident that the audi-

ence had become completely absorbed, and after the third act the excitement was like an inundation breaking through a dam: a frenzy of applause, of shoutitng, of celebrating. The actors hugged each other; an enthuisastic wire was sent to Chekhov who awaited the outcome in Crimea. And, of course, it was not only the success of *The Sea Gull*: this was truly the second birth of the Moscow Art Theater. By so justly rendering the mood of Chekhov's work, Stanislavsky and Nemirovich Danchenko initiated a new period in the history of Russian repertory and scenic art. They understood it so well that when the Theater later moved into its new building in the Kammerherr Lane, curtain, programs, tickets, and posters bore the sea gull as an emblem. It became the Theater of Chekhov, and it should have borne his name, rather than the name of Gorky, given to it after the 1917 Revolution by an arbitrary act of the Soviet government. What Stanislavsky wrote about these heroic times described the situation in literature as well as in the theater: "There are epochs when no new dramatists or actors appear on the horizon—then suddenly a whole group of playwrights, artists, and directors come to life and create a theatrical miracle. Later arrive the imitators and perpetuators. They take up the tradition and transmit it to the next generation. But tradition is capricious and is often transformed or deformed into trade routine and sheer skill." But at the time of *The Sea Gull* it was still a theatrical miracle: the Moscow Art Theater had found its true style. Chekhov's dramas had a musical quality, and their effects were gained by cumulative impressions, moods, and undercurrents; their elusive and allusive character broke away from narration in scenes or external manifestations of action. Chekhov admired the unity of the Moscow Art Theater production based on teamwork, discipline, and purposeful blending of all the aspects of a performance into one accord. He showed, however, his critical attitude toward naturalistic exaggerations. Of course the audience was thrilled when the swings in a garden creaked, or when one could hear the hoofs on a wooden bridge, but when in the second act of *The Cherry Orchard* the actors started killing mosquitoes in a rather noisy fashion, Chekhov remarked: "In my next play somebody will say, what a marvelous site, there are no mosquitoes." He preferred "minimization" and understatement in props and setting, as well as in acting and intonations. Holding back, reticence, intimation—in a minor key—was what he wanted on all levels of staging, and the Moscow Art Theater finally reached perfection in applying these rules to Chekhov's lyrical drama.

Despite *The Sea Gull*'s success, the Moscow Art Theater ended the season of 1898 with a 45,000-ruble deficit, but immediately found a generous patron in the liberal millionaire Savva Morozov who asked the shareholders to double their investments and offered to put 200,000 rubles into the enterprise. Later, all the actors and some writers (including Chekhov) became shareholders in the Moscow Art Theater Company, and since 1899 its finances have been assured, not only through support of its many wealthy friends, but also from box office receipts. It owned its new building and all the properties and costumes, and it could afford to spend large sums of money for salaries, fees, and production. It did not stage more than three to five news plays a year and largely relied on repeat performances of its well-established repertory. Chekhov's plays occupied a place of honor.

Immediately after *The Sea Gull* there was, however, a moment of confusion when Chekhov offered his *Uncle Vanya* to the Maly Theater. Fortunately, the latter's literary board asked the author to rewrite the third act. Chekhov refused and passed the play to Nemirovich Danchenko. *Uncle Vanya* was produced in October 1899, a year after *The Sea Gull*, and was a clamorous success. It was again a drama of nuance and subdued mood, depicting unhappy men and women, victims of their own illusions and weaknesses. The personal tragedy of Voynitsky, or Uncle Vanya, is caused by his meekness and credulity. He works like a slave on the estate which belongs to his niece Sonia, the daughter of his late sister and Professor Serebriakov, and sends all the income to the latter, because he believes in Serebriakov's genius. Only when Serebriakov and his second wife, the beautiful Yelena, visit the estate does Uncle Vanya understand that his idol is a parasite and a shallow egoist. In a fit of despair and jealousy, he makes a futile attempt to kill the man for whom he had sacrificed all his life—but he fails even there. Serebriakov's daughter Sonia loves the ironical and "superfluous" Doctor Astrov—who, in turn is passionately attracted to Yelena. And Uncle Vanya also adores Yelena. But all these loves and repulsions do not lead anywhere.

Sonia's Voynitski's and Astrov's loves are unrequited, Yelena does not leave her husband even though she knows what kind of man he is, and after Serebriakov's departure, Uncle Vanya and Sonia continue their unrewarding toil in order to make life easy for a despicable ingrate. At the end of the last act both sit in solitude and dejection with no hope other than that expressed by Sonia in her prayerlike monologue: a day will come when all their sufferings and tears will be redeemed and they will see the sky full of flying angels and shining stars.

This final note of dream and resignation fitted perfectly the general mood of *Uncle Vanya*. Futility and fatality, the unromantic fatality of everyday events, the overwhelming weight of boredom and banality are its central themes. What prevented this or any other Chekhovian drama from becoming completely desperate was the feeling of comprehension and warmth with which the author treated his unhappy figures. The autumnal landscape of these melancholic studies in illusion and frustration is always illuminated by the pale rays of compassion and humor. Chekhov never sits in judgment of his ineffectual heroes and luckless heroines, and he sympathizes with their grief or their wingless reveries.

Three Sisters, which followed *Uncle Vanya,* (first performance February 13, 1901), was quite similar in mood, but the play contained some new elements. It was written at a time when Chekhov was fully conscious of his own dramatic style and of innovations used in his plays by the Moscow Art Theater. After the success of *Uncle Vanya* he became strongly attached to the new enterprise. "The Moscow Art Theater," he wrote in a message to the actors, "is the best page of that book which some day will be written about the contemporary Russian stage. This theater is your pride, and it is the only one I love, though I have never been in it." Chekhov was at that moment in the Crimea fighting against tuberculosis. He could not come to Moscow, so the Moscow Art Theater decided to go on tour and bring the entire company, with all their stagehands and technicians, scenery, and costumes to their beloved writer.

Stanislavsky commented that only the wealthy Duke of Meiningen could afford such a costly adventure unprecedented in Russia—and particularly for such a young company; yet the actors and directors had such dash, ardor, and confidence that they surmounted all obstacles. They traveled during Easter vacation, and the spirit of spring and holiday reigned in the company. Chekhov saw *The Sea Gull* and *Uncle Vanya* in Yalta, and admired, among other actors, Olga Knipper, his future wife. Upon her return to Moscow, she interpreted most successfully the part of Masha in *Three Sisters*.

This new play by Chekhov, although not acclaimed as unanimously as *Uncle Vanya* at the time of its production (1901), belonged to the finest realizations of Stanislavsky and Nemirovich Danchenko. Later, it took the second place in the Chekhovian repertory (the first was held by *The Cherry Orchard*) and remained a favorite with the public for more than half a century.

Three Sisters is again a story of unfulfilled aspiration and individual dissatisfaction. Olga, a schoolmistress and a spinster, and her sisters—Masha, married to a trivial and boring man, and Irina, a young girl—stay in their brother's house in a dull provincial town and dream of the glorious past when they lived in Moscow with their late father, a general. They do not accept their present existence and long to return to Moscow—to them a symbol of happiness and beauty. But nothing can change the pattern of their destiny. Masha tries to escape from the tedium of her unhappy marriage into a dream of love for Colonel Vershinin, but the latter is not free and his regiment is about to move away from the town. Irina is ready to marry an officer of the same regiment, Baron Tuzenbakh, but this is a compromise and not a great love. Tuzenbakh, however, is killed in a senseless duel. All the sisters have high hopes for their brother, Andrey, but he marries a stupid little girl and is gradually engulfed in a quagmire of pettiness and laziness.

Most of the protagonists of *Three Sisters* are above their environment. The provincial town where they spend their fruitless lives is a somnolent, backward hole, and simply does not offer them any opportunity for cultural or human satisfaction. The three sisters, Vershinin, Tuzenbakh, and even old doctor Chebutykhin, a lost man and a drunkard, feel sharply the contrast between their needs and dreams and the low-grade Russian reality. They also wish to have some useful occupation, and their constant talk about work is not a self-recrimination of superfluous people but a sincere search for some significant activity, for a "cause" and for a faith. The three sisters dream of Moscow in the same way as the whole of Russian intelligentsia aspired to a radical change of their surroundings at the beginning of the century, and when Vershinin speaks of how beautiful life will be in two hundred years, his famous monologue is interpreted by the listeners not as mere resignation but as a sign of a profound dissatisfaction with the present conditions. Although this theme is not the leitmotiv of the play, it emerges more strongly in *Three Sisters* than in *Uncle Vanya*.

In *The Cherry Orchard* the expectation of a better future is embodied in the figures of the dreamer and "eternal" student, Trofimov, and Ania, whom he loves and whom he persuades to leave home to go with him to Moscow. Of course, both are secondary characters in a comedy that is mainly concerned with the decline of the "gentlefolks' nests" and with the fate of their superfluous inhabitants. Ania's mother, Madame Ranevskaya, owner of an estate adorned with a magnificent cherry orchard, has squandered all her money on lovers and now is forced to sell her property to Lopakhin, a representative of the materialistic, down-to-earth bourgeoisie. The procession of superfluous men is led by Gaev, the owner's brother, and the whole story revolves around the vain attempts of all these comic and pathetic characters to avoid the inevitable and forget about reality. The cherry orchard, of course, symbolizes the beauty and refinement of an antiquated, and therefore condemned, way of life; and the utilitarian Lopakhin, who wants to cut down the cherry trees in order to build apartment houses on the site, can hardly sense the lyrical, melancholic mood of those who have to pay for their former faults and surrender the estate to the newcomers. The last scene of the play, showing the empty house with its only occupant, the old servant Firs, whom the owners forget in their precipitated departure, had a double effect: it combined the feeling that "cherry orchards" were doomed with a compassion for those who had to fall under the ax.

Produced by the Moscow Art Theater in 1904 (January 30), with such actors as Kachalov (Gaev), Leonidov (Lopakhin), Moskvin (Epikhodov), Artem (Firs), and Knipper (Ranevskaya), *The Cherry Orchard* immediately became the most popu-

lar of all Chekhovian plays. More than any other of his lyrical
dramas it reflected the times of expectation and stir on the eve
of the 1905 Revolution. But, of course, its lasting success in
Russia, and later abroad, is not due to the description of a social
environment. Soviet critics of the forties and fifties tried to interpret Chekhov as a chronicler of his era and a critic of tsarist
Russia. They always looked for political allusions and symbolic
hints in the speeches of his characters, and forced the Moscow
Art Theater to present *Uncle Vanya, Three Sisters,* and *The
Cherry Orchard* as historical documents or socio-political illustrations for the study of a sunken world. It is significant that
after the 1917 Revolution such an intelligent and brilliant historian of literature as D. Sviatopolk-Mirsky predicted the disappearance of Chekhov's plays from Soviet repertory because of
their limited value as reflections of a given Russian environment.
This prediction, shared by many other less distinguished critics,
proved to be completely wrong. In the thirties, Chekhov was
resumed on the Soviet stage not only by the Moscow Art Theater
but by a number of other houses in Moscow and the provinces—
and since then he has never disappeared from the billboards all
over Russia. Millions of Russians cry and laugh at the sufferings
and antics of Chekhovian protagonists in *Ivanov, Uncle Vanya,
Three Sisters, The Sea Gull* and *The Cherry Orchard,* these
classics of the national stage. And these plays continue to attract
actors, directors, and spectators in Europe and America. Chekhov
represents new dramatic form, a special version of the psychological drama which supplanted the performance of external action in the Western world of the twentieth century. The themes
of his plays also have proved very modern: the defeat through
pettiness and trivial occurrences, the melancholia of broken fortunes, the impossibility of true communication between human
beings, the intricate web of love, aversion, boredom, and dreams
that entangles the lives of ordinary people—all these themes
proved to be universal and particularly appropriate to our era.
Painter of the intelligentsia, Chekhov spoke of those who do not
succeed in the battle for survival and do not belong to the
minority of victors and conquerors—and he knew how to make
the hearts of his audience vibrate with the pain of self-identification and the comfort of kindliness and pity. The great merit of

the Moscow Art Theater lay in bringing out not only the despondency but also the mercy and compassion of Chekhov's works. It also succeeded in giving them a marvelous scenic appearance and in creating a series of memorable characterizations —not only of the main protagonists but also of those secondary figures in whom the Chekhovian subtle genius of the light touch and of comic or pathetic detail reached its best expression. Chekhov's plays had a tremendous impact on the Russian stage and originated a whole school of staging and acting. Each performance of Chekhov in Moscow between 1898 and 1917 was an event and a lesson for provincial actors and directors. Later, foreign directors and critics flowed to Kammerherr Lane to learn the "Moscow Art Theater manner." The way *Three Sisters* or *The Cherry Orchard* were produced became a tradition and a symbol of a very definite artistic form. Even the works of minor dramatists who imitated Chekhov, such as Ilya Surguchev's *The Violins of Autumn* (1914), were transformed into spectacular successes—and the Moscow Art Theater remained unequaled for decades as the house of the psychological drama conceived and executed as a musical unit, within the framework of realistic scenery.

These accomplishments did not stop, however, the further search for new roads. Even though the Theater did find its most genuine self-expression and greatest artistic satisfaction in the production of Chekhov's works, the latter represented but one phase in its evolution. At the beginning of the century, Stanislavsky and Nemirovich Dancheko were in the full maturity of their craft and were eager to make experiments beyond those they had made in archaeological naturalism and psychological impressionism. With their usual dynamism and earnestness, they moved into a variety of ventures—covering the long road from the drama of social significance to the symbolist play of fantasy and intellectual speculation.

5

The evolution of the moscow art theater

THE MOSCOW ART THEATER was started in 1898 with a company of thirty-nine, limited financial resources, and hardly any technical equipment. At the beginning of the twentieth century it grew into a large, flourishing, well-organized, and perfectly directed institution with a company of one hundred and a large staff. Strict discipline imposed upon everybody from top to bottom, from directors to stagehands, maintained a rigorous order within the theater. It was also the most technically advanced Russian theater of the period: it possessed a vast turning stage, modern machines and electrical appliances, and its own workshops for scenery and costumes directed by trained professionals. Instead of bureaucratic red tape and a formal hierarchy, which undermined the Imperial Theaters, it was ruled by a community spirit and comradeship based on a unity of vision and a sense of responsibility freely accepted by all as participants in the "common cause." The enemies of the Moscow Art Theater often reproached its directors for an excess of planning and rationalization. They found it contrary to the militant, agressive beginnings of an enterprise bent on the renovation of the Russian stage. Yet the marvelous co-ordination that Stanislavsky and Nemirovich achieved in their joint venture would have been impossible without blue prints, a well oiled mechanism, and a great deal of attention paid to all concrete details. Many Russian and foreign spectators and writers referred to the "theatrical miracle" per-

formed by Stanislavsky. Of course, methods and principles were
essential in a great institution which had a distinct ideological
and artistic purpose. But above all, there was the vision of harmony as the guiding spirit of the whole company. The teamwork,
the careful planning, the unfolding of each performance with
clocklike precision, the suppression of any chance occurrences or
accidents did not stem from "the limitation of the actor's creative
imagination," as opponents of Stanislavsky used to claim, but
from the desire "to do things well" without relying on strokes
of genius. To some of the rebels, such as the actor Mgebrov, the
very polish of these performances—the fruit of dozens of rehearsals
—the uniform perfection, the invisibility of effort, the smoothness
and ease of each presentation, became a source of irritation. "It
was too cozy, too handsome, too holiday-like," wrote Mgebrov in
his highly temperamental memoirs. He forgot to add, however,
that this excellence which delighted the audiences and puzzled or
startled the critics was achieved at the cost of long, patient work,
by a series of trial and error, through painful concentration of
will and attention. As in all true masterpieces, the spectator was
not aware of how the smoothness was reached, and he did not
need to know what technical devices were invented to give him
a total vision of unity. In Andreyev's *Life of Man,* for instance,
the drapes on the stage were of black velvet, and stagehands wore
black velvet overalls (all stagehands always wore black velvet
slippers and gloves so that they merged with the stage).
In *Wit Works Woe,* in order to make the scene of the ball
in a Moscow mansion of 1820 look real and set the mood of
gaiety, special rooms were arranged behind the wings where the
actors impersonating the guests were met by bowing servants and
conversed before coming on stage—all this, of course, invisible
to the audience. All the supers acting as guests were perfumed,
wore excellent authentic dress, and talked French. One of them
relates that he had really had a good time: for him it was a true
ball, and a most enjoyable one. More important: these were not
tricks but means toward a convincing artistic accomplishment.

No wonder that from its very beginning the Moscow Art
Theater greatly revolutionized the Russian stage—and this before
its fame reached Europe and America.

The flowering of the Moscow Art Theater coïncided with an
exciting period in Russian history. The first years of the new

century were marked not only by tempestuous economic development but also by an awakening political conscience and by the intensification of liberal and socialist movements. In all classes of society there was a stir, a yearning for reform and self-fulfillment, an expansion of energy, a hope for a better life, which impregnated the air with suspense and a springlike spirit. The era of preparation between 1900 and 1904 culminated in the 1905 revolutionary explosion; and in 1906-1908, despite the governmental reaction and the alternation of concession and repression, Russia went through momentous conflicts of classes, interests, and ideologies, resulting in great social and political change. In these times of tension, unrest, and general activity, cultural life was also injected with a new animation, and daring literary and artistic movements spread all over the country. The Moscow Art Theater became both the center of new esthetic experiments and the symbol of liberal tendencies. In this twofold aspect, it faithfully expressed the yearnings of the progressive intelligentsia with which it was justly identified. At the same time, it assumed the artistic leadership that the Imperial Theaters were losing, and served as an example and an inspiration to numerous enterprises which marked the theatrical expansion in Russia at the beginning of the twentieth century. Its influence was felt not only in such well-established theaters as the Korsh in Moscow and the Suvorin in St. Petersburg, but also in the provinces where the number of good companies was growing steadily. This growth reflected, among other things, the process of class differentiation in Russian society and the emergence of new audiences issuing from the lower bourgeoisie and even the popular masses.

The influence of the Moscow Theater abroad was also augmenting: the proof of this came during its 1906 tour of Central Europe. The company went first to Berlin with five plays: *Tsar Fydor Ivanovich, Uncle Vanya, Three Sisters, The Lower Depths,* and *An Enemy of the People.* The German press received the Russians with hostility or indifference but their performances soon became a triumph—and not only in the German capital, but also in Dresden, Prague, Vienna, etc. At first, Nemirovich Danchenko wondered whether he should take the costly risk of a tour to other cities: the company had eighty-seven members, and needed seven railroad freight cars for settings and properties. At this critical moment, an unknown young man offered him a loan of 30,000 rubles: it was Nikita Baliev, the future director of "The Bat," a theatrical company of international fame.

Summoned by Lugné Poe, Nemirovich Danchenko went to Paris to study a tour of France but renounced it after having discovered that he would have to spend 25,000 francs on advertisements alone and that even the smallest notice in Parisian dailies had to be paid for.

II

After the affirmation of Chekhov's psychological drama with its subtle nuances and undercurrents expressed through realistic details, the same method was successfully applied to plays by Ibsen and Hauptmann—the two favorite dramatists of the Theater in the first years of its existence. Even though Ibsen had been previously introduced to Russia on other stages, including the Stanislavsky's Hunters' Club, it was Nemirovich Danchenko who was most efficacious in promoting the great Norwegian. Between 1898 and 1902, he produced five dramas by Ibsen and three by Hauptmann, and this out of a total of twenty plays. Ibsen's *Hedda Gabler, When We Dead Awaken,* and *The Wild Duck* were interpreted as psychological dramas of ideas and moral problems. But in *An Enemy of the People* (Doctor Stockman) and *The Pillars of Society* the elements of social criticism were emphasized. In those two works the Moscow Art Theater paid tribute to the political excitement of the period, thus becoming the mouthpiece of its own audience—the intelligentsia. The same tendency was patent in productions of Hauptmann: while his *Lonely Lives* was presented in subdued Chekhovian colors, the realistic treatment of *Drayman Henschel* and *Michael Kramer* contained strong social and political intimations. In any case, this was the way the spectators reacted to certain plays by foreign authors in which they detected situations seemingly relevant to Russian political conditions. Of course, allusions and intimations also could be found in Chekhov's *Uncle Vanya* and *Three Sisters,* but by no means could they be classified as social dramas. The latter were brought to the Moscow Art Theater by Gorky—and in the last forty years Soviet historians have tried their best to prove that this was an event of first magnitude, that Gorky's influence almost changed the whole direction of the Theater, and in any case was very profound and significant. Thus a myth has been created, and while it is imposed upon readers and critics in Russia, it is also often accepted in Europe and America. The facts, however, are more complex and quite different from "corrections of history" practiced by many Communist interpreters.

There is no doubt that the directors of the Moscow Art Theater were deliberately looking for social dramas, that they, particularly Nemirovich Danchenko, believed in the close link between the stage and contemporary life, and that they were sharing the progressive, liberal, or even socialist leanings of those throbbing years which preceded the 1905 revolution. Yet, a simple glance at the Theater's repertory between 1900 and 1917 shows most clearly that social drama was allotted an extremely limited place. In fact, it occupied the last place—in terms of quantity and quality. And there was only one year when the new productions of the Theater happened to be in this category: it was the 1902-1903 season with *Smug Citizens* and *The Lower Depths* by Gorky, and *The Power of Darkness* by Leo Tolstoy (if not a social drama, strictly speaking, it was a picture of Russian peasantry whose moral problem could be linked with that of Russia's backwardness). In 1901-1902, *The Wild Duck* and *Lonely Lives* were shown, and in 1903-1904, *Julius Caesar* and *The Cherry Orchard*. In the two seasons during which the whole country was ablaze with rebellion, the Moscow Art Theater offered to the public *Ghosts* by Ibsen, *Ivanov* by Chekhov, short symbolic plays by Maeterlinck, *Brand* by Ibsen, *Drama of Life* by Knud Hamsun and *Wit Works Woe* by Griboyedov; the only Russian contemporary play was Gorky's *Children of the Sun,* which was far from being a success. The truth is that only three of Gorky's plays were produced by the Theater in first twenty years of its activity, and only one of them, *The Lower Depths,* was acclaimed by the public and remained an organic part of the repertory. The two others (*Children of the Sun* and *Smug Citizens*) were hardly ever repeated. This does not imply that Gorky's plays were not produced elsewhere, and they certainly represented the school of the socio-political, topical drama on the Russian stage, but whatever influence he had was not channeled through the Moscow Art

Theater. Things changed after the 1917 Revolution, but this coincided with other radical changes in the conditions of theatrical
life in Russia. To contend, however, that Gorky exerted an influence on the Moscow Art Theater before 1917, and that the
impact of his plays was great in the life and formation of that
institution, is simply a distortion of truth and of history. Not only
were Chekhov and even Andreyev more significant than Gorky
in the evolution of the Moscow Art Theater, but productions
of Ibsen, Maeterlinck, or Hamsun represented much more important milestones in its development. This statement as well as
the subsequent criticism of Gorky as a dramatist is not intended,
by any means, to minimize either the literary merit or the enormous importance of his work in Russian literature and culture.

At the turn of the century, Gorky's stories of rebellious tramps
and romantic hoboes made him famous overnight. The very
material of his tales was new and refreshing: he was depicting a
peculiar world of the lumpen proletariat, of the "fourth estate"—
all those seasonal workers, Volga dockmen, bargemen, fisherwo-
men, and, in general, the "damned of the earth"—and he did it
not only in colorful strokes of a rather crude realism, but also
with strong romantic overtones, with a zest for life, and a sense
of protest which sounded like a trumpet after the tearful com-
plaints of the Chekhovian melancholy intellectuals. With Gorky
a new social class entered Russian literature, together with a bold
spirit of virile struggle and of down-to-earth criticism of existing
social conditions. Gorky became the embodiment of the imminent revolutionary tempest, and his poems in prose, such as the
Song of the Stormy Petrel, or the ballad of the fearless falcon
and the crawling water snake were, despite their dubious literary
qualities, known all over Russia as poetic images and symbols of
the insurgent wave. A man issued from the people, a self-made
writer who passed through all the ordeals of poverty and manual
labor in his childhood and youth, Gorky was considered the
mouthpiece of the rising proletariat, the representative of the
working classes, and he soon became the idol of the radical intelligentsia. His popularity was truly fantastic, and police persecutions only increased his fame.

Gorky was in the Crimea fighting his tuberculosis when the
Moscow Art Theater gave its guest performances in Yalta, and

Chekhov introduced him to Stanislavsky and Nemirovich Danchenko. The next winter the authorities let Gorky come to Moscow, and he visited the Moscow Art Theater during the performance of a Chekhov play. The public learned of his presence and jammed the foyer and the corridors, urging Gorky to appear on the stage. This insistence irritated the thirty-three-year-old writer. He came before the footlights and snapped at the audience: "Why do you want to see me? I am not the corpse of a drowned man or a ballet dancer, and your idle curiosity is simply disgusting if one thinks what a remarkable play is being offered to you." Friend and admirer of Chekhov, he fell under the strong influence of this writer's dramatic technique and showed it in his first play, *Smug Citizens,* produced by the Moscow Art Theater in 1902. Attracted by the theater since his youth, Gorky tried to organize a company in a small town in the Ukraine in 1897 but did not write a play until 1901. *Scenes in the House of Bessemenov,* later called *Smug Citizens* (the English title is not exact, the title in Russian means "The Philistines," or "The Small Bourgeoisie") had hardly any plot. The play presented in fragmentary fashion the conflict within the family of Vassily Bessemenov, a lower-middle-class man living in the "shadow of capitalism" and clinging to his money and social position. He defends his little world of property owners and law abiding citizens, and tries to assert his paternal authority over his wife and his children, Pyotr and Tatiana. The latter loves Nil, who has been raised in the family but now revolts against his surroundings. Nil belongs to the revolutionary proletariat, and the conflict between the young people and Bessemenov and his clique has a double meaning—that of the eternal clash between generations, and that of two opposing social forces. Personal relationships between the main protagonists emphasize the basic collision of customs and ideologies. Pyotr, attracted by the young widow Yelena, and Tatiana whom Nil cannot love, stand in the middle of the road while Nil and Polia, the girl he chooses as his companion, announce a new type of resolute fighter. The oppressive atmosphere of the Bessemenov house was depicted by Gorky in the traditional colors of critical realism, but the strong characters of Nil, Polia, and, in part, of Yelena were breaking away from the usual Russian passive types.

The production of the play was not an easy thing. The censors cut the dialogues and thus watered down their spirit of protest. But even this was not enough to secure an authorization for the production of the play: Gorky was considered by the police a "dangerous subversive." Nemirovich Danchenko had to set into motion all his connections, and finally, after having alerted some high-placed ladies and a few moderate dignitaries, he succeeded in getting the green light: *Smug Citizens* was allowed to be presented in Moscow on March 26, 1902. The authorities feared demonstrations and so replaced ushers with police agents, who looked ridiculous in tails and white ties—the regular Moscow Art Theater staff uniform.

All these extraordinary measures proved to be unnecessary; the public remained cold. As Stanislavsky later stated in his memoirs, the performance did not have a big success, and despite all the efforts of the actors, the audience failed to catch the social and political message of the drama. The same thing happened in St. Petersburg. Was it due to the cuts made by the censors? Apparently this was not the reason because *Smug Citizens* had great popularity in the provinces, and was acclaimed by the public in various cities, particularly in Odessa (with Nevolin applauded in Nil's part), Kiev, Kharkov, Orel, etc. Were the audiences of Moscow and St. Petersburg more sophisticated? This seems to be the case, for *Smug Citizens* lacked any striking qualities as a theatrical work. It read well when published in a literary almanac, but the stage revealed all its defects: it was a mediocre play, it followed Chekhov in its plotless structure and its absence of a central protagonist, and it lacked inner dynamics—despite excellent and, at times, strong character portrayal. Moreover, its sociopolitical tendency was not organic, i.e., ideas were not incorporated into the destinies of the protagonists. To speak about the production of *Smug Citizens* as a milestone in the history of the Russian stage, as an event of first magnitude, and as a turning point in the evolution of the Moscow Art Theater, as is now the custom in Soviet publications, is simply a falsification or a mythomaniac fantasy. The only good thing one can say about *Smug Citizens* is that it was a topical play, that it suited a certain mood of socio-political sensitivity, and that it had freshness because of the environment it depicted. Most Russian plays dealt with intellectuals, landowners, and impoverished noblemen (like Chekhov) or with government officials or other representatives of educated society. Ostrovsky brought in old-fashioned merchants. Gorky chose his heroes from the less well known lower middle class and from the fringe of the industrial proletariat. Yet the Moscow Art Theater dropped *Smug Citizens* when it became overshadowed by *The Lower Depths,* Gorky's second play and his sole and true theatrical triumph. It could be said that in the history of the Russian theater Gorky entered and remained as the author of that striking picture of the "scum of the earth," and that none of his subsequent theatrical attempts has ever reached the popularity and provoked the response equal to that attained by *The Lower Depths.*

This play was, in a way, a dramatization of Gorky's previous stories, and particularly reminiscent of the tale *Ex-Men* or *Creatures That Once Were Men.* The action took place in a flophouse inhabited by various human wrecks. The plot revolved around the love affair between Pepel, a thief, and Vasilisa, the wife of Kostylev, a pawnbroker and the owner of the flophouse, a brutal and disgusting individual. Vasilisa pressures Pepel to kill her husband, and he finally commits the murder, but the real motive for his action is not the attachment to his mistress but his deep love for Natasha, her sister, whom he hopes to liberate from the tyranny of Kostylev and the indignity of her environment. Although these motives of passion, love, and revenge do form the backbone of the play, the center of gravity of *The Lower Depths* lies in character and environment portrayal. All the inmates of this Russian Bowery are victims of social conditions and their individual failure to cope with life. Yet all of them dream of freedom and regeneration, and when Luka, a peasant pilgrim, comes to the grim dormitory and speaks to them of hope and future, they all have, at least for a moment, new illusions and new expectations. They all cling to Luka: Anna, the dying wife of a miserable locksmith, the alcoholic actor, the prostitute Nastia, the illiterate Tartar, and the baron, whom women and gambling have ruined beyond any remedy. What Luka is offering to all these unhappy creatures is a "saintly lie." He uses illusions and words as a physician uses drugs to relieve the pain of an incurable disease. When asked about the existence of God, Luka exist: if you do not believe in Him, He does not exist." In fact, Luka does not really help anybody, and after his disappearance, nothing has changed in the dark flophouse or in the existence of its inmates, and this arouses the anger of Satin, the only character in the play who rejects lies and preaches courage, truth, and strength. He wants to face life, to meet his misfortune head-on, and he detests the lulling illusions of the weak, the false and corrupting consolation dispensed by priests and masters in order to keep the masses in ignorance and submission. Although he himself has reached the lower depths of dejection and defeat, he refuses to surrender; and in a speech which became famous all over Russia and was sounded as an appeal to rebellion, he declared "'man'—it sounds grand" and glorified the struggle for human dignity. There is no doubt that Luka and Satin are two expressions of opposite philosophies, but it is also quite clear that the play itself leaves a wide possibility for the interpretation of each of these characters.

Stanislavsky avoided showing the bums of Kostylev's asylum as Nietzschean supermen. To him the main idea of the drama was that men who fall down and disintegrate, hoping to get some freedom at the bottom of the social ladder, actually become slaves of their misery and of their new environment. He therefore did not accentuate romantic traits in his impersonation of Satin—although certain passages of Satin's rebellious speeches did stir his audiences who saw in them direct allusions to the contemporary scene. On the other hand, Moskvin represented Luka as a sly and almost ambiguous peasant, devoid of Christian virtues which other actors saw in the Gorkian pilgrim. Davydov of the Alexandrinsky later gave an image of Luka as a kind and luminous Russian philosopher, but many artists in Russia and abroad identified him with supreme compassion and kindliness. Gorky himself went through a real change of heart about his own hero, and after the 1917 Revolution, tried to affirm that the character of the pilgrim was completely negative. In an article (1933) entitled "On Plays," Gorky said that he had written "some definitely bad plays" and sharply criticized Luka's philosophy of compassion, denouncing him as a dangerous and obnoxious individual. Some Soviet directors were so impressed by

Gorky's self-criticism that they began interpreting the pilgrim as an astute charlatan or a rascal. In 1939, Fyodor Kaverin made Luka a ridiculous and cunning old man, whose appearance on stage provoked laughter in the audience. Nothing in the text warrants such an interpretation. It is obvious, however, that Gorky, a convinced partisan of struggle and bitter truth, could not accept the attitude of "salvation through illusion" personified by Luka.

It is questionable whether Gorky was completely satisfied with the staging of his work by the Moscow Art Theater. The new element in the performance was the merging of grim naturalistic details with a certain romantic halo. Stanislavsky took his company to various dives and flophouses in the popular districts of Moscow, and the actors and stage designers followed life models faithfully. The settings of Kostylev's institution as well as the rags of the actors, were so suggestive that some spectators in the first rows were afraid of catching lice. The authenticity of the naturalistic detail was, however, counterbalanced by a non-Chekhovian manner of acting. This was in accordance with the main principles of the Theater: Stanislavsky and Nemirovich understood immediately that Gorky, despite his early apprenticeship in Chekhov's school, had written a drama which resembled Chekhov only in its lack of a consistent plot and in some impressionistic touches. Contrary to the shadowy quality of Chekhov's protagonists, drawn in delicate lines and water colors, Gorky's characters were sharp and full-blooded, and instead of being understated, they were treated in a romantically exaggerated way. There was a certain brutality and roughness in Gorky as a writer and as a dramatist, and his robustness, rhetoric, and social passion were alien to Chekhov's subtle objectivity and perfectly controlled restraint. In all his subsequent plays Gorky showed the same qualities and defects. He wrote some fifteen plays but he never produced anything equaling *The Lower Depths,* although one of his last plays—*Yegor Bulychev and the Others* is very interesting.

It is undeniable that all his work as a playwright made Gorky a most genuine representative of the socio-political drama. He provided Russian repertory with quite a few specimens of this genre yet, by a certain irony of destiny, they became available to large audiences only after the 1917 Revolution when their topical interest was gone and they could be interpreted only as historical documents, in a retrospective fashion. We will see later what their impact was on the Soviet theater. But as far as the Moscow Art Theater is concerned, his role was limited and came to an end soon after the success of *The Lower Depths* in 1902. In fact, two years later, the Moscow Art Theater rejected Gorky's next play *The Vacationists*. These scenes depicted Russian intellectuals by means of a rather complex love relationship: Varvara, disillusioned in her husband, abandons him for the writer Shalimov who is no better because he has renounced the ideals of his youth. At the same time, Varvara can not respond to the love of Rumin, a weak man who commits suicide. Her brother falls in love with Maria Lvovna, a doctor who, in turn, suppresses her own feelings because of her sense of duty and honesty. She is the only character in the play who understands the gap between all these members of the intelligentsia and the people. She makes long speeches on this issue, and the unfavorable light in which Gorky has depicted all his protagonists serves as an illustration of the thesis. *The Vacationists* opened a series of Gorky's attacks upon the intellectuals whom he accused of indecision, lack of courage, and alienation from the masses. It is curious that the drama made a point of the moral obligation of the writer who should use his art as a weapon and join the struggle for the "common cause." It is quite possible that, among other reasons for the rejection of the play, the Moscow Art Theater did not share the author's opinions on artists' social functions. *The Vacationists* provoked many discussions when staged by the Kommissarzhevskaya Theater in St. Petersburg (November 1904). Later, during the storm and stress of 1905, its performances in the provinces stirred up demonstrations by excited audiences who welcomed the play as a response to the problems of the day. While *The Vacationists* was being acclaimed in provincial theaters, and *The Lower Depths,* staged by Max Reinhardt, was approaching its three hundredth performance in Berlin, Gorky, sentenced to solitary confinement, was writing a new play in his prison cell. Finished in the spring of 1905, *The Children of the Sun* was produced on October 25, 1905, in the new Kommissarzhevskaya Theater where the director Arbatov gave it a strong symbolist flavor, and twelve days later by the Moscow Art Theater which interpreted it in a realistic vein but too much as a family drama. In the title of the play, Gorky refers to the intellectuals, such as the main protagonist, Protasov, a scholar who leads an artificial life behind the wall of abstraction. All the characters of the drama are unable to cope with their personal affairs: Protasov's wife is in love with another man, and his sister Liza goes mad after her lover commits suicide. In the last act, superstitious and ignorant peasants attack the villa of the "children of the sun," whom they accuse of spreading an epidemic in the region, and this senseless rebellion is as futile as the sterility of the isolated and impractical intellectuals. The message of the drama was not as obvious as that of *The Vacationists,* and *The Children of the Sun* never attained any success. No other theater, except the two mentioned above, ever attempted to produce it. Gorky, however, continued to write one play after another.

In 1906 Gorky published *The Barbarians,* another drama about the intellectuals with a rather confused plot. One could not understand whether the title meant that the protagonists were Barbarians or that new Barbarians would come and destroy the world of futility and distorted feelings depicted in the play. More psychological, it lacked the strength of other Gorkian dramatic experiments and was even poor in character portrayal except for Monakhova, the main heroine who commits suicide. *The Barbarians* was produced in Germany earlier than in Russia where it did not go on the boards until 1907 in St. Petersburg, with no success.

A worse fate befell *The Enemies,* a drama written the same year and banned by the censors because it represented the clash between the administration and the workmen of a textile factory. This was an eminently political piece with a frank emphasis on the socialist leanings of the Russian workers and on the divergence of opinions among the owners. While the Germans could see it in Berlin (staged in 1921-22 by Erwin Piscator), Russians were only allowed to read it in the literary almanac *Knowledge* published by Gorky and his friends. It did not arrive on the boards of the Academic Dramatic Theater (formerly Alexandrinsky) until 1933, and those of the Moscow Art Theater two years later (1935).

The Last Ones, initially entitled *The Father*—also banished from the stage and published in *Knowledge* was of more interest to the critics than to theater directors (produced in 1917-18, and revived in 1936), and it never attained success with the public. This blunt and often shocking portrayal of Ivan Kolomiytsev, a policeman, a cruel and corrupt man belonging to a family of decadent nobles, moving in a circle of lustful and greedy relatives, is drawn against a background which contained some of the themes and types used by Gorky in his novel *The Artamonov Business* (1925). It was meant to offer the picture of those who were attached to a condemned and dying old order. Much later, in the thirties, Gorky returned to this theme in his last plays in a more satisfactory manner. Of the two 1910 plays, *The Eccentrics* and *Vassa Zheleznova* (completely revised twenty years later), the former was a weak psychological drama of the intellectuals, with some good secondary character portrayals, while the latter depicted a monstrous woman ready to commit a crime in order to secure money for her children. *Vassa Zheleznova* deals with the passion for property and the lust for acquisition which overshadows all human feelings of the heroine. She moves amongst intrigues, plots, and amorous complications in a ruthless, abhorrent way, but Gorky fails to give her the vigor of a tragic figure. While some critics evoke Saltykov's novel *The Golovlyov's Family* in connection with *Vassa Zheleznova,* this writer wonders whether Gorky was not influenced by Saltykov's *Death of Pazukhin.*

Vassa Zheleznova marked Gorky's passage from the attacks against the intellectuals to the exposé of the lower middle class, of provincial tradesmen whom he knew so well. His next plays, *The Zhukovs* (1913) and *The False Money* (1915), with scenes from the lives of merchants, failed to attract the public and were hardly ever produced. *The Old Man* (1915), almost a melodrama, depicts a former convict who has fled from prison and remade his life under an assumed name and then commits suicide when threatened by his former prison mate. It was staged by Tairov in the forties with Gaideburov in the part of Mastakov, the runaway, but never became a part of Russian repertory and remained a forgotten work. After the 1917 Revolution, Gorky abandoned his activity as a dramatist and did not resume it until the thirties when he planned a tetralogy devoted to the fall of the tsarist regime. He finished two dramas, *Yegor Bulychev and the Others* in 1932 and *Dostigayev and the Others,* the sequel to the first, the next year; they both belong to the history of the Soviet theater, and we will talk of them in connection with their excellent production by Vakhtangov Theater in 1932.

As a representative of the socio-political and topical drama, Gorky undoubtedly made an important contribution to Russian repertory. Its influence, however, was felt much more after the 1917 Revolution than in the years when the Moscow Art Theater assumed the leading role in tsarist Russia. From a literary standpoint, Gorky's dramas belong to critical realism, and they reveal a curious combination of heterogenous elements: descriptive qualities of an Ostrovsky, some attempts at imitating Chekhov's psychological innovations, and Gorky's own sharp and, at times, thick and brutal character portrayal, enhanced by passionate hate and vigorous faith. Despite some merits, they all had two essential defects, except, perhaps, *The Lower Depths, Yegor Bulychev,* and, in part, *Vassa Zheleznova*: they lacked fundamental human conflicts presented in convincing dramatic form, and they were either rhetorical and bookish, or grossly exaggerated and somewhat primitive. It is interesting to compare them to Ostrovsky's comedies: while the latter are still alive, Gorky's plays appear dated and require a tremendous effort of staging and acting for their revival. Today, Gorky is acclaimed as the father of socialist realism and his plays, *post hoc,* are hailed as examples to be followed by Soviet dramatists. Unfortunately, the latter did try to imitate Gorky with definitely negative results. None of the plays conceived and executed in Gorky's tradition remained for more than a very few years in the Soviet dramatic repertory.

III

The appearance of Gorky's plays in 1902-1903 on the boards of the Moscow Art Theater represented the highest point in its preoccupation with the socio-political drama, and although in the momentous years of 1905-1906 Nemirovich Danchenko and Stanislavsky, as well as their whole company, felt strongly the impact of the liberal and revolutionary movement, they staged but one play with political overtones—*The Children of the Sun.*

Other plays by contemporary authors of the same period return either to Ostrovskian realism (*Vaniushin's Children* by Serghei Naidenov) or to imitation of Chekhov (*Ivan Mironych* by Evgeny Chirikov). Both plays were staged during the 1904-1905 season. One can see quite easily that the leaders of the theater were wavering at that moment between various literary and artistic trends. Stanislavsky and his friends understood very well that they had achieved great success in several directions: the initial historical drama of scrupulous realism, the Chekhovian psychological and impressionistic play in which realism found its own medium of understatement, and the production of character plays in a realistically expressive fashion (Gorky). But while those attainments were obvious and all pointed to the various interpretations of "truth on stage" or application of realistic principles to staging and acting, some of Stanislavsky's productions reflected his search in a different area. He himself defined it as the "line of fantasy and symbolism." There was a concurrence of circumstances which led to the development of this line: the emergence of symbolism as one of the leading literary and artistic movements not only in Western Europe but also in Russia; Stanislavsky's personal dissatisfaction with certain exaggerations of the realistic method; the spirit of search and experiment which animated the whole group of young men and women in and around the Moscow Art Theater; and the pressure of the public which always expected something new from its beloved center of artistic enjoyment. Thus general conditions and personal yearnings merged and led to an important phase in the development of the Moscow Art Theater.

Western symbolism was a reaction against realism in art, against the predominance of common sense and of positivism. The influence of Baudelaire and Verlaine, of Ibsen and Maeterlinck, of Oscar Wilde and later Verhaeren, was felt by a whole generation of Russians; it excited the young and provoked in them a renewed interest in spiritual and emotional life, in vague aspirations, and in universal problems. In 1900-1901, the production of Ibsen's work by Nemirovich Danchenko incorporated various elements of symbolist staging. The new tendency was even more visible in Stanislavsky's production of *Snegurochka* (*The Snow Maiden*) by Ostrovsky, a kind of national fairy tale (the opera based on this play, by Rimsky-Korsakov, was produced by the Mamontov enterprise). Formerly Stanislavsky used numerous symbolist settings and dramatic effects in dramas at the Hunters' Club. Now he emphasized them, interpreting *The Snow Maiden* as a poetic dream. The scenes representing winter and the farewell to the carnival with the burning of a straw idol and choirs and dances of peasant girls were conceived in the spirit of folklore realism and had an ethnographic flavor. But when all the rites were performed and all the artists were gone, in the sudden silence there was on stage the spectacle of a forest come alive as by magic. All the bushes in the foreground began to move, hands protruded from immobile trees, and everything assumed human form; the whole forest, actually made up of motionless supers, became filled with wood spirits, spooks, witches, vixen, goblins, pixies, elfins, and above all of them reigned a gigantic Father Frost followed by his playful daughter. For the sound effects of the live forest, seventy people made use of some two hundred special instruments behind the wings. Not less fantastic were the scenes in the palace of Tsar Berendey, with two painters working on its high ceilings, and a crowd of singers, fife and zither players, and reciters, for whom special music had been written by Grechaninov. The whole thing certainly transcended the limits of a national legend.

What annoyed Stanislavsky with this, as well as other performances, was the weight of the three-dimensional reality (including that of the actor), and the dominance of material details. All the tricks that thrilled the spectators, such as the snow avalanche in Ibsen's *Brand,* or the period furniture in Chekhov's comedies, or all the ethnographic paraphernalia in Tolstoy's *Power of Darkness* (staged in 1903 with such accurate reproduction of peasant environment that the tragic spirit of the drama was buried under the wealth of objects and settings) seemed too earthy and too mechanical. Stanislavsky longed for a more subtle and different way of representing spiritual reality. For several years, beginning in 1904 with *Ghosts* by Ibsen and ending in 1912-1913 with *Peer Gynt* also by Ibsen, and *Hamlet* under Gordon Craig's direction, Stanislavsky concentrated his search in the field of symbolist drama and made various experiments which took him far away from his initial scenic realism. During this period, the most significant Moscow Art Theater productions were those of Andreyev's dramas, Maeterlinck's *The Blue Bird,* and *Drama of Life* and *In the Claws of Life* by Knud Hamsun.

Leonid Andreyev (1871-1919) patronized by Gorky at the beginning of his career, started as a realistic story teller but soon evinced a morbid interest in pathological situations and grim metaphysical flights. This trend became accentuated after the defeat of the 1905 Revolution, when the pessimistic mood of the writer corresponded to the feeling of emptiness and desperation typical of the disillusioned and frightened intelligentsia and middle class in the aftermath of the short "spring of freedom." After 1906 and until his premature death in 1919, Andreyev devoted himself mostly to writing plays and attained a clamorous success. Between 1907 and 1914, Andreyev was perhaps the most popular dramatist in Russia, but his plays proved to be ephemeral and did not remain in the national repertory. His fame was as short lived as it was striking and boisterous. In the years preceding the First World War, each play by Andreyev was an event followed by heated controversy among critics and spectators, but his plays were forgotten before his death, never to be revived under the Soviets. As a fierce opponent of communism, Andreyev was banned from the Russian press for a long time, and it was not until 1960 that the reprint of his selected plays and stories was finally authorized. His works, however, sank into oblivion not only because of their political overtones: they were dated and could hardly appeal to the modern reader.

The number of dramas written by Andreyev is close to thirty and the most famous among them is *Life of Man,** produced by the Moscow Art Theater in 1907. This morality play presents five scenes which summarize human existence in a highly abstract and stylized form. The piece has neither plot nor characters, and the cast is designated by generic labels: an Old Woman, a Young Man, a Guest, a Drunkard, and so on. We see the nameless protagonist (the Man) being born; then he is shown as an ambitious youth, who dreams of fame and fortune, and with his young wife imagines that the bottle of milk, all they can afford in their poverty, is champagne, and the garret they have to inhabit is a ballroom in a palace. And when the dreams come true,

* (*He Who Gets Slapped* is as well known in the United States.)

and there is a ball in the house of a famous architect (the Man),
the reality of accomplishment is duller than the reverie of the
poor, and envy, gossip, malevolence, and wickedness surround
the Man at the apex of his success. The illusion of happiness is
but of short duration, and is destroyed by the misfortunes of
Man: his son is dead, he himself is ruined and old, death is
around the corner, his whole life was a brief nonsense, compar-
able to the feeble flicker of a candle which is lit for a while and
then extinguished by a gust of wind. This is one of the allegories
contained in the play (probably taken from folklore, and more
precisely from the *Tsar Maximilian* with its popular song—"man
burns like a candle, just blow, and out she goes"). But there were
other images to enhance the hopeless mood of the play, such as
the Old Women in whom one could easily recognize implacable
Parcae. In general, the idea of an iron blind fate dominated
Andreyev's creation, and one of the most important personages
of the play was "Somebody in Gray" who acted as a Master of
Ceremonies in this synopsis of life.

Stanislavsky interpreted this drama as a symbolic vision aimed
at showing the meaningless fatality of human existence, and he
staged the play in an abstract and expressionistic fashion. The
curtain was raised on a completely darkened house. A candle
was burning on a table at the left corner of the stage, where
Somebody in Gray, formless, almost invisible, sat reading the
author's commentaries on the action. His first words were to
the public: "You who came here, you who are sentenced to death,
behold the life of man." In the last act, the candle was blown
out—and this was the end of the life of man and of the performance. In order to emphasize the pessimistic mood of the play,
Stanislavsky used black background, and ropes to outline windows, walls, rooms, tables, seats, and other objects. The settings
were simplified and stylized—the whole design of the drama was
made in straight, rather angular lines; here again, Stanislavsky
emphasized the unity of his vision. In the third act, the ballroom
in Man's rich house was outlined by golden strings and the
costumes were made of gold or of somber fabrics. The shapes of
the guests were grotesque, and the voices of actors sounded hollow or matter of fact, almost expressionless. In the last scene,
Man's death in an inn, drunken men spoke hoarsely, old women

in black cloaks were ratlike, and in the back of the stage there were shadows and reptilelike forms. At the very end, all figures disappeared, a black mist invaded the stage—and out of it emerged Somebody in Gray to utter his final gloomy remark.

What worried Stanislavsky and his company, as well as some critics and many spectators, was the impossibility of creating living characters in a play which was based on generalities and abstract concepts. Actors became like masks or shadows, and this certainly went against the very essence of Stanislavsky's method and aspirations. He was not very happy about his own production, although greatly interested in various possibilities of simplification offered by symbolism. But two years later (1909), when Nemirovich Danchenko directed another drama by Andreyev, *Anathema,* a certain success was obtained, not so much because of stylization and innovation, but because the actors, and particularly Kachalov in the title role, created memorable images. This triumph of the actor had nothing to do, however, with the content of the drama. In Andreyev's vision, *Anathema* was the spirit of negation, a kind of combination of Mephistopheles, Satan, and the Nietzschean superman, with some elements borrowed from Byron protagonists, such as Manfred and Cain, while the central idea of this concoction reminded one of certain parts of *Faust.* The kernel of the play was the juxtaposition of the spirit of darkness with a poor little man, a Jew called David Leiser, who was supposed to embody compassion and humanity and who, despite all the ups and downs of his destiny, always remained kind and humble. The conflict between Anathema and Leiser was represented in a highly pretentious manner, partly in fantastic landscapes of celestial space, partly on earth; and the schematic expression of ideas, as well as constant reference to inflated symbols such as The Guardian of the Gate, or the lawyer Nullius (an incarnation of Anathema), were annoying and empty. Andreyev was tossing around all sorts of great metaphysical concepts, but the spectator felt that all his syllogisms were made of cardboard.

Attracted by nightmarish images, Andreyev wanted to instill fear and mystic tremors in terrified spectators. In *King Hunger* he reveled in horrible scenes of a revolt of the masses which, in their blind and bestial fury, destroyed cities and killed women and children. This allegory seemed to say, "This is where revolution will lead you" to the radicals, and "Look where you are going to finish" to the conservatives. Not less macabre are Andreyev's grim inventions, such as *Black Masks*, a play in which Duke Lorenzo fights a duel with his own double, or scenes in the utterly complicated *Ocean*, or even those of his so-called realistic plays. The trouble with Andreyev was that he did not hide his intention to horrify the spectator and, instead of using subtle means, shouted and threatened in a most rhetorical manner. Tolstoy made this deadly remark about Andreyev: "He wants to frighten me but I am not scared."

The only play in which the metaphysical horror derived from a more or less believable human situation was *Thought* (adapted from an early novelette). The Moscow Art Theater produced it in 1914, but as a purely psychological piece without using abstract devices. This corresponded to a shift in the direction of the Theater which, after its symbolist experiments, returned to the psychological and realistic drama. Andreyev himself also dropped allegories and wrote realistic or pseudo-realistic plays. *Life of Man*, produced by Meyerhold in Kommissarzhevskaya Theater in 1907, and by the Moscow Art Theater, made but rare appearances on the Russian stage, and *Anathema, Ocean, Black Masks,* and *King Hunger* never became part of the theatrical repertory, while other plays by Andreyev, conceived and written in a more conventional style, became box office successess all over the country. *Thought* represented (not chronologically) a bridge between Andreyev's attempts at philosophical abstraction and his pictures of contemporary life. Its hero, Kerzhentsev, believes in the power of human thought and his own superiority over ordinary human beings. He kills the husband of the woman he loves, and then puts to death a psychiatrist who has to examine him when he simulates madness. Kerzhentsev is finally confined in a mental institution, and begins to wonder whether he is actually mad. Or did he go out of his mind because he started simulating a mental derangement? Stanislavsky and Leonidov, both of whom impersonated Kerzhentsev, interpreted and staged the whole play as a clinical case of growing madness, and held the public spellbound by their sophisticated rendering of a complex psychological or pathological process.

Days of Our Life and *Gaudeamus,* both depicting the university youth of the time, with a certain emphasis on death and human futility, were written in 1908 and 1910 respectively; they had a brief but clamorous success just before the First World War—mostly in provincial theaters. Even more popular in Russia, as well as abroad, were Andreyev's dramas of lust and passion: *Anfisa* (1909), and to a lesser degree *Yekaterina Ivanovna* and *Professor Storitsyn* (1912). The rivalry of three sisters who love the same man assumes tragic accents in the first play; one of the sisters, Anfisa, is consumed by passion and poisons her lover, and her personal tragedy is portrayed against the dark background of the downfall of a family. *Yekaterina Ivanovna,* which the Moscow Art Theater produced as a drama of manners, had symbolic or hidden ulterior meaning but fell short of capturing its audiences because of its psychological shortcomings. It had an excellent first act: a jealous husband shoots at Yekaterina, his wife, whom he suspects of unfaithfulness. She is innocent, but the shot changes everything: Yekaterina is so offended and disgusted by her husband's suspicion and brutality that she gives herself to that very man whose name was erroneously linked to hers, and then gradually turns into a sort of glorified prostitute. The public could not understand why such a pure and innocent woman as Yekaterina should become what Andreyev made her, and the artists of the Moscow Theater failed to convey this to their audience. Nemirovich Danchenko tried to stage this play as a tragedy but didn't succeed in making acceptable the reasons and the meaning of the heroine's sudden change, and the play was a failure.

In general, Andreyev's plays had a strange fate. After a short-lived and brilliant appearance on the Russian stage, followed by violent discussions, they faded without leaving any trace and turned into shadows of the past almost at the time of their author's physical death. And yet most of them were well done, and there is no doubt that Andreyev had more craft and dramatic vigor than his former friend Gorky. Whenever his plays, such as *He Who Gets Slapped* (1915) were produced abroad, including the United States, they were acclaimed by the audiences of the twenties, and their resumption by college theaters after World War II showed that they had not lost their stage appeal. The bombastic, rhetorical, and artificial character of Andreyev's highly romanticized style remains, however, the main defect in his plays. In the same way as Gorky's dramas, the plays of Andreyev are a closed chapter in the history of the Russian theater and have a limited historical or illustrative significance.

IV

Stanislavsky and Nemirovich Danchenko understood perfectly well that their success in "atmospheric" impressionism and the Chekhovian play of "mood" and "aura," was due mainly to a symphonic unity of each performance, to a careful orchestration of all the components of a show, and to the consistency in ideological conception strictly adhered to in the production and in the acting. This facilitated Stanislavsky's experiment in symbolism. Nemirovich Danchenko remained much more conservative throughout all the years of search and experiment even though he did produce a few of the symbolists and introduced modernistic devices into the staging of his beloved Ibsen. During the 1904-1905 season, Stanislavsky staged three plays by Maeterlinck: *The Intruder, The Blind Ones,* and *Inside,* all written by the Belgian for the puppet theater, and the production, not very successful, was partly impressionistic and, as far as setting and props were concerned, reduced to "conventional simplicity," or highly stylized. But in the same season the Moscow Art Theater showed realistic or Chekhovian plays by Naidenov and Chirikov, and *Ivanov* by Chekhov. After the political interlude with Gorky's plays, including *The Children of the Sun* in 1906, the symbolist tendency became more visible during the next two seasons.

In 1906-1907, in addition to *Brand* (with beautiful settings by Simov, with Kachalov as Brand, and the handsome Ghermanova as Agnes, directed by Nemirovich Danchenko) , Stanislavsky showed *Drama of Life* by Hamsun, and this performance seemed a crucial one. In it he definitely shifted from direct expression of emotions to scenic images for conveying abstract concepts. *Drama of Life* was the second part of Hamsun's trilogy about Kareno, a Nietzschean dreamer and philosopher, an enigmatic symbol of intuitive human aspirations. He teaches the children of Oterman, a rich man who built for Kareno a glass tower on the seashore,

a hermitage of meditation, and a lighthouse at the entrance of a
perilous fjord. Oterman had promised to publish the writings of
Kareno but since the day a quarry of marble was discovered
on his lands, he became possessed by the demon of avarice. In
a fit of madness Oterman sets fire to the tower, but his own children as well as Kareno's manuscripts perish in the flames. His
daughter Teresita, the incarnation of lust and desire, vainly
attempts to gain Kareno's love and falls victim of a tragic accident.
And behind all these tormented men and women looms the old
beggar Tiu who tries to say something but is never listened to.
He acts as a silent Fate in the entangled lives of all the people
around him. The whole performance of the play had a weird,
almost mystical flavor, and its mood was conveyed to the audience
through strictly symbolic devices. The same symbolism impregnated the production of *In the Claws of Life*, the last part of
Hamsun's trilogy, staged by Stanislavsky three years later. Here
again action and dialogue were interpreted as signs of a trans-
cendent reality.

Since symbolic impressionism did not permit complete con-
cretization, Stanislavsky was always torn between certain scenic
approximations and extremist forms, which led to the renunciation of three-dimensional representation and to a replacement
of a live actor by a stylized marionette. His inner tact and stage
experience helped him, however, much more than any definite
theory. Sometimes, as mentioned before, the necessity of finding
adequate props and costumes defeated his initial intention. It
happened, for instance, in 1908 when he staged *The Blue Bird*
by Maeterlinck. This allegory conceived as a fairy tale, centered
on the two children, Tiltyl and Mitil who are looking for the
Blue Bird, a symbol of happiness and contentment. In their
search they come in contact with animals, birds, beasts, and
objects, and travel through the Land of Memory, the Kingdom
of the Future, the Farewell, the Awareness. The spectators were
enchanted with the staging of *The Blue Bird* and the whole of
Moscow was talking about the Cat with the plumed hat which
resembled his tail, or about the opulent clumsy Bread on his fat
white legs—but Stanislavsky wondered whether these cheap miracles were truly innovations, and whether the fairy tale mood was
reached through them or through the charming and extremely

suitable music by Ilya Satz, the talented composer of the Moscow
Art Theater. *Life of Man* and *Anathema* by Andreyev, and
In the Claws of Life by Hamsun were more satisfactory, because
the external devices in them fitted more organically with their
philosophy. The last in this series of symbolic pieces was the
production of *Hamlet,* directed by Gordon Craig, in 1911. But
elements of symbolism, of simplified or abstract settings, and of
experiments in new scenic devices persisted in many later productions until *Cain* by Byron in 1918-1920, which put a formal
end to the efforts of the Theater in the symbolist play.

In all his initial experiments in symbolism, Stanislavsky was
greatly helped and influenced by Leopold Sullerzhitsky (1872-
1916), one of his most brilliant disciples. An extraordinary person, greatly respected by Tolstoy, Chekhov, and Gorky, Sullerzhitsky had a most adventurous life comprised of dozens of jobs,
revolutionary activities, prison, and finally a conversion to Tolstoy's moral doctrines. He helped to bring the religious sect of the
Wrestlers of God from the Caucasus to Canada, remained with
them two years in the New World, and came back to Russia
without a penny. While completely destitute (he slept in public
parks and actually almost starved), he became a stagehand in the
Moscow Art Theater and soon struck up a friendship with Stanislavsky. An idealist with high esthetic and moral aims, he sought
truth and artistic inspiration by communion with nature, simplicity of living, and active love. Tolstoy said that Sullerzhitsky
had a genius for altruistic affection. He saw in the theater a
powerful means of bringing people together and provoking
in them genuine emotions. This concept explains his enthusiasm
for Stanislavsky's System, independent of his deep personal attachment to this man whom he loved and respected highly. Sullerzhitsky was one of the first apostles of the System, and he
taught it with the passion of a convert in the private Adashev's
School in Moscow which counted among its pupils many future
stars of the Russian stage, including Vakhtangov. Like Stanislavsky, Sullerzhitsky came to the conclusion that "theater as a
spectacle" should be ultimately replaced by "theater of true feelings." There is no doubt that he greatly influenced Stanislavsky
around 1910-1912. Appointed manager of the First Studio or
Workshop of the Moscow Art Theater, he became its guiding

spirit and trained a whole group of important actors and directors.

Yuri Zavadsky, one of the leading Soviet directors writes in the *Book on Vakhtangov* (1959): "Perhaps the Stanislavsky System would not have come into being without Sullerzhitsky and his naive infatuation with Tolstoy, Hindu philosophy, and Yoga, his live sense of reality, his extraordinary pedagogical talent, and his deep understanding of human beings and life. Sullerzhitsky influenced Stanislavsky enormously when the latter was working on his System, and also during the production of *The Blue Bird*."

Ilya Satz the composer (1875-1912) was also collaborating with Stanislavsky during the "symbolist interlude." A very nervous man who would ask his relatives to shut him in a room until he had finished the score, he used to hang around the stage for hours, watching the rehearsals and listening to discussions, trying to get impregnated with the spirit of the play and the character of its settings. He composed suggestive and impressionistic scores for the plays by Andreyev, Maeterlinck, and Hamsun, and, in general, emphasized the importance of the musical element by enhancing the mood of Stanislavsky's productions. Later, in his *Hamlet*, Gordon Craig showed how music, architecture, and painting could be fused into a symphonic unity. Even before him, the Moscow Art Theater used three-dimensional props and avoided flats and what it called false illusionism. Gordon Craig, the famous Irish director, actor, and theatrical innovator, brought with him the concept of reduced settings. He used screens of various sizes to build constructivist decor by placing them at different angles and in various architectural combinations. He also built huge columns, passageways, and staircases which played a most important role in grouping actors and in arranging scenes.* Some of his screens shone like gold, and the black-coated Hamlet, acted by Kachalov, was projected against this shimmering background of light. In Craig's interpretation the Danish prince was ageless, he didn't belong to any given period, and his tragedy consisted of the opposition of his spiritual reality to the realm of death around him—he alone was true to life; all the

---

* The leading idea of his production of *Hamlet* was a golden pyramidlike hill, on top of which were the king and the queen while courtiers in gold robes and suits were placed all along the tiers of the elevation in strict feudal order.

other characters were products of his morbid fantasy. The unity of Craig's production and the abstractness of his stylized settings made a profound impression on Meyerhold, Tairov, and other young men who were looking for new avenues. Craig, however, left Moscow before the completion of his *Hamlet;* this task was taken over by Stanislavsky. Although the Irishman and the Russian got along very well, there was a basic point of disagreement between them. Gordon Craig was more and more convinced of the necessity of eliminating any personal, purely subjective and emotional components in acting and dreamt of replacing the human face by a mask as in the Greek drama. Stanislavsky and Nemirovich Danchenko were not less preoccupied with fundamental problems of scenic art, but they were definitely centering their research on the psychological preparation and training of a live individual. Craig ended up with the theory of a glorified marionette obediently fulfilling the work assigned to him by a dictatorial director within a strict general outline.

Stanislavsky leaned toward theoretical rules derived from empirical experience, which later were simply referred to as his System. In Europe and America it was to become "The Method," and its fanatical supporters elevated it into sacred Tablets of Art to be accepted, adored, and followed without any compromise or correction. Of course, neither Stanislavsky nor his Moscow Art Theater could be held responsible for such exaggeration and idolatry. It has to be pointed out that all the Russian actors who brought the Method to the United States—Boleslavsky, Tamirov, Deykarkhanova, Solovyova, Baklanova, Bulgakova, as well as Lee Strasberg, the American promoter of the Method, knew perfectly well that this "grammar of acting" could not replace "inner truth" or an innate talent and that its basic precepts were not dogmatic principles but the result of trial and error. Stanislavsky later attempted to summarize his ideas in such books as *An Actor Prepares* and *Building a Character,* which, in the first half of the twentieth century, became for many a kind of theatrical bible; but he never stopped reassessing his own discoveries, and kept correcting and changing his methods all the time. At various stages of his own evolution he stressed this or that element of his theory, and it is therefore unnecessary and erroneous to present them as tenets of a canon. Besides, in the first years of the Moscow Art Theater, Stanislavsky was often torn between his duties as a stage director and his personal problems as an actor. In 1906 he felt so bad about his "wooden" acting that he took a vacation.

Nemirovich Danchenko devoted himself almost exclusively to directorial duties, which gave him more concentration and unity of purpose. But Stanislavsky, perhaps because of his dual role, had a wider outlook and more varied experience. Both agreed, however, on what must precede the technical preparation of an actor for a role, namely, the preliminary analysis of the play. Before anything else, all the members of the cast had to be quite aware of the basic idea of the work, as well as of its super-objective, its trunkline of action. From the moment a play was selected, the task of the director was to make clear all these essentials through discussion, criticism, and even contributions by literary specialists. It is well known that critics and historians were often invited by the directors to deliver lectures to the company. The whole character of a production depended on basic definitions. For instance, the superobjective for *Julius Caesar* was the death of the protagonist; the "through" (or trunkline) action, the rise and fall of a great man; while the ruling idea could be worded as "the greater they are, the harder they fall." (Hamlet wants to expose and punish the murderers of his father; this, in Stanislavsky's terms, is the "trunkline of action" in the drama.) All this formed the substratum or the ideological foundation of a production, and determined its style, including the settings and the general "line" of acting. The interpretation of a part had to fit into this general design. In the first place the actor had to understand and feel the character he was going to impersonate, and Stanislavsky always emphasized the importance of this aspect of the actor's work. He also believed in the study of what may be called the prehistory of a character, or its life before the play (the "pre-text" work). We know that what he called "inner truth" was intimately connected with the psychological (sometimes purely intuitive, sometimes strictly rational) interpretation of a personage. Mrs. Varvara Bulgakova told us that her husband Lev, a prominent Moscow actor, was dissatisfied with his interpretation of Smerdyakov in *The Brothers Karamazov*, staged in the 1910-1911 season. He had special difficulties in impersonating Smerdyakov after he killed his own father. Stanislavsky questioned Bulgakov's basic assumption: "You believe that Smerdyakov is suffering because he has committed a murder. But in reality the murder has released him. Don't suffer—rejoice." The part suddenly took a new dimension, and when Bulgakov followed Stanislavsky's advice, everything fell into shape, and the spectators watched with awe the mad joy of a murderer. It is often ignored that Stanislavsky attached the greatest importance to the actor's imagination. Through study, analysis, work of the mind, and imagination the actor finally arrives at what can be called a creative vision of his own part. Only then begins the problem of exteriorization or expression. It is in this area that the Method becomes most helpful. After the part has matured in the mind of the actor, and after he feels himself within the skin of the protagonist, he can divide the part into psychological bits united by the same feeling, and the rehearsals can begin. This is the moment when words and gestures come in. We can see that they represent the last moment in the long series of literary and psychological preparation. It would be unfair not to mention that Stanislavsky demanded certain prerequisites on which he does not seem to dwell sufficiently in his treatises: voice, diction, posture, physical deportment. Those who worked in the Moscow Art Theater know that he was almost fanatical on those subjects. They were taken for granted, in the same way as is the capacity of a piano player to produce sounds and hit a chord.

In general, Stanislavsky believed that his system had two aspects: one dealt with the preparation or training of each individual actor, and the second with his actual work as an interpreter. The actor, through all sorts of inner and physical exercises, had to develop his capacity to reach a state of creative concentration without which he would not be able to project himself properly. And here he had to control his unconscious forces. Stanislavsky knew well the importance of the latter but believed in the directing functions of the conscious and the superego.

The second, or interpretative, part of the artist's work had to be focused on a definite role and he had to become fully aware of its dynamics or inner unity of action.

The main problem was how to convey an emotion and create

an image which will be accepted as true and alive by the audience, thus infecting it with a scenic illusion and provoking the miracle of artistic communication. While Stanislavsky admitted the intuitive perception of a role and its imaginative stage creation, he was eager to offer the actor more solid foundations than sheer "temperament" or "passion" in the old romantic manner. The central point was the assumption that the actor actually experiences the emotions he wants to convey to the audience. By an act of volition the actor evokes in himself the genuine feelings of the role and keeps them through the use of certain techniques. Stanislavsky claimed that one cannot act an emotion; the emotion itself must come to the actor if he makes an effort of will and does something. "The actor must learn how to will what is assigned to him as an image." Whether in representing these emotions the actor referred to his personal recollections, using his affective memory, or whether he built a psychological state by an effort of his imagination, the stress was on the authenticity of his impersonation. The problem, therefore, was not how to represent love or lust or anger but how to feel angry, in love, lustful, and the exteriorization of these feelings or what we call acting, derived naturally from a psychological prerequisite. In short, Stanislavsky pondered not how to act but how to feel, how to experience emotions. He even contended that if the actor felt genuinely he would find the right intonation or the right gesture. Of course, Stanislavsky knew the difference between life emotions and stage emotions and he did not claim that an actor who impersonated Hamlet or Othello must have possessed in real life a strong capacity for passion, love, and jealousy. His thesis was that life emotions, transformed into stage ones, change qualitatively and quantitatively. They become poetic reflections and as such can acquire strength and sincerity which the actor might not express in real life. On stage the emotions become augmented, reinforced—gaining a quality of intensity which changes them into kinds of electric transformers of energy. It has been pointed out that in his theory of emotions Stanislavsky was strongly influenced by the French psychologist Théodule Ribot (1839-1916) whose *Psychologie des sentiments* was translated into Russian in 1888. Stanislavsky believed in desires as psychological motivations, and saw wishes and anxieties as the basic components of psychological process. He spoke not only of the "memory of emotions" but also about the six stages of the basic process: wanting, seeking, experiencing, impersonating, blending, influencing. It is quite possible that Stanislavsky and his disciples did not make a clear distinction between "sincerity," "authenticity," "truthfulness," etc., as used in life situations and in stage conditions. It is impossible to identify fully life emotions with analogous feelings on the boards. The latter are not a result of a real stimulant but are created by an act of volition which draws on affective memory, on creative capacity, on imagination, to link a rudiment of an emotion to illusory, fanciful circumstances and expand it into a larger, poetic feeling. To represent wrath or despair, the actor can evoke through his emotional memory a case where he felt those emotions to perhaps a much lesser degree than what he will offer on stage. Stanislavsky affirmed that an artist can live only his own emotions and is therefore bound to use in his acting his personal experiences, the only way of instilling the living soul into a dead part. In 1914, Evgeny Vakhtangov formulated this law even better than Stanislavsky: "The majority of feelings we know through our own emotional experiences, but they were originated in our soul in a different order according to a different logic than those necessary for an artistic image, and therefore the work of an actor consists in extracting the traces of those emotions from various corners of his own soul and then lining them up in a sequence which is required by the inner logic of the play."

Stanislavsky was aware of the fundamental duality of an actor's activity: to live intensely on stage, and not to dissolve himself completely in his part—to be passionate, if necessary, but without ever losing control of his creation. A great actor always combines extreme sensitivity with extreme self-mastery. Although Stanislavsky asked the actor to forget he was on stage, he understood that this was an unattainable ideal.

For many years Stanislavsky explored the most difficult problems of acting: how to create in oneself at the right moment the emotion required by the part?

His initial answer lies in the psychological truth of the artistic image. He often asked an actor to describe the day of the character he was going to impersonate, or to imagine what he would have put in a diary, or what his conduct would have been in a given situation. After the process of maturation, the behavior of the actor on stage depends on the completeness of his reincarnation. Stanislavsky preached that if an actor really wants to know why his beloved is cold, or really wants to see her eyes, he would be greatly facilitated in his intonations and gestures. Later, he conceded that, vice versa, certain gestures and intonations brought back the emotions, particularly when the actor was confronted with repeat performances, acting his part again and again. For instance, when playing the part of Krutitsky in a comedy by Ostrovsky, Stanislavsky himself met with a slight accident: the handle of the door he wanted to open fell on the floor. Without losing countenance, he picked it up, and looked at it for quite a while, thus creating a new suspense; and the effect of this accidental invention was such that he retained the accident and gesture in the following performances. In his lessons to young actors, Stanislavsky always pointed out that consummate actors never feared accidents: they turned them always to their own advantage, if they behaved exactly as the character they were impersonating would have behaved in this contingency. But he warned them of routine repetition of tricks. His ideal was constant renovation so that each performance would be different and unique in its nuances.

Soviet interpreters of Stanislavsky's System often claim that after the 1917 Revolution and under the influence of dialectical materialism, Stanislavsky ended up by placing the conditioned reflex in the center of his method. This is a gross exaggeration. Stanislavsky always attributed great importance to associative reflexes and he knew that emotions can easily come to life through action, or that gestures and intonations can originate from one's unconscious prior to the awareness of emotion by the actor. From the very beginning of his method, he emphasized the role of physical action for the release of tension on stage. When speaking of the support given to the actor by the setting, the music, the lighting, or by whatever could create a mood, he also warned about the way the actor entered the stage: it should have the same effect as entering a room in real life: "Touch the table next to your chair, relax, do not be tense." He knew that muscular strain fetters the movements and all creative effort. "You are an old man, but your voice is too young—breathe slowly, with a certain difficulty; your voice will become adequate to your academic age." These and hundreds of other small technical items led to the main rule: Do not wait for an emotion—it does not come to order; start with an action, and then you will create your "circle," your "public solitude" and find the stable "point" of creative concentration, which is detachment and control. Of course, Stanislavsky knew that action can be voluntary or unconscious, and that only in the first case can it be conducive to the birth of emotion, while in the second case certain impulsive actions derive from initially felt emotions. It is true that in the last years of his life Stanislavsky became very interested in what one could call elementary physical actions. He wanted the actor to control the "small truth" of such actions. "We actors forget how we walk in life, how we sit, eat, sleep, talk, look and listen, and we have to learn it all again on the boards just like the child learns to walk." But, of course, all these actions assumed an artistic value only if they were serving an ulterior purpose, as means to create an atmosphere of truth and thus help to exteriorize an inner meaning and a psychological image. For example, says Stanislavsky, in Pushkin's *Mozart and Salieri,* Salieri has to take a glass of wine, put in the poison, and offer the drink to Mozart, his friend and rival. How much all these physical actions depend upon the complex psychology of the reluctant murderer and how important it is for the actor to reflect in each gesture the contradictions and the inner struggle within Salieri's mind. And who can say where the physical ends and the psychological begins or vice versa?

In *The Brothers Karamazov,* Dimitry, blind with passion for Grushenka and believing that she is in his father's house, knocks down Gregory, the old servant. Dimitry was played by Leonidov, an excellent actor, but the scene did not come off until Nemirovich Danchenko made this remark: "You are looking for Grushenka on stage and all becomes false. Actually, she is not on the stage, and Dimitry's inflamed imagination pushes him further, into his father's quarters, and Gregory does not let him in, so he eliminates this obstacle without even noticing that he hits an old man, his childhood friend. The object of his fixation is beyond the stage and he wants to reach it with all the strength of his temperament." The way Salieri will hold the glass with the poison, or Dimitry will struggle with the old servant, is made up of a succession of movements and gestures and facial expressions and voice inflections—and each of them has to be true—and it is the task of each individual actor to bring to perfection and complete convincingness these multiple scenic elements. We speak of an "achievement" or of excellent "technique" if each beat is well measured and well executed. But the achievement of the small truth encourages the actor and facilitates his creation on a superior level. We come back to the basic principles: the necessity of genuine emotion, of a conception of the part, of psychological and ideological study. Stanislavsky's method aimed at an inner discipline of the actor, at the highest degree of artistic intelligence and at a perfect control of all external means. It is obvious that such a method did not deny the importance of natural talent but simply tried to develop it through a rigorous discipline of work, study, experiment, and conscious effort. We should not forget that Stanislavsky always had in mind the super-objective as the supreme goal of a performance: "to convey the emotions and the ideas of a playwright, his dreams, torments and joys." The trunkline or through action mobilizes all the psychic and physical efforts of the actor and gives consistency to the whole work, including its form, in settings, lighting, and structure of the stage. The unity of the physical and of the inner psychological is the key to the success of the whole—for a total production as well as the rendition of a part by an individual actor.

Nikolay Gorchakov reports that Stanislavsky made this remark to an actor: "You display actions all the time; this is all right, but you must also think on the stage, you must observe, listen, and reason—all this is action too, and even more effective than those which demand many gestures and shifting positions." As Alexander Popov, a Soviet director, aptly reminds us in his essay on the Moscow Art Theater, Nemirovich Danchenko, who was always concerned with practical applications of Stanislavsky's theories, spoke of the "second level" of a play which, in his opinion, was dependent upon the inner world of the actor. "The scenic image which the spectator takes home is formed not by external gestures and actions of the cast, but by the very essence of its contribution—and it has to be discovered by the audience. 'How magnificently acted,' 'how funny,' 'how pathetic'—all this we feel as a pleasure during the performance. But when it is over, tears and laughter are also over. If the performance were limited only to the magnificent acting, to the craft, the impressions from it would stop there. But what I take home is more than that, it is what the actor lives by, the most precious substance of art—and here lies the difference between the Moscow Art Theater and other theaters." The actor expresses himself in an infinite variety of combinations, but there is a core in his impersonation, and throughout all his lines and beats the spectator perceives a unity which tends to create a consistent image. In the same way, the whole play has a leading idea, a kernel, a vision, the unity of which is achieved by actors, settings, production; and it is this vision which will remain with the spectator, and raise the performance to the height of a momentous art experience.

V

The Moscow Art Theater was like a symphonic orchestra under a brilliant conductor. It had no soloists and its unity was essentially that of a highly professional team. Its opponents called it the theater of directors and claimed that the actor was sacrificed to the smoothness of the ensemble work. This accusation was, however, unjust: to achieve the miracle of co-operation and harmony, the Theater needed first-class actors, and, as we know, Stanislavsky directed his main efforts toward the training of each individual member of his company. He and Nemirovich Danchenko succeeded in assembling a group of men and women out of which, at one time or another, emerged all the best Russian actors and actresses of the twentieth century. Some of them, such as Meyerhold or Vakhtangov or Mikhail Chekhov, later broke away from the institution which had been their alma mater, but others remained loyal to it all their lives. And, of course, Stanislavsky himself was an excellent and highly talented actor. One can say that all members of the Moscow Art Theater, particularly in the first twenty years of its existence, were expert artists. But there were, of course, *primi inter pares,* the first ones among the equals. Kachalov, Moskvin, and Mikhail Chekhov were probably the most outstanding representatives of Stanislavsky's school, while Leonidov, Luzhsky, Artem, Vishnevsky, and Gribunin came immediately after the three leaders.

Ivan Moskvin (1874-1946), a pupil of Nemirovich Danchenko, played some forty-nine parts during his long career. One of his most remarkable impersonations was that of Tsar Fyodor in Alexey Tolstoy's tragedy. Even his unassuming physique lent itself to this part of a weak, sickly, and nice man, doomed to be the victim of ruthless politicians. Some critics believed that Moskvin was most successful in the parts of Luka in *The Lower Depths,* or of Snegirev in *The Brothers Karamazov,* or of Protassov in *The Living Corpse,* because his forte lay in representing humble little men. The design of his interpretations was strictly psychological, and he knew well how to make alive the image of the "simple heart." One of the secrets of his art was an intensity of emotions rendered through a series of light touches, always in the style of understatement. At the same time he revealed himself as an excellent comedian in such parts as the ridiculous Yepikhodov in *The Cherry Orchard,* or the hypocritical and cunning Foma Opiskin in Dostoevsky's *The Hamlet of Stepanchikovo,* or the bombastic liar Nozdrev in the adaptation of Gogol's *The Dead Souls.*

An entirely different type of an actor was Vassily Kachalov (the stage name of Shverubovich, 1875-1948). A handsome, tall, well-built man, he had a stirring voice with a rich range of modulations and inflections, and his parts ranged from melancholic Chekhovian to romantic figures, such as Hamlet—one of his most poignant and human creations in Gordon Craig's production. He came to the Moscow Art Theater from the provincial stage, and when he left Kazan, his former colleagues warned him that Stanislavsky's company was made up of apprentices and amateurs led by sophisticated and whimsical directors. His early training having been quite conventional, he had to work hard in Moscow to absorb new techniques. He soon developed into a striking actor. Even though he was acclaimed as Vershinin or Tuzenbakh in *Three Sisters,* and later gave remarkable characterizations of Russian intellectuals in various modern plays, his best parts were those of rebels and romantic heroes. He was a severe intransigent Brand, a sarcastic and analytical Ivan Karamazov, a fiery Don Juan in Pushkin's *The Guest of Stone,* and a tragic Cain in Byron's drama. While Moskvin's characterizations were typically

Russian, revealing a certain national flavor, a "sense of the soil" (for instance, in Luka of *The Lower Depths,* or as Pazukhin in Saltykov's drama), Kachalov was more intellectual and attracted by universal types. He was much better as a representative of the intelligentsia than of the people.

Kachalov's diction and sense of form made him an exceptionally good reader of poetry (very few actors can read poems without becoming too declamatory and emphatic). Kachalov showed all the shades of his refined art not only in reciting the classics but also the moderns, and those who heard him—as this writer did—reading, for example, Mayakovsky's poems, will always remember this unusual attainment of excellence.

Some critics reproached Kachalov for the unevenness of his performances. Despite his solid skill, he had to be completely absorbed by the part to give it all the impetus of his genius. In that, he could be compared with another prominent member of the company, Leonid Leonidov (1873-1941). A pupil of Lensky and an actor of varied experiences, Leonidov did not join the Moscow Art Theater until 1903. His first part was that of Pepel, the thief in *The Lower Depths.* A very temperamental actor interested in dark, passionate, or strange characters, Leonidov was acclaimed as Peer Gynt, as Soleny in *Three Sisters,* and as Man in Andreyev's *Life of Man.* An essentially tragic actor, he could also be very successful in comic parts which he did with great finesse. He considerably expanded his activities in post-Revolutionary repertory.

Before 1917 one of the most popular among other talented actresses of the Moscow Art Theater was Olga Knipper (1870-1959). Her reputation was enhanced by the fact that she became not only the interpreter of Chekhov's heroines but also his wife. Her sense of measure, of sober psychological nuance, a carefully prepared pattern of the role, made her an outstanding and typical representative of Stanislavsky's method. The spectators remembered that as Masha in *Three Sisters,* taking final leave from her beloved Vershinin (acted by Stanislavsky) she uttered but one word—"farewell"—but her posture, facial expression, the play of hands and movements of the body were such that although she did not cry, the spectators had tears in their eyes. One of her best parts was that of Ranevskaya in *The Cherry Orchard:* she interpreted her as a benevolent human being whose life has been very unhappy. While the images of Chekhovian women were often identified in the mind of theatergoers with the way Knipper made them appear on the boards, Knipper had a very rich stage experience, and it is known that outside of Chekhov's heroines, she interpreted some forty-two other roles, among them a memorable presentation of Natalia Petrovna, the protagonist of Turgenev's *A Month in the Country.*

Knipper belonged to actors who reach perfection through incessant labor and conscious preparation. She was less endowed by nature than Maria Ghermanova (1884-1945 ?), a beautiful woman with a caressing voice and innate qualities of a great actress. Knipper was at her best in what she herself called "fragile" parts based upon meticulous integration of details, while Ghermanova was attracted by characters which demanded more forceful expression. Her main asset was a combination of temperament and craft, and she showed it in Yekaterina Ivanovna of Andreyev's drama, and particularly in Grushenka (*The Brothers Karamazov*) whom she showed as a national image of femininity. Her Sofia in *Wit Works Woe* was not a well-bred, empty-headed miss but a dangerous, self-conscious coquette. Her career in Russia, however, was interrupted by her decision to leave her native country after the Revolution. She went to Prague where she directed the so-called Prague group of the Moscow Art Theater. In the twenties this was one of the most important theatrical establishments of the Russian *émigrés* in Europe.

The great achievement of Stanislavsky's system was that it did train excellent actors and actresses. The strength of the Theater did not consist in having a few quite outstanding men and women, but in forming a group of consummate performers. There were no inferior members in the company, no fill-ins, no second-rate understudies, and one could be sure that the smallest part in each play would be acted as seriously and as carefully as any of the leads. The theory and practice of the Moscow Art Theater had a tremendous impact on the level of acting in Russia. As a result of this educational influence, the degree of professional efforts in the field rose very high. The Moscow Art Theater, integrating the glorious past of the Russian stage, created a new tradition of unusual cultural standing which became a model for universal admiration in the first quarter of the twentieth century.

6

FROM "The WORLD OF ART" TO MEYERHOLD

THE MOSCOW ART THEATER was at the apex of activity and scored its greatest triumphs during the two decades between its beginnings and the 1917 Revolution. It tested its skill and strength in naturalistic representation, then created the drama of moods and impressions, went a long way into psychological realism, and, paying tribute to changes of mentality and attitudes among the intelligentsia, made some explorations in symbolist art. But throughout all its affirmations or experiments, it always remained faithful to the basic idea formulated by its two great leaders. However strongly Stanislavsky and Nemirovich Danchenko disagreed at times about the style of production and methods of acting, particularly in connection with the system of artistic training, they were both promoting the "theater of authentic emotion" (an inadequate translation of the term *perezhivanye* in Russian). This meant that they requested from the actor psychological truth in his gestures, words, attitudes, and all other forms of self-expression as the prerequisite of his performance, and that this theater based on truth and authenticity they opposed to what could be called "theater of show"—which put the emphasis on all the external, visual, and auditive devices. Being excellent professionals, they knew perfectly well the importance of the "materialization" of a play; Stanislavsky in his System demanded from the actor the full control of his body, diction, and purely histrionic qualities. But the differences between the two conceptions was deep, and the history of the Russian theater in the first quarter of the twentieth century, and even later, is filled with their struggle.

In two discussions with pupils in April 1922, E. Vakhtangov, who, in Stanislavsky's opinion was destined to become "the leader of the Russian theater," explained in these terms the difference between Meyerhold, the representative of the *avant-garde*, and Stanislavsky: "For Meyerhold a performance is theatrical when the spectator does not forget for a second that he is in a theater, and is conscious all the time of the actor as a craftsman who plays a role. Stanislavsky demands the opposite: that the spectator become oblivious to the fact that he is in a theater and that he be immersed in the atmosphere in which the protagonists of a play exist." Stanislavsky was pleased that the spectator came to the *Three Sisters* as if he were invited to be a guest of the Prozorov family. This was in his opinion the highest theatrical attainment; and he wanted to ban from the stage all theatrical trivilality. He branded as "theatrical" all that reminded him of the old theater, and "theatricality" was used in the Moscow Art Theater as a term of opprobrium. It is true that all he damned was truly vulgar, but, excited by the elimination of triviality, he also expelled the necessary theatricality which consists of presenting dramatic works in a theatrical way. Of course, Stanislavsky and Nemirovich Danchenko never renounced theatrical devices, and Chekhov's plays, where various musical effects were emphasized, were a good example of their practice while the production of other works obviously involved elaborate settings. It would be naive to claim that Stanislavsky ignored the specifics of scenic art. In its long career, the Moscow Art Theater experimented with all sorts of forms, including the so-called theater of scenic conventions. But it did subordinate the externals and the style of a performance to its human values and put above all these the actor's authentic interpretation. Stanislavsky and Nemirovich Danchenko aimed in different ways at the creation of believable characters. The problem for both of them was to find a balance between the organic vision and the scenic image by which it was communicated to the audience. Whoever tried to bring on the stage a scenic image without an inner human content was, in their opinion, guilty of a fundamental error.

But while the Moscow Art Theater was strengthening its position as the house of "authentic human emotion" and of "truth against empty esthetic shell," the whole movement in the arts was directed toward a greater emphasis on purely formal values; shape, color, and line played an increasingly larger part in the affirmation of "theatricality." And since opera and ballet in Russia were the centers of lavish productions, they promoted new developments in production ahead of the drama.

To understand fully what was going on in Russian theatrical circles at the beginning of the century, we should not forget that the Moscow Art Theater was neither an isolated phenomenon nor an exotic flower grown on ungrateful soil. On the contrary, it was closely related to many other manifestations of a new esthetic culture which summarized the finest achievements of educated Russian society of the period. It is for historians to say whether this blooming of the arts a decade or two before the fall of tsarism signified the supreme fulfillment of the dying nobility and old intelligentsia, the swan song of a condemned society. In any case, Stanislavsky, Nemirovich Danchenko, and their friends belonged to a group of pioneers who rapidly became a compact army. The modernistic movement stirred up creative energy in various areas, and The World of Art group played a particularly important role in the renaissance of visual arts. It included young people who felt that in the trinity consecrated by the liberal intelligentsia—truth, good, and beauty—the last component was disregarded. They initiated a crusade against the utilitarian, materialistic, or social-minded esthetics of a Proudhon or a Chernyshevsky and, in particular, sharply critized the paintings by the "itinerants" who paid more attention to social messages than to color and composition. In 1898, Serghey Diaghilev (1872-1929), a student in the aristocratic Law Institute, launched a magazine The World of Art and proclaimed in his leading article that "new climate and new ideas were born while precious scents were filling the air." This luxuriously produced and illustrated magazine became an event. It challenged academism and naturalism and opened a new window into Europe by introducing to Russian readers the latest artistic trends of the West, from impressionism to French cubism and, to a lesser degree, German expressionism. Each issue contained letters from Paris,

Rome, Munich, and other artistic centers, and articles by foreign contributors; problems of painting, sculpture, architecture, theater, and (at the beginning) literature, were given a large display. Promotion of the latest European fashion in all areas of the arts came along with a passionate exploration of the national past, especially of certain historical periods. *The World of Art* made important discoveries, mainly in the Russian icon and the eighteenth century, and painters such as Benois, Dobuzhinsky, Ostroumova, Somov, Lanceré, and others laid the foundations of what later became the cult of the old St. Petersburg and of Russian romanticism. They also started a whole movement in graphic arts and etching and began a series of beautifully printed monographs and illustrated editions. In 1902 Diaghilev was awarded a prize by the Academy for his book on Levitsky, a painter of the Yekaterina the Great era. The interest in Russia's artistic past opened new horizons for research, and a whole generation of scholars, more or less connected with the group, brought archaeology and art history to unprecedented heights (among them were Grabar, Kondakov, Rostovtsev, Muratov, and many others whose impact was strongly felt even in the post-Revolutionary period) .

In Moscow the members of this group joined hands with Mamontov's operatic enterprises, and also greatly contributed to the promotion of new modern music; Scriabin and later Rachmaninov, Medtner, Stravinsky, and finally Prokofiev came from the same circle. It was through The World of Art group and their friends that modern European music, from Wagner to Debussy, became widely known in Russia and was played at the evenings organized by Nurok and Nouvelle.

The most visible and immediate effect of The World of Art movement was the change it brought into painting. An exhibition organized by Diaghilev established the St. Petersburg group —Benois, Golovin, Somov, Bakst, Ostroumova, Lancére—as well as their Moscow colleagues, Serov, Vrubel, Korovin, Levitan, Maliutin, Kustodiev; and the same Diaghilev brought to Russia canvases by Renoir, Degas, Whistler, and many other modernists.

The various members of the group were much more united by the community of taste than by ideology, but there was also a unity of direction and inspiration in all their efforts, and they were close to unanimous in what they rejected; they all hated provincialism, naturalism, sloppiness of execution, substitution of social righteousness for craft, and replacement of excellence by virtuous intentions. One of the common traits of the new movement was its deep interest in the theater and ballet. In fact, painters and musicians of The World of Art made a very important, although underestimated, contribution to the renovation of theatrical arts in Russia.

We know that the impetus for this change was given by Mamontov who made an appeal to Vasnetsov, Vrubel, and Korovin for the scenery of his operas. This initiated a true revolution in the art of setting and décor: the magnificence of Mamontov's productions startled and delighted the public, and the Imperial Theaters followed suit and gave new luster to their musical and ballet performances. The drama was the last to profit from The World of Art.

At the beginning of its career the Moscow Art Theater, bent on naturalism, centered its attention on the authenticity of objects, furniture, and costumes, and on the replacement of optical illusion by realistic constructions (true windows, columns, and the like). In Chekhovian plays, however, Simov, the accredited painter of the house, helped Stanislavsky and Nemirovich Danchenko in creating a mood, an atmosphere through exact reproduction of environment. He succeeded in building perfect replicas of noblemen's estates of the late eighties with a strong touch of impressionistic devices, including backdrops and flats. (As a painter, however, he was mediocre and lacked originality.) Later began the period of mild stylization and symbolic settings, and The World of Art was called upon. By that time (1908-1910), the members of the group had acquired predominant positions in Russian theater; they imposed their settings, costumes, and make-up as well as their experiments everywhere, and greatly influenced the whole way of production. And while Alexander Golovin made his brilliant sets for the Alexandrinsky and other Imperial theaters, Denisov, Sapunov, Sudeikin, Bakst, Roerich, Benois, Dobuzhinsky, and their friends worked for the Imperial as well as for private stages in St. Petersburg and Moscow—and their disciples invaded the provincial enterprises.

One of the central figures, next to Golovin, in this flourishing of theatrical arts, was Alexander Benois (1876-1960), a painter, an author, a highly educated and cultured man, and a great lover of the stage. After his settings for *Die Götterdämmerung* by Wagner in 1903 and his successes with Diaghilev in Paris and London, he entranced the Russian audiences with his beautiful, highly stylized sets and costumes, mostly in eighteenth century plays (Molière and Goldoni). His refined art brought great changes into the production of ballets in Mariinsky Theater, and he turned Pushkin's little dramatic scenes into one of the most sophisticated performances of the Moscow Art Theater in 1915. Later he did *La Locandiera* by Goldoni for Stanislavsky in the same spirit of extreme elegance and charming taste, and in 1921, the *Queen of Spades*, the last work he staged in Russia before emigrating to France.

Mstislav Dobuzhinsky (1878-1958), whose paintings and drawings evoked the romantic enchantment of St. Petersburg, was greatly responsible for the success of Turgenev's *A Month in the Country*, and he made grim and impressive settings for *The Possessed* by Dostoevsky. Roerich did fantastic sets for Ibsen's *Peer Gynt* (all for the Moscow Art Theater). The best works of the group, however, were produced by Diaghilev, Meyerhold, and Tairov, particularly in opera and ballet. What was later called the Russian contribution to Western scenic art, originated with Mamontov's Opera and the Imperial Theaters and culminated in the renovation of the ballet. It coincided with the decline of Petipa, the undisputed master and choreographer of the Imperial stage, and the influence of Prince Serghey Volkonsky, Director of Imperial Theaters between 1899 and 1902. A man of high culture and exquisite taste, and an admirer of Jacques Dalcroze, the Swiss apostle of new rhythmics, Volkonsky promoted all sorts of reforms in the conservative environment of the Russian ballet, and his successor, V. Teliakovsky, also took a favorable attitude toward modern trends. At the end of the century the young and progressive elements in the ballet gathered around Mikhail Fokine (1880-1942), a fiery dancer and great choreographer of the Mariinsky. He waged a war against the stiffening regulations of classic ballet and introduced a great variety of free movements, either to replace the usual toe dance or to combine with it, and abandoned conventional steps and attitudes inherited from the Italian and French ballet masters. He did not reject the strict training and the scrupulous technique of the Imperial ballet schools, but he brought to them a new inspiration, a major range of means of expression, and an inventiveness of choreography which followed two main trends: naturalness of movements and steps, and stylization of the performance as a whole. Fokine disliked long shows in several acts with large displays of *corps de ballet* and involved plots, similar to the operatic ones, which were so typical of the great nineteenth century ballets (for example, *Swan Lake, The Sleeping Beauty* or *The Enchanted Forest*). He wanted the modern choreographer to choose more limited subjects in time and action and seek dramatic sharpness, plastic unity, and novelty in the very design of the dance. But he especially battled for the harmony among the pictorial, musical, and kinetic components of a show. Rejecting second-rate scores and "occasional" music, he reverted to great classics or modern composers, and his early successes comprised *Chopiniana,* Schumann's *Carnaval,* and *Aragon Chota* by Glinka. He made bold groupings of dancers and suggested steps inspired by the complete use of the body as means of expression, not of legs only as in the conservative ballet. Then came the *Armida's Pavilion* (1907) with Benois' stupendous sets, and experiments in dances with a strong emphasis on the erotic and on the fantastic (Fokine loved Hoffmann and made an adaptation of *Coppelia*). In the Polovetski dances from Borodin's *Prince Igor,* he stunned the audience, accustomed to the orderly routine of Italian pastorales, with wild leaps, barbaric exuberance of exotic folklore. and maddening rhythm of quick steps. The vitality of his choreography, projected against the background of a feast of colors, assured this performance a long life in the Russian ballet.

There is no doubt that Fokine absorbed certain influences from the West, but it must be pointed out in all fairness that Isadora Duncan with her choreography of the bare foot and the naked body, which went back to the Hellenic pattern, was not known in Russia until her appearance there in 1909, long after Fokine's experiments, including the use of lengthened tunics instead of the tutu and the replacement of the "steel toe" by the bare foot.

But the highest affirmation of the Russian ballet and the

fullest blending of music, painting, and dance was achieved by Diaghilev. The editor of *The World of Art* magazine organized exhibitions of art in Russia and abroad (that of 1905 showed Russian portrait painters) and initiated concerts of Russian music from Glinka to Scriabin in Paris. In 1909 he decided to bring Russian dancers and singers to Europe, and succeeded in arranging a series of opera and ballet performances in Paris, which marked a turning point in the history of the Western theater. These performances came as a revelation, as an unexpected discovery of great esthetic impact. The Countess Anne de Noailles, famous French poetess, reports in her memoirs twenty years after the Diaghilev "miracle" that she was late to the first night as she did not expect anything interesting, but the moment she entered her box at the Châtelet Théâtre she understood that this spring evening of 1909 was an extraordinary one, and that the spectacle before her eyes was something she had never seen before, something unbelievable and unique: "Everything that could enchant, inebriate and dominate a spectator was there, gathered on the stage and flourishing as naturally as flowers bloom and open up in some beautiful climate." The word "success" is inadequate to depict the enthusiasm that gripped Diaghilev's audiences during his six-weeks of guest performances in France. A contemporary compared it to a mass psychosis, to a delirium of bliss, to a paroxysm of ecstasy. What seemed quite extraordinary to the critics was the perfect amalgam of pictorial, musical, and dramatic elements of each performance, and the high quality of execution by brilliant and consummate singers, dancers and musicians. Of course, in *Les Sylphides,* this romantic reverie, the Parisians could admire for the first time a dancer who was destined for highest fame—Anna Pavlova. In *Armida's Pavilion,* besides Fokine, choreographer and dancer, they saw the beautiful and accomplished ballerina Tamara Karsavina; and in *Cleopatra,* "a choreographic drama," they saw the sophisticated Ida Rubinstein. The great ballerinas were supported by Mordkin, Bulgakov, and other great soloists—the most outstanding among them Nizhinsky, probably the greatest male dancer of the twentieth century. The whole *corps de ballet* was made up of first-class artists, and the total effect was overwhelming. One should remember that by this time the art of the dance was at its peak in Russia; it had many brilliant representatives, men and women, each with a strong artistic personality, and all endowed with a stupendous technique that no other country in the world could match—the fruit of a century of tradition, enhanced by an enthusiastic eagerness for renovation.

The opera performances were no less remarkable. Not only did *Pskovitianka (The Woman from Pskov)* by Rimsky-Korsakov, or the first act of Glinka's *Ruslan and Liudmila* reveal the freshness of the Russian national school of music, but the singers were quite out of the ordinary and did not resemble the usual Italian tenors and baritones: Fyodor Chaliapin, Russia's greatest basso, was endowed not only with a voice of extraordinary resonance and timbre, but also with a great artistic gift, and every part he sang was acted magnificently. His feminine partner was Lydia Lipkovskaya, an outstanding soprano. Other performers gave evidence of the high level of operatic art in Russia—a fact that truly surprised the French critics. No less astonishing for them was the lavishness of all performances: sets, costumes, and properties were a pure delight to the eye. During the next three years, 1909-1912, Diaghilev's opera and ballet conquered Europe. He added Piscasso, Matisse, Braque, and Cocteau to the staff of his Russian painters and costume designers in the same way as he induced Hindemith or Ravel to join Stravinsky, Prokofiev, and the older Russian composers. At the beginning his triumph was mainly due to The World of Art group and their friends. After the Revolution and until his death in 1929, Diaghilev continued to be in the center of Western ballet and opera; although his company was 90 per cent Russian—including Nizhinsky and his sister Bronislava, a brilliant choreographer, Karsavina, Mordkin, Miassin, Romanov, Danilova, Balanchin, Lifar, and others— he surrounded himself with the most outstanding French painters and composers and poets, and his enterprise turned into an international affair. Its impact became world-wide, and while it affirmed the glory of Russian artistic genius abroad, it stopped being an active factor in the development of the arts in the USSR. Thus began a tragic separation between the *émigrés* and their colleagues who remained in their native country. Because of Diaghilev, most famous Russian artists, including almost the whole of The World of Art group, found themselves outside of

Russia in the twenties, and next to them were other important figures who were not associated with the "king of the ballet," such as the ballerinas of the old school, Kshessinskaya, Yegorova, Trefilova, Spesivtseva and others. Whatever Russia owed to Europe in the performing arts was now paid back with generous interest by Diaghilev and by all the *émigrés* who became teachers and propagators of the achievements of their country. Diaghilev established a tradition of the Russian ballet and opera in Europe and America, and his influence was lasting and profound. In a way, it revolutionized the methods of production everywhere, particularly in terms of sets, costumes, décor, libretto, and the synchronization of music, dance, painting, and architecture.

In the first phase of Diaghilev's activities, Alexander Benois played a leading role with his settings for *Armida's Pavilion, Les Sylphides,* and *Gisèle* (1919, 1924, 1927, respectively) and Stravinsky's *Petrushka,* presented with a décor which evoked the old St. Petersburg. In 1923 Benois left Russia and again offered his settings to Diaghilev, for the Paris Grand Opera, and for London's Covent Garden. His *Coq d'Or* is probably the best example of his art which united eighteenth century grace and oriental splendor of colors in an amazing equilibrium. His sense of proportion enabled him to stop lavishness before it became ostentation, and stylization before it lapsed into abstractness. Some critics called this refined artist "a Westerner with a Russian soul."

Not less important was Leon Bakst (1866-1924), also a member of The World of Art. Not being able as a Jew to get a residence permit in St. Petersburg, he went to Paris where he provided Diaghilev with dazzling sets and costumes. There was an oriental, almost barbaric prodigality in his pictorial excesses or in his bright, sometimes blinding, tone contrasts. The richness of *Sheherazade* or the fantastic impressionism of *Daphnis and Chloe* matched the inventiveness of *The Spectre of the Rose* (1911) in which Nizhinsky excelled in his prodigious leaps and turns, and which owed its sensational success to Bakst's stunning choice of colors: the Spectre, in red, appeared in a white room and flew out through a green window. In *Saint Sebastian* he had Ida Rubinstein appear with a bow twice as big as herself. He liked strange accessories: a tray for the giants brought in by dwarfs, headdresses for the dancers three times bigger than the usual ones, a horseman in white on a white steed against background of violently bright sets, etc.

Alexander Golovin provided Diaghilev with sets and costumes for *The Firebird* and other ballets including the famous *Afternoon of a Faun,* the first showing of which in Paris provoked violent fights between its enemies and defenders. Golovin's pictorial luxuriousness was, however, quite different from that of Bakst. It had a more classical touch with a predilection for eighteenth century splendor and, at times, with a definite flavor of national Russian, even folkloristic, tradition.

After the 1917 Revolution, Diaghilev went very much beyond the circle of his former The World of Art friends and made an appeal to the younger generation. Cubists, futurists, and surrealists became his close associates, and he approached representatives of the French school headed by Picasso, Braque, Leger, and Matisse, and the Russians who had been working previously with Meyerhold or Tairov. Among the latter were Boris Anisfeld, Yuri Annenkov, and particularly Natalia Goncharova and Mikhail Larionov. Goncharova made the memorable *Little Wedding (Svadebka)* a work of rare taste and daring stylization, and Larionov, *The Jester (Shut),* a piece of strange inventiveness, both considered milestones in Russian post-Revolutionary scenic art. All the works of those painters who had freshly emigrated from Russia reflected the trends which prevailed in Soviet *avant-garde* theaters in the twenties.

I I

It has been said that the history of the Moscow Art Theater can be divided into clear-cut periods. The first, marking its greatest achievements and most fertile activity, comprised the two decades between its foundation and the 1917 Revolution; after that, it became almost silent for five years and lived on its previously accumulated capital, marking time and taking initiative in new forms only outside of its walls. After its trip abroad (1922-1924) a transformation took place, and since 1925-1926 it has tried to fall in step with the development of Soviet society, adding contemporary plays to its well-preserved old repertory, but ceasing to be a source of new inspiration. In the thirties, it became a sort of National Academy, a well-established and glorious institution, a citadel of psychological realism, offering an example of accomplished craft but having nothing new to say. Those who have seen plays produced by the Moscow Art Theater in the Soviet Union and noticed its conservatism can hardly imagine how alive it was fifty years ago. However, even during its best period it was much more attracted by the idea of perfecting its acquisitions than by traveling unknown roads. It is true that Stanislavsky experimented with various plays as far as repertory went, paying tribute to the social drama with Gorky and to symbolism with Andreyev and Maeterlinck. But both Stanislavsky and Nemirovich Danchenko agreed that their enterprise should not become a laboratory in new scenic forms, and that sheer experimentation should be taken outside of the theater itself. Thus in 1905, when Stanislavsky was particularly yearning for change, he decided to establish workshops for free experimentation. Originally his project dealt with the training of young actors destined to go later to the provincial stage and to spread the good word throughout the country. But he also wanted to try out plays which for some reason or another did not fit into the regular repertory. The workshop was called "Studio" and was given quarters in Pozharskaya Street. The direction of the Studio was entrusted to Meyerhold.

Karl Theodore Kazimir Meyergold, born in 1874 into a Lutheran family of German-Jewish extraction, became a Greek Orthodox in 1895 and took the name of Vsevolod Meyerhold. As a young man he became very interested in the theater, and in 1896 entered the drama class of the Moscow Philharmonic under Nemirovich Danchenko. Later he became a member of the Moscow Art Theater company; he played Treplev in *The Sea Gull* and other parts, without great success. He admired Stanislavsky and carried this love throughout his life despite many differences of opinion which separated him from the elder director. In 1902 he left the company, formed his own group, and went on the road acting in and producing plays by Ibsen, Maeterlinck, and Hauptmann. By that time, his taste and opinions were already formed: he was an antirealist, greatly attracted by symbolism and experimentation, and in politics he was a revolutionist of the socialist and populist brand. Tall and lanky, with sharp mobile face, deep-set eyes, and large sensitive mouth, he gave the impression of tense force. Propelled by sanguine temperament but able to channel his energy, Meyerhold could work like a maniac, and there was something of a sacred madness in his devotion to ideas, his love of abstraction and the intransigent, almost dogmatic way he sought to translate his theories into reality. What made him a difficult person was a combination of cold logic with a sort of furor, of clear intelligence with passionate fancy, and his capacity for constant change, for leaps from one experiment to another. Already in 1905 Stanislavsky apparently felt that his former actor was an extraordinary man and he asked Meyerhold to direct the Studio. But he underestimated Meyerhold's originality and extremism.

At that point, Stanislavsky was worried by the recent failure of Maeterlinck's one-act plays in the Moscow Art Theater, and he wondered whether some new scenic forms were necessary for their successful production. It was agreed that Meyerhold would work on *The Death of Tentagiles*. At the first meeting of the group it became clear that Meyerhold's interpretation of a new search went beyond the limits assigned by Stanislavsky. Meyerhold was firmly convinced of the futility of theatrical naturalism, and he was highly disrespectful toward realism and quoted Voltaire: *"Le secret d'être ennuyeux, c'est tout dire"* (The secret of being boring is to say everything). Enemy of detail, Meyerhold experimented with stylization: an oversized bed with an enormous canopy to represent a king's bedroom; a huge canvas across half the stage to form the setting of a painter's studio; several identical arbors painted green to suggest *bosquets* in which identically dressed girls sew the same kind of ribbon with an ivory needle, were to him an image of the eighteenth century.

In general, Meyerhold wanted the decorative principle to become the determining factor of a performance. Later, this formed the main problem: most of the *avant-garde* directors, headed by Meyerhold, maintained that a show was to be organized esthetically, and that this was the sole objective of any production. The actor was but a part of a pattern, and his acting was actually absorbed by the setting. Yet at the same time, Meyerhold dreamt in 1905-1906 of a "spiritual theater" and, in his opinion, the esthetic principle of scenic organization had to serve a higher purpose: "The time has come," he affirmed, "to attempt to stage the unreal, to render life as perceived in fantasy and visions." He tried to materialize these vague aspirations through hints and impressionistic devices. But what he did with *The Death of Tentagiles* and *Schluck and Jau* (by Hauptmann) left the spectators cold and disappointed Stanislavsky. Meyerhold used a background of ornamental flats and simple canvases, and accompanied the action by music. But his whole performance had a tendency to become a pantomime: "Word is but a design on the fabric of movement," he maintained. His actors, with their cold precise diction and well-organized gestures, had solely plastic value. For Stanislavsky this meant the elimination of the live actor and the transformation of the performance into a panoramic picture entirely determined by a dictatorial director. The difference in ideologies produced an inevitable clash between Meyerhold and Stanislavsky, and the Studio on Pozharskaya Street was closed. Meyerhold tried to organize his Society of New Drama and then was invited to the theater owned by Vera Kommissarzhevskaya.

Stanislavsky, however, did not abandon his idea of a workshop. A few years later when his System took on a definite shape, he wanted to test it in an enterprise where it could be in full operation. The latter was hardly possible within the Moscow Art Theater itself because Nemirovich Danchenko and the actors, although following the principles of Stanislavsky's theory, were often opposed to its application. Nemirovich Danchenko rallied definitely to the Stanislavsky's System around 1911 and applied it to the production of Tolstoy's *Resurrection* (an adaptation of the novel). At first, Stanislavsky sent his friend and pupil, Sullerzhitsky, to teach the System in the private dramatic school of Adashev, and then in 1911, began the planning of a workshop. A year later, always with the help of Sullerzhitsky, an excellent group of young men and women connected with the Moscow Art Theater gathered in a small place on Tverskaya Street. It was later called The First Studio of the Moscow Art Theater, and both Stanislavsky and Nemirovich Danchenko made speeches at its opening. The latter dwelt on the importance of intuition, and this warmed up the heart of Sullerzhitsky, who had been appointed the manager of the new venture. "All my life," said this devoted follower of Stanislavsky, "I hated reason when it tried to be the boss, but it can be an excellent servant if one learns how to use it." When somebody asked him whether Stanislavsky's System would not harm a talented artist because of its reliance on intelligence, Sullerzhitsky replied: "When they say that Mr. X. is wrong because his intelligence overcomes his talent or vice versa, I am inclined to surmise that he has neither intelligence nor talent." The members of the Studio had both, and they showed it. Among them were such great figures as Evgeny Vakhtangov, who immediately became a teacher and a leader, and Mikhail Chekhov, the nephew of the writer, while others, such as Gregory Khmara, Nikolay Kolin, Serafima Birman, and Boris Sushkevich, turned later into important actors and directors.

At the end of January 1913, the Studio presented *The Shipwreck of "Hope"* by Herman Heyermans, a Dutch playwright, to a select audience headed by Benois, Stanislavsky, Nemirovich Danchenko, and senior members of the Moscow Art Theater company. This was the first product of the workshop and, for Stanislavsky, who had supervised all the preparatory work, it was a test of his System, and he attributed to its merits the resounding success of the performance. Nemirovich Danchenko said he had the sensation of being at the christening of a son or a daughter of the Moscow Art Theater; the older generation of directors and actors felt that they had found their successors.

The play related the story of an old ship sent to sea, despite its poor condition, by a greedy owner who wants to collect the insurance. *Hope* sinks with all its crew, and in the fishing village, women and girls mourn their sons, husbands, and lovers. The main idea of the production was that simple fishermen, close to nature and away from the corruption of big cities, preserve their souls, while greedy acquirers lose theirs. This drama of covetousness and grief was staged as a page of life, each character being interpreted as a psychological portrait. Richard Boleslavsky, a handsome energetic man and a good actor, directed the play. He was less fanatical about the System than some of his companions and counterbalanced their excessive "depth of emotional experience" by a vivid sense of showmanship and by a youthful joy of creation. His zest for life and his love for the stage were truly infectious. On the other hand, Stanislavsky and Sullerzhitsky never missed the opportunity of stressing the importance of the "inner circle," of "emotional concentration," and other requirements of the System. Some members of the Studio joked about Sullerzhitsky's desire to create some sort of a theatrical monastery, but they were all impressed by his feeling of moral responsibility and his ideal of discipline and integrity. One can say that both Stanislavsky and Sullerzhitsky developed among their pupils the idea of artistic service and of the actor's moral mission, which greatly influenced the younger generation and kept the artistic standards in Russia far above the average.

There is no doubt that the Studio and its members became instrumental in spreading the Stanislavsky System in Russia and abroad (Boleslavsky, Kolin, and Chekhov later emigrated). But the evolution of the workshop led it away from its mother institution, and most talented actors such as Vakhtangov, Chekhov, Kolin, Diky, and others, deviated from the initial direction and went their own highly individual ways.

Vakhtangov soon became the central figure of the workshop. Evgeny Vakhtangov, born in 1883 in the Caucasus, son of a tobacco grower, broke with his family and came to Moscow in his early twenties to enroll in the university and dramatic schools. His love of the theater was not the usual infatuation of a young man, but a real passion. He later became a good actor, especially as a parodist, but he was first of all an illuminating and impassioned teacher and director. During his short career (1911-1922) he shaped with his word and example hundreds of people and created a whole following which preserved for decades a true cult of this extraordinary man, who was simultaneously a "pure heart" and the "leader image." By this time, the Stanislavsky System had gone from external to spiritual realism, to a search for expression of the most refined and invisible emotions. In 1913-1915 this "spiritual realism" was often tainted by Tolstoyan tendencies, including a negative attitude toward the upper classes and capitalist reality, affirmation of man's moral resurrection, pacifism, and belief in the forces of love and brotherhood. Vakhtangov was strongly attracted by these ideas, although he was much more conscious of political problems of the day: in 1905 he joined the Socialist-Revolutionist Party, and sympathized with its doctrine until his death. He was inclined to emphasize the forces which prevent man from becoming good, and this led him to the concept of the two worlds, that of live souls and that of dead puppets, and he put them into each of his performances. He believed that the Workshop had to have an idea, an end, outside of the sphere of art, and therefore he did not agree with the art for art's sake theory. "There should not be a performance," he said, "without answering what the performance is for, what purpose it fulfills."

In 1914, the Studio moved to a new locale. Performances open to the public were given in a room where the seats were elevated in front of a stage without proscenium or footlights. The actors moved very close to the spectators but were supposed to pretend not to see the audience and not to care about it. The next hit of the Studio was *The Cricket on the Hearth,* an adaptation of Dickens's tale by Boris Sushkevich, a solid, rational, and controlled director. It was probably the highest attainment of the workshop and the most spectacular theatrical event of the 1914 season. It expressed Sullerzhitsky's dream of a performance filled with "the love of mankind" and compassion for the "little man." It had sentimental, intimate qualities mitigated by humor, it radiated the warm hope in man and the victory of goodness over cruelty and greed and, at the same time, it presented characters on the verge of the grotesque, without fear of exaggeration. This was actually a step toward "theatricality," enhanced by the introduction of a "reader" or "commentator" (acted by Sullerzhitsky). Chekhov as the plumber and Vakhtangov as Tackleton gave a new tone to the whole performance. *The Cricket on the Hearth* became a favorite with the Russians and an organic part of national repertory.

In December 1916, Vakhtangov showed *The Flood* by Henning Berger, a drama depicting a group of people caught by a torrential rain in a cellar bar; they believe that there is no escape from the flood and that they all face imminent death. The money-grabbing Beer, the bankrupt Frazer, the shyster O'Neill, the prostitute Lizzie, the unemployed actor, the unsuccessful inventor—all feel united before death. All social barriers are knocked down and misfortune brings forth the human feelings of the stranded companions. In the second act, the purification through love is accomplished, they are united in truth and march toward death hand-in-hand. But this spiritual transformation is only an illusion; and in the third act when they learn that there is no more danger, everything comes back: vice, greed, meanness, and hatred. The psychological changes of protagonists offered, of course, great possibilities for actors. Vakhtangov and Chekhov, for instance, alternated in the role of Frazer, the bankrupt broker. Vakhtangov presented him as a man at the end of his tether, resigned to ultimate defeat. Chekhov, on the contrary, showed a man who was agitated by a sort of inner tremor, and while drowning never lost his fighting spirit and the hope to float again to the surface.

The excellence of the acting was not the main merit of *The Flood*. Vakhtangov appeared in it as a director of genius. He knew how to achieve a complete fusion between interpretation of characters and scenic devices, and he subordinated the whole performance to his own idea of human nature. This gave unity to the play in the sense of what he called "spiritualized realism," but it was in truth a particular form of expressionism. Each part had sharp, slightly exaggerated contours, and every means of communication, every stage detail was carefully determined by the main idea. A year later, the same principle inspired *Twelfth Night* directed by Kolin (under Stanislavsky's supervision). The beautiful Olga Baklanova played Olivia; Boleslavsky, Sir Toby; Kolin, Malvolio. The whole play was interpreted as a challenge to boredom and pessimism, as an explosion of gaiety and free spirit. It was shown to the public in December 1917, in the midst of the revolutionary upheaval, and at this moment, the First Studio was confronted with new tasks and problems.

III

One of the determining factors in the life of the theater in Russia between 1906 and 1925 was the role of symbolism. For twenty years symbolists reigned in poetry, greatly influenced prose, and tried to reform the drama.

The actual number of plays offered in those years by Russian symbolists was rather limited, but this was compensated for by

Western production. Andreyev, of course, headed the list. Fyodor Sologub, (1863-1927) an exquisite poet and a typical decadent, had his *Hostages of Life* staged by the Alexandrinsky in 1913 and obtained a certain success by the dramatic adaptation of his *Little Demon,* an outstanding novel in Gogolian tradition. His more poetic and less popular pieces, *Nocturnal Dances, Vanka the Butler and the Page Jean,* were produced for limited audiences by *avant-garde* directors, such as Evreinov. *Famira-Kifared (Thamira of the Cither),* a "Bacchic tragedy" by Innokenty Annensky (1855-1909), one of the symbolist masters, was produced by Tairov in 1916 as a "satyr's drama." The contributions to the repertory by the leaders of the symbolist movement, Vyacheslav Ivanov and Valery Briussov, were almost nonexistent; (Prokofiev, however, made an opera out of Briussov's novel *The Angel of Fire).* Alexander Blok wrote for the theater, but his lyrical dramas were very seldom offered on the boards. The scarcity of repertory was not, however, proportionate to the real influence of symbolism on Russian theater. Not only were all the plays by European symbolists constantly shown throughout the country, but symbolist overtones were widely spread in works by minor Russian dramatists, even if they were classified as realists. The experiments by *avant-garde* directors were all inextricably connected with symbolism. The whole artistic atmosphere in Russian educated society after the failure of the 1905 revolutionary movement was permeated with symbolism and estheticism. Sociologists believe in the causal connection between this period of political depression (1906-1914) and the success of decadent and purely esthetic "art for art's sake" trends. It is, however, impossible to dismiss as escapism the whole direction of artistic life in Russia, as well as in Europe, during the first decade of the century. Whatever the national characteristics of the movement in Russia after 1906, it belonged to a much larger antirealistic current. And particularly in the theater, the most interesting and freshest innovations were definitely antinaturalistic and directed against academic realism. In the fourth issue of *The World of Art* magazine, Briussov attacked the Moscow Art Theater and reproached it for "the unnecessary faithfulness to life." "Imitation of nature," he wrote, "is a means but not an end of art. Theater that simply aims at accurate rendering of reality is meant for people with little imagination. Art is inevitably determined by a set of conditions and patterns. The stage, with all its limitations and its three walls is basically conventional. We must bring to it a set of consciously established esthetic conventions, and the theater should take them for granted." After 1906, discussions about the direction and character of theatrical art assumed extraordinary width and intensity in general and in the specialized press, as well as in numerous public debates. It coincided with the predominance of the symbolists and their allies in criticism. In fact, they replaced the sociological publicists almost everywhere and were instrumental in shaping the esthetic opinions of Russian educated society, not only in big cities but also in the provincial periphery. But aside from the general bent toward stylization and experimentation, the leaders of the "new wave" failed to agree about the most burning issues of the scenic art. In particular, they sharply disagreed about specifics and about the relationship between a play as a literary phenomenon and its theatrical embodiment.

Yuli Aikhenwald, a popular lecturer and impressionistic critic, provoked a tempest around 1910 by his "negation of the theater." He affirmed that since a play was a work of literature, the theater could but illustrate it, and the stage, therefore, was as good as a book with pictures. According to Aikhenwald a discriminating person prefers to read a play in the solitude of his room where he can give free rein to his imagination; for in a performance, which is a coarse materialization, a poetic image is reduced to a limited corporeal form. However genuine the theatrical attempts to overcome matter, the latter always triumphs because every production deals with objects and human concreteness. Besides, the teamwork of actors kills creativity: the latter is an individual act, and collective creativity does not exist. God is alone, and He never had assistants for His creation—He did not need them. An actor has no creative initiative as long as he is compelled to repeat other people's words. And this brings us to the analysis of the substance of a performance. Each art has its own medium of expression. Literature uses words; music, sounds; dance, movements; painting, line and colors. But the theater is a hybrid, and is compelled to combine literature, music, painting, architecture, dance; what it offers is necessarily fictitious and ephemeral. It can exist only if supported by other arts, and its effectiveness depends on the quality of a mixture concocted by its directors, actors, and painters. One may ask what is the best definition of theater, but perhaps the answer is that it lacks its own proper substance.

The resonance of this extremist attitude was amplified by the fact that it had been launched by somebody who for years held the job of theatrical reviewer in leading monthlies and dailies. Aikhenwald's opponents, such drama critics as Kugel, Efros, Lunacharsky, and others, claimed that theatrical syncretism is a great asset, and that the fusion of esthetic forms, far from being a mark of weakness, explains the appeal and the lasting influence of the stage. Some symbolists, headed by Vyacheslav Ivanov, suggested that the modern theater be brought back to its religious origins and promote "choral art of congregate action" as an expression of national and spiritual culture. Ivanov's "temple theater" envisioned a breaking away from the contemplation and passivity of the audience and dreamt of the union of spectators, actors, dancers, and choruses in "a common ecstasy." The Greek theater was offered as an example of this Dyonisian drama. Ideas of Nietzsche and Wagner were avidly discussed in theatrical foyers. Some mystical-minded actors and writers spoke of ballet and dance as "prayer and liturgy" which bring the spectators closer to divinity. Sologub advanced the theory of "active audiences" and their "collective creation" which, in his opinion, as well as in that of many of his friends, would abolish the footlights and all the other barriers between the stage and the spectators.

On the other hand, Sologub suggested that the author (or a reader as his substitute) be brought into each performance to read all the remarks and descriptions of settings. The actors would be assigned to recite the dialogue, interrupted by the author's comments. To sustain this proposal, Sologub's followers quoted Goethe who believed that listening with closed eyes to a simple nondeclamatory reading of Shakespeare was the best way to enjoy and to appreciate his tragedies and comedies.

No less heated was the controversy dealing with the respective functions of actors and directors. The variety of opinions among the representatives of the *avant-garde,* Meyerhold, Tairov, Kommissarzhevsky, Evreinov, ranged from the support of dictatorial "single will' to the "dematerialization" of the actor and his replacement by a human puppet. The only thing, however, in which everybody concurred was the rejection of fake or make-believe and the acceptance of theatrical "conditionalism" or conventions. This attitude was strengthened by what the Russians found in European scenic theory and practice. Georg Fuchs, of the Munich Art Theater, questioned in his books (*Die Schau-buehne der Zukunft,* 1899, and *Die Revolution des Thaters,* 1909) even the physical arrangements of theaters inherited from the Renaissance, and recommended, among other things, the return to the arena and amphitheater performance. He also warned against the identification of theater with literature and sociology: "You see Ibsen's *A Doll's House* and you discuss the problem of feminine emancipation instead of evaluating the play as a dramatic and esthetic phenomenon." The Russians were also attracted by the three-dimensional sculpturesque settings and geo-metrical designs made by the Swiss, Adolphe Appia, who treated a stage as an architectural problem. Work by Jacques Copeau, Charles Dullin, Firmin Gemier, and other French innovators also pointed away from the academic theater. Wagner's operas were interpreted either as expressions of universal myth in folk-lore or manifestations of a deep religious feeling, and their criti-cism by Nietzsche also had a large resonance. The endeavors of Isadora Duncan to restore Greek dances and choruses, and Max Reinhardt's showing of *Oedipus Rex* in a circus provoked great interest in Russia. And finally, the two-fold aspect of Gordon Craig's theories strongly impressed the leading Moscow and St. Petersburg directors. They often quoted this passage from Craig's *The Mask* (1908) : "The actor must go, and in his place must come the inanimate figure, the 'super-marionette.' " The symbol-ists also liked Craig's belief in theater as an expression of the mystical essence of the world, the latter being translated symbol-ically as the spirit of the play; (for instance, he suggested that for *Macbeth,* instead of elaborate settings, there should be just a rock and mist) . While Fuchs spoke of the actor's body as the bearer of rhythm, Craig found it too fortuitous and unreliable, too subject to incidents and accidents, and his verdict was cate-gorical: The human body and the human face are but inferior means of communication. The ancient world and the Eastern civilizations knew it too well and therefore used masks and pup-pets as higher theatrical material.

All these ideas, in their pure or altered form, were set into practice by various theatrical enterprises between 1906 and 1917, and their effects were widely felt in the Soviet era.

IV

One of the earliest and most important experimental ventures of the period was the theater established by Vera Kommissarzhevskaya, the great Russian actress. In a way, she was not only the promoter of the symbolist theater, but its poetic image and the emblem of the times. Innumerable devotees adored her as the high priestess of new art, and no other Russian star of the twentieth century has wielded such power over audiences. Legends have been created around this fragile little woman who was herself like a flame, and knew how to inflame others. Like Anna Pavlova, her contemporary, she appeared a superior being, who could easily transcend the law of gravity and the weight of matter.

Daughter of a prominent opera singer and sister of Fyodor, a leading theater director, Vera Kommissarzhevskaya (1864-1910) was brought up in an environment of writers, composers, and artists. Married at nineteen to Count Muraviev, a painter, she separated from him two years later, and never had a satisfactory personal life. She acted as Betsy in Stanislavsky's production of Tolstoy's *Fruits of Enlightenment* in 1891, and then went on the road with provincial companies (Sinelnikov in 1893, Nezlobin in 1894-1896). She began with small parts in comedies and vaudeville, and gradually acquired a varied experience (she played more than one hundred parts in five years); but she did not become known until she devoted herself to serious dramatic roles, mostly those of sophisticated and suffering young women. She was not pretty, but her mobile, slightly irregular and extremely expressive face had a charm all its own, and there was grace and strength in her slim, frail figure. This is how a contemporary described her stage appearance: "Her wide-open, deep, and sad blue eyes fixed the spectator, and there was a silent question in them. Her low melodious voice, vibrating like a string, pulled you away from this world of misery, promising the solution of all problems but never fulfilling the promise, stirring, moving, disturbing. Her spell was like witchcraft, and enchanted spectators deposited their love at her feet. Her acting went beyond art, revealing a live, tormented soul." "I have a sick soul," she wrote, "and I am burning it from both ends in order not to feel eternal pain." All her audiences sensed that pain, and some critics saw in it an unconscious foreboding of the disaster which was awaiting the doomed Russia. In any case, hundreds of thousands responded enthusiastically to her impersonations, particularly the university youth for whom she became an idol. But fame did not come to her easily. She was thirty when she finally gained recognition, and she spent long years of doubt searching for her own identity and adequate means of artistic expression. It has been often stated that Kommissarzhevskaya always played herself, and that this extreme subjectivity was her asset as well as her handicap. Her professional training was long and varied, she never shrank from parts imposed upon her by directors, and showed that the range of her impersonations was quite wide. But there is no doubt that she reached the height of her art only when she brought to life the image of a unhappy, searching, and sensitive woman—in other words, when she portrayed herself. Her acting was breathtaking when she appeared as a slightly morbid, restless creature, languishing in the prison of trivialities and dreaming a marvelous escape into a heaven of light and perfection. On such occasions, her audiences went through a memorable experience of shattering truth and intensity. Not each performance, however, was of the same caliber. She was often uneven, sometimes pale and weak, and she could not display every evening the same miraculous self-identification with her part.

Kommissarzhevskaya often portrayed with great success gay, simple-minded girls, but she was at her best in highly dramatic, even tragic, parts. As a person of poetic temperament and rare sensitivity, she was hardly ever satisfied with what existence offered her, and she constantly looked for something she was not able to define. On the stage, she continued her relentless inner dialogue, and her intonations with notes of despair, the inflections of her breaking voice, the gestures of her small hands, and the brisk motions of her body—all the tense aura around her plunged her audience into a state resembling a mystical trance. What made so remarkable her impersonations of Ibsen heroines, for example, Nora of *A Doll's House,* Hedda Gabler, Hilda of

The Master Builder, or Sonia in *Uncle Vanya,* was the way she used the text as if it were only an excerpt from some long confession; she seemed always to be alluding to a "sub- or super-text." She gave the impression that what one saw and heard on the stage was not a complete revelation of the personage, and that there was much more to it, hidden and hinted at. Basically an actress of symbolist techniques, she elevated into symbolic significence the most prosaic and realistic dramas. In this way, she instilled new life into old plays. In *Without Dowry* her Larissa, depicted by Ostrovsky as a gypsylike girl brought up in disorderly and not too virtuous surroundings, did not resemble a bit the image fixed traditionally by such great realistic actresses as Fedotova, Yermolova, and Savina. Kommissarzhevskaya created a new Larissa, a nature of idealistic purity pitted against hypocritical bourgeois morality, suffering from vulgarity and injustice. In the third act, when she sang an Italian air by Tosti, she revealed Larissa's solitude, her unhappy love, her desperate fate, bringing tears to the eyes of the spectators. Since then, all Russian actresses sing this song. The provincial girl she impersonated grew into a great figure of sacrifice and love of freedom.

In 1896, Kommissarzhevskaya was invited to join the company of the Alexandrinsky. She stayed there six years and excelled in many roles. The theater-goers could never forget her Marguerite in *Faust* (January 1899) ; the scene in prison was astonishing in its tragic force and psychological nuances—remarkable for emotional restraint and complete avoidance of tricks or exaggeration. Rosie, in *The Battle of Butterflies* by Hermann Sudermann, Hilda in *The Master Builder,* and Nina in the unsuccessful first version of *The Sea Gull,* also belonged to her best interpretations.

Despite her growing popularity, Kommissarzhevskaya felt that her artistic freedom was limited by the rules and regulations of the Imperial stage, and she resigned in 1902 from the Alexandrinsky, thus breaking what was considered a brilliant career. After twelve performances in the Suvorin Theater, which brought about a true delirium on the part of the public, she went on the road to make money for her own theater. Known as Kommissarzhevskaya Theater, it opened in 1904 in St. Petersburg in one locale, and then two years later moved to another on Officers Street. Her brother Fyodor acted as director and producer, and at the beginning Kommissarzhevskaya, who sympathized with the radical intelligentsia, played in Gorky's dramas (*The Vacationists* and *The Children of the Sun*). She also presented to the public dramas by young writers, Chirikov and Yushkevich, and showed her great interest in the symbolists. The search for new forms made her turn to Meyerhold, and in 1906 she engaged him as director of her enterprise. Symbolist writers, modernist painters, *avant-garde* composers, made the house on Officers Street their home, and it became the center of the leftist movement in the arts. Each performance caused violent discussions and even scandals. Some prejudiced spectators became so incensed against this "mad senseless theater" that they even opposed such innocent reforms in it as the division of orchestra seats in even and odd numbers. But the followers of new trends and the youth, particularly university, conservatory, and art students, gave all their support, not only to regular performances, but also to Saturday special evenings (recitals of poems, separate dramatic scenes, modern music).

Meyerhold, who came to the Kommissarzhevskaya Theater after his rift with the Moscow Art Theater, found himself in a friendly atmosphere. Here he was given the opportunity to put into practice all his ideas of a nonrealistic theater. Forging ahead with his customary passion, he simply failed to notice that Kommissarzhevskaya was not only the owner of the theater, but also a great actress who wanted to perform in congenial parts and not simply attract audiences by the magic of her name. It must be granted that whatever Meyerhold did, it was daring and significant, even though not always understood and accepted by the public. On the first night of *Hedda Gabler,* chosen for the opening on November 10, 1906, the new curtain by Bakst, representing a Greek temple and a sphinx (symbol of religious sources of art and of Eastern wisdom) was pulled aside, and the spectators were confronted with an antirealistic production. *Hedda Gabler* was built on the principle of correspondence between moods and colors, so dear to the hearts of French symbolists. Each character had his own color and a fixed set of gestures. A contemporary described it as follows: "The stage seemed filled with bluish-green-silver mist. The background was blue. On the right side, a huge transom, the whole height of the stage, represented a window. Underneath stuck out the leaves of a black rhododendron. Outside the window, the air was greenish-blue. In the last act, the twinkling of stars pierced the bluish mist. On the left, the whole wall was occupied by a huge tapestry representing a silvery gold woman with a deer. Silver lace decorated the top and the wings of the stage. Greenish-blue carpet covered the floor. The furniture, including a grand piano, was white. Green-white vases held large white chrysanthemums. White furs were thrown over a strangely shaped sofa, on which Hedda reclined—in a sea-watery green dress. It shimmered and flowed at her every movement, and she resembled a sea serpent with shiny scales." Other performances of modern plays were organized in a different key, presenting various aspects of production and forming exciting chapters in the history of the Russian stage. But critics doubted whether all this prodigality of inventiveness and decor was helpful to the "intense acting" to which Kommissarzhevskaya was accustomed.

Meyerhold's technical innovations were consistent with his general outlook. He abolished the "stage in depth" and replaced it by a "scenic platform," he brought the backstage closer to the *avant* scene. The movements and attitudes of actors were determined by the concept of a bas-relief. And since the aim of the director was not to convey concrete individual feelings, but purified "extracts" of emotions, purged from naturalistic vestiges, actors had to fit into the general picture, to become part of a visual unit. They were trained to talk in a monotonous recitative keyed to three *leit* notes (leading notes), and moved slowly, rhythmically in what resembled a ritualistic procession. Most of Meyerhold's productions were staged on one level, on a narrow band closed in the back by decorative screens. Flat canvases often replaced all settings. It was obvious that Meyerhold tried to bring his stylization as close as possible to the main lines of a puppet show, externally, at least. His more profound aim was to convey the feeling of fate and to provoke the "shudder of mystery." In that sense *The Death of Tentagiles* was a model play: the sisters who try to save their little brother Tentagiles do not know why he has to perish, they are fighting against unknown forces—the Old Woman who might be Death or Mother Earth, or the Invisible King, or the Heavy Door which is inexorably shut behind the victims. The pre-ordained order of the Christian God coincides here with the Fate of the ancients. And the whole drama can be summarized by the French nursery rhyme: *Les petites marionettes font, font, font leurs trois petits tours et puis s'en vont* (the marionettes make, make, make their three little turns and then are gone).

Pelléas and Mélisande was interpreted as a fairy tale. Settings were childishly simple; the king's tower was just a frame covered with gray paper. Kommissarzhevskaya, as the princess of the blond tresses, acted as if she were in a dream, walking with open innocent eyes in the midst of jealousy, blood, and the grim inevitability of injustice and death, but the abstractness of the whole production limited her acting.

Meyerhold's experiments stirred curiosity and gave vast material for discussion, and partly for imitation and adaptation by milder followers or pseudo enemies, but they failed to captivate the general public. They seemed too sophisticated and transcendental. Besides, they systematically reduced acting to such a strict pattern that the personality of Kommissarzhevskaya was definitely sacrificed.

The only play in which the inventiveness of the director matched the creativity of the leading lady was *Sister Beatrice,* also by Maeterlinck, with music by Liadov and settings by Sudeikin. It is the story of a nun who falls in love with a prince and elopes from her convent. The statue of the Virgin stepped down from her pedestal to take the place of the fugitive and to hide her sin. After many years, suffering and disappointed in earthly love, Beatrice came back to her convent, and the Virgin returns as a statue to her recess. Nobody notices the change, and Beatrice, who had felt like a criminal and expected severe punishment, could lead a peaceful life and die as a saint surrounded by loving companions.

This miracle play (see also *Notre Dame des Epines Fleuries* by the French romantic, Charles Nodier), was set by Meyerhold in blue, green, and gray. Contrary to the individualization of the crowd, practiced by the Moscow Art Theater, he treated groups of nuns like choruses who stepped down from church murals of the Middle Ages. Identically dressed, making identical sober gestures, they moved like a unit and formed a pictorial background. Other groups also had pictorial or statuesque quality.

In the second act, that of the miracle, the stage was brilliantly lit, and the Virgin seemed to irradiate light, her brocade robe shone through the gauze, while a sonorous voice addressed a crowd of beggars and cripples off stage.

Kommissarzhevskaya was extraordinary as the Virgin and Sister Beatrice. In a red-brown torn dress, prostrated on the stone floor before the statue of her guardian, she told, in a poignant monologue the story of her failings and pains, the eternal story of feminine illusions and deceptions. The scene of her death resembled the descent from the cross of the early Renaissance.

One of the most surprising attempts made by Meyerhold was the staging of Blok, the leading symbolist poet. Blok's poetic dramas, *The Little Showbox, The King in the Market Place, The Rose and The Cross, The Song of Destiny, The Stranger,* and others, usually dealt with the split between dream and reality and depicted the corruption of beauty, soiled by vulgarity and coarseness. Highly allusive, often esoteric, based on melody, rhythm, alliteration, verbal complexity, his plays were meant to be read. Critics considered them delicate flowers which would wilt in the heat of footlights.

The Little Showbox, produced in 1906 (décor by N. Sapunov, music by Mikhail Kuzmin, the poet), was particularly difficult because Blok hit in it the "pseudo mystics" and was bitingly ironical and ambivalent.

The play opened with the reunion of sophisticated talkers and the appearance of a strange maiden. Pierrot sees in her Columbine, his dream, but the arguing intellectuals believe she is death or its symbol. Where is the truth? Is Pierrot a fool or an unhappy lover? And is it not the gay Harlequin who succeeds in snatching away the mysterious Columbine?

The next scene is a masquerade, lovers dance with their mistresses, maskers laugh and flirt. Pierrot wonders whether Columbine is made of flesh or of cardboard. Harlequin claims in his song that nobody knows how to love, life is like a sleep, and he wants to break the spell and get into the live world. But when he jumps into it through the wide window, he finds but painted paper and falls flat on the floor. Then Death comes to the ball and all the maskers flee; only Pierrot walks toward her with outstretched hands, and Death is transfigured into a lovely girl.

Now the author himself walks in, but when he is about to rejoice at such a happy ending, everything disappears: Harlequin dies, bleeding with cranberry juice; Pierrot is left alone and he knows for certain that his beloved, Death or Lady Beautiful, is made of cardboard. Is it Pierrot's diseased mind that turns everything into cardboard? Perhaps Columbine is the eternal feminine, the image of Beauty and Spirit? The audience was left with all these questions when all the settings were pulled up to the fly-house, announcing the end of the show on an empty stage closed in by blue canvases. Meyerhold himself acted as Pierrot, a sharp angular figure, pathetic and ironical at the same time. As a director he definitely scored a great success. The originality of the production lay in an open rejection of scenic illusion, in a combination of live actors with marionettes, and the use of the childish, primitive techniques of Punch and Judy in contrast to the complexity of symbolic content. Of course, one could say that the sonorous recitation of Blok's verse jarred somewhat with the cardboard settings and the wry expressions of the masks. But *The Little Showbox* had a completeness and an appeal that even the hostile critics (and they were in the majority) had to acknowledge. Selected audiences of writers, poets, and intellectuals were puzzled and delighted by the performance, and professionals, independently of their own opinions, had to recognize that Meyerhold was bringing something new to the Russian theater.

In 1907, plays by Western dramatists, such as Wedekind, Hofmannsthal, and Pszybiszevsky (*The Winter Fairy Tale*) alternated with pieces by Sologub, Remizov, and other Russians. But despite extraordinary efforts in scenery and production, and the contribution of such talented young painters as Sapunov, Sudeikin, Anisfeld, and Dobuzhinsky, the theater was not a favorite with the general public, and could hardly go beyond the borders of a laboratory. Besides, the conflict between Meyerhold and Kommissarzhevskaya was steadily deepening. She could go along with his innovations and his choice of symbolic and "spiritual" plays even if the audience did not understand them, but she certainly disapproved of his tendency toward the marionette. Meyerhold's most important purpose was to give scenic form to abstractions; for Kommissarzhevskaya, the essence of the theater resided in acting and she fought against the "dematerialization" of the actor, which her director always had in mind. Besides, Meyerhold barred her from quite a few of his important productions; she did not have a part in Blok's *The Little Showbox,* and was refused the leading part in Wedekind's *The Awakening of Spring.* Meyerhold felt she was too old for the role of an adolescent. Further collaboration between the two became impossible, and Kommissarzhevskaya asked Meyerhold to leave. He was offended and brought his case before an "honor jury," but lost it. Another "innovator," Nikolay Evreinov, was called in to replace him in the Kommissarzhevskaya Theater. But neither Evreinov, nor Fyodor Kommissarzhevsky could save the situation. The ban of *Salomé* by Church censorship was the last blow and the theater was obliged to close its doors in the spring of 1909.

Kommissarzhevskaya again went on the road, to America and then on a tour of Russia. She wanted to act freely and she also hoped to make enough money to reopen her theater. The journey through Russian provinces was tiring and hectic. Despite thunderous ovations, she felt depressed and upset. In Tashkent, she caught pernicious smallpox and died on February 10, 1910. Her remains were shipped to St. Petersburg, and thousands attended her funeral.

V

V. A. Teliakovsky, who, in 1907, was Director of Imperial Theaters, writes in his memoirs: "When the painter Golovin came into my office and told me that Meyerhold had been fired from Kommissarzhevskaya Theater because he almost killed everybody there in his innovator's frenzy, I immediately said to Golovin that I wanted to see Meyerhold without even consulting my artistic advisers. Golovin wondered why I wished a meeting with Meyerhold, and I replied that he must be a very interesting fellow if everyone railed at him. Next morning, Meyerhold came, rather surprised by my summons, and he must have been even more surprised when he left with the appointment as one of the director-producers of the Imperial Theaters. I did not ask the specialists about him for a very simple reason: what could they tell me except to raise a protest and then say, 'Not even a private theater could stand the man, so why do you bring him here, into our temple of art?' " The news that Meyerhold was going to produce dramas and comedies on the imperial stage stunned the theatrical world of the two capitals. Was Meyerhold's acceptance a sign of a renunciation or of a compromise?

At this moment, Meyerhold was passing through a new phase of his artistic search. He realized that he had to bring about less controversial, tamer performances for the government theaters and pursue his more challenging experiments on the side. But he did not need to make any deals with his conscience. His recent experiences shattered his faith in the symbolist "theater-temple." He was also through with statuary, hieratic, pictorial, or linear stasis, and he wanted to get away from Craig's marionettes and Maeterlinck's abstractions. What attracted him most at this point of his career were the circus and the music hall, bright and brilliant forms of spectacular show, with an emphasis on tragic farce and comic grotesque. Instead of mystical illumination through symbols and intuitive glances into the mysteries of life, he aspired now for a dynamism leading to loud joy, to a union of actor and spectator in a gay revelry of light, color, and movement. The latter was emerging now in his theoretical concepts as the language of modern times in complete accordance with contemporary physics. Were not space and time expressed in movement? And should not all the "messages," whether social or moral or philosophical, be replaced by movement as the most authentic manifestation of being? Meyerhold started his "training of the actor," being more and more attracted by pantomime as the pure spectacle of gestures, attitudes, and musical rhythm with no literary superstructure of words. He also aimed at suppressing all the barriers between the stage and the audience: stairs led from the stage into the auditorium, actors came from the orchestra, walking through the aisles. In the House of Interludes, a theater where Meyerhold tested many of his ideas, the hall was arranged as a tavern, with spectators sitting at separate tables, and dances being performed in their midst.

Basically, the same spirit animated Meyerhold's production of Molière's *Don Juan* in the Alexandrinsky Theater (1911), for which Golovin made beautiful settings and costumes reproducing the magnificence of the Louis XIV Versailles. Curtains and footlights were abolished. A half-moon proscenium went deep

into the house, the stage was lit by huge candelabra standing on
the floor and by chandeliers hanging from the ceiling, and all
lights were on in the theater during the performance so that
the whole house had the aspect of a festive ballroom. The prompt-
ers were placed on the stage behind screens, valets in liveries
brought in chairs, little blackamoors were running back and
forth arranging the accessories, and at the appearance of the
Stone Guest, they all hid under the tables. The whole performance with its open artificality had a gay, dancing rhythm. Don
Juan (Yuriev) was "fluttering through life," among courtiers,
beautiful women, rich tapestries, and a procession of guests, to
the sound of Lully's music. It was a triumph of "theatricality" as
opposed to the "drama of authentic emotions," a challenge to
the Moscow Art Theater, to the psychological school, and to the
profundity of the symbolists—a show for the pleasure of the
senses.

Meyerhold tackled the same problem in *The Masquerade* by
Lermontov, to which Golovin again contributed luxurious settings, re-creating the atmosphere of the Romantic period in
Imperial St. Petersburg of the thirties. This time, however, instead of superficial gaiety, there was the grim intensity of crime
and passion. In the scene where Arbenin, the jealous husband,
is looking for Nina, his wife whom he erroneously suspects of
betrayal, Meyerhold made him rush through a throng of maskers,
with their jokes, jumps, dances, and revelry gradually turning
from a whirlwind of gaiety into a tornado of menacing faces,
horrible snouts, threatening muzzles, while the tempo of their
movements was increasing, becoming a monstrous saraband and
reflecting the diseased imagination of the frantic husband. The
whole performance was based on the main theme of the play:
Nina is innocent, but Arbenin gives her poison and kills her.
There is a complete disparity between truth and appearance, and
Meyerhold plays on the juxtaposition of suspicion and reality,
of lies and integrity, of pretense and candor. *The Masquerade* is
one of his most astonishing achievements, and it would have been
celebrated much more if it had not had the bad luck of being
presented in St. Petersburg on the eve of the Revolution. It
looked like a splendid last curtain for the old regime.

Very close in manner to *The Masquerade*'s scenes was his

production of *Columbine's Scarf* (Schnitzler-Dohnanyi) in the House of Interludes (1910), interpreted as a pantomime. Columbine, engaged to Harlequin, spends the last evening with Pierrot, whom she pretends to love. Pierrot offers to die with her and takes the poison, but Columbine betrays him even in death and escapes to the wedding ball. During an old-fashioned quadrille, the white sleeve of Pierrot flashes in the doors and windows, and the dance becomes a nightmare for the frightened Columbine. A big-headed conductor, four incredibly ugly musicians, and other strange creatures grimace round her; she tries to flee but now Harlequin pursues her. He discovers Pierrot's corpse, understands the whole situation, and forces her to stay with her dead lover. Columbine goes mad, drinks the fatal cup while dancing, and falls inanimate next to Pierrot.

Meyerhold, who loved Hoffmann, used here all the Hoffmannesque devices: mystification, doubles, hobgoblins, devils, monsters; combinations of mad laughter with macabre horror; the whole mood of fantasy expressed in short scenes of complete unreality (settings and costumes by N. Sapunov).

In all these highly successful productions, Meyerhold tried to underline the elements of whim and artificiality. He was at that moment highly interested in the "conscious conventions" of the Chinese and Japanese theater and always spoke of the oriental stage where servants pile two chairs, one on top of another, to represent a mountain. In 1910, he applied this method to performances at The Tower, the apartment of Vyacheslav Ivanov, the "king of symbolist poets," in front of a most exclusive audience. In *The Adoration of The Cross* by Calderon, Meyerhold used primitive devices of the Spanish itinerant theater. Later, in 1915 in *The Stranger* (*Unknown Woman*) by Blok, he emphasized the grotesque in the first act where actors brought their own plates and glasses to the tavern; in the second act they constructed a bridge by joining wooden pieces they carried from the left and the right wings. An astronomer observed a falling star from this bridge: a stagehand with a lighted torch at the end of a bamboo pole made a circle of flame, and another stagehand in the opposite corner extinguished it in a pail of water. Painted canvases and bamboo canes served as décor.

After the closing of the House of Interludes, he continued his experiments in various workshops under the name of Dr. Dapertutto, (Dr. Everywhere), a name well suited to his manifold activities. The interest in *commedia dell'arte* was not on his part a mere esthetic hobby: in its tradition, Meyerhold discovered the principle which he wanted to oppose to the Moscow Art Theater school of thought. Stanislavsky denied the fixed *emploi* and fought against stock character parts; such divisions as "lover," "noble father," "ingénue," "*raisonneur*," inherited from the French, simply did not exist for him. He believed that an actor could act in different capacities insofar as he could reach the core of a character by the effort of "inner penetration" and "authenticity of emotions." Meyerhold denied the possibility and even the validity of such a transfiguration and defended the *emploi*, the stock character, as the foundation of "conventional" theater. In the *commedia dell'arte* each actor was assigned his part, a Doctor from Bologna or a Captain Spaventa, and could perfect this image (or mask) by repetitive stage appearances. Meyerhold's ideal was a man who could be a mime, a dancer, a juggler, a comedian, an acrobat. He therefore attached the greatest importance to the physical training, to the development of the body, voice, and movements. In the magazine *Love of Three Oranges* which he published in 1914, he glorified Gozzi and the techniques of the *commedia dell'arte*. In general, he claimed that the theater *is* technique. Already by 1907, he maintained that one makes an error when speaking of "Ibsen's or Shakespeare's or the Renaissance theater" because one actually refers to literature and to historical periods. Shakespeare can be presented in a naturalistic or a symbolistic manner, and this is theater. It therefore should be quite clear that a play becomes theater only the moment it is performed, and only from that moment and depending on the way it is done, it belongs to the history of scenic forms. It might be added that most of the ideas Meyerhold developed after the Revolution matured in him during the decade which preceded the fall of the old regime.

Between 1908 and 1917 Meyerhold emerged as one of Russia's greatest theatrical directors. His road, however, was not very easy. He caused scandal and often provoked hate. The theater critic Kugel called him a monster; the artists of the Imperial

Theaters were reluctant to work with him; and for Davydov he was "an enraged kangaroo escaped from the zoo."

And still even his worst enemies had to recognize his energy and originality. He worked relentlessly, traveled abroad to learn from foreign artists or to take on an occasional directional job (production of *Pisanella* by Gabriele D'Annunzio with Ida Rubinstein in the Paris Opera in 1913); he wrote articles and books (*About Theater,* 1912), or gathered material which later became incorporated in his further publications, *Emploi of the Actor,* 1922, and *Reconstruction of the Theater,* 1930. And, of course, he continued to direct not only dramas but also operas and ballets. In 1911, Mussorgsky's *Boris Godunov* with Chaliapin in the title role, was presented under his supervision, and in the same year he showed an enchanting performance of Gluck's *Orpheus and Eurydice* with Sobinov, the tenor, and Fokine's choreography, which spread his fame even outside of Russia. Less successful was his *Elektra* by Richard Strauss. But then again, in 1917 he achieved true success in *The Masquerade* by Lermontov, which brought to an end the pre-Revolutionary phase of his diversified career.

7

GREAT DIRECTORS

BEFORE 1917, two men represented opposite tendencies in the
Russian theater: Stanislavsky was universally recognized as the
leader of the realistic and psychological trend; and Meyerhold,
highly disputed, was rejected by the majority of critics and
actors, but impressed the public and professionals as a great
innovator. His later work carried his name well beyond national
borders. Yet he and Stanislavsky were not the only great directors
of the time, and others should be added to the list. Fyodor Kommissarzhevsky, Nikolay Evreinov, Alexander Tairov, and a little
later, Evgeny Vakhtangov, emerged as leaders of a vigorous
movement of renovation. Quite different in their theories and
practice, and less extremist than Meyerhold, they all, however,
departed from theatrical realism and looked for new forms of
scenic expression. All of them were what the Russians called,
from the French, *régisseurs,* which was a combination in one
person of director and producer. These directors-producers held
an almost unlimited control over actors, budget, and repertory.
In fact, they exercised greater freedom, independence, and authority than most of their colleagues all over the world. In many
cases, such as in the Moscow Art Theater they also had very
solid ground under their feet: a theater building, a large stock
of props and costumes, a fixed repertory. They did not depend
on "angels," grants, or boards of trustees. This situation insured
continuity of work and opened vast possibilities for experimentation.

The two greatest directors, Stanislavsky and Meyerhold, were also professional actors: the leader of the Moscow Art Theater an outstanding one, and the "rebel," a good one. Other directors, such as Vakhtangov, also went through the experience of acting but for them it was a secondary activity, as in the case of Kommisarzhesvky.

Fyodor Kommissarzhevsky (1874-1954), ten years younger than his famous sister, started his work in Mamontov's Opera, and later went to Nezlobin's (doing an adaptation of *The Idiot* by Dostoevsky). He was also active in his sister's theater, although his ideas did not coincide with those of Meyerhold. In 1908, this thin man with a pale waxlike face (later he wore a beard for a time), was an esthete who found greatest delight in books, precious objects, and beautiful surroundings. A man of few words, he listened to discussions with a strange smile, and got the reputation of being cautious, almost shy, but when called upon to assume responsibilities, he revealed strong convictions and an original mind bent on philosophical problems. Enemy of rationalism and deeply affected by the religious currents of symbolism, he rejected the theater of the "fourth wall" but also disagreed with the "inhuman formalism" of a Meyerhold. In his opinion, theater was a vital human necessity, a place where, as he said, "people have always gathered in order to understand themselves, to share their joys and sorrows with others, and where they have found spiritual comfort and warmth of togetherness." Yet his idea of "togetherness" was different from the "conciliation" or "sobornost" of a Vyacheslav Ivanov, or the free communion of individuals proposed by Georgy Chulkov, a mystical anarchist. For Kommissarzhevsky the *raison d'être* of any performance lay in the common emotional and spiritual experience of the audience. He claimed that this experience can be provoked only through live actors, hence his opposition to marionettes and the "dematerialization of the actor." The task of the director is to give unity and meaning to the performance by revealing the ideas and feelings contained in a play. He used to say that "every play, even the most naturalistic one, has music concealed in it." All the elements of a show—acting, sound, lighting, properties— had to be tied together and serve harmoniously for bringing

forth the inner essence or the spiritual reality of a dramatic
work. Thus, theater develops the mind instead of stupefying it.
Sheer entertainment, theater of pure show without anything for
the mind and the soul, is a low form of artistic activitiy and
should be dismissed by serious directors. Modern theater must
look for plays which reflect ideas in the Platonic sense. The central idea or spirit of the play must illuminate the whole performance and determine its form as the most adequate means of
expression and communication. And the task of a director is to
discover this essence by studying not only a particular play, but
the whole work of a playwright in order to understand his vision
of life and his intimate convictions, and this requires a long and
highly specialized effort. It is not a technical, but an intellectual
and a spiritual, assignment. As a result of this search, the director suggests the style of the play, the manner in which it should
be acted and produced. Of course, the manner should change
according to the author and his work.

This point of view led to extreme individualization of performances and made each work by Kommissarzhevsky a separate
and often highly exciting and original unit. He tried out various
kinds of plays in his sister's enterprise, then in his studio which
later was transformed into a small theater. He was one of those
who, like Meyerhold, understood the value of Remizov's plays,
so intimately connected with folklore and verbal research. He
produced Remizov's *The Devil's Show* as a combination of folkloristic ritual with symbolic and mystical allusions but failed to
convince the public of the beauty and profundity of Remizov's
drama, as he also failed in his interpretation of Andreyev's
Black Masks; he presented, however, a most unusual *The Master
Builder* by Ibsen. Some of his concepts seemed quite startling.
He believed, for example, that Molière's plays should never be
acted as realistic (he understood that no comedy could be presented in a completely realistic way) ; some of its protagonists
should be slightly "above" life while others should be treated
as dolls and automatons (servants, the physician, the bourgeois);
his *Le Bourgeois gentilhomme* was an extremely successful production. He also did very well with Ostrovsky, whom he interpreted not as a chronicler of a certain class and period, as a

painter of environment, but as a timeless explorer of the antithesis between matter, the oppression and abuse, and spirit, the
ray of joy. Unlike other directors, he saw this light not only in
concrete actions of some protagonists, such as Katerina in *The
Storm,* but in all the dances, songs, games, and rituals of old
Russia, frequently introduced by Ostrovsky in his plays and
usually considered as interludes or technical devices for "relief."
Interpreting them as essential parts of the action, as true "rays
of sunshine" piercing the reign of darkness, he rendered Ostrovsky much gayer, more affirmative and picturesque. He worked
with Evreinov on *Judith* by Christian Gebbel (written in 1840),
then on Goldoni's *La Locandiera;* in Nezlobin's theater in Moscow his productions included *Princess Turandot* by Gozzi, and
the first part of *Faust.* After 1910 he founded his own theater
in memory of Vera, where he showed plays by Remizov, Kuzmin,
Sologub, and other modern poets, mostly symbolists, although he
did not approve of an exclusively symbolist theater and made
his stylization quite personal. One of his best productions was
Vanka the Butler and Page Jean, by Sologub, whose extrava-
ganza in nine scenes dealt with a well-known itinerant subject:
the love of a lady in high station and her page or attendant, but
it was shown in double sequence, how it might have happened
in France in the eighteenth century and how it actually did
happen in Russia at the same period (Vanka's affair with a
princess), and this presentation of one plot in its twofold aspect
gave Kommissarzhevsky a marvelous opportunity for erotic and
unexpectedly tragic treatment of fairly stylized episodes. Also
remarkable was his production of Dostoevsky's tale, *The Bad
Anecdote.*

Kommissarzhevsky always experimented in "adequate scenic
forms for dramatic images." Endowed with a strong musical
feeling and a sense of rhythm, he was very attracted by operatic
art. His staging of *Tales of Hoffmann* by Offenbach became a
classic, imitated by many theatrical producers and even by the
movies. He built stairs from the proscenium to an elevated stage,
and put on them groups of students who listened to the performance but would occasionally get involved in the action and
become protagonists. Hoffmann himself, as well as other characters, played the piano set on a platform.

After 1917 Kommissarzhevsky produced *Fidelio, Parsifal,* and other operas and established a workshop called "a synthetic school" (drama, opera, ballet). In addition to professional training, his two hundred pupils had to learn all the other arts in order to become "universal actors." They took part in all the performances of the "New Theater" (1918-1919) in which Kommissarzhevsky produced *The Barber of Seville, The Tempest, Tales of Hoffmann,* and other "dramatizations of music."

Kommissarzhevsky's influence on the Russian theater was very powerful. Vakhtangov took from him many ideas and devices, and he left a profound imprint on a whole generation of actors and directors. Unfortunately, for the art in Soviet Russia, he left his native country in the early twenties and emigrated to Europe and then to America, where he acquired international repute. His production of various plays at Covent Garden in London, his activities in Shakespeare repertory at Stratford-on-Avon, his presentation of Pirandello, the first of its kind outside of Italy, his teaching in dramatic schools in England and the United States, and his production of various plays and operas in New York of which *Turandot* and *Wozzeck* at the City Center were his last, are some instances of his multiform attainments. All these contributions belong, however, to the history of the Western and not that of the Russian theater.

II

Another outstanding innovator of the pre-Revolutionary era, Nikolay Evreinov, was in many ways the opposite of Kommissarzhevsky. Playwright, producer, director, actor, musician, theoretician, this extraordinary man published dozens of books, from a monograph on Aubrey Beardsley to the history of corporal punishment in Russia; he graduated not only from the exclusive Imperial Law Institute but also from the conservatory where he wrote compositions under the guidance of Rimsky-Korsakov. He combined versatility with social graces: born into an aristocratic family in 1879, he had excellent manners and was a brilliant conversationalist. In private life as well as in his artistic activities he was charming and striking, unpredictable and fanciful, pungent and witty. His friends called him "fount of life and mis-

chief," and whoever came in contact with Evreinov was captivated by his improvisations, his passionate interest in the most
diverse fields of art and knowledge, and by his inexhaustible
creativity. A slight, thin man, always on the move, as if he were
about to run or to fly, he talked incessantly in a pleasant high
voice, mixing projects and jokes, philosophical digressions and
quips. His big green eyes twinkled and laughed in his pale,
elongated face framed by straight long "artist's" hair. With his
feminine mouth and the perfect design of his arched eyebrows
he resembled a pre-Raphaelite portrait; to some he seemed to
come out of one of Hoffmann's tales. Despite all his energy and
dynamism, there was, however, something fragile and quaint in
his whole figure, in the gestures of his graceful, thin hands, in
the childish impishness of his remarks. In whatever he said or
did he was completely sincere and utterly artificial.

He started a career of civil service but abandoned it because
of his passion for the theater, and began writing and producing
plays. He was twenty-nine when in 1908 he formulated his ideas
in a sensational article which read like a manifesto. With slight
variations and additions, his position remained unchanged until
his death in 1953.

Evreinov opposed the concept of the theater as an esthetic
phenomenon and claimed that theatricality is an organic urge,
therefore prehistoric and pre-esthetic. The play instinct, observed
on all levels of animal life is as basic as hunger or sex; it pre-
cedes in man any notion of beauty. When a savage puts a feather
in his hair or a necklace around his neck, he obeys the universal
play urge. But unlike Schiller, whose theory of art as play he
knew very well, Evreinov stressed the fundamental distinction
between art as self-expression of the creator, and the instinct of
theatricality which coincides with the common desire not to be
oneself, to change, to become another, to be different, to assume
an imaginary personality. A girl who puts on an unusual dress
or wears a new make-up, children involved in the game of cops
and robbers, participants and spectators of public ceremonies,
military parades, receptions, masquerades, manifest in all their
diversity one and the same theatrical drive. A large part of life
is theater, and we constantly act on life's boards. Consciously or
unconsciously, everyone plays his part, and conformity to social

rules in a drawing room has the ordinance of a performance, and "to be consistent" to oneself means merely to remain faithful to a part one has chosen or which has been imposed.

Granted these premises, the so-called naturalistic and realistic theater becomes the most absurd thing. The audience, Evreinov used to say, does not need an object but its image. This is what should be called "the reality of the stage." Simplicity and naturalness on the stage is an antitheatrical crime. The true aim of scenic art is "theatricalization of life." The release of theatricality expresses its superiority over "real raw feelings," over life, and also over esthetic exclusivity. Instead of senseless make-believe and other cardboard attempts at "faithfulness to life," we should recognize and cherish all the aspects of the play instinct. Their fullest development is the aim of the theater. To serve its purpose, the theater should by no means try to make the audiences *forget* they are witnessing a performance. On the contrary, it must render them highly conscious of this fact and make them enjoy the empasized, unadulterated, and intensified expression of theatricality.

The relationship between life and art was placed by Evreinov in the center of his esthetics, and he resolved this problem in the same way as Oscar Wilde, establishing a basic and incontrovertible difference between the two realities and maintaining that art influences life and not, as vulgar common sense pretends, vice versa. In *About the Most Important,* one of his best and most widely known plays, Evreinov makes his hero, Paraclete, form a company of actors and send them all "into life" to play the parts he has chosen for each of them. The actors succeed in changing the destiny of unhappy inmates of a poor boarding house, some of whom are on the verge of committing a crime or suicide— and the sheer intervention of acting gives new dimensions to human existence.

According to Evreinov, the whole evolution of European theater toward realism in the nineteenth century was a big mistake which should be simply erased from the history of art. To renovate the contemporary stage we should return to those periods of the Western past when nobody was ashamed of or tried to hide the basic incompatibility between life and artistic creation. Evreinov conceived a grandiose plan to resurrect glorious theatrical manifestations of other times and lands "in their cultural totality," showing also the theatrical devices and tricks and thus educating the public. This ambitious project was materialized but in part in the Ancient Theater (1907-1908) he organized in St. Petersburg, together with Baron N. Driesen and N. Butkovskaya. A. Sanin, the former associate of the Moscow Art Theater, and a number of The World of Art painters, including Benois, Chembers, Bilibin, Roerich, Prince Shershavidze, and others, collaborated with Evreinov in his new and exciting venture. The Ancient Theater was greatly appreciated by professionals and the general public. It offered medieval miracles: *Three Magi*—eleventh century, *The Miracle of Theofilus* by Rutebeuf—twelfth century, *Robin and Marion,* a thirteenth-century pastorale by Adam de la Halle, *Two Brothers,* a fifteenth-century morality play, and two sixteenth-century farces. All these performances also showed the theatrical audiences of the period. For Adam de la Halle's play Dobuzhinsky transformed the stage into a castle hall filled with knights, ladies, servants, and minstrels. The leader of the comedians' itinerant company came in to start all the preparations for the performance, bringing all the props, a wooden horse on four small wheels among other things, and disclosing all the tricks of the trade.

The second season of the Ancient Theater in 1911-1912 met with even greater success. It was mainly devoted to seventeenth-century Spanish playwrights (Calderon, Lope de Vega, Tirso de Molina). The stage usually represented a Spanish town with a background of foreboding mountains and a public square, in the midst of which a platform for the actors was erected. Costumes, often inspired by Velasquez, and dances were magnificently executed. In general, in his productions, Evreinov emphasized visual effects. "Words," he said, "play but a subordinate role on the stage, and we hear more with the eyes than with the ears."

During the same years Evreinov made experiments in *commedia dell'arte* together with K. Miklashevsky, another enthusiast of the Italian eighteenth-century comedy. Evreinov adored improvisation, called it one of the most satisfying forms of the "theater for oneself," and was always attracted by the performance for which only a synopsis of the plot was given to the actors who otherwise had to rely on their own wits and imagination in dialogues and *mise en scène*. Unlike Meyerhold, the Doctor Dapertutto, who was mainly interested in devices and stock characters of the *commedia dell'arte*, Evreinov thoroughly enjoyed its humor and creative freedom. In general, while most theater directors were deadly earnest and often dogmatic in their search for new forms, Evreinov, with his harlequinades, personified the spirit of gaiety and pleasure. His philosophy, as well as his theatrical practice, was highly affirmative and full of joyous vitality.

In 1908 Evreinov was asked to replace Meyerhold in the Kommissarzhevskaya Theater. Although as firmly opposed to realism and to the "authenticity of emotions" theory as his predecessor, Evreinov nevertheless was alien to Meyerhold's dogmatic intransigence, and he did not care for abstractions and mystical flights. But even more important, particularly for Vera Kommissarzhevskaya, was Evreinov's refusal to replace the imperfect live actor by a perfect marionette. He was interested in romantic eccentricities, in the intensification of theatrical conventions, in the exaggeration of actors' personalities, in the grotesque, and in the spirited. His productions (*Francesca da Rimini* by D'Annunzio, plays by Wilde and Sologub) were coldly planned and lavish in style.

The Crooked Mirror, a theater of "smaller forms" which delighted the Russians for ten years (1908-1918) and which Evreinov directed with zest and genius, became one of his most striking enterprises. He knew how to give scenic expression to irony and humor, and the comic sketches and parodies of his theater rendered it nationally famous. The way he staged *Vampuka* (book by Volkonsky, music by Ehrenberg), a parody of *Aida* but actually a biting exposé of all the routine and silliness of Italian opera, became a model for numerous imitators. Titles of his skits and bits from their dialogues, were repeated throughout Russia as colloquialisms (used even today in Soviet journalism). *Stepik and Maniurochka, The School of Stars, Karaghez, The Eternal Dancer,* and many others, written and staged by Evreinov, created a new trend in Russian repertory, that of a short play, based on comic situations and verbal quips. Some critics compared The Crooked Mirror to Gilbert and Sullivan, but Evreinov catered to a more sophisticated public and his road

was definitely that of subtle irony and satirical grotesque. It
originated a whole style and idiom which could be found later
in all variety shows, skits, sketches, and other "small forms."
Talented young painters, including Radakov and Annenkov, and
writers such as Averchenko, Potyomkin, and Teffi, worked with
Evreinov.

Despite his hectic activities (he also directed operas in the
St. Petersburg House of the Musical Drama established by Lapitsky, and at Zimin's), Evreinov found time to write plays and
to develop his theories. In a book entitled *Monodrama* (1909)
and in the three volumes of *Theater for Oneself* (1915-1917),
he claimed that since nobody can express himself fully in words,
the theater offers the only complete means for release. Every
spectator recognizes and identifies himself with the actor. The
protagonist or the principal character of a play might be called
"Ego," and the spectator, his "Alter Ego" or his double. Actually,
we become the personages we see on the stage. Thus is created
"monodrama" in which the external performance corresponds to
the inner one. In order to achieve the purpose of self-identification, we do not need elaborate settings and we should avoid the
dispersion of attention caused by too many objects. The latter
can be used only as reflection of subjective moods. It is the individual who gives them scope and meaning. The spectator should
see external reality through the eyes of the protagonist, and
what is happening on the stage must become the personal, intimate drama of the audience.

Evreinov wrote such monodramas for The Crooked Mirror as
The Spectacle of Love, Backstage of the Soul, etc. In his book
Theater for Oneself he amplified his favorite theme of the "theatricalization of life," requesting everyone to introduce into everyday existence the colorful entertainment of acting. He said that
his own aim was "to put festive dresses on Her Ladyship Life,
and serve her as a tailor."

After the Revolution, Evreinov's activities lasted for but a few
years and he emigrated in 1925. Although he still was busy with
various theatrical ventures abroad—French, Czech, and Russian
ones—and made interesting productions, his career as a director
was virtually closed after he left Russia. He wrote books and
plays, some of which have been staged in many countries, charmed

his friends by the fireworks of his paradoxes, but all this could not be compared with what he did in Russia between 1908 and 1925, the period of his most valuable theatrical attainments and his most effective influence.

III

Alexander Tairov (1885-1950) had been director of the same theater for thirty-five years, and in terms of duration and consistency his work can be compared only to that of Stanislavsky and Nemirovich Danchenko, although the range and scope of his activities were much more limited and their impact less obvious and less profound.

Tairov abandoned his law studies and started as an actor at twenty. At one time he was associated with the Itinerant Theater of Gaideburov and Skarskaya (Vera Kommissarzhevskaya's sister) who tried to organize a popular stage for the masses and produced social and naturalistic plays with religious undertones. Following this, he served as an actor under Meyerhold in the Kommissarzhevskaya Theater; in 1911-1912 he joined Nezlobin's dramatic company and, in 1913, Mardzhanov's Free Theater. He experienced failures and frustrations and felt that neither naturalism nor its antithesis, theater of conventions, offered a complete solution. At one time he spoke of "the end of the theater" as the result of this impasse but gradually succeeded in working out his own theory which contained a remedy for what he called the "current disease."

Tairov's point of departure was the distinction between art and life as two different categories, and the consequent repudiation of naturalism and symbolism as two equally erroneous extremes. Theater, maintained Tairov, should not imitate life: the actor does not need to take "models from life" or look for a "psychological truth through authentic experience" which is unattainable. He cannot be a camera eye, his acting must be art and not a "family scene" or a "snapshot," and the fusion of stage and life is senseless. It is also unreasonable to make theater a pulpit for philosophical illumination, or make it speak an esoteric language studded with allusions and emblems. Theater is an art in its own right, it has to be affirmed in its specific and exclusive form, and acting is creation. As such, it produces and determines emotions on the stage, only they are essentially different from those experienced in life. What we call stage emotions and what we enjoy and admire in a theater belong to a "stage image," a child of fantasy, brought into existence by the creative power and imagination of the actor. A true impersonation is actually the exteriorization of imaginary emotions and inner images. The process by which these images are created seems mysterious, it is different each time and with each actor, because of its strictly personal nature. From that point of view "universal systems of acting" (Stanislavsky) or elimination of the live actor (Meyerhold) are equally wrong and have to be abandoned. A theater in which theatrical arts are restored brings forth the actor's special creativity under the supervision of a director who builds a "stage atmosphere": the latter is of enormous help to the actor and its inner rhythm gives consistency to the performance. In fact, a performance must be organized as an esthetic whole, and music is the safest means to find the right style and spirit of a show. Everything, from speech to gestures, must follow a pattern found and determined by the director. The text is only a pretext, and literature is not theater. A written play is similar to the book in an opera. Hence the right of the director to cut and change any given text.

In a way, Tairov was ready to accept pantomime as the highest theatrical form, and in this he seemed to agree with Meyerhold. But the difference between the two became quite obvious as soon as Tairov, after an association with K. Mardzhanov, a director and an impresario, continued the latter's Free Theater and opened in 1914 the Kamerny (or Chamber) Theater, the place of his theories and practice for the next three decades.

It is typical of the period that most innovators went beyond the requirements Stanislavsky formulated for an actor in his System. The "universal actor" of Kommissarzhevsky, like that of the Moscow Art Theater, was supposed to possess intellectual qualities and a knowledge of all the arts. Meyerhold, who later created his theory of biomechanics, Evreinov, and particularly Tairov, attached primary importance to the physical attributes and training of an actor. Tairov was even accused of paying more attention to the exterior of his actors than to their talent, and to choosing "models," male and female, for his company. When asked what kind of actor he hoped to produce, Tairov quoted the demands of the ancient Hindu theater: "freshness, beauty, pleasant face, red mouth, good teeth, a neck round as a bracelet, arms of handsome form, gracious stature, powerful hips, charm, dignity, nobility, pride, without speaking of genius." In his opinion, the training of dramatic actors had to begin at the age of seven or eight, just as in the ballet. In his own school adult pupils had to learn fencing, acrobatics, and juggling; clowning was also taught; physical education included voice, mimics, gesture, suppleness and strength of the body. In general, Tairov insisted that the actor acts mainly with his body and gestures, that his gait, way of walking, and all his movements are, perhaps, more important than his diction, although the latter had also to conform to strict rules of music and rhythm. The actor, moving on the stage, must be treated as a three-dimensional phenomenon. The stage itself has to be considered architecturally and not pictorially, as had been the custom in realistic as well as in symbolist theater.

In the past, said Tairov, painters made settings and decorated flats and drops. Now comes the turn of architects to build constructions, and Appia and Craig understood that space should be used from a dynamic point of view. Geometrical forms can express the "lines of a play." The problem of the stage floor should also be solved radically: it cannot be flat and horizontal. Stairs help, but one should not forget that the floor is the keyboard of an actor; it must change for each performance, presenting a variety of levels, inclined surfaces, and divisions of areas. In general, all the externals have to be considered functionally, they are there to help the actor and to serve a decorative purpose. The same is true for costumes and make-up.

Tairov opened his Kamerny in 1914 when Russia was already at war with the Central Powers. For the first night, he chose *Sakuntala* by Kalidasa the great Sanskrit poet, adapted by the symbolist poet Balmont, and filled the stage with half-naked bodies, with processions and pantomime scenes, all of which struck the audience by their perfect rhythm and design. Kalidasa's story of a king who falls in love with the daughter of an ascetic living in a forest, but later loses his memory and fails to recognize his beloved, was treated by Tairov as an opera-ballet. In his further productions he again used either half-naked bodies, or actors in tights, and fused gestures, dance, music, and words into one rhythmical whole. He never tired of emphasizing the role of music for the modern stage; each of his performances could be understood in terms of harmony and composition. His actors recited in a sing-song manner, and it was a compromise because actually Tairov would have liked them to sing. The stage was "constructed" with settings made by steps, cones, pyramids, and blocks of stone. Every one of his presentations was a hit: *The Playboy of the Western World* by Synge, *Life is a Dream* by Calderon, *The Fan* by Goldoni, for which Natalia Goncharova made the settings before leaving Russia and joining Diaghilev. During the 1915-1916 season he produced *The Marriage of Figaro*, Rostand's *Cyrano de Bergerac,* and Rémy de Gourmont's *The Carnival of Life.* They were followed in 1916-1917 by Shakespeare's *The Merry Wives of Windsor, The Jest* by Sem Benelli, and *Famira Kifared* by Innokenty Annensky. The music for most of the plays was by A. Porter, a Frenchman who lived for ten years in Russia, and the decor of Sudeikin, A. Lentulov, and Alexandra Ekster an extremely talented and original cubist painter.

One of Tairov's most revealing productions was *Famira Kifared* in 1916. The play, by Innokenty Annensky, a refined symbolist and Hellenic scholar, represented a legend on which Sophocles had presumably written a tragedy. Famira (Thamira), son of a king and the nymph Argiope, has been abandoned by his parents and becomes a musician, a player of cither or lyre (Kifared—of the cither) living in solitude in the mountains. His mother comes to him when he is twenty. She now loves him passionately, and when he enters a contest with a Muse, makes him lose it: he would have married the Muse had he won. Famira recognizes his own artistic inferiority, loses his musical gift, and blinds himself as a punishment for competing with divinities; his foolish mother is turned into a bird. This tragic story contains many allusions to the role of the artist, his devotion to art to the exclusion of love, and the incomprehensible ways of fate.

Tairov built his performances on two notes or rhythms: one was employed to represent Famira and his art, and it was a dignified and noble motif of Apollonian clarity; the second accompanied satyrs and bacchantes who romped on the stage and gave the play its Dionysian character. The main action was continually interrupted by choral interludes; bacchantes, arm in arm, danced and moved according to a pre-established design. Ekster provided a cubist landscape—rocks, pillars, blue steps, stones, conical cypresses evoking mountains, Greek temples, and sacred woods. Sculptural forms and the human body, mostly naked, and ingeniously painted in the case of menads and satyrs, changed shape and color under an elaborate system of lighting to which Tairov attached supreme importance. The stage had several levels, but ideologically as well as physically the action was divided into two distinct parts: Famira was in the center up-stage, the seat of tragic doings and undoings, while sileni, satyrs, and menads were assigned the lower level for their dances and antics.

Tairov's company counted some twenty-five members, among them the handsome Alisa Koonen, a former Moscow Art Theater actress, an unusually talented interpreter of tragic parts, endowed with a rich voice and rhythmic power. The tall, thin Nik Tseretelli, an excellent actor, was, on the contrary, at his best in harlequinades and grotesques. Other actors, whatever their individual qualities, were molded by the director who subjugated them and exerted complete control over them. They submitted to it with a sort of enthusiastic devotion, being entirely won over to Tairov's ideas and overwhelmed by his personality. Unlike Meyerhold, who could never be a good teacher and whose impatience played him bad turns in his relations with actors and pupils, Tairov was an excellent educator and a professional leader. Meyerhold was often abrupt and made blunders in handling people. Tairov possessed great knowledge of human nature and an ability for persuasion and diplomacy, and therefore was much more successful with pupils, actors, and, later, with party officials. This short man with a round face, big mouth, and clear eyes which seemed light because of his dark complexion, knew exactly what he wanted. He was pugnacious, insistent and consistent, and all his theories were clear-cut, leaving no place for vagueness and half-truth. His work was very neat, he showed great concern for every detail. Meyerhold, with the exception of the productions on the imperial stage, was often sloppy; he mainly cared for the general lines, for great ideas, but he was not particularly fastidious about their materialization. Tairov, on the contrary, invariably offered a finished product of highest quality, he never left anything to chance, and all his performances resembled a well-ordered, faultlessly executed concert which he conducted with an expert and firm hand. Theater as art found in Tairov a consummate "maker" and producer. Whatever he did, he did well, and nobody, even his worst enemies, would dare accuse him of amateurishness. In fact, his Kamerny Theater, which on the eve of the Revolution found itself at the opposite pole of the Moscow Art Theater, was probably the only one that could compete with Stanislavsky's house professionally.

IV

The influence of the innovators was mainly felt in Moscow and St. Petersburg, and to a lesser degree in smaller towns. Still, between 1908 and 1917 their ideas spread all over the country and were discussed in the most remote corners of Russia. Companies on the road could hardly handle new stage settings, but they did present symbolist plays and what was called at the time, "decadent moods." Theatrical life was very intense; regular theaters functioned well not only in European Russia but also in Siberia and on the periphery, and great performances of big theaters, from the Moscow Art Theater to that of Kommissarzhevskaya and Meyerhold, brought the notion of latest developments to provincial audiences.

In the years 1914-1917 "small forms" often called "theater of miniatures," had a vogue in the provinces, mainly due to Evreinov's The Crooked Mirror, and Nikita Baliev's The Bat. The Bat began in 1908 as a private club for Moscow artists and their friends, and then expanded into a public cabaret with refreshments, still bearing the character of an exclusive night club. Wit and horseplay, songs in costumes, farcical sketches, one-act plays, and dance numbers made it highly popular. It differed from The Crooked Mirror: the latter specialized in satire and parody while The Bat had a more varied repertory, and its numbers covered a broader territory. It grew into an important theatrical enterprise, and excellent actors, painters, and writers became associated with its gay, spirited performances; Vakhtangov, for instance, staged for it his *Lead Soldiers* with Shostakovich's music. In 1920 Baliev went abroad with his company; he had great success in Paris, and later in New York, presenting new currents of Russian art on a small scale.

In direct connection with "small forms" were performances in clubs and artistic gatherings. Most popular was The Stray Dog, located in a cellar on Mikhailovsky Street in St. Petersburg, organized by Boris Pronin. Later, there was the famous Comedians Inn, called the Russian Montmartre, with murals painted by Sudeikin, Sapunov, Yakovlev, B. Grigoriev; artists from leading theaters came into these clubs for supper after performances and often improvised entertainments for themselves and their friends. Writers, poets, painters, and stage directors formed the main clientele of The Story Dog, or Comedians Inn, or other dens, and many original ideas and projects were born in those cellars. In a certain way, various "literary and artistic clubs," patronized by the intelligentsia in large towns, served also as centers for theatrical improvisation and experimentation. One can argue that these were greenhouses, typical of an exclusive upper-class culture. Such an objection may sound true from a historical and social point of view, but, as we will see later, all the ideas and aspirations cultivated by artists and intellectuals before the Revolution came to the surface and played a decisive role in the first years of Soviet rule.

Despite the popularity of new trends from 1908 to 1917, they changed but little in the theatrical life of Russia. Realistic acting, with more or less realistic repertory, prevailed on the boards in the majority of enterprises. The country looked at the Moscow Art Theater, the Alexandrinsky and Maly Theaters for guidance and example of professional standards. The problems of repertory was, however, more complex. While such theaters as the Suvorin, Korsh, Nezlobin, and a few others, without counting the *avant-garde,* did renovate their repertory, most houses in the provinces as well as in the capital, continued to offer second-rate plays by skillful dramatists such as Sumbatov, Nevezhin, Shpazhinsky, Krylov (in the Alexandrinsky or Maly), and less prominent companies staged works by the epigoni of Russian realism (Timkovsky, Tikhonov, Ryshkov, Shcheglov, Protopopov, and Baryatinsky). The story of a society lady involved in a crime (*Vera Mirtseva* by Lev Urvantsov), or a comedy with historical accessories (Yuri Beliaev with his *Lady from Torzok* and others) were box office successes.

Plays of Chekhovian mood, describing small dramas of little people, were in great demand, and this explains why Nemirovich Danchenko and Kommissarzhevskaya produced such second-rate pieces as *Ivan Mironych* and *The Jews* by Evgeny Chirikov, or *Autumn Violins* by Ilya Surguchev. Certain mannerisms and lyrical aspirations were mistaken for modernism in *Listen Israel, Voice of Blood,* and *Nu* by Ossip Dymov (1878-1959). Two Jewish dramatists came to the fore in the prerevolutionary years: David Aisman with *The Wives* (1908) and Semyon Yushkevich, whose realistic dramas with symbolist flavor were produced by the Moscow Art Theater (*Miserere,* 1910) and by Kommissarzhevskaya *(In The City).* Other plays by Yushkevich also gained popularity around 1910. Sholem Asch's *God of Vengeance* was also very popular around 1908. The symbolist drama was provided by Andreyev who dominated the provincial theater until 1917, and by a vast foreign repertory which included Ibsen, Hamsun, Maeterlinck, Sudermann, and dozens of other less significant playwrights. And, of course, the classical repertory continued to occupy its usual place on all boards.

Great progress was made in the opera and ballet. Modern painters and producers brought new brilliancy to performances even on secondary stages, while those in Moscow and St. Petersburg, particularly in the Imperial Theaters, reached a high degree of luxury and technical accomplishment. It was also the period of most prominent singers such as Chaliapin, who sang in St. Petersburg's People's House as well as in the Mikhailovsky, of Leonid Sobinov, the popular tenor, Alexander Smirnov, and Ivan Yershov, prominent in Wagnerian operas; no less known were women singers: Medea Figner, Maria Kuznetsova, Lipkovskaya, Felia Litvin, the greatest interpreter of Wagner, and many others.

Among the popular actors, the Moscow Art Theater led the way with Stanislavsky, Kachalov, Moskvin, Artem, Luzsky, Leonidov, Gribunin, Serebriakov, and with the actresses Knipper, Ghermanova, Lilina, and later Gzovskaya.

The Maly Theater in Moscow had such accomplished realistic artists as Yablochkina, Sadovskaya, Pashennaya, next to the old Yermolova, Fedotova, and Nikulina, while their male counterparts counted Lensky, Samarin, Sumbatov, Sadovsky, Ostuzhev.

Alexandrinsky had still the "old guard": Michurina-Samoilova, Korchaghina-Alexandrovskaya, Yuriev, Khodotov, Apollonsky, and Davydov. The stars of the Korsh and the Suvorin Theaters were Blumental-Tamarina, Dalmatov, Svobodin, and Polevitskaya. Quite a few young actors emerged at the beginning of World War I (1914): Mikhail Chekhov, Vakhtangov, Sushkevich, Alisa Koonen, Ghiazintova, Birman, and others whose names became known after 1917.

This is by no means a complete list and the aim of this enumeration is only to show that on the eve of 1917 Russia possessed numerous excellent, experienced actors in her more than two hundred regular theaters. The theatrical culture of the country was very high, and most of the well-known artists had a large following and numerous pupils. There were also a great many free-lance actors who did not attach themselves to any particular institution and who went on the road with different companies and appeared as guest artists in various cities. Among them was Pavel Orlenev (1869-1932) whom enthusiastic fans compared with Mochalov. In his early twenties he played simpletons in farces and vaudeville until Stanislavsky, who appreciated his techniques, recommended him to Suvorin. In the latter's theater he made a sensation in 1898 interpreting Tsar Fyodor in A. K. Tolstoy's drama, as a tragic figure. He emerged as an interpreter of extreme and pathological characters, and his highest attainments were Raskolnikov and Dimitry Karamazov in the adaptations of Dostoevsky's novels, as Osvald in *Ghosts,* as Brand, as Solness in *The Master Builder* and as other protagonists of Ibsen whom he adored. A man of enormous drive, he was afflicted by almost pathological nervousness and alternated periods of great elation with cycles of black depression and heavy drinking. Whenever he portrayed morbid, neurasthenic individuals, he held audiences under the spell of his psychological portraiture. Critics and onlookers spoke of his uncanny intuition, but Orlenev did not rely on his innate dramatic gift; whether sober or drunk, he worked relentlessly to polish his parts technically. His devotion to art was total, and he had his own philosophy in which modern symbolism and the dream of "a third reign" of joy and beauty mingled with the idea of "the theater for the people." He believed in the actor's and playwright's message, particularly in a moral and philosophical message. Unfortunately, he had no time or patience to concentrate on anything but his acting. He led a disorderly life, like Kean, and roamed like a gypsy through the regions of Russia. His guest appearances had great impact on the provincial theater to which he always brought modern repertory. He also played abroad: in America, where he went twice (his wife Alla Nazimova, a dancer and an actress was at one time popular in Hollywood), and in Norway where he played Ibsen's heroes to the delight and surprise of the natives. After the Revolution his fame declined, and poor health prevented Orlenev from creating a theater for workers and peasants.

The Russian theater between 1900 and 1917, during the last years of the Empire, showed a tremendous strength and intensity. The search for new forms, the perfection of established institutions, the number of talented performers, the innovations in the drama, in the opera and in the ballet, and the involvement of professionals as well as of the public in problems of further theatrical development, placed Russia at the head of the scenic arts in the Western world. By the end of the nineteenth century the Russians surprised and enchanted Europe and America by the revelation of their literature; at the beginning of the twentieth century they amazed them again, this time by the disclosure of their music and their advanced theatrical culture.

Of course, it was not a culture of the masses or for the masses, and this point became a crucial one after the Revolution. Whatever was achieved in the Russian theater in the twentieth century, and particularly by its innovators, was done by the educated classes and primarily by the intelligentsia. It can be argued that in a country where only the privileged had free access to culture, and millions of peasants, workmen and the middle classes were forcibly kept in ignorance, it was the intellectuals and the nobles who, in creating art, literature, music, and theater, expressed the essence and the aspirations of the silent and oppressed people. The educated minority spoke for the masses and acted as the representative of the whole nation. If this was the case, the theory which views all the fine attainments of Russian artistic culture before the downfall of the Tsar as "flowers on a tomb," as a last blossoming of a marvelous plant with rotten roots, doomed to die at the first gust of the storm, should be taken with a great deal of skepticism. It might be mentioned that all the cultural fulfillments in other European countries in the nineteenth and twentieth centuries were also not for the masses, and their promoters and creators belonged to the educated minority, recruited mostly from the nobility and the bourgeoisie. This did not prevent them from expressing the national spirit and the ideals of their respective countries. It is impossible to say that the high level of French theatrical achievements, for example, was the work of large democratic groups. In reality it resulted from the efforts made by the artistic élite, just as in Russia. Everywhere it is a minority that fights for new forms in the arts and creates and promotes new sensitivity, which it passes to the masses after the long and difficult period of incubation and experimentation. The same happened in the Russian theater —and, as we will see, the impetus of the movement initiated by this minority, by this experimenting élite, was powerful enough to overlap into the revolutionary period until the official doctrine denied the rights of a creative minority and tried to substitute for it artificial pseudo-democratic products. The clash between this doctrine and the efforts of true creators who either rebelled against it or attempted to avoid it by a hypocritical conformity, is the content and the tragedy of theatrical life in Russia between 1917 and the present day.

8

THE FIRST YEARS OF
THE REVOLUTION

THE MARCH 1917 REVOLUTION brought but a few immediate changes in the conditions of theatrical life in Russia. The most important was the abolition of censorship, that very scourge of the repertory which, on the eve of the cataclysm, hit the historical drama *Pavel I* by Merezhkovsky and the production of innocent topical plays. The Imperial Theaters were reorganized on the basis of autonomy and elective administration, mostly modeled after the French Comédie Française. Professional unions of actors grew like mushrooms. Some of them, such as those of the Mariinsky Opera, refused to admit into their midst the ballet people even though the latter argued that the success of some operas, such as *Prince Igor*, were mainly due to dances (notably to the famous Polovetski dances). The leading directors—Stanislavsky Meyerhold, Tairov, Evreinov, and Kommissarzhevsky—welcomed the downfall of tsarism. But the Provisional Government of Kerensky, although formed by intellectuals, did not do anything special for the arts, probably believing that there were more important matters—such as war and the struggle for peace—to attend to.

It must be pointed out that the Bolsheviks understood better than their democratic adversaries the purport of theater as a means of propaganda. As soon as they seized power in November 1917, they immediately established administrative agencies with special tasks in the field of the arts. Since a large portion of the educated classes were opposed to the new government, Lenin's Soviet of People's Commissars could expect only resistance and sabotage from the majority of actors and directors. This was particularly true of the former Imperial Theaters where performances were even suspended as a gesture of protest against the Communist rulers. Many theaters adopted the "wait and see" tactics. In 1918-1920, when civil war was raging in vast territories, theaters in the provinces stopped functioning. In big cities the lack of fuel and electricity often created unsurmountable material barriers for regular performances. One should not forget that for five years (1918-1923) Russia was the ground of bloody struggle, terror, and famine, and that normal life seemed a distant dream, while surrounding reality was a fantastic succession of privations, sufferings, arrests, executions, and destruction. In these appalling conditions the theaters also went through incredible adventures.

Already by November 22, 1917, the Council of People's Commissars published a decree by which all the theaters were put under the jurisdiction of the Art Department, created within the Commissariat of Education. This was the first step toward nationalization. In December, Anatoly Lunacharsky, the Education Commissar, a well-educated man, himself a writer and a dramatist, invited some 120 writers, painters, and actors for a conference on the arts under the new regime, but only five came, among them, Mayakovsky, Blok, and Meyerhold. In January 1918 a Theatrical Section headed by Olga Kameneva (Trotsky's sister) was established "in order to create new theaters in connection with the socialist reorganization of State and Society." Meyerhold was appointed head of the Petrograd branch of this national center. Moscow theaters, as well as theaters in the provinces, depended on local Soviets. Imperial and Academic theaters were administered by boards of directors, five appointed by the Education Commissariat and five elected by "theater collectives" which included everybody, from the first lady to the ushers and sweepers. The Theatrical Section prepared the transfer of all theaters from private to state ownership, and its efforts were finally crowned by a law, signed by Lenin on August 26, 1919. It declared the unification of all theaters under a Central Theatrical Committee entitled to administer them and to approve their repertory; buildings, settings, costumes, etc., were declared national property, or socialized. The existing theaters were divided into two categories: the first comprised well-known and established institutions with regular and "politically mature" companies, and the State was to give them instructions about repertory "in order to bring them closer to the people and its social ideals," but they were to be administered on the basis of autonomy; while the second category included private theaters of various shades and was to be controlled in a much stricter way. The State assumed the financing (i.e., government subsidy) of all theaters of the first category. The Party Congress of the same year (September 1919) affirmed that "there are no forms of science or art which are not connected with the great ideas of communism and with the infinitely varied work of communist economy." In order to "bring to the working masses all the treasures of art created on the basis of exploitation of labor," free tickets were distributed to soldiers and workmen by various professional organizations. This began to bring new audiences to all Russian theaters. In 1919, actors were drafted to give performances for the Red Army; in 1920 on the Western front (in the 16th Army alone, 149,470 soldiers saw 259 professional performances). This trend continued steadily. Professional artists were also giving regular performances in workmen's clubs or in factories and even in the villages. In 1920-1922 this movement took on large proportions.

The period between 1919 and 1923 was filled with a struggle between the Central Government and the autonomous theaters, which all fought for larger independence and often escaped Party controls. During these years problems of civil war, foreign intervention, economic reconstruction and consolidation of power overshadowed all subsidiary issues, such as entertainment and artistic activities; and although the Communist Party consistently strengthened its positions in the arts, it was forced by circumstances to grant a great deal of freedom to theatrical enterprises.

Of course, one of the main reasons for such liberalism was the lack of a clear-cut theoretical line. From the beginning of the Revolution, the Party considered cultural change as a logical result of social and political transformation. The divergence of opinions on this problem was extremely sharp among the Communists themselves, and particularly among those artists and intellectuals who professed their sympathy toward the new regime and called themselves its allies and helpers.

What added to the confusion on the morrow of the establishment of the Soviets was the actual situation in literature and the arts. Lenin and the majority of his former companions were inclined to brand all the religious- or mystical-minded symbolists as "enemies of the people and reactionaries" but it was the symbolists, such as Blok, Briussov, Bely, Chulkov, Remizov, and Zelinsky, who supported the Revolution in Theatrical Sections or in Literary Conferences. Consequently the continuation of symbolism in poetry, prose, and theater had to be tolerated; moreover, in 1918-1922, some Communist officials themselves were directly or indirectly connected with the "modernist" movement.

Even more complicated was the situation with numerous groups, mainly formed by young people, who vociferously claimed to be the true heirs of the old bourgeois culture and the only candidates for the creation of a new Soviet art. And here again, the opinions varied. Should it be a theater circus for thousands of people, or pageants in the streets; should the performances be based on folklore, on universal myths, on revolutionary history, on concrete examples of class struggle; and what did Lenin mean by saying that "truly popular art" will be one of the immediate results of the Revolution?

The extreme position was taken by the group of Proletcult, led by Alexander Bogdanov, an old Marxist, and at one time Lenin's opponent. He claimed that the past should be completely rejected and a new culture created by the triumphant proletarians. In his zeal he was promoting half-baked works by old and young artists whose main merit was their humble origin, and whose great artistic aspirations were not to resemble the contemptible models of the "bourgeoisie." The Proletcult people did not know what to offer as a substitute for the old, and therefore they experimented in various directions from "cosmism," which wanted to expand the range of art beyond the earth into the unlimited space of the universe, to "populism," which spoke of the "faceless" crowd as a new hero to replace the former "bourgeois egotistic individualism." In the theater, Proletcult hoped to supersede old bourgeois plays by "mass shows," and in this it got the support of other left wing groups, including Meyerhold. The Communist leaders, although highly suspicious of Bogdanov and of Proletcult, favored the idea of popular mass performances and quoted the words by Romain Rolland: "A happy and free people needs festivals more than theater houses." Of course, the initiators of monumental "living panoramas" under the open sky looked at festivals in a different way. Symbolists, such as Vyacheslav Ivanov, still talked of "choral action," "show of conciliation," and used religious or typically populist terms, while the Proletcult saw in street processions and public festivals, including masquerades and allegories, manifestations of class collectivism. Some of them confessed, not without embarrassment, that they would have liked to stage the myth of Prometheus. But only a few local festivals were actually organized by the Proletcult people; for example, the anniversary of the November Revolution in 1918 in Moscow and Voronezh. Most spectacular performances which took place in 1920 were directed by such "formalists" and "decadents" as Serghei Radlov and Evreinov. The latter staged in Petrograd *The Storming of the Winter Palace,* reproducing the highlights of the Bolshevik uprising and their attack on the seat of the Provisional Government with the help of sailors from the warship *Aurora.* Eight thousand people participated in the show, an orchestra of five hundred musicians played revolutionary songs, and a real blast from the *Aurora,* anchored on the Neva River, enhanced the collective action in which performers and spectators mingled freely. For his work, Evreinov got a fee in the form of a fox fur coat, and his assistants, the painter Yuri Annenkov, Petrov, and others, got a dozen eggs and half a pound of tobacco each, a real bounty in those hard times.

Thousands of supernumeraries and actors swarmed in other "living panoramas," such as *The Blocus of Russia* by Radlov or *Forward World Communism* also by Radlov and his friends. In these grandoise shows, stage directors gave their orders from "posts of command," by phones, megaphones, and through signals. For the celebration of May 1, 1920, *The Mystery of Freed Labor* was staged between the portals of the former Stock Exchange in Petrograd under the auspices of the Politburo of the Red Army, directed by Alexander Kugel and Yuri Annenkov.

Two thousand performers milled in this monumental pageant attended by thirty-five thousand spectators who heartily applauded the actors impersonating the Pope, the Sultan, the Banker, the Merchant as symbols of capitalism: the crowd also enjoyed the ballets and fireworks of the liberated proletariat.

Evreinov was obviously inspired by the Festivals of the Great French Revolution, and by the Russian eighteenth century festivities. In the apotheosis he had the "Tree of Freedom" around which all nations were united in brotherly celebration while the soldiers of the Red Army replaced rifles with sickles and hammers. Every part of the action was accompanied by music: the procession of slaves by Chopin's "Funeral March"; the New Bright Reign by excerpts from Wagner's *Lohengrin;* and the group dance around the tree by Rimsky-Korsakov's *Sadko.* Of course, some critics did not miss the chance to reproach Evreinov that he had borrowed allegories from a "bourgeois revolution." But those were extremists: the public enjoyed the tree, Rimsky-Korsakov, and the Red Army soldiers very much. Other festivals (*World's Commune, Action of Third International,* etc.) had the same character of big strokes and loud settings. The fashion of these shows spread to the farthest corners of Russia. Nikolay Okhlopkov, who later became one of the most important Soviet directors, staged as a young man a *Struggle between Labor and Capital* in Siberia, on the public place of Irkutsk, with the participation of armed forces and workmen's unions. This is how the local paper described the end of the spectacle: "Banners appear on the stage. Artists impersonating the victorious proletariat board automobiles and drive around the square, acclaimed by dozens of thousands of spectators." Performances which staged episodes of the Civil War, particularly the victories of the Red Army over Denikin and Wrangel, often involved ten thousand soldiers whose task was to give an exact replica of military action. But neither those naturalistic pageants nor the symbolic and heavily allegorical parades directed by the left wingers lasted for a long time. They wilted by 1921 and began to disappear by 1922, when the only important pageant took place in a small town and enacted the 1905 strike by the workmen of Ivanovo-Voznesensk.

The open-air demonstrations reflected the desire for large,

monumental and popular spectacles opposed to the chamber atmosphere of the psychological or bourgeois stage. They aspired to a posterlike, crude, and noisy theatricalization of the public meeting and of current events. One understands immediately how such a tendency, by the law of contrasts, could fascinate a refined esthete like Evreinov or other sophisticated directors who enjoyed tremendously the experience of festivals.

A different approach, however, came from the Proletcult headquarters. First of all, its leaders declared a complete break with the past, and this meant the rejection not only of "bourgeois realism or symbolism" but also of "bourgeois actors." In his book-manifesto *Creative Theater* (1919), which had four reprints in two years, Platon Kerzhentsev, theoretician of the movement, wrote: "Any attempt at forging a socialist theater by the hands of the geniuses among bourgeois actors will be as fruitless as analagous efforts, for instance, to create a socialist magazine by bourgeois journalists. The task of proletarian theater is not only to train good professionals who can act well in the plays of socialist repertory but to release the creative instinct of the masses." And since this "creative spirit" of the proletariat was supposed to be expressed in general form, without any emphasis on concrete historical conditions or human characters, Kerzhentsev's position was not very far from a proletarian version of symbolism.

A slightly different attitude was adopted by the Proletcult followers such as Boris Arvatov, who saw in the Soviet theater "a laboratory of new social life making models of objects, conditions of existence and men; a theater as production, as factory, as construction." This group found itself very close to futurists, constructivists, and suprematists, who by the way, were far from being sons and daughters of proletarians.

After having organized mass performances, and three shows in Petrograd, Proletcult opened its Central Experimental Theater in Moscow (1920 until 1923). It had local branches and thousands of clubs and amateur groups all over Russia. Under the influence of what was going on in Moscow during these years, the Proletcult abandoned its symbolic-allegorical monumental line, and followed the trend announced by Meyerhold, Annenkov, Radlov, and others: cubism and futurism in externals, techniques of circus and music hall in composition and acting.

Among the significant shows of the First Workmen Theater of the Proletcult were a highly allegorical *Legend About a Communard* directed by A. Mgebrov and V. Chekan, *The Dawns of Proletcult* (a staging of poems made by V. Ignatov), and *The Mexican* based on Jack London's story and staged by Serghei Eisenstein, the future film director, assisted by V. Smyshliaev. The climax of this last performance, studded with circus tricks and buffoonery, represented a boxing match between capitalism and socialism; the victory of the frail-looking proletarian over the Hercules-like servant of the bosses opened the road to the Mexican Revolution.

Another Eisenstein show in 1923 was a fanciful modernization of Ostrovsky's *Even a Wise Man Gets Caught* (other title: *Enough Stupidity For a Wise Man*). Its sly protagonist Manefa became an *émigrée* in Paris, a theosophist, and a clairvoyante by profession; other typically Russian figures were replaced by General Joffre and Lord Curzon. During the performance a dud exploded among the public, creating a panic. The stage represented an arena, and dialogues were going on while the actors tried to keep equilibrium walking on a tight rope. In the middle of the play a short film was projected to show the theft of Glumov's diary. Eisenstein, who at this time was studying Japanese, must have borrowed the device from Tokyo theaters: in 1919-1920, the Japanese often alternated the action on the stage with projection of explanatory films. But on the whole, the actors followed Meyerhold's biomechanics, and Eisenstein's theory was not very different from the practice of that famous director. Eisenstein believed that a theatrical performance should be a free montage of autonomous attractions or entertainments bent on producing a cumulative thematic effect. Hence the combination of tricks taken from the circus, music hall, and Grand Guignol, the Parisian theater of horrors and suspense. His predecessors in the movies, mainly Kuleshov and Dziga Vertov, preached "factography," and in *The Battleship Potemkin*, the film which made him famous, Eisenstein followed their principles derived from the LEF (Left Front) movement and from *The Thing* group.

The Proletcult was patently "sociological"; it fought for a
theater of agitation and propaganda, but since it wished to find
new forms for revolutionary content, its roads crossed those of the
avant-garde. This was one of the most interesting phenomena of
the period: all the "left wing" tendencies in art, born and formulated under the tsarist regime, received new impetus from the
Revolution and flourished stupendously between 1918-1923 and
even later. Their Communist opponents were perfectly right
when they recognized the "alien" origin of all those currents
which declared themselves arch-revolutionary and claimed to be
the best expression of Soviet mentality. The years of the New
Economic Policy (1922-1928) also favored freedom in the arts,
experimentation and eccentricity—and only by the end of the
twenties, when a new offensive in all fields marked the consolidation and the hardening of the Communist rule, was the *avant-
garde* badly mauled and finally destroyed by police methods.

In the early twenties the *avant-garde* had its heyday. The
Proletcult, for instance, succeeded in attracting large groups of
youth, including Communist youth organizations, and it backed
Theaters of Working Youth (TRAM in Russian). In those
amateur theaters the classics were always replaced by shows of
political actuality, inspired by Meyerhold. Many TRAM staged
plays on various forms of industrial production, about extracting
oil in Baku, cotton-growing in Tashkent, woodcutting in Arkh-
angel, toolmaking in Moscow; but they used for them techniques
of the *avant-garde*. When the government decided to quash the
Proletcult, the TRAM were the last to be liquidated: even in
1930 they numbered seventy theaters.

The groups which mostly influenced the Proletcult and other
revolutionary formations in the first decade of the Soviet Regime,
were cubists, cubo-futurists, constructivists, and imagists. All of
them were close to each other and had personal as well as ideological ties. Their origin lay in the years 1912-1914, when young
painters affirmed themselves as distinct and often hostile to The
World of Art movement and followed more recent and radical
French and German esthetic currents. Aristarkh Lentulov, Alexandra Ekster, Pyotr Konchalovsky, Nikolay Kulbin, were mostly
cubists and, in 1910, formed the Moscow group called "The
Knave of Diamonds." In 1912, a dissident group, the "Donkey's

Tail," exhibited works by Kazimir Malevich, Vassily Tatlin, Marc Chagall, and Mikhail Larionov. Some of them evinced an interest in the art of the icon and in popular woodcut prints; in general, they showed a more "national" and expressionistic spirit. Quite a few of these painters became prominent in stage design. They all were mixed with the group of cubo-futurists which comprised Mayakovsky, Velemir Khlebnikov, Vassily Kamensky, Nikolay and David Burliuk—poets, writers, and painters who wanted to "drop all the classics from the ship of contemporary art" and who began to launch the slogans of Western futurism and, later, dadaism: "Set words free, destroy all grammatical structure, cultivate speed and modernity, be aggressive, repudiate all tradition, search for daring and startling forms of expression, and act as new barbarians in renovating creative life." The cubo-futurists were connected with an important group of young scholars, mostly around the "Society For the Study of Poetic Language" which included Victor Shklovsky, Roman Jakobson, Boris Eichenbaum, Yuri Tynianov, and many others. They initiated the formalist movement in literary criticism and history and became highly influential in the first years of the Revolution.

Most of the cubo-futurists and related groups were strongly "urbanistic." They hailed the civilization of speed and machines, extolled the movies as the most marvelous form of art, dreamt of skyscrapers, and saw in the cult of steel—precision instruments and modern technology—a valuable counterpart to the rotten sentimentality of the romantics and of nineteenth-century decadent "softies." These ideas were taken up after 1918 by the constructivists who wished to make art as well-planned and regulated as technical conveyances, and felt that beauty should be functional. In 1923, Mayakovsky and other futurists and constructivists affirmed in their magazine, *LEF* (The Left Front of the Arts) and *New LEF* the necessity of functional and utilitarian art; a group which published (with Ilya Ehrenburg and Lissitsky) the magazine *The Thing* wanted the writers to produce "real things" instead of old-fashioned elegies and the sighing and crying stories. LEF felt that literature should become factual reportage, documentary and journalistic, and be as efficient in life as any other human activity. Both groups made a god of dynamics.

In all these trends there was definitely a stress on the destruc-

tion of the old esthetics. When the Revolution proclaimed the
end of capitalism and of the bourgeois state, the *avant-garde*
interpreted the victory of the proletariat as the trumpet call for
the attack on the Jericho walls of realism and traditionalism. The
theater, of course, was part of the general scheme.

In 1918-1919, the center of the *avant-garde* in Petrograd was
The Art of The Commune, a publication which became a laboratory of new theories and ideas. Mayakovsky, Nikolay Punin,
Ossip Brik, and Nathan Altman, all of whom played important
roles in the IZO, (the Governmental Section of Figurative Arts) ,
contributed to *The Art of The Commune.* Its theatrical section
backed the Proletcult and Meyerhold. Later, the *Theatrical
Messenger* continued the same line. The talented painter Yuri
Annenkov, who also was an excellent writer, formulated the
program of the iconoclast: theater should be liberated from
literature and dramatists and be affirmed in its own right; self-
centered acting technique should be fully accepted. While music
hall performances are closer than anything else to the pure
essence of theatricality, mechanization of modern culture and
technology must find their expression on the stage.

Anennkov produced in Petrograd (1919) *The First Distiller*
adapted from Tolstoy's play, in which the discovery of alcoholic
drink was represented as the Devil's invention to dominate men
and turn them into swine and beasts. He used it merely as a
scenario and introduced into it new protagonists, a Vertical Devil,
a Jester of the Elder Devil, accordion players, acrobats, and
turned scenes in hell into a series of fantastic tricks for which
circus artists, including a red-haired clown, were invited. This
was chronologically the first "modernization" of a work by a great
writer from the "classical past." It exploded like a manifesto and
had a resounding echo. The theater of Popular Comedy in
Petrograd (1920-1922) under the leadership of Radlov and Solovyov, specialized in improvising *buffonades* and in presenting
classical plays in music hall disguise (Lope de Vega, Molière,
Calderon) . *Stenka Razin,* by Vassily Kamensky, was filled with
acrobatic acts and farcical episodes. At the same time, actors of
the theater larded their parts with topical hints and revolutionary slogans: this was their contribution to current events.

Yutkevich, Kosintsev, and Trauberg openly declared that they were going to cultivate "eccentrism" in their Theater of Free Comedy. To show how appreciative they were, not only of the music hall but also of the movies and detective stories, they staged a play about Musichall Kinematografovich Pinkerton, (which in Russian sounded like a Christian name, a patronymic, and a family name) turning it into a game of gags and circus entertainment. The Factory of the Eccentric Actor, an independent institution, gave in September 1922 in Petrograd *The Marriage* by Gogol and thus announced it: "Electrification of Gogol, Music Hall, Americanism, and Grand Guignol." Kosintsev believed that "the tempo of the Revolution is that of scandal and publicity" and wanted to use "circus, movies, music hall, dime novels, posters, and American dances" for propaganda purposes.

While cubist and futurist painters made décors for various well-established theatrical institutions, (Ekster and Yakulov for Tairov, Nivinsky for Vakhtangov, Altman and Chagall for the Jewish Chamber Theater), their comrades were active on experimental stages in Moscow and in the provinces. Tatlin, Rodchenko, and Popova taught in dramatic schools and hailed the new world of wheels, machines, and gadgets as the source of inspiration for the constructivist art, industrial, functional, and the only one truly allied to the proletariat and its revolution. During the NEP (New Economic Policy) this tendency was doubled by great admiration of America as the land of highest urbanization and constructivism.

At one point, imagists headed by Serghei Essenin also claimed that they had something to contribute to the theater of the Revolution; they dreamt of it as poetic and experimental in literary forms. They failed, however, to create their own scenic technique.

It can be safely stated that the first decade of Russian revolution was under the sign of antirealism in the theater, and that all the new trends conceived in the pre-Revolutionary period were developed and intensified after 1917. Some of their leaders came to the fore as genuine representatives of the new proletarian era, combining extremism in form with sharp political propaganda; others, such as Tairov, for instance, or some urbanists and imagists, avoided political commitments.

In the years 1918-1924, any new theory, any eccentric proposal, any crazy attempt at innovation, would find enthusiastic

followers and material opportunities. This hardly seems possible
if one thinks of the misery and devastation which struck Russia
in the first years of the Communist rule. But to understand what
happened, one has also to imagine the atmosphere of excitement
and adventure which reigned in those unbelievable and heroic
times. Hundreds of new theatrical ventures sprang up all over the
Soviet territory, and amateur movements took the form of an
avalanche. By 1927 there were twenty-four thousand theatrical
circles in Russia. Dramatic schools were swamped. When a
theatrical studio was established in the provincial town of Voronezh, in 1919, nine hundred candidates came to entrance exam-
inations; in Irkutsk, in Siberia, the opening of a dramatic school
attracted three hundred applicants. And similar things occurred
in other places. While workmen's and peasant's clubs promoted
the amateur movement, more sophisticated groups in large cities
repeated futurist or Proletcult slogans, admired Meyerhold as
the leader of Russian theater, and made all sorts of experiments
"to find an adequate theatrical language for the new Communist
society." Not less amazing was the attitude of the general public.
The interest in the theater resembled an epidemic. Never and
nowhere had such a phenomenon been witnessed in modern history. Regular theaters drew huge audiences and so did dramatic
groups and improvised stage platforms. Of course, free distribution of tickets among workmen and soldiers was an important
factor; another factor was the general desire for entertainment
in dire times of starvation and misery. Living conditions were
awful, and theater offered some kind of escape to thousands
of hungry, worried people. But there was also an explosion of
creative instinct, a wish for self-expression, for artistic activities,
a novelty for the large masses, which explains the emergence of
dramatic groups in factories, in villages, and in the Red Army
and Navy. In 1920, the armed forces alone had some 1,210 theaters, 1,800 clubs, and 911 dramatic groups. *The Theater Messenger* of 1919 (No. 6) tells of the town of Kargopol in Olonezk
region, with a population of four thousand: it had a theater and
a theatrical bulletin. In all corners of the former empire of the
tsars one could find experimental workshops and dramatic
schools; every local Soviet had theatrical sections, while every
plant or military unit organized amateur performances. "The

whole of Russia recites," said Shklovsky, "and here live cells get transformed into theatrical cells."

In large cities, crowds stormed the auditoriums, and Moscow and Leningrad theaters, on top of the regular schedule, gave performances in the suburbs. Legitimate companies formed itinerant groups for villages and small provincial towns. Actors went on these trips willingly because they were paid not in worthless money but in bread, lard, and butter, the most precious products of the era. The Mariinsky Theater of opera and ballet, for instance, sent a group of singers and dancers to workers' clubs every Saturday, and its itinerant company had 170 performances on the road in ten months; in the 1920-1921 season they gave 225 shows for labor unions. Some statistics indicate that more than 3,000 theatrical organizations functioned in Russia during the terrible years of the Civil War, 1918-1922.

In his often quoted book *The Knight's Move,* Victor Shklovsky relates: "In this terrifying world made of frost, stale herrings, rags, typhoid fever, arrests, bread lines and armed soldiers, one first night followed the other, and every evening theaters were jammed. Toward the middle of a show the huge unheated houses were warmed up by the breath of the audience. Lights would flicker and often go out, there was little current and no coal. Isadora Duncan danced by the light of torches brought on the stage while thousands of voices, hoarse from the cold, sang 'Bravely forward, keep your step, comrades' in the dark house. In operas, members of orchestras played with their fur coats on and fur caps over their ears, and steam came from brass instruments as if they were locomotive pipes or smoke stacks. And dancers in tights and tulle skirts danced in polar draughts." (*Khod Konia,* Berlin 1923). Yablochkina of the Maly Theater tells in her memoirs that she and her colleagues played Ostrovsky's *Wolves and Sheep* at 5° centigrade. They wore furs and boots, caps and mufflers, the make-up froze on their faces, costumes became hard and icy, but the audience, wrapped in blankets and shawls, sat patiently through the performance and apparently enjoyed it.

Was it escape from reality, a glance into a new world of fiction, a discovery of an artificial paradise by people who for centuries had not been admitted to the entertainments of the upper classes, or a kind of collective curiosity, that inextinguishable Russian desire to learn and experience new things? Whatever the explanation, from 1918 till 1924, this collective psychosis assumed striking proportions, creative inventiveness rose in a fountain-like jet. These were the years of experimentation and establishment of new enterprises, such as children's theater, the Jewish Studio Theater, schools of acting craft and direction, dramatic courses, and dozens of workshops, where most fantastic theories were tested, such as N. Foregger's Free Workshop, B. Ferdinandov's Workshop of Experimental-Heroic Theater, The Factory of the Eccentric Actor, Mchedelov's Studio of Improvisation, and Meyerhold's State Institute for Directors. Public and private discussions on the theater were enhanced by books and magazines printed on something that resembled wrapping paper, and with an ink one could hardly read. In 1921-1922 forty theatrical magazines were published in Moscow and Petrograd (later Leningrad) —three times as many as before the Revolution.

In the feverish atmosphere of the Civil War and general upheaval when nothing seemed too radical or impossible, when proportions were magnified and energies multiplied, and later, during the years of NEP, when the arts enjoyed relative freedom, experimentalists and innovators prevailed among professionals, and they enchanted the public. But next to them were gathering hostile forces. The emergence of popular multitudes and of new mass audiences raised the problems of repertory and the level of theatrical performances. Lenin and his friends were not so much interested in finding a new revolutionary art as in using the stage as a political platform and as a means of "enlightenment" of the people. They were perfectly satisfied with realism and good old plays by Ostrovsky and Gogol. Lenin and "reasonable Communists" hoped to instill the existing theatrical institutions with Party spirit, and they did not care for Mayakovsky or Tairov or Meyerhold. The clash of the two tendencies was inevitable, but it did not occur until the end of the twenties. In the first, most fruitful, most sensational, most colorful decade of the Revolution, the *avant-garde* still had a dominant position. Its universally recognized leader, Meyerhold, was given a free hand to promote and realize his most extravagant projects.

II

Meyerhold began his activities in 1917 in an official capacity: he was deputy chief of the Petrograd Theater Section which succeeded in drafting for its membership the leading symbolists: Bely, Briussov, Chulkov, Ivanov, and Blok, the latter appointed chairman of the repertory committee. All of them were old friends, but Meyerhold looked for new ones among cubists and futurists. He soon got a small army of young followers—painters, actors and poets—who belonged to the *avant-garde*. His first theatrical venture in 1918 was the staging of Mayakovsky's *Mystery Bouffe* in Petrograd's conservatory. Vladimir Mayakovsky, a futurist, wrote it as a half-comic popular pageant, with crudely drawn, posterlike figures. He parodied the Bible and imagined a new flood and a new Ark, the "unclean" being the proletarians of various races and professions, and the "pure" including the exploiters of all kinds, from the Abyssinian Negus to the fat Russian merchant and the German officer. After the unsuccessful attempt of the exploiters to impose their rule upon the "unclean," the latter throw the "rulers" overboard and find their way to the promised land—after passing through hell with inoffensive devils and through paradise with boring angels. He who brings them to the end of the journey is neither Devil nor God, but Man, and his Sermon on the Mount, a travesty of the Gospel, deals with bread and fruits of the earth, and jeers at the decoys of religion. In the land of plenty, hard and soft rolls grow on the trees, and workmen are freed from want and capitalist abuse.

This political farce with its coarse facetiousness, belly laughter, and loud, slapstick-comedy jokes was conceived by Mayakovsky as a propaganda piece. The Biblical subject was used in a polemical, antireligious sense, and its revolutionary intent was emphasized by a hyperbolic style. It began a whole series of "social message" works in which primitive characters were crudely painted in black and white.

Meyerhold staged this "heroic, epic, and satirical picture of our epoch" (according to the subtitle), as a county fair show on the occasion of the first anniversary of the 1917 Bolshevik

Revolution. The painter Malevich put on the boards a huge blue
hemisphere representing the terrestrial globe and some cubic
forms intimating the Ark. The hell was a gothic green-red hall;
the paradise, a gray cardboard construction with multicolored
clouds; and the promised land, a structure of machines. The
actors, not very good ones, recited in a monotonous psalmody
but they often succeeded in getting across the punch lines to
the public. One of the famous ones was the definition of the
democratic republic made by a capitalist to a proletarian: "It
is like a doughnut: to me the doughnut, to you the hole."

The critics did not like *Mystery Bouffe,* and accused Meyerhold and Mayakovsky of making a "vulgar circus," a crude show
box; the Communists found the farce "too abstruse for the proletarians." It was a quite a few years before they changed their
opinion.

In 1919, Meyerhold, who had gone on the road, was caught
by the Whites in the South and arrested while trying to escape
from the port of Novorossiisk. Beaten up and thrown in jail,
he owed his life to the intervention of important friends: his
companions of the abortive escape were executed. As soon as the
Reds defeated the Whites, Meyerhold joined the Communist
Party and arrived in Moscow attired as a typical Civil War commissar, wearing a leather jacket and a gun on his belt. This did
not surprise his intimates: from his early youth Meyerhold had
sympathized with the socialists and had hailed the revolutionists.

Now he launched a new movement: "October in the Theater."
(The overthrow of Kerensky's government took place on October 25, old style, or November 7, new style; hence the confusion
—the Russians talking of the October, and the rest of the world
of the November Revolution.) "The time has come," said Meyerhold, "to make a Revolution in the theater, and to reflect in each
performance the struggle of the working class for emancipation."
Only new forms could do the job, and this idea was enthusiastically accepted by his young followers: in this atmosphere of general excitement and enthusiasm, they all wanted to navigate
toward unknown shores. Through Meyerhold's influence the
theater of the Revolution in 1920-1924 became definitely the
theater of the *avant-garde*—and this was the most striking event
of this period. In no other country had the experimentalists

(later called "formalists") such vast testing grounds and such
financial and material possibilities as in Soviet Russia, and this
despite the fact that Lenin and his old guard were conservative
in art.

In 1920, Meyerhold was appointed the head of the Theatrical
Department in the Education Commissariat; this meant that he
was given power and authority. He also directed the Russian
Socialist Federative Soviet Republic Theater Number One. Of
course, Party leaders did not like his total repudiation of the
past or his extremism, or his extravagance. But was he not using
the theater as a means of political propaganda? And was he not
the leader of the intellectuals whom he drafted for the service
of the Revolution? His workshops, his "flying theaters" sent by
train or on sleighs to villages and provincial towns, were but a
part of his vast activities.

In Moscow he took an old unheated building, which looked
like a hall for political gatherings (formerly Zon's Operetta House
on Sadovaya Street), and established there his headquarters with
complete disregard for comfort, in the ascetic spirit, typical of the
Civil War period. There he began a series of memorable performances, drawing huge audiences of workmen, soldiers, and
intellectuals. The admission was free of charge.

He began with *The Dawns* by Emile Verhaeren, which he
changed completely, making it a contemporary play with hints or
even direct mention of current events. A messenger who came on
the stage in the course of the performance read bulletins from
the Southern Front where the Red Army fought against Wrangel,
and the news of the storming of the Isthmus of Perekop was
met with an ovation: detachments of soldiers with Red banners
rushed to the stage to express their joy. On some evenings, it
looked much more like a political meeting than a theatrical
show. Meyerhold welcomed this as a sign of the unity between
the actors and the spectators. Impatient to produce plays, Meyerhold hardly trained his actors and they were rather bad, but the
settings were interesting: cubes, ropes, mobiles, red circles, golden
circles, triangles of shiny metal. Actors in roughly painted gray-
silver, cotton clothing recited, standing on top of cubes, and
the cold voices of the chorus rose from the orchestra pit.

The first night of *The Dawns* provoked heated debate, and

Krupskaya, Lenin's wife, published a virulent letter against this "modernization and distortion of Verhaeren" questioning whether the cubist and abstract style of Meyerhold's staging was actually "proletarian." Even more explicit was a letter from the Central Committee of the Party of December 1, 1920. It attacked the Proletcult, Meyerhold's friends. Their philosophy was branded as "bourgeois" and dependent on Mach, the Austrian physicist and psychologist and the target of Lenin's previous polemics. Futurism was accused of "corrupted senseless taste, alien to proletarians." Two months later, Meyerhold left the Theatrical Section and became a free-lancer. He probably felt the same way as Ehrenburg, who said (in Berlin) in 1922: "In Russia, revolutionaries in art are zero (O) in social life; and revolutionaries in social life are reactionaries in art (– minus) ."

Disregarding the opposition of certain Party circles, Meyerhold produced *Mystery Bouffe* again (May 1, 1921) in a new version, closer to the concrete political situation, with topical hints and figures, such as the French Premier Clemenceau in a top hat, striped trousers, a shirt-front made of pages torn out of a French book; in subsequent performances, he wore yellow spats, gloves, and a rose. Most of the costumes were made out of pieces of newspapers, the actors talked from a box on the proscenium and other constructions, a clown interrupted the dialogue with his antics. Igor Iliinsky gave a satirical image of a frightened and indecisive Menshevik. The décors were by Malevich. A few weeks later, during the Third Congress of the Communist Internationale, *Mystery Bouffe* was given in a circus arena in German, with an expensive *mise-en-scène,* for which the organizers were reprimanded by Party authorities. Meyerhold immediately disassociated himself from this unhappy enterprise. His version ran one hundred times and was repeated in the provinces but never attained great popularity.

While engaged in polemics and debate, Meyerhold concentrated in 1921 on the preparation of actors for his own company, according to his new theory of biomechanics. During these years, thousands of young men and women had invaded all the dramatic schools, and he therefore had no difficulty in finding eager pupils. He trained them quickly enough to show in April 1922 *The Magnificent Cuckold* by Crommelynck (*Le Cocu magnifique*) .

This comedy, which lampooned a miller who looks for his wife's lover and makes all the male population of the village pass through her bedchamber, was by no means a revolutionary subject, but Meyerhold used it in order to test his latest innovation, biomechanics. The stage was completely denuded, no curtains, no rafters, no backdrops. It was occupied by a mill-like construction (by Lyubov Popova) with platforms, stairs, wheels, rolling discs, windmill sails, a trapeze, a viaduct, and inclined surfaces. On this truly constructivist stage, actors in blue overalls ran, jumped, and moved like acrobats. Instead of "true emotions" they presented movement and acted like athletes, exhibiting all sorts of physical exercises with the exactitude and inventiveness of drilled professionals. The idea was quite clear despite all the cheap jibes of silly critics: Meyerhold's daring premise was that the truth of human relationships and behavior, the essence of man, is expressed not by words but by gestures, glances, steps, and attitudes. "The mute eloquence of the body" can do miracles; "word is but an embroidery on the canvas of movement."

In Crommelynck's comedy, Dr. Dapertutto made a comeback, and the acting through movement was alternated with buffoonery, farcical numbers, and musical surprises: Iliinsky, an excellent actor, wearing two red bands, made a marvelous clown, and in the third act a brilliant jazz orchestra was introduced. There were other amusing gags and the whole performance had real go, a brio, and was enhanced by very good acting: in addition to Iliinsky there was Babanova, a gifted and charming actress, and some young people Meyerhold had succeeded in forming. The brilliance of the production was matched by sobriety and economy of means.

Each of Meyerhold's following shows was an event and a subject for debate. In *Tarelkin's Death* by Sukhovo-Kobylin, he accentuated the parody in an eccentric way. V. Stepanova's decor was abstract, consisting of lines and geometrical forms, but the style of the show resembled that of a popular farce. The actors displayed marvels of agility, and did clownish numbers. Wearing blue-striped overalls, they all struggled with objects which suddenly came to life, fell to pieces, jumped into the air, or exploded thunderously. There were also shots, flights across the stage on steel ropes, and circus properties with magic surprises. When

reproached for all these eccentricities, Meyerhold, in heated polemics with his critics, defended his right to modernize productions with jesters' devices and the techniques of the circus.
In a less successful performance of *Earth On Its Hind Legs*
(from *The Night* by Marcel Martinet) the combination of circus, music hall, playroom, gymnasium, and slapstick comedy
reached new extremes. Trucks, motorcycles, or bicycles on the
stage, or whole detachments of Red soldiers marching with full
war equipment including small cannons, certainly added to the
strange aspect of the boards and of the house.

By 1923, despite Lenin's opposition to all sorts of *avant-garde*
formalism and violent attacks in the Communist press, Meyerhold's position was very strong. Himself a member of the Party,
he had powerful supporters in the government, including Bukharin, Rykov, Frunze, and Lunacharsky, and enjoyed tremendous
popularity with the youth. Delegations from all regions of Russia flocked to Moscow to see his performances and to learn
about his biomechanics. The debate surrounding his work kept
alive theatrical life in the Soviet Union and made it well-known
abroad. The beginning of the New Economy Policy, with its
loosening of Party controls and more liberal atmosphere in the
arts, also strengthened his position. In 1923, he was given a big
theater named after him—the TIM (in Russian: *Teatr imeni
Meyerholda*), and was granted the title of People's Artist for the
twenty-fifth anniversary of his activities on the Russian stage.
He was also the head of the State's High Workshop for theater
directors; his former and present pupils included Iliinsky, Alexandrov, Eisenstein, Okhlopkov, and many others. His influence
was growing steadily, and he had large financial and material
means at his disposal. He could go abroad and get acquainted
with the recent trends in Western art. And he was training for
leading roles Zinaida Raikh, the woman with whom he was
passionately in love, the former wife of Essenin. Although Meyerhold was not a true educator, he did an extraordinary job with
Raikh: an extremely attractive and intelligent woman, endowed
with charm and sex appeal, she certainly was not gifted for the
stage—and still Meyerhold made an actress out of her.

In these best, most glorious years of his life, Meyerhold resumed his work with the classics. Probably no other show raised

so much indignation and debate as his version of Ostrovsky's *The Forest* which he broke into thirty-three episodes and treated in the spirit of cinematographic techniques; his "trunkline" was the exposé of Russian landowners, but this theme actually expanded into a satire of the upper class in general.

He turned the two actors of *The Forest,* the Happy one and the Unhappy one, into Don Quixote and Sancho Panza, and presented the rest of the cast as grotesques: they wore multicolor wigs, and behaved like clowns. The setting was basically constructivist, and a long suspended stairway led from the house onto the stage, dividing the latter into two parts; the Spartan uniformity and shabbiness of the earlier shows changed now to a display of bright colors and props. Instead of symbols and abstractions, real objects were put in—tables loaded with food, mirrors, pails, and plates. Was it a reflection of the material improvement under the NEP? Some critics, quite erroneously, interpreted this new trend as a return to the times of Meyerhold's lavish productions in the Alexandrinsky.

It was during the NEP, between 1922 and 1928, that the Russians, keenly interested in the West, had cultural exchanges with Europe and America and could compare their own artistic efforts with movements abroad such as futurism, dadaism, surrealism, and expressionism. German expressionistic plays and writings were quite popular in Moscow and Leningrad. Even more influential was the "urbanistic" tendency. The *avant-garde* admired machinism and Americanism, American films were extremely popular, and the fox-trot and shimmy made their appearances on the dance floors of Soviet night clubs. At the same time, all these manifestations of Western life and art were officially condemned as typical of capitalist corruption and decline. This created an ambiguous situation whenever European or American life was represented on the stage. For example, Meyerhold's *Give Us Europe,* a large potboiler in seventeen episodes with 95 parts alternatively interpreted by 45 actors, depicted the struggle between two firms: the bad capitalist American and the good Russian socialist. "Clean" parades of Soviet mariners and athletes were pitted against the scenes of moral dissolution in Europe; and although Meyerhold presented the latter in a satirical and sometimes farcical manner, the spectators obviously en-

joyed the dancing girls and beautifully dressed ladies from the
Western Cities of the Plain. Stepanova offered a new décor for
the show: rotating wooden shields, the position of which could
be rapidly changed, thus offering a variety of backgrounds; there
were also other combinations of mobile walls.

A new phase in Meyerhold's experimentation was offered in
January 1925 in *The Teacher Bubus,* an inferior play by the
Soviet dramatist Alexey Falko (then thirty-two years old). Except
for *Mystery Bouffe* this was the first play from modern Soviet
repertory. *Bubus* had a strong political ring: it is the story of
a weak intellectual in some undetermined European country; he
hesitates in accepting the Revolution unconditionally because he
is disturbed by its cruelty and intransigence, but his attempts
at reconciling the bourgeois and the proletarian ends with his
becoming a weapon in the hands of the former. Here again
Meyerhold showed the decline of refined and resplendent Europe
against a contrasting bare décor. This time he experimented
with a closed stage: the boards on which the actor moved were
circumscribed by a pavilion made of bamboo canes which rustled
and stirred. The objects were real, and some of them, such as
carpets, were quite luxurious; a fountain was used as a symbol
of lavishness. But the main innovation was the music: *Bubus*
was staged as a dramatic symphony, accompanied by forty-six
excerpts from Liszt and Chopin; long pauses between dialogues
had a musical intent, and each performer had his own rhythm
of speech and movement, almost a melodic line. The tempo of
the whole performance was slowed down, and silence before
speech had a definite, impressionistic "pre-acting" value.

Some biographers intimate that certain ideological doubts
crept into Meyerhold's mind at that time; like many other Communists of the first hour, he did not approve the atmosphere of
the NEP, the resurrection of middle-class mentality, and the vul-
garization of Soviet society. This was the moment when a great
many writers and intellectuals favored humor and satire to stig-
matize the narrow-mindedness, greediness, and backwardness of
social strata which prevailed in the NEP era.

At the same time, after the death of Lenin, the struggle within
the Party became intensified, and under the steady pressure of
Stalin, his rivals were eliminated, first of all Trotsky. The en-

thusiasm and the gaiety so typical of Meyerhold's creations at the dawn of the Revolution were gone, those years of heroic and cosmic hopes seemed very distant and his new mood was reflected in the plays he offered to the public.

Meyerhold's new enterprise, the TIM, was well organized, and reposed on solid foundations; it also possessed a company of trained actors and the preparation of each new show now became more careful.

In April 1925, Meyerhold presented another modern play, *The Warrant* or *The Credentials* by Nikolay Erdman, a very talented young man (born in 1902). His satirical comedy depicted Pavlusha Guliachkin, a kind of Soviet Khlestakov, who spreads the rumor that he has special credentials giving him extraordinary powers; he even shows this document with duly affixed seals, stamps, and signatures. All the "ex-people" who dream of the return of the old regime, all the former bourgeois, gather around Pavlusha, and a rich NEPman decides to give his daughter in marriage to this important official of pure proletarian extraction. At the end everything explodes: it comes out that Pavlusha is the son of a middle-class bourgeois across the Moscow River; he is a rogue, a crook, and a liar; his warrant that empowered him to arrest half of Russia is a fake, and is confiscated by the true members of the secret police.

Erdman certainly ridiculed and exposed the remnants of the defeated classes, but he also hit the Soviet bureaucracy, the fear inspired in ordinary citizens by Party credentials, and the whole regime of suspicion and oppression which spread over Russia under the Red banner. Meyerhold showed the "former people" in concentric circles, looking like wax figures from Mme. Tussaud's museum, but he mixed satire with a threatening feeling of doom, and parts of his staging were openly grim. So was the make-up of most protagonists, who looked like horrible masks. Quite striking was the ball at Pavlusha's wedding to the NEPman's daughter: a brassband orchestra played well-known pre-revolutionary tunes, white-gloved waiters served champagne, and toasts were made to "the members of the reigning house." At the same opening night, April 20, 1925, some of the spectators interpreted the hints and allusions of the play as direct comment on recent events and shouted, "Down with bureaucracy," "Down with Stalin." Later, Meyerhold was reminded of this fact as a proof of his connections with the right wing and Trotskyite opposition. His attempt to stage another play by Erdman, *The Suicide,* was thwarted by the authorities: after the dress rehearsal *The Suicide* was banned by the Party Central Committee. During the subsequent purges Erdman was arrested and disappeared into the darkness of Siberian concentration camps.

Meyerhold made his assistant, Fyodorov, produce another topical political play, *Roar China,* by Serghei Tretyakov, a futurist writer who made a propaganda piece in a posterlike, coarse manner. But at the end of the same year (1926), which was opened by *Roar China,* Meyerhold resumed his adaptation of classics and produced the most controversial *The Inspector General,* "a grandiose suite on Gogolian themes" in fifteen episodes, each having a separate title. He did not hesitate to transform the text and even, in parts, the plot of Russia's beloved masterpiece. His aim was to create a synthetic and symbolic picture of the country. Instead of a small provincial town, he transferred the action to a big city, probably the capital itself, made the mayor a general, his wife a lady of dubious virtue from high society, and Khlestakov an expert adventurer, well-versed in politics and the intrigues of the court, yet behaving like a harlequin. The latter was accompanied by an enigmatic travel companion, an officer who does not figure in the cast of the original comedy. The enormous half-moon stage of mahogany had fifteen doors. The main action was placed on a sloping 16 by 20-foot platform which emerged at the right moment out of the darkness with actors and props ready. Costumes, furniture, candelabra, and settings were all resplendent with gold and glitter as in Golovin's days, and accompanying scores and old love songs were arranged as period pieces. The music was by Gnessin and the settings by Kiselev. In the scene where the officials bribe Khlestakov, instead of a succession of individual interviews with the imposter, Meyerhold staged a stunning show: all the fifteen doors in the circular wall were thrown open, and the officials appeared, each offering money with an outstretched hand. In the scene of the ball, guests came onto the stage from the house, and the end was treated in a Hoffmannesque manner: at the exposé of the swindle, the mayor went out of his mind, was put in a straight jacket by policemen and carried away on a stretcher, while his wife collapsed in a dead faint. Then a white curtain with the announcement of the arrival of the authentic inspector general in gold letters was lowered, then raised again over the stage where, instead of living actors, painted clay mannequins, arranged in a mute scene of distress and astonishment, gave a frightening spectacle of a panopticon. The acting of Garin (Khlestakov) and of Babanova (the mayor's daughter) was excellent, in tones of easy and elegant grotesque, but Anna Andreyevna, the mayor's wife, interpreted by Raikh, was heavily erotic: this was the way Meyerhold made his wife play most of her parts.

Meyerhold's *The Inspector General* was a momentous event. It probably had more detractors than defenders, but its impact on dozens of directors was prodigious. Some of them simply copied Meyerhold; others imitated him in a more or less disguised fashion. If they were not as daring as *The Comrade Khlestakov*, put on by D. Smolin in 1922 (with Mayakovsky poetry as part of the dialogues), they were still quite eccentric. In 1927 Igor Terentyev staged *The Inspector General* in the House of the Press in Leningrad and made the costumes of the protagonists emblematic: the postmaster wore stamps and envelopes, the head of the public hospitals had a skull painted on his sleeves, and the round-faced pair, Dobchinsky and Bobchinsky, were transformed into garrulous women. A W.C. was placed in the center of the stage and actors in turn took refuge in it.

It is interesting to note that of the three "adaptations" or, as the public called them, "distortions" of classics by Meyerhold— *The Forest, A Profitable Job* (Ostrovsky), and *The Inspector General*—the first and the third became parts of national repertory: in 1936, just before its director fell into disgrace, Meyerhold's theater had its 1500th performance of *The Forest,* and *The Inspector General* was shown not only in Moscow but also in the provinces and in Europe (in 1928 at the theatrical festival in Paris to which Meyerhold's and Vakhtangov's companies were sent by the Soviet Government). *The Inspector General* provoked a tempest of indignation, and thousands of people claimed in the press and in public debate that Meyerhold had committed a sacrilege and should not be permitted to distort in such an offensive way the consecrated, great masterpieces of Russian litera-

ture. Luncharsky and Andrey Bely defended their friend coura-
geously, but the number of his enemies grew steadily after the
memorable performance of 1926. His next "adaptation" of *Wit
Works Woe* (1928) was definitely milder and did not attract
much attention. Some critics believe that *The Inspector General*
was Meyerhold's last great creation, and that after 1927 his inventiveness and brilliance went downhill.

One of his many problems was that of the repertory, and in
May 1928 in a telegram to Mayakovsky begging for a comedy,
he wrote: "Theater is perishing, there are no new plays." As
we will see later, there were plenty of them, but their flat, down-
to-earth realism simply horrified and disgusted Meyerhold.

Mayakovsky's *The Bedbug* was produced in February 1929.
It was a great success with the public but not with the critics:
the official press attacked the author for his text, the producer
for his staging, and the musician, Shostakovich, for his score.

The Bedbug, written in prose, was directed against the revival
of the triviality and vulgarity that flourished under the NEP. Its
hero, Prisypkin, dreams of refined existence after the privations
of civil war, calls himself Pierre Skripkin (*skripka* in Russian is
violin) and marries Elzevira Renaissance, daughter of a barber
and herself a manicurist. A fire breaks out during the wedding
party, the jet of water from firemen's hoses freezes immediately
in the winter sub-zero temperature, and dead drunk Prisypkin
becomes a block of ice in the cellar of the house. He is discovered
fifty years later, intact with his guitar, butterfly tie, pomaded
hair, and a bedbug on his collar; and he is brought back to life
through the miracles of refrigeration, anabiosis, and Soviet
science. For the society of 1979 he is a curious specimen and so is
his bedbug. Both are placed in a cage in the zoo, the *philisteus
vulgaris* and the *cimex normalis* of olden times. The citizens of
the Communist paradise look with amazement at those remnants
of the NEP period while Prisypkin plays the guitar and sings
sentimental songs. Yet his last words are rather ambiguous; he
recognizes his brothers in the crowd in front of his cage and
shouts at them: "Citizen brothers, where do you come from,
how many are you, have they thawed all of you?" In Meyerhold's
production Prisypkin addressed this speech to the house, facing
the spectators.

Prisypkin was interpreted by Igor Iliinsky. He was clownish, pretentious, and sad, one of the best fanciful images of that gifted actor. *The Bedbug* was a satirical grotesque, and its text fitted perfectly into the form given it by Meyerhold, although some critics wondered whether it was absolutely necessary to add trapezists and trained dogs to what was already going on on the stage. The costumes and decor of the first act, in which Prisypkin and his future mother-in-law buy various items and food for the wedding and talk to vendors, was treated as nineteenth-century vaudeville by the group of cartoonists known as *Kukriniksy*. The wedding was a buffoonery, and the settings for 1979 were made in silver tones with wide use of glass, metal, and linoleum by Rodchenko. By giving a quasi-realistic treatment to the episodes of the NEP and a purely constructivistic one to the vision of the future, Meyerhold ably stressed the difference between the old and new, not only in mentality but also in art.

He was confronted with almost the same problem in *The Bathhouse*, Mayakovsky's next comedy, which he produced in March 1930 in a rather hostile atmosphere. The first presentation of *The Bathhouse* in Leningrad's People's House by Vladimir Liuche in January was received very coldly by the public, which did not laugh, and by the critics, who sneered. *The Bathhouse* was a sharp attack against Soviet bureaucracy impersonated in the comedy by pompous Pobedonosikov and his secretary Optimistenko. They were pitted against Chudakov, an inventor, who puts together a time machine in which one can go backward or forward, into the past centuries as well as into the centuries to come (the influence of Wells's famous story is obvious). While Chudakov is fighting against bureaucratic obtuseness and stupidity, a Phosphorescent Lady drops from the year 2030 for a twenty-four-hour visit. She is ready to take with her those who are willing to travel into the future at the speed of a year a second. Pobedonosikov also wants to go along but is kicked out by the Lady: people like him do not belong to the future.

Meyerhold emphasized the biting satirical spirit of *The Bathhouse* defined in its subtitle as a "drama of circus and fireworks." Chudakov, the inventor, and his friends wore overalls, went around with a light, dancing gait, the diagrams of their machine were neatly designed geometrical lines; whereas the bureaucrats were clumsy and overstuffed, they sat in heavy armchairs, and the only modern items on their tables were numerous telephones. The Phosphorescent Lady of the future with her close-fitting raiment, looking like a constructivist dream, and quite a beautiful one, was played by Raikh.

The main décor was made of a fixed platform around which rotated huge circles. Long strips with slogans descended from the rafters. In the third act, there was a dialogue about art and theater which sounded like a challenge to what the Communist press was writing about realism. And then there was a frank parody of the ballet *The Red Poppy* by Glière, acclaimed at the time as a true manifestation of revolutionary art. In Meyerhold's parody, it was just a repetition of dated Imperial ballets. Polemical verse and various slogans on the stage challenged the outdated realism of academic theaters and the bad taste of Communist leaders.

The play and its production were surrounded by an atmosphere of hostility. Mayakovsky commited suicide less than a month after the performance. And then *The Bathhouse* was taken off the boards for a quarter of a century. In fact, it was not until 1955 that Mayakovsky's comedies were again offered to Soviet audiences. Between these two dates, 1930-1955, lay the twenty-five years of Stalin's era. It banned experimentalism in art and curbed all the innovators—including Meyerhold.

9

FROM INNOVATORS TO CONSERVATIVES

IN THE FIRST POST-REVOLUTIONARY DECADE Meyerhold embodied the new spirit of the Russian theater. Various factors concurred in placing him at the center of all theatrical events: his past experiences and the discussions they aroused, his consistent and intransigent antirealistic stand, his relentless energy combined with creative imagination, and his privileged position in the Communist Party. He was inventive, daring, and powerful. All the innovations of the Soviet stage, all the experiments of the *avant-garde* either sprang directly from him or were somewhat linked with his activities. He represented, moreover, that very antirealistic movement in the arts which swept over all of Europe on the morrow of World War I; and through him, Russia maintained her ties with the West. In the twenties Soviet literature, art, and theater still continued to move ahead in the mainstream of European culture. Their themes and ways of expression were national and topical, and certainly mirrored the social and political scene of the Revolution, but their basic artistic tendency reflected the general trends of the century, the direction which was common to all Western countries. The break between Russia and the West came later, in the thirties, when the doctrine of socialist realism was invented as an exclusive art form in opposition to the "decadent and hostile" culture of European and American capitalism.

The minority of youth and talent which responded enthusiastically to Meyerhold's daring exploits was also fascinated by his theories. Meyerhold was a visionary, and in his book *Reconstruction of the Theater*, he outlined his ultimate objective: the merging of cinema, radio, circus, music hall, sport, and comedy into a super-show which would express the urban age of technological progress. He believed that this new form would become the art of the future socialist society. In pursuing this dream, Meyerhold found fabulous technical solutions, mainly in the field of theatrical kinetics. This, probably, was one of his weaknesses: driven by his own dynamism and looking for expression in action and movement, he minimized the part of contemplation and stasis in esthetic emotion. Bent on creating a spectacle of speed, agility, surprise, and humor, making a constant appeal to the senses and to fantasy, he certainly neglected, and at times deliberately overlooked, the intellectual, ideological elements of a play. He was a highly intelligent man, and an intellectual, but he did not want ideas to be discussed on the stage or expressed through scenic media. They were secondary, let alone unnecessary, for a successful show. In general, his artistic intent was not ideological—and this originated his rift with Party theoreticians.

Meyerhold was so absorbed by his struggle against tradition and so passionately involved in demolishing—often with malice and sarcasm—old-fashioned theatrical forms, that his negation appeared more convincing than his affirmations. As an iconoclast and a rebel he was clear-cut, consistent, streamlined. As a builder, he knew how to make ordinary theatrical material look new and strange. In this, he followed the formalists who claimed that the basic device of all arts consisted precisely in rendering objects, words, and images unusual, singular, and eccentric. But he was rather vague or incomplete in many ways. It is customary to say that Meyerhold was also a bad teacher, that as a producer he often bungled details, that he often did not aspire to perfection and was satisfied with mere outlines, however sparkling they were, that he squandered the riches of his inventiveness instead of making rational, well-organized use of them. This, however, should not be accepted without critical reservations. When he so wished and when he did care, Meyerhold could work out a finished product, well balanced, carefully planned, and skillfully proportioned, such as *Masquerade, The Inspector General, The*

Forest, and others. His main defect, his Achilles' heel as he himself used to say laughingly, was his impatience which prevented him from becoming an educator. Unlike Stanislavsky, he did not form actors, and he did not leave behind him a Meyerhold System or school of acting. He had his methods of production, his discoveries and tricks, his scenic images, but not a routine of training. This is the reason why he could never build a superior company. Here again, the main difficulty lay not alone in the deficiencies or peculiarities of his temperament. In Meyerhold's theories and practice the actor was not a free agent; his role was reduced to fulfilling the assignment given him by the director. There was no room for an actor's individuality in Meyerhold's scheme. One is left with the impression that he always cherished the idea of a marionette or a docile performer in a mask. The live actor had for him a purely functional, not creative, value. Hence the mechanical character which marred his less successful productions. Added to his attitude toward the ideological content of the plays he chose, his attitude toward actors explains why many of his performances, while being significant theatrical events, lacked intellectual or even deep emotional impact. It is obvious how this was bound to cause conflicts in a country ruled by a doctrinaire ideology which aimed at permeating all the arts.

Tairov, the second great director of the twenties, was very close to Meyerhold in his negation of the past and his revolutionary aspirations, but he chose a less spectacular road and, unlike his master and rival, he firmly believed in the creativity of the live actor. His performances were orchestrated; he compared actors to instruments, and the director to the conductor who should know every beat of the play. He sought for a melodious unity, for a rhythmic theme, and since he believed in music as the underlying principle of all scenic activity, he made words, movement, lighting, and psychological touches serve as a background for a perfect concert. In the twenties the public went to the Kamerny Theater as one goes to the ballet. Critics often said that, for instance, Alisa Koonen "danced beautifully through her role," or, "Tseretelli's design had delightful variations in minor key." The harmony of Tairov's productions pleased the senses, and the general impression received by the audiences was always that of esthetic gratification, regardless of the dramatic or comic content of the play: Tairov avoided the grimness or madness of Meyerhold's tragedies and the fantastic distortions of his grotesqueries. Some adversaries of Tairov dubbed him superficial, lacking in depth or emotional power. Others compared his enterprise after 1917 to an island protected from the stormy ocean by a coral reef. In 1918, at the height of the revolutionary cataclysm, he presented Oscar Wilde's *Salomé* to haggard, starved audiences which jammed the frozen hall. Alexandra Ekster, the leading stage designer of the Kamerny, applied to this performance her theory of "dynamic costumes." Each costume expressed the rhythm of characters' motions and gestures, it was like a make-up for the body or a mask for the face. Ekster's costumes moved on the stage; she spoke of the "delaying velvet, the speedy, agile silk, the heavy-paced brocade." She decorated costumes with paint and achieved surprising effects of color and tone by manipulating a complex lighting system. Ekster's "music of painting" and "rhythm of forms" was particularly potent in *Salomé* where Tairov made large use of background curtains in color. When John the Baptist uttered his prophecies, the silver-black curtain was pulled aside revealing the fatal pit. When Salomé consented to dance, making Herod shout with pleasure, the backstage curtain was torn and disappeared, disclosing a red curtain which seemed to bleed under the drunken rays of the moon. Alisa Koonen, a passionate, aggressive Salomé, wore a black dress with red veils, and her figure was projected against a blue background. Monsters, demons, goats, and leopards were painted on the stage curtain. The settings were cubistic: scaffoldings, spiral staircases, inclined surfaces. Pieces of material, multicolored curtains, and costumes of different textures fitted into the general atmosphere of the play.

The contrast between the audience in rags and the silk and brocade displayed on the stage was again very pointed in *Adrienne Lecouvreur,* the story of the French eighteenth-century actress and her unfortunate loves. The elegance of the Royal Court and Theater stressed the idea of the producer: he wanted to lift his spectators above the coarseness of their present-day life.

This tendency, however, was dubbed anti-Revolutionary. Already in 1918, when Tairov showed two plays by Paul Claudel—*L'Échange* and *L'Annonce faite à Marie*—he was reminded by

Zavadsky as Calaf in Vakhtangov's
production of *Turandot*, 1922.

A sketch for *Turandot*, Act I, by Vakhtangov and Nivinsky.

Vakhtangov's production of *Dybbuk* for the Habima Workshop, 1922.

M. Chekhov as Eric in *Eric the XIV*,
First Workshop, 1921.

Vakhtangov in 1917.

The Moscow Art Theater Company in the United States in 1922. In the front row, Morris Gest, Moskvin, John Barrymore as Hamlet, Kachalov, Stanislavsky, Ethel Barrymore, Arthur Hopkins, Robert Edmond Jones; in back, Baliev and his wife.

Scene from Ostrovsky's *Storm* at the Kamerny Theater, 1924.

Koonen as the commissar in Vishnevsky's *Optimistic Tragedy*, 1933.

A model for Meyerhold's production of Ostrovsky's *The Forest,* 1924.

model for Meyerhold's oduction of Mayakov-'s *The Bathhouse,* 1930.

Iliinsky as Akim in *The Power of Darkness* by L. Tolstoy.

Meyerhold (center) at a rehearsal with Erast Garin and Zinaida Raikh.

Scenes from Tchaikovsky's opera *Queen of Spades,* produced by Meyerhold in 1935.

Three Sisters, Act I, the Moscow Art Theater, 1940; sets by V. Dmitryev.

Three Sisters, Act I, the Moscow Art Theater, 1940; sets by V. Dmitryev.

Vishnevsky's *The Last Decisive*. Scene in which twenty-seven seamen die defending the lives of millions.

A scene from Mayakovsky's *The Bedbug*, 1955.

Two scenes from Mayakovsky's *The Bathhouse*, 1955.

Finale of Trenyov's *Lyubov Yarovaya* at the Maly Theater, 1926.

A scene from Gorky's *Yegor Bulychev and the Others* at Vakhtangov Theater, 1932.

Pashkova as Bulychev's daughter Shurka in Gorky's *Yegor Bulychev and the Others.*

Sets by Ryndin for the prologue of Khrennikov's opera *Mother*,
Bolshoy Theater, 1957.

A scene from Pogodin's *Aristocrats*, Red Army Theater, 1956.

Nikolay Mordvinov as Othello.

Shakespeare in Soviet Russia: a scene from *The Taming of the Shrew,*
directed by Alexey Popov.

Soviet actors Yulia Borisova and Nikolay Plotnikov in *Alone,* by Alyoshin, 1959.

Zavadsky applying make-up to his pupil Vera Maretskaya, a popular Soviet actress of the 1950s.

Soviet actors Nikolay Gritsenko and Irina Korovina in the French play *Sixth Floor* by Gehry, 1958.

Set by Yanov for a pig-iron plant in Karpov's *Proletarian Outskirts*.

Communist censors that the name of Claudel is "the banner of imperialist, reactionary bourgeoisie." Between 1920-1922 he was constantly under the fire of indignant critics, but since Lunacharsky placed Kamerny in the category of "academic theaters" Tairov felt strongly protected, at least for the time being.

Tairov's main experiments in the twenties ranged from farce to tragedy, which he considered the highest achievement of scenic art. When he staged Racine's *Phaedra* in 1921, he divested it of all the layers of the seventeenth century and restored the plot to its archaic origins. The settings were conceived in the spirit of that massive severity which later marked Tairov's passage from flamboyant colors to the sobriety of architecture. Greek soldiers were treated like columns against the backdrop of blue sky, forms were primitive and the stage platform was like the deck of an ancient ship, the costumes of the protagonists fell in majestic folds. It was at this stage of his career that he came out with his notes of a director and repeated what he formulated before the Revolution: the play was but a pretext for acting, and the actor was the bearer of elemental human emotions. But he attempted political camouflage when he fed the journalists with catchwords about Phaedra being "consonant with the Revolution in her heroic pathos" or when he affirmed that such productions as *Princess Brambilla* by Hoffmann, which he called "a capriccio," reflected "the joy felt by the proletariat over its victories." He aimed at "pure musical joy" in *Giroflé-Girofla,* an operetta by Lecocq, also produced in 1922. In both of these revivals of nineteenth-century compositions, he experimented in light touches alternated with elements of grim irony in Hoffmann, and of farcical fantasy in Lecocq. *Giroflé-Girofla* remained in the history of the Soviet Theater an example of stunning lighting effects: in the scene where punch is burning in a bowl, the flames transformed actors' costumes into a phantasmagoria of shades and colors.

In 1924 Tairov, helped by the surrealistic painters, the brothers Sternberg, produced Ostrovsky's *The Storm.* Some critics saw in this performance an answer to Meyerhold's famous production of 1915 and even talked of Tairov's conversion to realism, because he interpreted Katerina's tragedy as being determined by her environment. But the settings, the costumes, and the whole treatment of the drama was actually surrealistic—heavily stylized, using realistic details only for symbolic purposes.

Yet there was a change in Tairov at that period. He was getting away from his musical dreams and from what his adversaries called "pure estheticism." While continuing to adhere to his main principles of construction and rhythm, he concentrated on plays which either reflected the West or were strongly permeated with the spirit of urbanism. Beginning with his show of Chesterton's *The Man Who Was Thursday,* he leaned almost exclusively on non-Russian repertory. He went with his company to Europe in 1923, 1928, and 1930, and the success of his performance was one of the reasons why the Soviet government allowed him to continue his experiments.

While his production of Eugene O'Neill's *The Hairy Ape* (1926) contained elements of anti-West propaganda, the settings were a genuine expression of his concept of dynamics and constructivism. He contrasted the half-naked bodies of stokers, the mass scene in the boiler room accompanied by the roar of machines, to the caricatured bourgeoisie who danced the fox-trot. For his basic décor he used a suspended cabin which was turned into a boiler room, the street, and the police station. On the other hand, *Desire Under the Elms* (the same year) was interpreted as "a pure tragedy and the conflict of eternal elements." Tairov defined its scenes as "heavy with existence but without any reality."

In the numerous plays produced between 1922 and 1930 (and they included, among others, *St. Joan* by Shaw, *Antigone* by Walter Hasenclever, who made Creon a brutal tyrant and Antigone a democratic pacifist, and *All God's Chillun Got Wings*), he sought sculptural brevity in visual form, and a mixture of buffoonery with tragedy which did not always come off. He felt that he should follow the general trend and produce plays by Soviet dramatists. First he tried to compromise and showed another European drama, *Conspiracy of Equals* (Babeuf's conspiracy, under the Directory) a concoction by M. Levidov, a Soviet journalist. This was not a good political move. Neither was Tairov's production of *The Purple Island* by Mikhail Bulgakov, another author who did not enjoy any favor with the authorities. In 1929, in his letter to the playwright Bill-Belotserkovsky, Stalin defined Tairov's theater as "deeply bourgeois and alien to our culture" and spoke of the *Conspiracy of Equals* and *The Purple Island* as "trash." One could say that by that time Tairov had to srtuggle between two contrasting forces; his desire to continue experimentations in style and form, and the necessity of conforming to the growing demands of Communist dogma. Because of his flexibility, diplomatic talent, and use of current terminology which enabled him to put the label of "socialist realism" on completely different and often most conflicting plays and productions, he did succeed in surviving through the thirties and even the beginning of the forties, but in the last twenty years of his activities, he could but rarely show the full impact of his innovations and reveal the true meaning of his artistic aspirations.

I I

The First Workshop entered the Revolution of 1917 under the moral and organizational leadership of Vakhtangov. Although still committed to Stanislavsky's System, he was getting more and more inclined toward independent search for new forms. Between 1905 and 1911, Stanislavsky himself had experimented in his productions of Maeterlinck, Hamsun, Hauptmann, and Andreyev. This was the period of tests in what could be considered Stanislavsky's laboratory. But then Stanislavsky got away from experimentation and concentrated on finding and formulating the laws of the actor's inner work, within the structure of realistic art. Vakhtangov, however, came now to those very problems of "theatricality" and "external technique" his beloved master seemed to have abandoned, and he wanted to continue from the very point Stanislavsky had left off. By the way, the leader of the Moscow Art Theater saw in Vaktangov his successor and followed with approval his pupil's theatrical exploits. As far as his own search for a new means of expression, he made a last attempt in 1920 with Byron's *Cain*, but it was a failure.

Since 1913, Vakhtangov had been associated with a students' group, called Mansurov Studio. Their first show, *The Lanin's Estate*, by Boris Zaitsev, was far from being a success, but this did not discourage the young actors, and Vakhtangov worked with them for three years trying to teach them that "a performance is

the expression of the will of a creative collective." By concentrating on exercises which dealt more with technique, he brought
corrections to the System. As in the First Studio, he warned his
new followers against the identification of creativity with consciousness, and stressed the role of the unconscious in any artistic
activity. Each rehearsal, in his opinion, should offer material for
the next one, and this material is reworked by the unconscious
in the interval between the two. Unlike Stanislavsky, he believed
that the profound knowledge of a character did not lead necessarily to the "truth of emotion," because the latter can be also
projected on the stage through improvisation, not alien to the
commedia dell'arte, or through the unconscious. He followed
eagerly all the theories and practice of Meyerhold and Evreinov.

After several private performances, the student group became,
in March 1917, Vakhtangov's Moscow Dramatic Studio, and
three years later it was incorporated into the Moscow Art Theater as the Third Workshop. In the same year Vakhtangov, despite
serious illness, worked with feverish activity. His production of
Ibsen's *Rosmersholm* in 1918 was not too successful although it
had an excellent cast, including Olga Knipper and Grigory Khmara, but Vakhtangov derived great satisfaction from teaching in
several workshops, such as Gunst, Armenian Operatic, Local Proletarian, Cooperative, etc., and taking over the leadership of the
Habima, a Jewish workshop, where, with Naoum Zamakh he
produced one-act plays by Sholem Asch, Peretz, and other Yiddish writers (without knowing a word of either Yiddish or
Hebrew). He continued also to direct the new Studio Two,
another offshoot of the Moscow Art Theater.

Between 1918 and 1920, Vakhtangov prepared and produced
four shows which assured him his place among the great directors, and he became one of the luminaries of the Russian stage.
All of his productions came as surprises to the public.

The first "revelation" was *The Miracle of Saint Anthony* by
Maeterlinck, on which Vakhtangov had worked since 1916. The
play represented the saint as a tramp who resurrects Hortense, a
rich old woman. The relatives, gathered in the house for the
spoils, do not like the miracle and are highly suspicious of the
man who performed it. Only Virginie, a servant, recognizes the
saint in the old tramp because she is a "simple heart" and there-

fore endowed with a second sight. The heirs, however, call the police, and Anthony lands in jail. In the second variant of the play shown in 1921 in the Workshop Three, Vakhtangov stressed the sharp irony of this satire, and exaggerated the contrast between the bourgeois pettiness and the isolated bearers of a spiritual truth. The rhythm of the performance was precise, almost "geometrical," but lively and engrossing. The whole treatment was expressionistic. No gestures, grins, or laughs "as in life" were allowed. All the acting had to serve one single purpose, had to fit into a carefully prepared, mathematically calculated general design. Instead of illusory truthfulness, Vakhtangov showed schematic, grotesque attitudes. The crowd was treated as a unit, and not as an assemblage of sharply individualized persons, as Stanislavsky required it. In the scene where Anthony appears in Hortense's house among the guests and heirs, all of them were dressed in black, in contrast to his white robe. The resurrected woman was attired as an old doll. Settings were highly functional and subordinated to the central theme of the entire composition. All this corresponded to Vakhtangov's desire "to have a theater of sharp expressive forms instead of a theater of real figures." What made Vakhtangov's productions different from those of Meyerhold or the constructivists was the fusion of psychological acting with the acceptance of conventions, and the great awareness of stylistic unity. Vakhtangov displayed inventive fantasy and affirmed the theatricality of a show, but he also stressed the intrinsic and human value of the master actor. His belief in the "purifying, elating role of art and in the necessity of bringing joy on earth" gave all his endeavors a major optimistic overtone. The company he formed included such excellent actors as Yuri Zavadsky, Boris Zakhava, Nikolay Akimov, Alexander Popov, and many others who later occupied important positions in the Soviet theater.

In his productions, Vakhtangov used different devices. For instance, he based his preparatory work for *The Feast During The Plague,* by Pushkin, on the principle of scenic sculpture dear to the heart of constructivists. People around the feast table were molded in large gray cloth with holes for their heads. The "breath of the plague" was implied by the "lack of bodies." This was his typical device: the replacement of objective reality by that created by the subject. The world was expressed according to the views and emotions of the individual, and if it looked twisted or deformed, this was the fault of the subject. Thus the priority of man's vision over reality was asserted, and it also meant the superiority of spirit over matter. This explains why Vakhtangov, the enemy of "mechanization of life" in the Sullerzhitsky tradition, remained alien to urbanism, industrialism, and technological devices promoted by constructivists and other innovators of the *avant-garde*. No wonder that while he was attacked for his "idealistic" philosophy by the Communists, he was also denigrated by the left-wing theatrical extremists.

Vakhtangov firmly believed that the actor needs inner justification based on the truth of emotions, but he made an important addition to the thesis: the emotions have to be brought to the audience in a augmented, often exaggerated, form, such as grotesquerie, fantasy, or buffoonery, in a particular *expressive* form which suits the stage, within the framework of its conventions. The author writes a text, and the director-producer gives it life and form according to the means at the disposal of a given theatrical collective. The director suggests costumes and make-up, gait and intonations, he supervises the movement and the speech of the actors, and he gives unity and wholeness to the performance. Together with the cast of a play with whom he works incessantly, he brings out the content (or hidden intent) of the text, and he does it in terms of his own time. Vakhtangov interpreted "actuality" as the spirit of the era, without any compromise with the topical and flashy. Soviet art critics and historians try to represent Vakhtangov's interest in popular theater and his political radicalism as pro-Communist. This is one of the usual "corrections" of truth. Vakhtangov was a socialist and he welcomed the Revolution, but his convictions were not determined by the Communist theory. "The people alone," he wrote, "have the vigor and the seed of future creation, and artists should go to the people's soul, and this will bring forth true beauty." He favored the theater for "large masses" but for its repertory suggested the life of Moses, great epic subjects, the Bible, or works by Lope de Vega, Byron, and Verhaeren. He was so deeply interested in Western culture that his main accomplishments were with foreign authors (Maeterlinck, Strindberg, Gozzi). And he was definitely hostile to any propaganda on the stage. This is the reason why his productions were so embarrassing to Soviet critics: they did not know how to catalogue them or how to hide their obviously expressionistic character; neither could they deny their lasting influence on the best Soviet directors. It is also impossible to disguise the fact that Vakhtangov took a great deal from Meyerhold and from those who were condemned by the Party as "obnoxious formalists." It is highly significant that three years after the Revolution, a producer educated by Stanislavsky and the Moscow Art Theater, rejected "the performance of environment and of psychological and domestic sentimentality." Vakhtangov called his new method "fantastic realism." A few months before his death he addressed Meyerhold in a letter as "dear beloved Master," thanked him "for all you do for the theater," and assured him of his own and his company's "enthusiastic love."

The imprint of new tendencies was most visible in Vakhtangov's production of *Eric the XIV,* by Strindberg, the drama of a pathological prince who behaves on the throne in a puzzling and shocking manner. Here again Vakhtangov opposed the bloodless courtiers, the automatons of bureaucracy, and the "dead souls" of aristocracy to the madman who is alive despite all his eccentricities. Eric seeks life in the taverns of poor people and wants to marry the daughter of a simple soldier. Vakhtangov presented the courtiers as puppets or ghosts, in an abstract and almost monumental immobility, while their subjects, the artisans, workmen, and soldiers were treated with ethnographic realism and colorful details. The main idea of doom and ruin was accentuated by physical signs. Eric is born for misfortune, and his tragedy is foretold in the first act by sharp angular streaks of lightning against the background of black settings. The columns in the throne room are bent, gold ornaments are rusted. Labyrinths of stairs and passages, wrong perspectives, and flexed objects correspond to Eric's insanity. Vakhtangov represented reality through the diseased mind of his hero. Most figures looked symbolic: the Dowager Queen flapped around like a bat, the court jeweler wore a gold brocade dress, the henchman, in a dirty red jacket, a dagger and rope at his belt, held an ax in his hand. The performance, the last Vakhtangov gave in the First Work-

shop, also became memorable because Mikhail Chekhov impersonated Eric in a most stunning manner, bringing forth the inner
torment and contradictions in his own palace. Vakhtangov
claimed that the "actuality" of his production lay in the theme
of crumbling monarchy, the agony of which was pitted against
the vitality of popular masses; but the Communists looked with
suspicion at this expressionistic performance with its cubist
décors by Ignaty Nivinsky, music by Rachmaninov, and with
Chekhov's tragic interpretation of morbidity and madness. In
1922 the First Workshop went abroad, and *Eric XIV* created a
furor in Berlin.

In 1922, Vakhtangov directed in the Habima Theater *Hadib-
buk* or *Dybbuk* by Solomon Rappaport (S. An-sky), who told in
simple terms the story of two Jewish lovers: Leah, daughter of
the rich Sender, and Khanan, a poor young man, student of the
Cabbala. When Khanan learns that Sender is going to marry
Leah to another man, he dies, but his spirit enters his fiancée's
body. At the wedding Leah rejects her new bridegroom, and is
brought to a godly man, a "zaddik," to be exorcised. The zaddik
succeeds in expelling the ghost, or dybbuk, from the girl, but
her soul also disappears and her body dies. This mystical legend
was interpreted by Vakhtangov as a philosophical poem. His pupil
Zavadsky says: "It acquired an astonishing force of truth, it told
of monstrous injustice of life, of the poor and the rich, of the
despair of the former and the smugness of the latter, and of love
triumphing over death—and all that in unique forms of scenic
expression." Zavadsky himself and the painter Nathan Altman
assisted Vakhtangov, particularly in the make-up of the actors:
faces were painted like canvases in plain colors. Vakhtangov
subordinated movement, lighting, costumes, and music to the
same passionate rhythm, and he contrasted the young couple to
the world of immobility, superstition, and mean wealth which
make them perish. Khanan and Leah, in her white dress, are
victims, their fate is tragic. The air in Sender's house is heavy
and stifling, there is no sun, no joy, the ghetto suffocates any
breath of life with its century-old iniquity. This was embodied
by the ten members of the Hasidic sect; they wore long, black,
belted jackets, soiled by grease spots, and moved in unison,
making identical gestures with their hands, palms outward. Quite

extraordinary was the grisly dance of the beggars at the wedding. A hunchback, a blind woman, an idiot, a tubercular—each had his own mask and his own deformity. When these bundles of decrepit flesh covered with rags started to move and gesticulate with outstretched hands, the nightmarish dance seemed a saraband of Death. Whoever saw *Dybbuk*, even without understanding a word of the language in which it was presented, was immediately plunged into a horrible and fascinating dream. Here, Vakhtangov's art reached the limits of its disturbing and touching vision of mankind.

In order to show the full range of his possibilities, Vakhtangov shifted from the tragic mysticism of *Dybbuk* to the pure joy of *Princess Turandot,* because, as he said, "we need a festival." This fairy tale by Carlo Gozzi revolves around a beautiful and capricious princess who gets rid of her suitors by asking them to solve three riddles and by beheading them after their inevitable failures. But Calaf, the enemy Tartar prince in exile and in disguise, wins the contest and the cruel Turandot, who falls in love with the victorious stranger. The action of the play was set in the Great Violet City of China, and its characters, partly comic, partly fantastic, were derived from the Italian *commedia dell'arte. Turandot* attracted Vakhtangov by its very incongruity combined with poetic charm. He put into its production, his last work, all his fantasy and vitality. Mortally ill, well aware that he would not last long, he turned this production into a farewell to the world of whim, brightness, and color. He knew well other interpretations of *Turandot,* but he rejected Schiller's stylization, or Kommissarzhevsky's fusion of psychology with the Chinese fairy tale (1912), or the pageant of the wonderful Orient imagined by Max Reinhardt in Berlin's Deutsches Theater. He did not want a "temperance league performance" but sought something romantic and ironic, a flight of fantasy in which to alternate laughter with lyrical touches. He used the play for discarding the "truth of life" method and for replacing it by open emphasis on theatrical tricks and devices. Of course, this was not an original discovery, he was merely continuing in the wake of Evreinov and Meyerhold who had hailed the techniques of the *commedia dell'arte* before the Revolution. But his *Turandot,* which appeared a loose improvisation, was planned to the minutest particular. Vakhtangov, who had two hundred rehearsals for three or four performances in a year, was an extraordinary organizer and an indefatigable worker, and his art was precise and perfect.

Vakhtangov's *Turandot* started with the four traditional maskers of the Italian comedy coming forward and telling about the play. Then men and women in evening attire paraded on the proscenium, making jokes and laughing. These were actors, and they put on their costumes and applied their make-up in front of the audience, using whatever they could find for their respective parts: a towel made a turban, a shawl was transformed into a dress, and a piece of silk served to represent the magnificence of the court. A platform with an inclined surface was used as boards, and stagehands bustled around with décor or signs which indicated that the action took place in a palace or on a square. They forgot a white chair in the middle of the street, emphasizing the conventionality of the whole thing. The riddles Princess Turandot asked her unhappy suitors to solve were no less inconsistent, and so were all the scenic details. The actors made no secret about their trade, they seemed to shout to the spectators: "Look, we are acting, we are protagonists and maskers; now we stop acting; hello people in the house, we enjoy seeing you." This was an entertainment done with elegance and *brio,* mixing buffoonery with mastery and craft, and maintaining throughout the whole evening a gay, genuine rhythm.

By making *Turandot* a celebration of merriment and wit, Vakhtangov created a contrast to the gloominess of the times, and his colorful joyful art exploded in the dark Moscow of 1921 as a challenge to the ascetic constructions of Meyerhold and the abstract logic of Tairov. The night of the *Turandot* dress rehearsal Vakhtangov felt very ill; he had a temperature of 102°, but he continued to direct and to correct, and sat in the theater for hours, muffled up in a fur coat, a wet towel around his head. After that night he could not get up from his bed, and he only heard of the tremendous success of his beloved *Turnadot*: he was too sick to go to the performance. He died three months later.

Vakhtangov brought to the Russian theater a special kind of expressionism. In a way, his position was between the extreme of the *avant-garde* and the realistic psychologism of the Moscow

Art Theater. He was not interested in experimentation for the sake of testing new devices, for he believed in the necessity of an inner truth for the actor and director. But he was greatly conscious of the particular character of theatrical reality, not to be confused with life reality, and he tried to project its organizational, and consequently esthetic, elements. What made his influence so deep and lasting was a combination of personal and professional qualities. He was not a theoretician, but was an outstanding teacher and a man completely devoted to his art. He liked people, and his friends adored him. Warmth and human understanding gave a particular glow to all his work. Many performances directed by Meyerhold or Tairov were dazzling, brilliant, absorbing, but none of them, unless they were outright tragedy, had Vakhtangov's human touch. At the same time, his productions were technically perfect, bordering on virtuosity, the result of stubborn relentless labor. Vakhtangov, who had been formed in the school of Stanislavsky and Nemirovich Danchenko, left these high standards of artistic probity as a legacy to his numerous pupils, and his name became the symbol of professional integrity. Directors and actors, such as Zavadsky, Simonov, Zakhava, Shchukin, and many others, continued his tradition and formed a whole Vakhtangov trend in the Russian theater. The Third Workshop was transformed into an independent Vakhtangov Theater in 1926, and it became one of the best professional houses in the Soviet Union.

III

After Vakhtangov's death in 1922, Mikhail Chekhov and Boris Sushkevich assumed the leadership of the First Studio, and in 1924 it became an autonomous enterprise under the name of the Second Moscow Art Theater. In the first years after the Revolution, the Studio showed such plays as *The Daughter of Yorio* by Gabriele D'Annunzio, *The Taming of the Shrew* and *King Lear*, and in 1919, *Balladine* by the Polish romantic, Yuli Slowacki, directed by Boleslavsky. In 1924 the Studio staged *Love—A Golden Book*, a historical drama by Alexey Tolstoy, directed by Serafima Birman, but after sixty performances the Repertory Committee recommended that it be taken off as "too

light": at that time, the former Count and *émigré* Alexey Tol-
soy was not yet recognized by the authorities as the "leading
Soviet writer"; this title was bestowed on him much later in the
thirties.

The First Studio soon found itself in a difficult situation. It
did not produce a single Soviet or Revolutionary play and kept
itself apart, outside of the debates on art for the masses. Naturally,
it was not very popular with the Communists, and it was tolerated mainly because of its association with the Moscow Art Theater and its high professional rating: it had an excellent company
headed by M. Chekhov. Left-wing critics also disliked it; for them
it was a second edition of Stanislavsky and a stronghold of conservatism. To make things worse, the company became divided
by a feud between Chekhov and Alexey Diky, a talented producer
and Vakhtangov's pupil. In 1924-1925 Chekhov staged *Hamlet,*
and Diky produced *The Flea* by Leskov in Evgeny Zamiatin's
adaptation. In the Stalin era the struggle between the two groups
was depicted as a conflict of ideologies: the good Marxists rallied around Diky, and the reactionary idealists behind Chekhov.
But in 1924 this was not true. In fact, Diky was not at that time
a follower of socialist realism. In any case, his *Flea,* which had
a tremendous success with the public, was an expressionistic show,
stressing the ironic and grotesque aspects of a racy script. It was
based on the story of a left-handed Tula artisan who outsmarted
the proud Britishers and put horseshoes on the feet of a metal
flea Alexander the First had received as a present in London.
While lampooning bureaucracy and smugness, it hailed in a
highly humorous fashion the inventiveness and intelligence of
the Russian people. It was full of phonetic quips, word play,
popular wit, and bold jokes, and the spectators enjoyed it as an
excellent entertainment. It was presented in the style of the
nineteenth-century popular colored prints (the French *Images
d'Epinal*), and its staging as a "show-box" corresponded to the
sophisticated spirit Zamiatin gave to his adaptation. *The Flea,*
however, was censored as "formalistic nonsense" and banned because of Zamiatin: in the late twenties he became the main target
for critical attacks as "the enemy of the Revolution and denigra-
tor of Soviet reality"; he emigrated to France in the thirties.

Chekhov's style was quite different from Diky's grotesques. This extraordinary actor was more interested in symbolism and Eastern philosophy than in technical issues of the Soviet stage. And although the Studio was now called the Second Moscow Art Theater, Chekhov's ideas and productions were becoming less and less akin to the Stanislavsky System.

Mikhail Chekhov, a nephew of the writer, was born in 1891, and joined the Moscow Art Theater at the age of nineteen. As an apprentice he accepted the System and concentrated on "truthful emotions," but later found his own method of acting, mostly under the influence of Sullerzhitsky's idealism and Vakhtangov's techniques. Yuri Zavadsky contends that it is difficult to say whether Vakhtangov influenced Chekhov or vice versa. "They complemented each other in their imagination, creative originality, and temperament. It is well known that Vakhtangov worked with Chekhov when the latter prepared his best parts, including that of Khlestakov for the Moscow Art Theater." As the fisherman Kobus in *The Shipwreck of "Hope"*, or as Kaleb in *The Cricket on the Hearth* he already displayed surprising craftsmanship, but his real triumph came in 1921, with his uncanny portrayal of Prince Eric as a man born to be unhappy, torn by contradictions, and gliding toward madness. *The Inspector General* was staged by Stanislavsky as a satire without any stress on a definite historical period, and Chekhov used this general framework to create of Khlestakov a symbol of emptiness and evil, an embodiment of that very "void" Gogol always identified with the Devil. It was a grotesque acted with an open use of hyperbole in gestures and intonations but with such subtle shadings and such psychological refinement that the effect of the performance was stunning. Chekhov made Khlestakov frightening, abnormal, and universal. The spiritual tension and depth of this interpretation was carried over to the spectators with such hypnotic power that they remained spellbound and shivering. On opening night Vakhtangov whispered in amazement: "And this is the same man we meet every day?" Chekhov's companions were not less impressed with the actor's combination of ardent temperament and complete control of himself on the stage. The impetus of passion, the intensity of emotions he put into his part were often bordering on the pathological, yet he always saw himself acting, and even maintained that such a split was a prerequisite of true art. His power over the audiences reminded one of that exerted by a Salvini or a Paganini. Serafima Birman, his colleague of the First Studio says in her memoirs: "His talent is almost inexplicable, he is a phenomenon nobody has succeeded in deciphering." What added to this feeling was the diversity of his impersonations. Each of his parts was a surprise not only for the spectators but also for his fellow actors. The text of a play was for him but a springboard from which he made his creative flight. Out of the fusion between Chekhov and the literary character he was to interpret, a third and new image was usually born as different from the dramatic intention of the playwright as from the normal personality of the actor. Some critics maintained that his creations were the result of a constant struggle between the playwright and the actor. The writer of this book, who had long talks with Chekhov on this subject, feels that the actor was not struggling with the playwright but rather trying to discover certain elements which were deeply buried in the text or hardly obvious to ordinary readers. For instance, Chekhov made Khlestakov a metaphysical image of vulgarity and triviality with strong mystical overtones, but was not the mystical horror of nothingness inherent in Gogol's work? Those who have seen Chekhov in the stage adaptation of his uncle's sketches probably remember how he lifted comic and pathetic episodes to the height of an all-embracing vision of human suffering and limitation. His humor in impersonating comic figures was irresistible, but he was particularly impressive in tragic parts. An infallible artistic taste prevented him from exaggeration in the grotesque and in the display of strong emotions. He made Muromskoy in *The Case* by Sukhovo-Kobylin into a tragic figure, thus broadening the image of the ruined nobleman and offended father. In 1924-1925 he presented *Hamlet* as a man so crushed by the growing sense of grief and so despairing of himself and of mankind that he approached insanity, and displayed many signs of mental and emotional derangement. The Communist press was infuriated by such a subjective and depressing Prince of Denmark: they would have preferred an image which would have been helpful to the "cause."

In his early twenties Chekhov became critical of Stanislavsky and wondered what an artist could add to an accurate copy of nature. He came to the conclusion that naturalism was not art, and that the creative state was not concentration on emotional authenticity (*perezhivanye*) as Stanislavsky contended, but an inspiration stemming from the actor's vision of a dramatic work and of his own role in it. This inspirational, often purely intuitive, vision determined all the details of acting which should not be worked out separately or in advance; they would naturally fall into a design if the leading idea and the artistic concept were right. This concept does not come from crude emotions or from the coarse unconscious. It must be the expression of a man's highest aspirations, or what he calls the "loftier I" (a kind of super-ego), opposed to the "baser I" with the latter's daily sensations, ambitions, and illusions. This idealistic and dualistic philosophy derived from Chekhov's study of symbolism and Steiner's anthroposophy. A friend of Andrey Bely, who had been the exponent of both trends in Russia, Chekhov produced at the end of 1925 the adaptation of Bely's esoteric, symbolic, and fantastic novel *Petersburg*, in which he impersonated Senator Ableukhov. The Senator was the embodiment of the geometrical and mechanical order opposed to the chaotic anarchical strivings of the revolutionaries. His own son, associated with the terrorists, makes an attempt on his father's life. The whole atmosphere of tension and maddening contradictions of the old regime and of the budding upheaval were rendered by Chekhov in frightening, ironic, and, at times, prophetic overtones.

Mechanization and materialistic reduction of complexity to mere biological or economic processes were Chekhov's main enemies. He dreamt of a theater which would bring to the audiences lofty images of spiritual purification and religious experience through suffering and sublimation. He taught acting to the young members of The Second Moscow Art Theater and other pupils, but he also communicated to them the gist of his artistic convictions (later expanded in two books: *The Road of the Actor,* 1924, and *The Techniques of the Actor,* 1946). His philosophy, however, seemed highly objectionable to Communist authorities. Everyone concurred that he was a stupendous actor, perhaps of the Mochalov kind, with one basic difference: his intuitive inspirational acting was far from slipshod improvisation, it was supported on the boards by excellent professional training and a careful co-ordination between speech and movement. But he was politically suspect, he felt himself to be an "inner *émigré*," and he knew that neither his name nor the privileged position of the Moscow Art Theater could save his enterprise from an inevitable undoing. In 1927 Diky and his friends (numbering sixteen) left the Second Moscow Art Theater, and in a public declaration condemned Chekhov's methods of idealism and inspiration. The meaning of this warning was unmistakable, and Chekhov left Russia. He knew that for those whose medium of expression is language, for writers and actors, foreign soil could never be propitious. He lived in France and later in the United States, charmed Russian *émigré* audiences by casual appearances in Paris and New York, created some excellent characters in Hollywood films, made interesting experiments in a workshop in Connecticut established by Beatrice Straight, and wrote memoirs, but his role in the Soviet theater in which he made a resplendent and meteoric career, ended in the late twenties.

After Chekhov went into exile, the Second Moscow Art Theater was taken over by Ivan Bersenev who began producing plays of the Soviet repertory. Despite the high quality of the company (among others, Azarin and Cheban), it never gained the favor of the Communist government and was liquidated in 1933 during the great offensive against "the remnants of idealism and formalism in the arts." The company was incorporated into the Theater of Moscow Council of Trade Unions which at that time was directed by Evsei Lyubimov Lanskoy.

IV

Under the influence of new trends, workshops grew in the first years of the Revolution with surprising rapidity. Most of them went for experimentation and followed Meyerhold, Tairov, the futurists, the constructivists, and other innovators. The Free Workshop, led in 1922 by Nikolay Foregger, tried to present sounds and movements of the new city, industrial gestures, dances of machines, and "music hall in proletarian attire." Boris Ferdinandov, a member of the Kamerny Theater company, and the imagist poet Vadim Shershenevich founded the Workshop of Experimental Heroic Theater in which they showed *Oedipus Rex* next to Mérimée's *Jacquerie,* a drama of the fourteenth century peasant revolt, literary parodies, and mystery plays such as *The Lady With the Black Glove*. In the latter production, the actors were placed on triangles, ladders, and stirrups on a huge wooden cube serving as the stage platform. A blowing of horns and wailing of sirens accompanied the action. "The theater of today," declared Ferdinandov, "as our whole life, tends towards three things: America, Boulevard (in the French sense) and Machine . . . we must create an art without capital letters, pedestals and fig leaves." Mchedelov's Workshop of Improvisation devoted itself to the Italian *commedia dell'arte,* and its esthetic credo could be easily discovered from its declaration of 1925: "Lately we spend so much time discussing ideology and the social impact of art that we have lost the feeling of theater as such, in its own right." But improvisations in the seventeenth-century style appeared pale and tame in comparison to daring flights of more revolutionary workshops, such as, for instance, the Factory of the Eccentric Actor established in 1922 and bent on justifying its name. The leaders of the Factory, together with the youth of the period, were greatly interested in movies and particularly in the American film industry. They announced a futuristic version of Gogol's *Marriage* on their posters as, "Marriage or an Extraordinary Adventure of Charlie Chaplin," and their political show bore a cinematographic title "Foreign Trade Commissariat on the Eiffel Tower." Workshops in the cities of Kharkov, Odessa, Rostov, Kostroma, Irkutsk, and many other regional centers followed the example of Moscow and Leningrad and joyfully soared into most unusual combinations of drama, harlequinade, music hall, and movies.

Less extravagant were workshops connected with already established theatrical enterprises. Some of them were established prior to the Revolution and continued their activities into the Soviet era. Such was the case of the Second Workshop of the Moscow Art Theater directed by V. Verbitsky after 1916. It showed some nine plays, including *The Green Ring* by Zinaida Hippius, *Youth* by Andreyev, and *The Pattern of Roses* by Sologub in the provinces, and in 1924 it was incorporated in the Moscow Art Theater. Alla Tarassova, the leading lady of the Workshop, a bright actress with an excellent voice, attractive stage presence, and great psychological skill, emerged later as one of the most prominent members of the Moscow Art Theater Company. Khmelev, Batalov, Prudkin, also worked in the Second Workshop. Stanislavsky lectured after the Revolution in many of the innumerable Workshops. Among them were the Chaliapin, Gorky, Griboyedov, Gunst, and other studios.

While the Third Workshop gave origin to what later became Vakhtangov's Theater, the Fourth Workshop, established in 1921 by Vassily Luzhsky, E. Rayevskaya, and G. Burdzhalov, all actors of the Moscow Art Theater, seemed to follow at first the principles of "healthy artistic realism based on simplicity and truth, depth and fullness of content, acting and production" (Burdzhalov's formula) and sought people's audiences, but the presentation of Somerset Maugham's *Promised Land* and Pavel Muratov's *Café* in 1922 and 1924 revealed the antirealistic tendencies of the company. After the death of Burdzhalov in 1924, Mikhail Tarkhanov took his place and turned to the classic (Molière and Ostrovsky) and to the then emerging Soviet repertory. His policy, however, met with the opposition of a majority which wanted a more modernistic line and spoke of "conventions and symbolism." Tarkhanov, after a brief struggle, left with a group of followers.

Although the Workshop in 1927 assumed the name of Realistic Theater, its new director, Fyodorov, instilled the spirit of the *avant-garde* in *North-East* by Shcheglov, the next year. Hostile critics complained that in this production the sounds of the foxtrot drowned out the text, while the American music hall tricks and gags obliterated serious acting. In 1930, L. Volkov's production of *The Good Soldier Schweik,* adapted from the famous satire by Yaroslav Hashek, as a grotesque and *bouffonade,* and the showing of an exotic play the next year, with all the achievements of formalist techniques, provoked the wrath of the authorities. A new director, Nikolay Okhlopkov, was appointed. Although freshly graduated from Tairov's Kamerny, he declared himself a partisan of "proletarian and political repertory" and was therefore trusted by the Communists. Okhlopkov, however, started by combining revolutionary plays (*The Run* by Stavsky, *Mother* by Gorky, and *The Iron Stream* by Serafimovich) with scenic innovations. He was against the "veracity" of the Moscow Art Theater, and much more attracted by the methods of the Japanese Kabuki, by the Italian *commedia dell'arte* or by the

Greek theater. One of his most radical innovations was transferring the action from the boards to a podium built in the middle of the house and surrounded by other platforms, steps, bridges, and balconies which served as a stage for various episodes of the show. Okhlopkov's theater got the name of State Realistic Theater of Red Presnia (Presnia, a proletarian district of Moscow), because of the enthusiasm provoked by revolutionary plays among its spectators, and this explains how Okhlopkov was permitted even under Stalin to proceed with his innovations, provided he did not go too far and kept a strict ideological line in his repertory.

Slightly different was the road of Yuri Zavadsky (born 1894), Vakhtangov's pupil and one of the most brilliant and outstanding Soviet directors. This talented and highly educated actor and producer established his own Workshop in 1924 in the hope of rejuvenating the Moscow Art Theater by offering it the achievements of Vakhtangov, and of strengthening his own company by keeping them in touch with the excellent acting traditions of the past. In order to facilitate the fulfillment of this ambitious project, Zavadsky joined the Moscow Art Theater company and created a brilliant Chatsky in Griboyedov's *Wit Works Woe* and a gay Almaviva in *The Marriage of Figaro*. Stanislavsky was very impressed with his acting and entrusted him with the direction of Pushkin's dramatic scenes which Zavadsky presented in highly stylized manner, stressing the sharpness of certain theatrical devices.

The same tendency prevailed in the *One Does Not Play with Love* (*On ne badine pas avec l'amour*) by Alfred de Musset, presented in 1926 as a highly stylized reconstruction of the Romantic era. Only the production next year of *The Simple Thing* by Boris Lavrenyov depicting the Civil War, met with the approval of the Communist critics. After that every performance of Zavadsky's company was severely reproved for being expressionistic, formalistic, and antirealistic. They continued, however, to attract general attention and to count among the highlights of each theatrical season. Their success was also due to excellent acting by the beautiful Vera Maretskaya and the sensitive Nikolay Mordvinov. In 1932 Zavadsky presented Ben Jonson's *Volpone* as an exposé of the power of money over human beings, a gay satirical comedy, with Mosca as a central figure. The production comprised a series of expressionistic devices. In the first act, the protagonists wore medieval dress; in the second Russian merchants' coats; and in the third, tails and evening gowns, thus stressing the idea that money has ruled over the centuries. As in *Princess Turandot,* stage hands changed the settings, speaking and behaving like actors. In *The Devil's Disciple* by Bernard Shaw, an actor impersonating the author came to the stage at the end of the play and made a speech to the public. Ostrovsky's *The Wolves and the Sheep,* was stylized as if it were being given in the 1950s. All these performances were great successes, but the authorities decided that Zavadsky and his company needed to be "exposed to Soviet reality" and sent them to Rostov-on-Don, in a sort of honorable semi-exile or civic training quarantine.

Other, more conservative workshops felt the strong influence of modernism. Ruben Simonov (not to be confused with the well-known movie actor, Nikolay Simonov), who in 1930 became the director of the Vakhtangov Theater, founded a workshop in 1928. For six years he worked with a group of talented and enthusiastic actors, showing plays of classic and Soviet repertory. They were, however, reprimanded for "the ironic way of acting, sharply grotesque forms, unrestrained use of music, dismemberment of plays into mutiple episodes" and other expressionistic and formalistic sins. The authorities stopped the workshop's activities in 1934, and by 1937 the members of the workshop were incorporated into the Theater of the Komsomol (Communist Youth).

A similar fate befell the Workshop of the Maly Theater, led after 1925 by Fyodor Kaverin. Despite its origin, the Workshop rejected the realistic and conservative tradition of its Alma Mater, and resolutely adopted a "colorful, sonorous way of acting, a certain exaggeration of images, and, on the other hand, following the laws of theatricality and subordinating everything on the stage to the general rhythm; and making all the objects, together with the actors, visible to the spectator, as parts of the action" (from the Workshop's declaration). Communist reviewers were indignant: here was the outgrowth of the respectable academic theater, here were young men and women of Soviet society, some of them members of the Party—and "the stage looked like a permanent masquerade, an endless theatrical phantasmagoria, a hunt for caricature and eccentricities." Particularly obnoxious to the censors was the 1926 production of *Kino-novel* by Georg Kaiser, the German expressionist. It showed a young man who comes to Europe from America and lures his foster brother into going with him to the United States, the promised land of plenty and freedom. Such an obvious deviation from the anticapitalist and anti-American pattern, on top of the ostentatious display of "formalistic devices," provoked a series of protests in the press, especially when the Workshop went on the road and showed Kaiser's piece in various provincial towns. In 1936 the Workshop (then called New Theater) was merged with a Moscow district stage, and finally disappeared by 1941.

It is very typical of the period that the breath of revolt and innovation spread over the theatrical enterprise fostered by the Party for political propaganda. The main effort of Communist leaders was focused on the Red Army and the village. The propaganda themes usually comprised the struggle against external and internal enemies, and the glorification of Communist ideas and current governmental measures. Animated diagrams showing statistics of growth, colorful "dramatic posters," and "literary montage" of patriotic or polemical verse was introduced into skits and shows for soldiers and peasants by amateur actors who had secondhand information about the "innovators," such as Meyerhold and Vakhtangov. The all-union organization of the "Blue Blouse" which spread songs, oral newspapers, propaganda and slogans impersonated by live actors, limericks, pantomime and other theatrical forms throughout the whole country, was strongly attracted by the *avant-garde* theories on the rejuvenation of the theater by the circus and the music hall. It took considerable time to eradicate all these "formalist elements" from the propaganda theaters. By 1926 the Russian Republic had some twenty thousand dramatic circles, and about two hundred and eighty thousand amateur actors who played to twenty-five million spectators a year. Enormous pressure was exercised on all the provincial and village stages by the Department of Agitation and Propaganda to make them homogeneous and fall in line with the realistic theater. The process was long, but the emergence of a new Soviet repertory and the growing importance and influence of traditional Academic Theaters as models of higher art finally brought all the amateur and propaganda activities to the same uniform level of safe conservative representations.

By the middle of the thirties the workshop movement was completely extinct. But its role in the history of the Soviet theater is undeniable, and it was in the workshops that the attainments of the *avant-garde* were preserved and handed over to the younger generation of Russian actors and directors.

It is highly significant that a large number of workshops were connected not only with various leftists' ventures but actually came from the Moscow Art Theater and other academic boards. It showed how deeply the ideas of innovation had penetrated the whole theatrical world in Russia. No wonder that their development could be stopped only by artificial means of intervention from above and by governmental support of conservative institutions.

V

Those who did not share the extremists' views and did not believe either in the sudden creation of a new proletarian art or in bold experimentation were also divided by conflicting tendencies. The gigantic scope of the Revolution, the complexity of events, the grandiose perspectives opened up to the Russian people, and the messianic mission ascribed to Communism favored a "return to romanticism," considered by some intellectuals as the most appropriate style for such extraordinary times. Consequently, the theater was asked to represent heroic deeds, great canvases, tragedies by Sophocles and Shakespeare. Gorky with his wife, Lunacharsky, and Blok sponsored the Great Dramatic Theater in Petrograd. Blok, who acted as the chairman of the board of directors, made introductory speeches for the opening nights of *Don Carlos* by Schiller, and of *Danton* by Maria Loevberg. In 1919 the State Model Theater run by Fyodor Stepun, a writer and a philosopher, and two professionals, V. Massalitinov and V. Sakhnovsky, staged Shakespearean tragedies, and *Oedipus Rex* by Sophocles, the latter with harmonious settings by Georgy Yakulov. In these tragedies the actors talked in a special way, with diction and voice inflections obviously borrowed from the Greek Orthodox liturgy.

The partisans of romantic drama soon came out with a more general support of "great art." In this they found a response from very different quarters. All the anti-Communist-minded members of the educated classes welcomed it as a barrier against "crazy leftism" and "revolutionary barbarism," and numerous representatives of the new order felt that the classics might offer a healthy fare to the popular masses. The lack of contemporary repertory was another factor in favor of this "return to the classics." The movement which was spread over all theaters that shunned risky experimentation took on such proportions that in the starved Moscow of 1919, soldiers and workmen could, on a single night, choose six Shakespeare plays (*The Merchant of Venice* at the Maly, *Twelfth Night* at the Moscow Art, *The Merry Wives of Windsor* at the New, *A Midsummer Night's Dream* at the former Korsh, *Measure for Measure* at Experimental, and *Hamlet* at Coliseum). Of course, the problem remained whether new audiences were mature enough for such offerings. Some claimed that Shakespeare and Schiller were much too difficult for the popular masses. Others believed that theaters should simplify their methods and even their repertory in order to meet new audiences half-way. The old controversy about "absorbing the culture of the past" or creating new theater corresponding to social changes was still going on among high Party officials, as well as among artists and intellectuals. Lenin had conservative taste in literature, he could not understand poets such as Mayakovsky, whom he disliked heartily, and he had great respect for the Moscow Art Theater and the former Imperial institutions such as Maly and Alexandrinsky. Most of his companions, with the exception of Lunacharsky and, partly, Trotsky, shared his views. Lenin and his friends never forgot that theater can be used as a political weapon, and they insisted that it should have a basic educational purpose: the enlightenment of the masses. The classics seemed to fulfill this purpose, and realistic performances of Gogol, Ostrovsky, or Griboyedov were welcomed by the new rulers.

In a certain way, well-established theaters simply were compelled to show what was at hand. They hesitated to resume dramas and comedies by Artsybashev, Vinnichenko, Andreyev, Surguchev, Urvantsev, and other pre-Revolutionary "bourgeois favorites," and preferred the safe refuge of classics. Besides, mass audiences greeted with enthusiasm the traditional repertory— and this was what actually decided the issue. The policy of the Communist Party in the theater was determined not only by theoretical discussions but also by the demand of the mass audiences, which understood and enjoyed old-fashioned productions much more than the extravagant audacities of revolutionary pioneers. This was one of the disappointing lessons of the Russian Revolution. After a turbulent decade of daring experiments sustained only by the intellectual and artistic "elite" (a word nobody would have dared not only to utter but even to think of in those times) the regime which boasted to be the most progressive in the world firmly identified itself with theatrical conservatism.

In 1918-1920 the Alexandrinsky Theater underwent a period of struggle and reorganization, changed directors and administration, and did not resume its place in Petrograd, later Leningrad, until the early twenties. It still had an excellent company of veteran actors of the old school—mostly for character roles: Davydov, Gorin, Uralov, Goryainov, Vivienne, Sudbinin, Korchagina, Michurina and others. It produced comedies by Ostrovsky and repeatedly showed Fonvizin and Turgenev.

The Maly Theater under the leadership of Yuzhin, for whom even the Moscow Art Theater was too "fanciful," placed itself at the head of the "back to the classics" movement. In its first season after the Revolution, 65 per cent of its repertory was classical plays, and later occupied 98 per cent. Between the 1919-1920 and 1926-1927 seasons they showed fifty classical plays in three thousand performances attended by two and a half million spectators. Plays such as Ostrovsky's *The Forest* was shown 235 times, Gorky's *The Lower Depths*, 223 times, and Alexey Tolstoy's *Tsar Fyodor*, 153 times. Maly was still The House of Ostrovsky, and its celebrated actresses, Yermolova, Yablochkina, Sadovskaya, Leshkovskaya, Pashennaya, and their male partners, Pravdin, Turchaninov, Ryzhov, Yakovlev, and many others, continued the tradition in numerous and applauded performances. No less successful were Maly's guest performances in the provinces where it helped to reaffirm the principles of realistic acting and staging.

In 1920 the fiftieth anniversary of Yermolova's career turned into a festivity of the traditional theater: the old actress, then sixty-nine, was named People's Artist of the Republic by the Kremlin: thus was initiated the usage of awarding ranks and decorations to the "laborers of the stage." This was done on Lenin's suggestion, and the Moscow Soviet took active part in the celebration. The "leftists" did not spare their criticism of the Maly, "this reactionary museum or old-age asylum," and in 1921 Meyerhold recommended closing this citadel of outdated conservative art. Yuzhin answered, defending traditional forms and classical repertory in its "inviolable integral form" and attacking "distortions of great works of art" and sterile formalism. This was but the beginning of a long struggle in which the academic theaters finally won over the innovators.

A more complex situation developed in the Moscow Art Theater. On the morrow of the Revolution it continued to draw on its old repertory of classics: Griboyedov, Pushkin, Ostrovsky, Saltykov, Tolstoy, Gorky, and Chekhov. The new times made Kachalov accentuate Chatsky's "decembrist" spirit of rebellion in Griboyedov's comedy, or emphasize certain intimations of the future in Chekhov's plays. The latter, however, had but a very small place in the repertory until 1937 when a great Chekhov revival took place in the Soviet Union. Following the romantic trend, Stanislavsky produced Byron's *Cain* in 1920. Leonidov in the title role created a strong, tragic figure of a rebel against God. Despite brilliant auditory effects and excellent recitation, the play proved to be too sophisticated for the audience and terminated its run after eight evenings.

Many members of the company interpreted this failure as a sure sign that romantic symbolism and experimentation had outlived themselves. Still, the production of *The Inspector General* in the next season showed that Stanislavsky did not abandon his search for new forms. For instance, he presented an original solution of the space problem: the performance began on a narrow strip of a platform which gradually expanded, and this corresponded to the growing rhythm and meaning of the comedy.

Of course, its success was mainly due to Chekhov's interpretation, but other actors were also at their height: Moskvin as the sly mayor, and Lilina as his trivial and coquettish wife. It did not prevent, however, some Communist critics from condemning Chekhov's interpretation. S. Danilov wrote that "his Khlestakov was a psychopathological type with a deranged system of associations, a man who jumps from anger to apathy and finally becomes a nightmare of morbid imagination."

It was during these years (1919-1921) that the Moscow Art Theater strengthened its ties with the Maly Theater, including the exchange of artists for individual performances and a common front for the defense of realism. The attacks from the left which denounced the Moscow Art Theater as a "remnant of bourgeois estheticism and middle class complacency" consolidated the alliance among academic theaters. And here again Lenin's firm support of the Moscow Art Theater played its role.

It must be added that Stanislavsky was definitely opposed to what he called "formalist exaggeration." He expressed his opinion quite clearly when he said that the spirit of the times has been formed by suffering, struggle, and heroic deeds, in conditions of starvation, fighting, catastrophe, unheard-of cruelty. ". . . and this great life of the spirit cannot be rendered by external sharpness of form, it cannot be expressed by acrobatics or by constructivism, or by loud luxury of production, or by poster-like painting, or by futuristic daring. Nor do I accept the opposite extreme—the utter simplicity of settings which ends in their complete elimination, or artificial noses and circles painted on faces, and other exaggerated external devices justified by the fashionable theory of the grotesque."

While resisting the attacks from the innovators, Stanislavsky and Nemirovich Danchenko also stood firm in 1920-1922 against the Communist suggestions of including contemporary plays in their repertory. In a letter to Lunacharsky (published only in 1932) Nemirovich wrote: "We accept the Revolution but we are afraid that this music of the new world will not find for a long time an expression in dramatic literature. In any case, we do not see it yet—and if we, the theater, will be offered dry, artificial, imperfect, stammering material, we will not be able to make it sound right—regardless of the fact that it may be strongly tuned in to high revolutionary ideas. We cannot lower our art and ourselves . . . it is impossible to force the musicians of high musical culture to play unripe, lifeless scores written by school boys."

The Moscow Art Theater was spared this plight at least until 1924. Two events contributed to this situation. In 1919, during the Civil War, a group of fifteen members of the Moscow Art Company who gave guest performances in the south of Russia, were affected by the changing fortunes of the fighting and found themselves in the territory occupied by the Whites. Only a few of them succeeded in returning to Moscow, but the majority retreated with the Whites, then went abroad and remained in Europe. This was the case of such prominent actors as Ghermanova, Sharov, Khmara, and others. Some of them formed the Prague Group of the Moscow Art Theater and gave successful performances to *émigré* and Czech audiences. Ghermanova remained the central figure in that group, while Khmara and a few others went to France and Italy.

Another important happening was the authorization given by the Soviet government to Stanislavsky to take his company abroad. They left Russia for almost two years, from August 1922 to September 1924, and gave guest performances in Europe and America. While this tour had a most vivifying effect on the artists and enhanced enormously the reputation of the Theater throughout the world, it suspended its activities at home for two seasons. The absence, however, spared the artists many unpleasant things, as they missed two years of material distress and political terror. Stanislavsky's old friends and companions, whom he met in Prague and in other Western cities, tried to prevail upon him to become an *émigré* but he refused and returned to his native land. He arrived in Moscow at the height of NEP, (New Economic Policy) and found a theatrical life of great intensity and variety. The general loosening of controls in the arts favored the *avant-garde* enterprises. German expressionists played an ever-growing role in their repertory, and the collection of Georg Kaiser's plays published in 1922, was followed by those of Ernest Toller and then by Franz Werfel, Walter Hasenclever, Carl Sternheim, and others. Their hero was the little man suffering from his social environment, and Russian dramatists, such as Erdman, Faiko,

Olesha, Bulgakov, showed the same kind of protagonist and his protest (or antirevolt) in Soviet circumstances. Meyerhold portrayed him against constructivist structures, Chekhov showed him in deep introspection, and the Dramatic Theater of the Revolution and other experimental stages treated him as the product of an urbanistic civilization.

On the other hand, hundreds of local theaters throughout the country simply restored the pre-Revolutionary repertory, numerous dramas about sex and jealousy, and they pretended to march with the times by showing sensational pseudo-historical "exposés" of the Imperial Court and its alleged intrigues and love affairs. Most of these concoctions were on a very low level, morally and esthetically. There was everywhere a strong tendency toward light entertainment highly appreciated by the NEPmen, this ephemeral offshoot of free trade. Operetta, vaudeville, dancing, flourished in 1923-1927 in the same forms as before 1917, particularly on the boards in provincial towns. At the same time, the Agitation and Propaganda section of the Commissariat of Culture continued its slow but insistent work of socialization. In 1922-1923, 33 per cent of all theaters belonged to the State, 36 per cent were called co-operative, and 31 per cent remained in the hands of private producers. But three years later, in 1925-1926, the socialist sector grew to 63 per cent, the co-operative one went down to 27 per cent, and the private one shrunk to a mere 10 per cent.

In the ballet confined to the former Imperial, now Academic, Theaters of Moscow and Leningrad, hardly anything changed in the pattern of classical dancing, and Mme. Vaganova continued to train pupils in the traditional way. Some new developments took place in the opera. The down-to-earth, naively realistic Theater of Musical Drama of the old capital was supplanted by the more sophisticated Musical Studio founded by Nemirovich Danchenko in 1920. It started with a spirited and beautifully produced *The Daughter of Mme. Angot* by Charles Lecocq, and continued with other operettas, reaching the peak with Offenbach's *La Perichole* with Olga Baklanova and a young lively company, and *Lysistrata* adapted from Aristophanes. Later, they presented *Aleko* by Serghei Rachmaninov, a greatly transformed *Traviata* and *Carmen,* and ended up in the thirties with operas by Soviet composer Dzerzhinsky (*The Quiet Don*) and Khrenni-kov (*The Storm*). But in the early twenties this theater, which had began as a workshop, evinced a strong bent toward styliza-tion and the grotesque and interpreted musicals as comedies with songs. Good acting and suggestive settings greatly con-tributed to its success.

Stanislavsky also was instrumental in the opera. In 1918 the Bolshoy Theater established a Musical Workshop, and asked Stanislavsky to help raise the level of dramatic performances. Directed also by V. Alexeyeva and O. Gzovskaya, with N. Golo-vanov as orchestra conductor, the Musical Workshop became an autonomous Opera House and supplied directors and artists to other enterprises. It remained a more conservative institution than the Nemirovich Studio, which was interested in the union of various theatrical genres—music, dancing, acting, and singing— as equally important ingredients of a show and, in general, showed a more radical tendency. It became the State Musical Workshop Theater of Stanislavsky in 1924, and was later merged with Nemirovich's venture. It showed a great many operas of the old repertory, including *Werther, La Bohème,* etc., under the competent musical leadership of Vyacheslav Suk.

The Association of New Music promoted new means of mu-sical expression analogous to the *avant-garde* in dramatics. Various opera houses presented Western modern scores in ur-banistic settings and emphasized in them elements of industrial progress (particularly in *Pacific 231* by Arthur Honegger.) Modernistic trends were obvious in the production of the Lenin-grad Academic Theater of Opera and Ballet which showed *Salomé* by Strauss, *Love of Three Oranges* by Prokofiev, *Johnny Plays* by E. Krenek, *Wozzeck* by Alban Berg, etc.

The Bolshoy Theater in Moscow became the house of national opera and presented Glinka, Tchaikovsky, Dargomyzhsky, Boro-din, Mussorgsky, Rimsky-Korsakov, Serov, and others. It main-tained a high level of musicianship under the guidance of A. Pazovsky and A. Melik-Pashayev. Sobinov, Petrovsky, Nezhda-nova, Davydov, Medvedev, Rumiantsev, Dzerzhinskaya, Gorshu-nova, and other trained singers formed the core of Bolshoy's company. It had good conductors such as Kondraty Kondrashin, Serghei Sakharov, and others. But its vast repertory was mostly made up of well-known operas of Russian or foreign origin, and the lack of new works was badly felt in the twenties. Contemporary composers such as Andrey Pashchenko or Ivan Shishov tried to offer operas with strong political flavor. *The Eagles Revolt* about Pugachev's eighteenth-century uprising, by the former, and *Artist of the Toupée* on the subject of Leskov's story of the times of serfdom, by the latter. Neither of them gained any success with the public. Vladimir Deshevov's *Ice and Steel,* a heroic musical chronicle of the Civil War, also failed to provoke any lasting interest.

Some *avant-garde* Communists of the Monumental Theater Workshop in Leningrad decided in 1924 to use the music of "bourgeois" operas for a revolutionary content, and they made *A Fight for the Commune* out of Puccini's *Tosca,* shifting the action from Rome of 1806 to Paris of 1871; in the new book, General Galliffet kills a Russian girl. Meyerbeer's *The Huguenots* was transformed into *Decembrists,* the protagonists of the military uprising in St. Petersburg in 1825. These and other similar attempts failed miserably, but their promoters firmly believed that music of the past could fit any subject like an extensible glove. By the end of the twenties, however, such extravagancies ceased completely, and this coincided with the emergence of some new operatic material written by Soviet composers on various themes, including the classics. It is well known, for instance, that Shostakovich's first operas were done on Gogol's *Nose* and Leskov's *Lady Macbeth of the Mtsensk District.*

Although a number of opera artists, including such singers as Chaliapin, Smirnov, Petrovsky, Pozemkovsky, Kuznetsova, and others became *émigrés,* those who remained in Russia could insure a smooth functioning of opera houses. The Bolshoy Academic Theater in Moscow and the Academic Theater of Opera and Ballet in Leningrad, as well as the Maly Opera Theater in Leningrad, which later became a laboratory of Soviet opera (conductor, S. Samosud), offered a series of good performances drawing on national and foreign repertory. Leningrad had such good singers as Slavina, Lavrova, Lemeshev, Petrov, and good directors, such as Dranishnikov. The Opera Studio of Leningrad Conservatory became an important factor in post-Revolutionary musical education, under the guidance of Ivan Yershov, great singer, actor, and teacher. He had to start from scratch in an auditorium which lacked plumbing, settings and properties, lighting, and had not been heated for three years. But in 1922-1923 the Conservatory Theater gave eleven, and the following season, eighteen performances including *The Sorochinskaya Fair* by Mussorgsky, with S. Maslovskaya, a very good singer. A parallel Opera Studio was organized by the Moscow Conservatory. In general, the heroic efforts of musicians who tried to maintain the high level of musical culture in Russia bore excellent fruit and helped to form a new generation of singers and instrumental performers.

A new fact of the twenties was the renaissance of the movies. On the eve of the Revolution Russia had a large film industry with some thirty independent producers who put out hundreds of pictures. They all relished kinodrama which imitated the theater, mostly of the psychological or drawing-room kind. In 1919 the cinematographic industry was nationalized, and its production dropped considerably. The only picture worth mentioning during these years is *Polikushka,* an adaptation of Tolstoy's story with Moskvin in the main role. To keep the movie theaters open, the government had to import foreign films, and during the years of NEP, Russian spectators could see a large number of popular American and European pictures. In 1924 they were imported in the amount of three million gold rubles' worth. By that time a group of young directors, artists, and cutters gathered around Dziga Vertov, friend of Meyerhold, Mayakovsky, and other leaders of the *avant-garde,* declared war on the "esthetic cinema" and began a series of documentary films without any scenario or artistic aim. Vertov's "camera eye" theory insisted on the exploration of life, on "authentic reality, observed or surprised outside of the set and the studio," and his films did possess a directness, a forcefulness, and a sense of rhythm which he transmitted to his pupils, among them Pudovkin. Another teacher of the young was Kuleshov, professor at the First State Cinematographic School. Trauberg, Kosintsev, Romm and other prominent directors were impressed by Kuleshov's rejection of any theatrical tradition in the movies, which he treated as an independent art. He believed in cutting as the most important part of picture-making and worked on details of cinematographic

theory. Like most of the stage innovators, he paid great attention to the gait and movements of the actor and coined the
paradox that the legs and arms and not the face were essential
to the screen. His films, *The Great Consoler* and *According to
the Law,* were utterly formalistic and opposed to Vertov's search
for "life content" in a documentary style without actors and
props.

Discussions and controversy about films were as violent as those
about the theater. By 1925 two main currents had become quite
distinct. Eisenstein, with his *Battleship Potemkin* partly inspired
by Griffith's *Intolerance,* made an intellectual picture incorporat-
ing *avant-garde* tendencies and Vertov's factography but elevating
concrete details to the height of a social epic. There was a passionate breath in his presentation of sailors as a collective, in his
sudden opposition of contrasting shots, in his symbolic exaggerations and close-ups, as well as in his general, almost abstract
over-all views, or his analytical differentiation of images. He was
doing in his films what Meyerhold was achieving in the theater
and Mayakovsky in poetry. (Mayakovsky himself was making
scenarios at that time, and was greatly impressed by such Western
films as *Metropolis* and *Dr. Caligari's Cabinet.*)

The other school was representated by Pudovkin who soon
became the promoter of realistic movies. What he did in *Mother*
(from Gorky's novel) or *The End of St. Petersburg* (1927)
showed his close link with the theory and practice of the Moscow Art Theater. He liked precision of the subject matter and
of the working blue print, and relied mostly on individual actors
and an emotional succession of well-related and rhythmical
images. His technique was particularly revealing in *Storm over
Asia,* made in 1929. The third important director of the period,
Dovzhenko, became better known in the thirties and hardly participated in the feverish activities of 1925-1929 when Soviet pictures reflected the general movement of the artistic *avant-garde.*
It is significant that the movies turned to revolutionary subjects
almost at the same time as the theaters to which young writers,
formed during the first years of the Revolution, contributed a
new repertory in the middle twenties.

10

TWO ÐECAÐES OF
SOCIALIST REALISM

IN THE EARLY TWENTIES the Soviet theater felt painfully the lack of its own repertory. The pale and inefficient attempts at reflecting the Civil War on the stage made, for instance, by A. Vermychev (a Red commander killed by the Whites) who wrote *In the Trenches* and two other plays, had but historical interest. Anatoly Lunacharsky turned out many plays, some of them on the figures of the distant past (*Thomas Campanella, Oliver Cromwell*), but his half old-fashioned, half modernistic approach could hardly inspire directors and spectators. Upon his return to Moscow, Stanislavsky, fully aware of the situation, turned to historical events of revolutionary significance, and in 1924 the Moscow Art Theater produced a rather mediocre *Pugachev's Uprising* by Konstantin Trenyov, and *Nikolay I and the Decembrists,* an adaptation of a novel by Dimitry Merezhkovsky, an *émigré* and a religious thinker, who could hardly be welcomed by Communist critics. Another solution seemed to be the staging of already existing stories and novels. In fact, from 1925 on, dozens of such adaptations were produced in Soviet theaters: *Virineya* by Lydia Seifullina, who depicted the protest of a peasant woman against family restrictions and her growth into a revolutionary; *The Badgers* by Leonid Leonov, centering on the conflict between the anarchical and the organized forces in the village, personified by two brothers; *The Rout* by Alexander Fadeyev, a most impressive and successful picture of Red guerillas encircled by the Whites and the Japanese, and fighting their way out; and *The Wind* by Boris Lavrenyov, another chronicle of the Civil War—those and many other adaptations were very popular in the twenties. Most of them had all the drawbacks inherent in hasty dramatizations of narratives.

One of the most significant contributions to the new repertory was made by Vladimir Bill-Belotserkovsky, born in 1885 and author of several mediocre plays. "Bill" preceding his family name, was the remainder from the years he lived in America. His *The Storm* produced in 1925 by E. Lyubimov-Lanskoy in the Moscow Trade Union Theater, was a big success. The critics hailed it as "the great event in the history of the Soviet theater." It initiated, indeed, a whole trend in dramatic literature. Composed of four acts and eleven episodes, this Revolutionary pageant had a cast of fifty; its stock characters were defined only by their social functions and served as representatives of competing forces and classes. The play represented a provincial town wrangling with the usual problems of the military Communism period: epidemics of typhoid fever, famine, reluctance of peasants to pay taxes in foodstuff, plots and conspiracy of the Whites, indecision of fearful intellectuals, general confusion, struggle, and terror. The chairman of the local Soviet, assisted by a lame but energetic sailor, succeeds, however, in dominating the situation, thanks to his vigilance, will power and devotion to the cause, and the sheer physical strength of workmen who back him up the whole way. He is killed while squashing an uprising of the Whites, but the sailor, although deeply affected by the death of his friend, shouts jubilantly: "We have won, we have won!" The curtain falls on this symbolic outcry. Written in a naturalistic style, structured artlessly and in a crude fashion, with attempts of comic relief by obvious jokes and coarse humor, *The Storm* had no true literary merits, but it appealed to audiences because of its almost photographic rendering of well-known situations, its heroic spirit, and its bright splashes of color. Its very defects—lack of depth and character portrayal in black and white —were a challenge to actors who had to give flesh and blood to the schematic figures of the cast. In a way, *The Storm* was a model play, and its pattern was later repeated in hundreds of other similar works, with slight changes due to the degree of individual talent.

Another variant of revolutionary drama was offered the next year by Konstantin Trenyov (1884-1945) in his *Lyubov Yarovaya,* produced in 1926 by the Maly Theater where it had two hundred performances, and then by the Moscow Art Theater. For the Maly Theater this was a decisive step: actors and directors turned definitely to realistic plays on contemporary themes. While *The Storm* represented a rather primitive romantic-heroic trend, Trenyov's drama aimed at psychological realism and attempted a more complex characterization. Lyubov Yarovaya, a school teacher whose husband Mikhail was reported missing in World War I, recognizes him among the officers of the White troops which rescue her native town from the Reds. But Lyubov has become a Communist sympathizer and Mikhail is her class enemy; and while he is trying to arrest and execute the leaders of the Red underground, she helps them, and comes to open or hidden clashes with the man she loves. In the conflict between old affection and new faith, the latter triumphs, and when an insurrection overthrows the Whites and Mikhail is arrested, Lyubov is a stranger to him.

Since the whole action is unfolded against the background of conspiracies, involving spies and fanatics, escape from prison, and breathtaking adventures, the play has many striking climaxes and thrilling episodes. The two main characters, however, remain pale and conventional. Secondary figures are much more colorful, and they actually save the drama. The most popular among them is the sailor Shwandya, an ardent follower of the Communists but a liar, a rake, and a reveler, portrayed in the best farcical tradition. Highly satirical also are a former chambermaid who became a hoarder and a black market speculator, a police colonel, an absent-minded professor, and an empty-headed and cowardly liberal. By a strange twist, the stenographer Panova, a moral nihilist, ready to do anything for comfort and security, appears as a much stronger and more complex character than Lyubov herself, and Soviet actresses had to tone her down on the stage lest she occupy the first place. Trenyov attempted to draw the new strong man in the Commissar Kishkin, one of those unbending heroes in leather jacket who, as Pilnyak put it, were destined to mold the "friable soft Russia" by fear and compulsion. This second-rate melodrama became a hit all over the country for more than two decades.

Boris Romashov's *The End of Krivorylsk,* staged in 1926 by the State Drama Theater (the former Alexandrinsky), began a whole series of "satirical melodramas." Its success was mainly due to an excellent cast: Rashevskaya, Timé, Pertsov, Apollonsky, and other veterans of the stage put life into stock characters drawn by the playwright according to a pattern which was to be followed by dozens of imitators. Romashov wanted to show the decline of the old in a provincial town, Krivorylsk, where speculators, hoarders, spies, and counterrevolutionaries try to win over Muglanova, a girl who has left her family but had not yet succeeded in getting rid of "the curse of the past." The finale shows the victory of the young Communists and the renaming of the town as Leninsk. All the negative characters were ridiculed and provoked the laughter of spectators, but the comedy had a serious political intent; this division of a comic play into the two distinct parts was later jelled into a tradition.

These three archetypes—the heroic-romantic chronicle of the Revolution, the pseudorealist and slightly more psychological melodrama, and satirical comedy—served in 1925-1926 as a prelude to the further development of Soviet repertory. Only a few plays also stood out at that period as specimens of a different kind. One was *The Credentials* by Nikolay Erdman, first produced by the State Drama Theater and then by Meyerhold (see Chapter 8). Others were Mayakovsky's *The Bedbug* and *The Bathhouse;* Katayev's comedies *The Embezzlers* and *The Squaring of the Circle;* Yuri Olesha's *Three Fat Men* and *Conspiracy of Feelings;* and Bulgakov's *Zoyka's Apartment* and *The Purple Island,* all of which presented an independent trend of truly satirical and gay comedy without artificial morality; and this was the reason why all these plays had but a short-lived career and disappeared in the thirties.

Another instance of a well-constructed drama which refused to imitate schematic posters was Mikhail Bulgakov's *The Days of the Turbins* adapted by the author from his novel *The White Guard.* This was the first serious attempt to show the Whites, not as monsters and villains, but as honest human beings with idealistic and patriotic motivation. Of course, its success was partly the result of the controversy which the staging of such a "counterrevolutionary play" by the Moscow Art Theater had provoked in the official press. Fortunately, Stalin believed that there was no harm in showing "that the enemy was intelligent and strong," and he backed the Moscow Art Theater in its daring "encounter with the contemporary theme," as some Communist critics called the new production. Incidentally, the public was thrilled to hear the Imperial Anthem sung on the stage, and to see old army officers and monarchists portrayed in a true-to-life manner. Actors of the Second Workshop gave excellent portrayals of those young men and women who found themselves in 1918 in Kiev between the Germans with their Skoropadsky puppet government, the Ukrainian nationalists, and the advancing Bolsheviks. Written in traditional, realistic fashion, *The Days of the Turbins* was not a great work of art, but it remained a milestone in the history of Soviet repertory because of all the stir it aroused. Its production was at one time banned in Moscow, then the ban was lifted in 1932, but Bulgakov, who wrote thirty-two plays, was persecuted and reduced to silence. He owed his salvation to Stalin's protection which enabled him to work during the last years of his life as theatrical editor at the Moscow Art Theater. He died in 1936.

After *The Days of the Turbins*, Stanislavsky and Nemirovich Danchenko decided to stage a truly revolutionary drama. They chose *Armored Train 14-69*, dramatized by Vsevolod Ivanov from his own tale. It was again the heroic romanticism of the Civil War, but this time the background was highly exotic: Siberian Far East, peasant guerillas led by the illiterate but intelligent Vershinin, Nezelassov, a White officer torn by his scruples and borebodings and trying to save his armored train, a Chinese ready to sacrifice himself for the Revolution, and Peklevanov, a wise Communist who works underground to capture Vladivostok from the Whites, but dies at the moment of victory. The theme of the leading role assumed by the Party in organizing the elemental movement of anarchical peasants gave an ideologolical substratum to those scenes of combat and mass revolt. Kachalov gave a stunning interpretation of Vershinin as a pure Russian type, and other actors, Prudkin, Knipper, Vishnevsky, also ex-

celled in colorful and moving portraitures. But this performance
was more than a tribute to the revolutionary repertory and the
proof of political loyalty. It signified a definite step toward realistic productions in almost naturalistic vein. It looked as if the
theater had gone back as far as its style was concerned, and the
down-to-earth, "true-to-nature" settings by old Simov transported
spectators to a quarter of a century ago.

After 1926 plays on contemporary themes by Soviet dramatists
became an organic part of the repertory, and a must in the Academic and other theaters. They belonged to several well-defined
categories. In the first place came the romantic-heroic drama of
the Civil War, such as the dramatization of novels by Dmitry
Furmanov (*The Revolt* and *Chapayev* which also served for
films), or *The First Cavalry Army* by the popular Vsevolod Vishnevsky (1900-1951), staged by Diky in 1930 for The Red Theater.
Vishnevsky depicted in short schematic episodes the story of Sys-
soyev who rose from an ignorant soldier in the Imperial army to
the high conscience of a seasoned Communist.

A second group included melodramas with a sprinkling of
psychological motivation, particularly for showing the reasons
which compelled members of the old ruling classes to join the
Revolution. Typical of this kind was *The Break* by Boris Lavrenyov. It portrayed Bersenev, the old commander of a warship (obviously the *Aurora*), who, after an inner struggle in
which he is backed by his daughter Tatiana, married to a counterrevolutionary, finally decides to move his armored cruiser from
Cronstadt to Petrograd in order to help Lenin and the Bolsheviks in their struggle for power. Another important figure of the
play was the Commissar Godun, a very conventional character
of virile strength whom the art of Monakhov, an excellent actor,
transformed into a believable human being when *The Break*
was staged by the Bolshoy Dramatic Theater in 1927.

Of a higher dramatic quality were the plays by Alexander
Afinogenov (1904-1941), mainly devoted to the problem of the
intelligentsia under the new regime. His *The Eccentric,* produced
by the Second Moscow Art Theater in 1929, and by the State
Dramatic Theater the following year, showed Volghin, a young
nonpartisan intellectual, working in the administration of a provincial plant and organizing a "club of enthusiasts" to raise the

production and to fight the backwardness and the apathy of their environment. Another play by Afinogenov, *Fear,* produced in 1929 by the Moscow Art Theater, was a political drama presented in terms of an intellectual and psychological conflict which made it of a better quality than the trivial dramatizations of Communist primers. The hero of the drama, Professor Borodin, believes that fear is an eternal biological stimulus of human conduct in the same way as are hunger, love, and hatred. In his Institute of Physiological Stimuli, and particularly in his Laboratory of Social Behavior, he openly contends that the Soviet Regime is based upon fear, a theory eagerly backed by his assistants. An honest and unsuspicious man, Borodin has no inkling that most of them are scoundrels and saboteurs, connected with "interventionists." He is above politics, but they use him as a tool in their underground activities, until the truth is revealed to the professor. But there is more in his discovery. He finds out that the counter-revolutionaries, the old classes, the reactionaries dread to lose their privileges and therefore act through fear, while the Communists are fearless in their sacrificial struggle for the liberation of mankind. Klara, an old revolutionary who makes a speech against Borodin at a session of the Institute, is also instrumental in the old professor's change of heart. Leonidov, by his subtle rendering of Borodin's ideological problems, and other artists of the Moscow Art Theater who made the drama natural and intimate, succeeded in hiding the obvious defects of Afinogenov's work.

The atmosphere under NEP favored the emergence in the late twenties of a whole group of plays which consciously shied away from primitive psychology, posterlike history, and flashy Revolutionary naturalism. The trend was visible in completely different plays. Yuri Olesha in his *Conspiracy of Feelings* drawn from *Envy,* one of the most striking novels of the period, raised the problem of emotions versus reason in the new order, and opposed the optimistic health of limited supporters of the regime to the psychological twists, anxieties, and dreams of individuals who did not want to become sheer numbers in a collectivist society. The conflict between individualism and the all-leveling pattern of the Communist regime were raised with equal sharpness in Olesha's *The List of Benefits,* staged in 1931 by Meyerhold. His heroine, the actress Goncharova, keeps a balance sheet of benefits and crimes performed by the Soviet government, and comes to the conclusion that the new regime, despite a number of good points, is not propitious for free creation. She goes therefore to France in the hope of finding abroad a favorable atmosphere for her acting. But she soon discovers that Western art is corrupted by money and commercialism; in her grief and disappointment, she joins French workmen in a political demonstration and is accidentally killed by the police in Paris. A third play by Olesha, *The Three Fat Men,* a kind of Hoffmannesque fairy tale on the theme of class struggle and the proletarian duel with capitalism, was produced by the Moscow Art Theater as a sort of modern substitute for *The Blue Bird,* but it failed to become a success despite elaborate settings and refined directing. The Communist press attacked it viciously.

A place apart was occupied by Leonid Leonov, one of the outstanding Soviet novelists who wrote eleven plays in a consistent effort to gain laurels on the boards. Most of his works did have an ideological and psychological complexity which compared favorably with most of the current productions, but they were often marred by the playwright's desire not to miss the bandwagon of latest political developments. One of his best works was *Untilovsk,* produced in 1928 by the Moscow Art Theater, which saw in it a traditional exposé of middle-class pettiness and provincial stagnancy in which the elements of life and progress are vaguely embodied in a few young Communists. The whole emphasis of *Untilovsk* is on the grotesque image of the old way of life. The central figure of the drama is Chervakov, a man from the underground, a cynical philosopher of disintegration and annihilation, who believes that "everything on earth has the hole in which it is destined to disappear, just like a man is gulped up by his grave." He therefore denies the value of any effort and laughs at such naive concepts as progress. Chervakov's opponents were not portrayed too convincingly, and the play remained a gloomy picture of greed, bestiality, and nihilistic pessimism. Critics gave a very simple explanation for the prevalence of negative aspects in Leonov's image of darkness: he was but a fellow traveler, not a Communist. Yet they had to acknowledge that even members of the Party appeared stronger in their denunciation of evil than in their affirmation of the new Gospel.

Alexander Bezymensky (born in 1898), a fiery supporter of the new order, and a Communist Youth leader provoked a true scandal with his dramatic pamphlet in verse *The Shot,* whose main protagonist, Prishletsov, was a theoreticician of red tape and double dealing, surrounded by soulless bureaucrats and boot lickers. Only Meyerhold had the courage to produce this sudden disclosure of the regime's shortcomings; and this, of course, originated fierce attacks against the "decadent director" and the "Trotskyite author." Kerzhentsev, who became in 1936 the head of the Central Committee of the Arts, claimed that in Bezymensky's play "the Party was represented as a bureaucratic meeting place of stupid little bourgeois." The wrath of the detractors abated, however, after Stalin called *The Shot* "a model of revolutionary art for the present," and since then the comedy has had a successful run in provincial theaters.

No Communist authority, unfortunately, approved of another play in verse, *Commander of The Second Army* by Ilya Selvinsky, the constructivist poet, also produced by Meyerhold. The latter disregarded the heavy, clumsy style of the drama but was attracted by the legendary stature of the main hero who had in him something of the ancient Scythians. The image of this heroic leader and his warriors clad in Caucasian sheepskin coats and fur caps probably inspired the dances of partisans later choreographed by Moisseyev.

The hero of this drama, the rebellious and temperamental Chub waged a losing fight against dogmatic military bureaucrats and thick-headed soldiers, and finally collapsed because of his colorful personality. A quarter of a century later, in 1954, a Communist theater historian wrote that the following plays were inspired by "the false and mendacious idea that the victory of the proletariat and the growth of socialist forces lead to suppression of individual rights and potentialities, and to dissolving of personality and its leveling in the collective: certain works by Bulgakov, *The Conspiracy of Feelings* by Olesha, *The Lake Lyul* and *The Teacher Bubus* by Faiko, plays by Erdman, and *Commander of The Second Army* by Selvinsky." Most of these plays were produced by Tairov, Meyerhold, The Second Art Theater, Bolshoy Drama Theater, and Theater of the Revolution. They also entered the repertory of numerous theaters in provincial towns which followed the example of the *avant-garde* in Moscow and Leningrad.

II

The New Economic Policy (NEP) came to an end by 1928, when the Communist Party, led by Stalin's firm and ruthless hand, began its offensive. The abolition of both compromise and liberal concessions marked the beginning of a five-year plan for the industrialization of the country, and a bitter battle in the villages for the introduction of collectivized farming. New goals demanded heroic efforts, the return of austerity, and a sharpening of class conflicts. In the militant and aggressive atmosphere of these years, dogmatic Communists felt that an all-out onslaught was needed also in literature and the theater. This meant an attack against "fellow travelers," nonpolitical art, complacency in ideology, and a strict control of any aspect of artistic expression. Between 1927 and 1932 this program was carried out mainly by the organization of proletarian writers and its sections which were active in the theater and in the arts. The VAPP or All-Union Organization, and RAPP, the Russian Organization, became synonymous with the effort made by the most opinionated Communists to curb writers and artists. The extremists maintained that everyone was needed to help the industrialization and collectivization, and they planned specific assignments for poets, novelists, and playwrights. They also dreamt of brigades of artists working with the same discipline and under the same kind of guidance as any group of proletarians and peasants. In the same way as the political and social struggle against "the remnants of bourgeoisie in the village and the city," the assault against "the capitalist, decadent, and formalist spirit in literature and the theater" was launched like a military operation. The members of the VAPP and RAPP had their friends seize important posts on editorial boards, in the Ministry of Education, and in various governmental cultural agencies, while they also got into many administrative theatrical bodies, either as managers or representatives of controlling organs. At the beginning of the thirties some eighty thousand reliable men of the Party functioned as censors and control officers in publishing houses, magazines, newspapers, and theaters. Each new play had to be approved by a special agency for the repertory, but the visa for the actual production could be obtained from responsible officials only after the dress rehearsal. It often happened that a drama or comedy which passed the preliminary barrage of censorship was then banned because its scenic realization disclosed its hidden political harm.

In 1923, the Twelfth Congress of the Party demanded dramas on contemporary themes "using the episodes of the heroic struggle led by the working class." Quite a few of the plays in the new Soviet repertory seemed to have responded to this appeal. But VAPP and RAPP estimated that plays loyal to the regime were outbalanced by those hostile to it, or by neutral ones. Now, according to the theoreticians of proletarian organizations, the nonpolitical theater had no right to exist. Hence their fierce charge against the Moscow Art Theater, Maly, Bolshoy and all the Academic Theaters accused of "neutralist academism." No less violent were the denunciations of "formalists Tairov and Meyerhold," and of the "non-Communist *avant-garde*." The general offensive was launched "against the spiritual and artistic NEP," but there were also some specific accusations. RAPP declared that Stanislavsky's company was good only for "progressive bourgeoisie," Maly Theater played to the aristocracy and merchants, while Meyerhold and Tairov pampered the Bohemians, the liberal intellectuals, and other remnants of Russian symbolism and decadence.

By 1930 the intolerant fanatics openly called for "the dictatorship over literature" and other arts. According to them, every work of art had to express a "party attitude" toward reality. The ideological content being the only determining factor of form, they maintained that controls in the theater should therefore "include not only the text of a play but also its interpretation and staging." Of course, RAPP could not go as far as it wished with great directors such as Stanislavsky, or even Meyerhold, because both had a strong backing among Party dignitaries, but its campaign against individuals and institutions often brought about administrative measures of repression, including arrest, banishment, and police surveillance. After 1927 each theater in Russia was administered by a Council, and generally the manager was a Party member. The Department of Agitation and Propaganda also assumed censorship functions—and the whole set-up offered great opportunities to the leaders of the intransigent group. They also succeeded, by threats and persuasion, in attracting into their fold a number of poets and novelists who either really were or pretended to be of proletarian extraction; and they boasted of such playwrights as Afinogenov, Kirshon, Pogodin, Vishnevsky, and Bill-Belotserkovsky.

In 1931 RAPP organized a conference on theater at which it was confirmed that dramatic art should be considered a weapon of the working class in its struggle for power. A project to establish a chain of RAPP theaters to supplant all the existing theatrical establishments was approved by the conference, and a declaration, called "RAPP'S Theatrical Chart" was highly publicized.

The inflexible and ambitious policy of the "proletarians," failed, however, to bring them complete victory. Several factors worked against them and finally caused the collapse of RAPP. First of all, the "proletarians" were comprised of many heterogeneous elements, from former Trotskyites to rabid Stalinists; they had so many groups and sub-groups feuding with each other, and their aim was so patently that of unlimited power, that they often clashed with the high echelons of the Party, and almost threatened to become a foreign body within the organism of an ideological collective which, in order to be monolithic, ruthlessly suppressed factions or cliques. Secondly, despite loud shouts and noisy boasting, these violent and smug young men did not produce anything worth-while, and their best literary achievements were name-calling and polemics verging on informers' reports to the proper authorities. Of course, there were better elements among the "proletarians" and many of the members of VAPP and RAPP sincerely believed in "Communist art," but they were not too successful in producing its samples. Between 1928 and 1931, when their influence reached its peak, the proletarian playwrights, for instance, could hardly match those very fellow travelers whom their organization was condemning so vehemently. It is true that

Bezymensky's *The Shot* and Afinogenov's *Fear* were written by members of RAPP. But the first play was produced by Meyerhold who was under RAPP's fire; and *Fear* was presented to the public on most reprehensible boards—those of the Moscow Art Theater. Other "hits" of the same year, 1929, were by Selvinsky, Olesha, Vsevolod Ivanov, Lavrenyov, and Glebov. (*Inga*—a play by the latter was about a factory girl who has difficult love and family problems and aspires to a greater feminine freedom.) None of these dramatists belonged to RAPP. The next year, *Bread* by Vladimir Kirshon and *Wrath* by Evgeny Yanovsky, both representing class struggle in the village between the kulaks and the partisans of collectivization, had but an ephemeral success. A few years later Kirshon was denounced as a Trotskyite and his plays were banned (he died in exile, or was executed, in 1937). Other plays of the five-year plan were documentary reports in scenic form and did not remain in the repertory; this included such "plays" as *The Bridge of Fire* by Boris Romashov (1929) and *On the Line of Fire* by Nikolay Nikitin about the building of a power station.

At the same time, the exaggerations of RAPP and particularly of its vociferous "On Guard" group seemed pointless to many intelligent Party leaders. They felt that the so-called fellow travelers, on the whole, supported the regime and honestly tried to reflect contemporary life in their works. In the theater they renovated the repertory and, despite their diversity, did not show any opposition to the basic principles of Communist revolution. On the other hand, the "proletarians" either were sterile or, in the case of "leftists" and successors of Proletcult, leaned toward formalism, factography, and experimentation of the most dubious kind. In gatherings of proletarian writers, one could notice that some of them, such as Fadeyev and Libedinsky, or Afinogenov and Kirshon, who defended psychological realism and traditional literary schools, were much closer to fellow travelers and non-Communist writers than to their own colleagues from RAPP. And discords and intrigues of numerous splinter groups certainly did not favor creative work. Moreover, the tactics of RAPP either silenced nonproletarian writers or provoked strong discontent in their midst. Most of them felt that their loyalty to the regime was above suspicion, but they did not want to be treated in

RAPP's coarse manner and be disciplined like soldiers. In general, writers, actors, painters, and musicians felt as if RAPP pushed them into enormous barracks administered by brutal and stupid corporals.

III

All these circumstances, thoroughly discussed by Stalin and his friends, led to a spectacular resolution of the Central Committee of the Communist Party (April 23, 1932) which announced the suppression of RAPP and all other proletarian or nonproletarian literary and artistic organizations, and their replacement by a single Union of Soviet Writers in which the Communists would form their own faction. An analogous change was ordered in all other areas of the arts, including the theater. This decision put an end to the pretentions and abuse by RAPP and restored the rights of all Soviet artists, regardless of their "class origin" or general opinions. Such a measure assumed that all the writers and artists had rallied to the regime and were ready to serve it. And organizational centralization made it easy to control them and shape them into a homogeneous body.

At the beginning it looked as if this reform, considered as the victory of the Party's moderate wing, brought more freedom and various material advantages to artists. But it soon became clear that organizational unity imposed on all "workers of intellectual labor" was reposing on ideological unity. By 1934 this was definitely fixed in the formula of "socialist realism," which was proclaimed a "historically superior and qualitatively new step in the development of the arts." Thousands of articles and books offered interpretations of this esthetic commandment, but it would be appropriate to use the definition of socialist realism made by the Writers Congress in 1934 upon suggestions of Andrey Zhdanov, the Party spokesman: "Socialist realism being the basic method of Soviet literature and criticism, requires from the artists truthful, historically concrete representation of reality in its revolutionary development. Moreover, truth and historical completeness of artistic representation must be combined with the task of ideological transformation and education of the working man in the spirit of Socialism." This doctrinal assertion reigned supreme in Soviet arts until 1953, with a short interval during the war years, when writers were allowed more leeway. It meant that all playwrights, actors, and directors had to march in the tight boots of socialist realism. Whoever failed to conform or showed a dangerous deviation toward symbolism, intuitivism, romanticism, idealism, or other bourgeois trends, was branded a cosmopolitan, a lackey of capitalism, or an "inner *émigré*."

Theoretically, the formula of socialist realism was contradictory and vague since it confused such different concepts as aesthetic method, artistic intention, requirements of a school, and political demands. But in practice it became an inviolable tablet of the Communist credo, and it required political conformity and traditional form. Stalin expressed it in slightly different terms: "Literature should be national in form and socialist in content." Actually, "national" meant "patriotic" and "realistic." The official introduction of the formula signified the banishment of experimentation and of artistic *avant-garde*, as well as obedience to strictures of representational art, ranging from sheer naturalism and factography to psychological realism in an old-fashioned manner.

It is easy to see the impact of socialist realism on dramatic repertory and on acting and production.

The first requirement demanded that the plays reflect contemporary reality and topical themes. The second imposed on the dramatist the task of portraying a positive hero, "the bearer of the socialist ideal of the world's transformation." To quote B. Rostotsky, a Soviet theatrical historian, "Literature and art of previous periods could not know such a hero as he did not exist yet in real life"; and in depicting him, Soviet writers created new art.

It is quite logical that these demands were expanded to Soviet producers and actors: to stage plays and to portray people within the structure of socialist realism, achieving an educational result and giving the high image of the new man in a new society. The cliché of virtuous and strong-willed Communists began long before the adoption of socialist realism as the obligatory official dogma. Fellow travelers and proletarians alike made wooden masks instead of live people when dealing with the "new hero." This defect was patent in Vsevolod Ivanov's *Blocus*, (1929), a tendentious chronicle of the Cronstadt Rebellion in 1921 and its suppression by the Red Army, or in Lavrenyov's *Enemies* (1929), or in plays by Leonov. A stereotype was introduced and in one way or another most of the Soviet playwrights followed it for two decades. Another organic disease was the monotonous similarity of dramatic conflicts. Most of them were reduced to the clash between the old and the new in a posterlike manner.

Between 1932 and the beginning of the war against Hitler in 1941, Soviet repertory showed signs of life only if and when the dramatists dared to pour something fresh into consecrated molds or tried to get away from the prescribed formulas. In this category, the best specimens probably were plays by L. Rakhmanov, Afinogenov, Leonov, and partly Korneychuk. Rakhmanov turned the well-known and successful film *The Deputy of the Baltic,* into a play entitled *Restless Old Age* (1937), in which he represented an old scientist, presumably the academician Timiryazev, who gave his support to Lenin in the first year of the Revolution.

Afinogenov scored two hits with his *Far Taiga* (1935) and *Mashenka* (1940). The first concerned Malko, a sick Red Army commander in the Far East on his way by train to Moscow. A mechanical failure of his private car detains him for a couple of days on a siding at a whistle stop. Malko forgets about his mortal illness and stirs up the whole staff of the tiny railroad station and makes them realize that all of them belong to a huge collective of their country. He gives meaning to their work and brings them new hope. Particularly interesting is his ideological duel with the second switchman, a former deacon and sectarian turned atheist. Malko might die in three months, but he loves life and affirms it by all his deeds and words, while his adversary, paralyzed by the inevitability of death, denies the sense of any human endeavor and lapses into pessimistic nihilism. (In the initial draft of his play Afinogenov wanted to concentrate on this contrast, but Gorky convinced him to allot it but a secondary place.)

Maschenka had a poetic and naive charm of its own, and was very successful as a lyrical and psychological drama. Its heroine, a young grandchild of the grumbling Okayemov, an old misanthropic professor, comes to stay with him. He meets her without any pleasure, but gradually yields to her youth, honesty, and vitality. She transforms his existence, gives it a new meaning, and the old hermit ends up as an active participant of contemporary life. Staged by Yuri Zavadsky in the Theater of Trade Unions, it owed its immediate hold on Moscow audiences to V. Maretskaya, an excellent Mashenka, and Lyubimov-Lanskoy, a subtle interpreter of Professor Okayemov.

Platon Krechet (1934) by Alexander Korneychuk, winner of literary awards, became a success, not only because of the Party career of its author who occupied high posts in the government of the Ukrainian Republic, but because of his portrayal of the young Soviet intelligentsia, a new and attractive subject. Platon Krechet, a surgeon of proletarian origin and a former stoker, fights against physicians who are remnants of the past and block the way to reforms and bold scientific experimentation. He is shown as a man completely dedicated to his "service to the people," in contrast to Communist bureaucrats of the Public Health Service, but he is helped by Beresta, a true and prominent Party member.

Konstantin Simonov's *The Lad from Our Town*, also had its moment of popularity in the early forties. The author's hero, Lukonin, is an embodiment of patriotism and bravery. A typical representative of Soviet youth, he volunteers in the Red Army when there is trouble in Manchuria, then goes to fight in Spain. A romantic halo of adventure and combat saved Lukonin from becoming one of the customary stock characters.

The patriotic theme was strongly promoted in the years preceding the war, and this explains the place occupied by historical plays such as *Peter the First* by Alexey Tolstoy (from his novel), and *Fieldmarshal Kutuzov* (1939) by Vladimir Solovyov who, a few years later, was awarded Stalin's Prize for his *The Great Sovereign* in which he portrayed Ivan the Terrible as an outstanding and highly patriotic statesman.

In the middle thirties, at the beginning of purges and trials followed by terror and suspicion, Soviet dramatists either represented life around them as a ceaseless holiday or invented superficial conflicts. Dozens of plays were devoted to the activity of secret agents, spies, and diversionists. The worst of them degenerated into cheap thrillers and detective dramas, such as the popular plays by the brothers Tur and Leo Sheinin. But even such a talented author as Leonov could not resist the temptation, and revised his work to conform to the social command of his time. His first version of *Orchards of Polovchansk* was a lyrical and philosophical drama, almost with Chekhovian undertones. These features attracted the Moscow Art Theater which included the play in its repertory. Leonov wanted to show Makaveyev, the creator of gardens, as a man of purposeful and fruitful life, in opposition to Pylyaev, a superfluous man who made a mess of his existence. But this interesting idea was sacrificed to a melodrama: in the second version Pylyaev became a secret agent, and the conflict was reduced to a disclosure of "subversion." *The Wolf* (1938), by Leonov, again used saboteurs, policemen, disguised spies, and all the paraphernalia of a detective potboiler. Only in *An Ordinary Fellow,* a comedy (1940), did Leonov show less eagerness to be a political conformist. In this satirical piece, based on the traditional mistaken identity device, he portrayed Ladyghin, a pompous, boasting man, proud of his high connections. When Svekolkin, a friend of olden times, comes to visit him with his shy, unassuming daughter Annushka, Ladyghin suggests that he introduce Svekolkin to his friends as a VIP. Svekolkin consents to play the role, and Ladyghin makes a big fuss about him, admiring the dignity and poise of Svekolkin's act. But at the end Ladyghin makes a startling discovery: Svekolkin is a *true* VIP, a well-known scientist and a high functionary. The spectators obviously preferred such comedies to the grim and tendentious illustration of the slogan that the growth of socialism was necessarily accompanied by an intensification in the enemies' activities.

Another group of plays on "a given subject" were numerous attempts to bring Lenin to the stage and to glorify him as the father of the Revolution, and eventually Stalin, shown as the "faithful disciple and companion-in-arms of Lenin, the great continuator of his immortal work, leader and teacher of the Communist Party of the Soviet Union, of the Soviet people and of workmen of the whole world." (This quotation is from the Soviet Dictionary, Vol. 3, Moscow, 1955). After Trenyov's *On the Banks of the Neva,* in which Kniazev, a soldier, talks to Lenin on the phone, and Korneychuk's *Truth,* the most important and widely staged plays about Lenin were those by Nikolay Pogodin (pen name of Stukalov), a talented dramatist, born in 1900. He came to the theater from journalism, and all his plays, particularly the early ones, seemed to be dramatization of factual reports on current events. For example, *Tempo* (1929) depicted the building of the Stalingrad Tractor Plant before the construction was finished. The desire to bring to the spectators the "hot" problem of the day was also obvious in *The Poem of the Ax* (1930), devoted to the fabrication of stainless steel, or in *My Friend* (1931), in which the main protagonist, Gay, is the new hero: completely absorbed in his task to set going a factory, he struggles against egotistic climbers, dull bureaucrats, sluggish workmen, and even his own wife. The most popular in this series of plays was *Aristocrats* (1934), a half-serious, half-comical play about the building, by forced labor, of a canal between the White and Baltic Seas. Thieves, bandits, and other convicts, the aristocrats of crime, at first do not want to work but gradually become involved in collective action and are transformed and morally regenerated. Kostya the Captain, the main protagonist of the play, even receives official awards for his zeal. This theme of "reforming human character" through toil was current in the thirties, and numerous novels and plays exploited it. By the way, some of them were akin to "miracle plays," the conversion of former villains to Communism being similar to the change of sinners into good Christians. The underlying idea of all the novels and plays on that subject was to prove that Soviet society did create new men and new morality. What redeemed Pogodin's play from becoming an illustration of a thesis were his humor and his technique: *Aristocrats*, like Pogodin's other works, replaced the "trunkline action" of a single plot by a sequence of short episodes or dramatic scenes, each having its own climax and resolution, very much like cinematographic shorts. Excellent dialogues and unity of the main theme tied all these separate skits into a scenic whole. The novelty of this structure attracted directors and actors. *The Poem of the Ax* and *My Friend* were successful productions of the Theater of the Revolution, under the direction of Alexey Popov, and the Vakhtangov Theater produced *Tempo* and *Aristocrats*, the latter under the imaginative direction of Nikolay Okhlopkov, with Ruben Simonov, an outstanding actor, in the part of Kostya the Captain.

In 1937 the Vakhtangov Theater produced with great success

Pogodin's most popular drama, *Man With a Gun*. Shadrin, a soldier who comes to Petrograd in October 1917 and gets involved in the Bolshevik Revolution, is the main protagonist of the play, but the climax consists of his encounter with Lenin in the corridors of Smolny, the headquarters of the first Communist government. Before departing for the front, Shadrin also meets Stalin, whom Lenin telephones from the Smolny. Boris Shchukin, an excellent actor who also portrayed Kostya the Captain in *Aristocrats,* played the difficult part of Lenin. In his interpretation he tried to avoid any false romanticism. His Lenin was simple and human, without being sentimental and without ceasing to embody the Revolution. Thus his meeting of Shadrin, a peasant in soldier's uniform who stood guard at Smolny, symbolized the alliance between Leninism and the popular aspirations of the masses.

The Moscow Art Theater, under the guidance of Nemirovich Danchenko, staged *The Chimes of Kremlin,* Pogodin's second drama of the Lenin cycle. A. Gribov impersonated Lenin but, unlike Shchukin, he stressed not the physical image of the great leader but his psychological portrait, the strength of his personailty, the sweep of his general vision, the dynamism of his purposeful effort. In *The Chimes of Kremlin* Lenin's characterization has a wider range than in *Man With a Gun.* In the former, he is shown in the country, hunting and talking to children and women who pray for him as if he were a tsar. He walks at night on the banks of the Neva, accompanied by a sailor who is in love with the daughter of Zabelin, an electrical engineer, and he summons the same engineer to the Kremlin where the project of Russia's electrification is studied by Stalin and Dzerzhinsky, the head of the Cheka (the political police). And there is a long scene in which he chats with an old Jewish watchmaker, who is going to repair the silent chimes of the Kremlin and make the bells play "The Internationale." The image of Lenin is projected against the backdrop of famine and devastation that hit Russia in 1920—and this is painted realistically, with the opening scene bearing a slight resemblance to the beginning of Mayakovsky's *The Bedbug.*

The humor of *The Chimes of Kremlin* is subtly changed into a more serious, sorrowful mood in the last play on Lenin, *The*

Third, Pathetic, in which the news of the leader's death, treated
as a tragic leit motif, is replaced by hope in the future. The play
was written in 1955.

Pogodin, a prolific dramatist, wrote a great many plays on
topics from contemporary life. His *Creation of the World* (1946)
showed the reconstruction of a town ruined by the war and the
role of devoted Communists in this gigantic task. His *Missouri
Waltz* (1950), ridiculing President Truman, followed the official anti-American line. And his *The Three Who Went to Unploughed Lands* came immediately after Khrushchev's appeal to
young men and women, exhorting them to develop agriculture
in the southeast steppes of Asiatic Russia. By the way, many
critics found Pogodin's portrayal of Soviet youth far from being
flattering and accused him of flippancy and irony. None of these
plays, however, equals the suspense and humor in *Aristocrats* and
the Lenin cycle.

Another dramatist who portrayed the Communist great men
was Vsevolod Vishnevsky. His *The First Cavalry Army* enhanced
the pathos of revolutionary heroics and portrayed collective rather
than individual protagonists. *The Final Decisive . . .* (staged in
1931 by Meyerhold) showed the beginning of a war against the
capitalist invaders, who had wiped out a detachment of twenty-
seven fighters. One of them, before dying, writes "162 million
less twenty-seven" to indicate that the population of Russia can
afford any loss of human lives. *Optimistic Tragedy* (1932) produced by the Kamerny Theater, was again a lyrical-heroic chronicle in pseudo-classic style. The "saga" element of the play was
made quite patent by the figure of the Narrator who made comments, tied in all the scattered episodes of the drama, and, at the
same time acted as chorus and author's voice. The play showed
an anarchical group of Baltic Sea marines who, under the influence of a ruthless woman commissar, accept the stern Party
discipline and all die in the battle against the Whites. Their
end is a tragedy, but the final victory of the cause for which they
gave their lives makes it optimistic, and the narrator conveys
this conclusion to the audience.

Among other plays by Vishnevsky, *The Unforgettable 1919,*
written in 1949, belongs to fictional distortions of history which
were so frequent in Stalin's era. The play represents Lenin as

always accompanied by Stalin. The play ends with a telephone call from Stalin, who announces to Lenin that he has crushed the Cronstadt Rebellion and thus saved the Revolution. Based on complete falsification of historical facts, the play is simply a glorification of Lenin and even more of Stalin. It has a flavor of flattery and a ring of mendacity.

In the thirties there were other plays bent on open praise of Stalin (his youth, in the plays of a Georgian dramatist, and his role in the 1905 Revolution, in *Prologue* by A. Stein).

On the whole, comedies were less affected by propaganda aims, and very often they paid the necessary tribute to ideology either in the denouement or in some speech by the *raisonneur* of the play. A good example of Soviet comedy is Vassily Shkvarkin's *Father Unknown* produced by the Theater of the Satire in 1933. The plot of this hilarious farce is centered around Manya, a young girl who wants to become an actress and to play the role of a pregnant girl abandoned by her lover, and this leads to all sorts of foolish and comic situations. Shkvarkin's comedy actually belongs to the long series of Soviet vaudeville. Very few of the Russian playwrights in the thirties and forties went beyond this simple, and often primitive, form of humor. True comedy of manners or of characters was a rarity. As soon as the Soviet comedy verged on satire it had to abide by the regulations of socialist realism and preach definite political tenets. In many cases, however, the so-called ideological content of a play was extremely thin and only served as protective covering.

IV

The return to normalcy, the consolidation of the Soviet regime, symbolized by the 1936 constitutional law and the economic development of the country, favored a huge growth of theatrical enterprises throughout the Soviet Union. By the end of the thirties, there were 387 theaters in Russia proper, and some 500 in the other ten republics of the Union (at that time the USSR had eleven republics). These included nonprofessional and amateur companies. The achievements of national theaters in non-Russian regions were truly amazing: in the Ukraine and in Georgia, the already existing institutions were developed and expanded, or new ones sprang up, but in some Central Asiatic Republics, such as Kazakstan, Uzbekistan, and in small Caucasian autonomous regions, such as Ossetia or Chechnia, national theaters were either resurrected from the dead or created by enlightened national patriots on the basis of ancient traditions. There is no doubt that since the thirties, guest performances of these national theaters in Moscow and Leningrad had a certain influence on the art of the stage and on costume design in Russia.

What presented a novelty in comparison with the pre-Revolutionary past, was the ever-growing net of Red Army and kolkhoz theaters, and the development of the amateur movement. More than two hundred and fifty thousand people took part in the latter's activities in some four thousand clubs and local theatrical collectives.

The administration of all the theaters was definitely centralized in 1936 when a All-Union Committee of the Arts with a Central Direction of Theaters was created. In its structure and jurisdiction, the latter resembled the Imperial Direction with an essential difference, however: the tsarist officials administered but a few establishments and had no power over any of the 153 non-Imperial theaters which existed in the Empire in 1913, while the Soviet bureaucrats ruled over all theatrical enterprises of the country. In 1938, the stabilization of all companies as permanent units, regardless of their size, actually froze the personnel and made it difficult to move from one company to another without governmental authorization, and this strengthened the hold of Central Direction over actors and producers.

Of course, the controls were mild when it came to such theaters as the Moscow Art Theater, or the former Maly and Alexandrinsky. Besides, by the end of the twenties, artists and intellectuals in Russia accepted the existing regime as a permanent one and theaters voluntarily followed the general trend of social service and ideological drama. The actors enjoyed material benefits at an increasing rate, and the place of honor they occupied in Soviet society, the sensational growth of eager audiences and their enthusiastic response to any kind of scenic entertainment, created uncommon conditions for the development of theaters and for the training of companies. In terms of numbers—in regard to enterprises and spectators—there was what the Ameri-

cans call a boom. Less obvious was the tendency toward artistic
uniformity. In the early thirties, however, the implications of
socialist realism and of complete nationalization of theaters, became quite evident. The Party concentrated on two main tasks:
consolidation of realism in existing institutions, and elimination
of the *avant-garde* with its dangerous experimentation. And in
pursuing this policy, the governmental agencies found themselves in a favorable situation. There is no doubt that the masses
of new theatergoers were genuinely interested in plays on contemporary themes. They loved to recognize themselves on the
stage and to relive the episodes of the recent past, glorified and
sanctified by the playwrights. It took them quite a few years before they got tired of clichés and of poor and monotonous sermons
in dramatic form. But their disappointment did not manifest
itself until the late forties.

On the other hand, the best Russian companies remained
faithful to realistic tradition, and they joined forces with the
Party in the struggle against formalism and the *avant-garde*. It
is true that their interpretation of realism did not coincide with
official formulas, but it was closer to them than to the eccentricities of the *avant-garde* or the innovations of "seekers."

This was the case of the Moscow Art Theater, despite the fact
that its leaders were alien to the Communist ideology. Stanislavsky and Nemirovich Danchenko were aware of the situation,
and their immediate aim was to preserve the achievements of
Russian theatrical art and to maintain its integrity and high
standards. Future historian will discover that this task required
many compromises, and that on many occasions the two directors
were subject to pressures from the Kremlin which were friendly
in form but quite firm in substance. The Moscow Art Theater
added a number of Soviet plays to its repertory, and staged them
loyally, bringing out their political message. From *Armored
Train* 14-69, to *Platon Krechet* and *Lyubov Yarovaya*, from Leonov's dramas to *Earth,* a play about peasant life by Nikolay Virta,
or *Chimes of the Kremlin,* the Moscow Art Theater attempted to
choose what it believed were the better specimens of contemporary dramaturgy. Its efforts were sincere, particularly when represented by Nemirovich Danchenko, who had come to the conclusion that a new society had emerged in Russia and that the

theater had to adjust itself to changed conditions. Hence his statements about the help received from the Party and the truth of socialist realism, which shocked some of his friends in the late thirties, particularly after the death of Stanislavsky in 1938.

During the last years of his life, Stanislavsky concentrated on giving the final touch to his System and to his writings. He occupied again a central place in the Russian theater, and the principles of his System became a kind of Ten Commandments for the stage. Communist theoreticians recognized Stanislavsky's System and interpreted it in terms of dialectical materialism. They particularly liked the theory of physical action and linked it to Pavlov's conditioned reflex. In any case, the vast majority of Soviet companies looked at Stanislavsky and the Moscow Art Theater as the true interpreter of realism.

In 1932 both Stanislavsky and Nemirovich Danchenko came out with sharp criticism of formalistic innovators and defended realism on the stage as the only sound and healthy method, and as a "national tradition." This was in conformity to their previous announcements in which they condemned "excessive experiment." Already in 1926 they had staged Ostrovsky's *The Burning Heart* as an answer to Meyerhold, affirming the theater of actor, of artistic truth, and of psychological treatment of characters in opposition to the *avant-garde* theatricality and expressionism. In 1927 the Moscow Art Theater revived *The Marriage of Figaro* as a period piece, and presented Beaumarchais' play in careful décor, using the revolving stage for the swiftly changing twelve episodes of the play, and combining precision of historical restoration with psychological study of each part.

In 1935 they turned to Gorky and presented his *Enemies* as a violent clash of proletarians and capitalists. The production was schematic, but actors transformed a deficient text and poor plot into scenic reality through their creation of characters. Kachalov as Bardin, the liberal hypocrite, Knipper as his loquacious wife, and Tarkhanov as the old general, made the play a relative success.

The next year Stanislavsky and N. Gorchakov, his pupil, made a fascinating performance out of *Molière* by Bulgakov, in period settings by Williams. The plot of this play, written in 1931, revolved around Molière's domestic drama: the great playwright married his own daughter Amande, whom Madeleine Bejart, his former mistress, passed off as her sister. Bulgakov followed the biographical pattern, his Molière was old, in disgrace with the court, crushed by the ban of *Tartuffe,* and he died during the performance of *Le Malade imaginaire.* But the central event of the play was the cabal of hypocrites who poisoned Molière's life, suppressed freedom, and emasculated artistic creation. This part of Bulgakov's drama was topical, and his outburst against the officials had a ring of actuality. No wonder that *Molière* was called "a blunder on the part of the Moscow Art Theater" and severely criticized by the press. The directors had to close it after seven performances. Since similar incidents occurred with other plays of contemporary authors, the leaders of the Theater felt much safer when they dealt with classical repertory. Stanislavsky died before he finished the staging of *Tartuffe,* which was not presented until the following year, 1939. Great success was achieved by *Wit Works Woe,* by an adaptation of *Anna Karenina,* and the revival of *Three Sisters.* In Griboyedov's comedy the ensemble was excellent: Kachalov as a "socially significant" Chatsky, Masalsky as a cold and handsome Molchalin, and Moskvin as the liar, Zagoretsky, enchanted their audiences. *Anna Karenina,* with A. Tarassova in the title role (she worked on it for two years), Khmelev as Karenin, and M. Prudkin as Vronsky, was interpreted as the tragedy of a sincere and passionate woman crushed by the hypocrisy and malevolence of high society. And *Three Sisters* was staged in the same pale hues as it had been during Chekhov's lifetime. When, however, the Moscow Art Theater was allowed to give performances in Paris in 1937 and showed *Enemies, Three Sisters,* and *Anna Karenina,* the old Muscovites, now *émigrés,* found great differences between the present day and the former Moscow Art Theater. One of the reasons for their disappointment was the "historical" flavor of all those plays which some three decades earlier had still been "contemporary." And they found the "middle generation" of actors, such as N. Khmelev, A. Tarasova, K. Yelanskaya, O. Androvskaya, A. Stepanova, B. Dobronravov, A. Gribov, and B. Livanov, very talented but not reaching the artistic perfection of the older favorites. It is also true that the Moscow Art Theater's realistic production, which was so fresh and exciting in 1900, now appeared rather dated.

The Maly Theater was another mainstay of realism in the thirties. Its traditions presented sufficient guarantee of aesthetic soundness for the authorities, and the administration was eager to make adjustments for contemporary repertory and for the modernization of the classics. It must be said, however, that in *Armored Train 14-69* in 1935, or *On the Banks of Neva* in 1937, and the plays by Leonov, Panferov, and Korneychuk in the following years, the Maly simply fulfilled its obligations; but its representation of life never went beyond second-rate illustrations or, when the directors were eager to prove their political loyalty, beyond heavy stressing of social significance in the classics. Even Communist critics dubbed "vulgar sociologism" the attempts to interpret all the businessmen as ruthless acquirers and all the poor teachers as enlightened precursors of the Revolution. Such faults of taste were committed even in Ostrovsky's plays, and this despite the fact that the Maly was instrumental in the revival of Ostrovsky throughout the country. (In 1939, thirteen thousand performances of Ostrovsky's plays were offered in Russian theaters.) The best attainments of the Maly were the classics, and in its search for an adequate expression it even went to "formalistic deviations" such as the excellent production of *Tarelkin's Death* directed by A. Diky in 1936. The stage of the traditionally realistic theater was suddenly filled with phantasmal policemen, werewolves, and grotesque officials. Diky claimed that this conveyed to the spectators the irreality of the whole tsarist regime, but the audiences saw in the performance a tragic farce held together by artistic unity of conception. In a completely different style, and more typical of the Maly, was *The Inspector General* (1938) with Yakovlev as a cunning, intelligent mayor and Iliinsky as a "diminished" Khlestakov. The settings by Yuon aimed at an historical reconstruction of the 1830s. Similarly, in *Wit Works Woe*, the same year, Lanceré showed in his settings and costumes the Moscow of 1820, and the director and the artists revived the social environment of the period and presented historical vignettes, with an exciting Chatsky (M. Tsarev).

In the foreign repertory the Maly scored a success with *Othello*

(1935). A. Ostuzhev, pupil of Lensky, in the title role, acted with great emotional intensity representing the Moor as a pure idealist, an ardent believer in his vision of love and femininity. *Uriel Acosta* which Stanislavsky produced in the nineties at the Hunter's Club, was staged by the Maly as a romantic and revolutionary play, with settings which faithfully reproduced seventeenth-century Holland.

Despite all these successes and the good quality of the company, the Maly went through various tribulations because it lacked unity of direction. In 1938 it turned for help to the Moscow Art Theater, and I. Sudakov, who had been Stanislavsky's assistant in *The Days of the Turbins* and Nemirovich Danchenko's in *Lyubov Yarovaya*, was dispatched to the Maly to lead the whole enterprise. He gave a more resolute push toward socialist realism and staged a large number of plays by contemporary Soviet authors.

V

The main trouble with the theaters in the thirties was the discrepancy between good companies and poor plays. Soviet Russia had a large number of excellent interpreters and talented directors, old and young. Very often they succeeded in supplementing the deficiencies of a text by their imaginations, elevating a sketchy, dull character to the height of a lively, artistic figure, but such miracles could not happen all the time. Most theaters, such as the Moscow Art Theater, the Maly, the former Alexandrinsky, now the State Academic Pushkin Drama Theater, the Vakhtangov, and many others in Moscow and Leningrad were compelled to offer potboilers in their pursuit of Soviet repertory. They could not do otherwise because of the double pressure of political and theatrical considerations. Contemporary repertory was a necessity for any theater that did not want to get congealed in the classics, and it was also a proof of loyalty constantly required by the totalitarian regime. In their desperate search for plays which reflected current events, theaters produced numerous adaptations of best-sellers. In 1932-1934 novels by Furmanov, Fadeyev, Gladkov, Katayev, and many others were staged throughout the country. The few good works by Soviet playwrights were taken up by almost every theater, and one could see, for example, *Aristocrats* or *Man With a Gun* or *Armored Train 14-69* simultaneously presented on dozens of boards. And still the percentage of Soviet plays in comparison with pre-Revolutionary repertory and the classics was rather low.

Another problem was the adherence to the theory of socialist realism. It was a kind of obligatory gesture on the political level, but it left unanswered the question of its scenic manifestation. What production could qualify as meeting the requirements of the prevailing doctrine? Apparently the evaluation depended upon the degree of intensity and clarity by which the social message and the socialist intent of the play was conveyed and this opened a vast field for debate. In theory, all theaters declared themselves on the side of socialist realism, and this included institutions with a strong *avant-garde* tradition, such as Tairov's Kamerny or Vakhtangov's. Actually, throughout the thirties, directors, formed in the twenties, came to the fore and made frantic efforts to preserve some of their convictions within the framework of socialist realism. The whole history of the Russian theater of the period is filled with this losing battle against insipid uniformity. This explains how from time to time there were brilliant or extremely interesting productions which did not seem to fit into the general pattern: those were the last vestiges of the twenties. Directors such as Sushkevitch, who was active in the Maly between 1932 and 1936, Okhlopkov, Zavadsky, Akimov, Zakhava, Yutkevich and others, less known, succeeded from time to time in presenting productions which bore the imprint of the experimental era. Such was *The Inspector General* (1939) in Vakhtangov's Theater with Ruben Simonov, who impersonated Khlestakov as a light-headed dreamer, while the whole performance had the flavor of hilarious vaudeville. The death of Shchukin, one of the Soviet's best actors, on the eve of the dress rehearsal, deprived the performance of a remarkable mayor.

In the same theater I. Rappoport directed an excellent *Much Ado About Nothing,* with Mansurova and Simonov bringing gaiety to the whole performance. In 1940, in the patriotic *Field-marshal Kutuzov,* Okhlopkov used a stage framework of an arch, building columns of a portico in the style of the early nineteenth century and introducing music and choral singing. *Don Quixote* adapted by M. Bulgakov as a picaresque play, was acclaimed in the Leningrad State Dramatic Theater in 1941, with Nikolay Cherkassov in the title role, and on the Vakhtangov boards in Moscow where Ruben Simonov gave a different interpretation of the Knight of the Sad Countenance. His was a gay, warm portrayal within the framework of resplendent settings by Williams.

In many other theaters one could easily discover discrepancies in the style of production. Actors and directors quarreled and fought with each other because of different theories and tendencies. While some of them tried to preserve the spirit of the twenties, others wanted to return to stark realism or even naturalism and accepted socialist realism as the only command of the epoch.

Interesting productions were shown at the end of the thirties by Alexey Popov in the Central Theater of the Red Army, created for the armed forces. In 1937 the whole company went to the Far East and in seven months gave 576 performances to local garrisons. The next year in Moscow, it made a hit with a spectacular *Suvorov,* and it also proved what it could do in the non-military genre: *The Taming of the Shrew* was successfully interpreted as a "realistic historical comedy." Two years earlier, the same Popov had staged *Romeo and Juliet,* with Babanova, in the Theater of the Revolution (merged in 1942 with the Moscow Drama Theater). A group of Meyerhold's pupils, who left the Master's company for personal reasons, joined Popov in his efforts and brought some noticeable refinement to the production of Shakespeare. In the ballet, however, despite the modern flavor of Prokofiev's music and the art of dancers such as Ulanova and others, *Romeo and Juliet* was presented in traditional settings of "historical Renaissance," with conservative period costumes.

While such large enterprises as the Moscow Theater of Trade Unions specialized in contemporary repertory presented with naked black-and-white tendentiousness, sparks of inventiveness and artistic initiative were at times visible on secondary stages such as the Theater of Satire with Victor Khenkin, Lenin's Communist Youth Theater, and others to which good actors from "liquidated" institutions were attached by governmental order.

A special place in the theatrical life of the thirties and forties was occupied by Gorky's plays. Since 1928 they had become a must on billboards of hundreds of theaters, and although the audiences took many of them as sheer pictures of a distant past, they were extolled as models of socialist realism. Nemirovich Danchenko presented *The Enemies* with an emphasis on the simplicity of its protagonists, opposed to the "psychologism" of the twenties.

The most successful productions of Gorky were *Vassa Zheleznova* which he revised, giving a more tragic accent to the greedy and unscrupulous mother (excellent interpretation by Serafima Birman), and *Yegor Bulychev and the Others* which he entrusted to the Vakhtangov Theater. The main figure of this late play is Bulychev, a rich merchant who has cancer and is obsessed by the idea of death. He is condemned because of an incurable disease, but so is the world to which he belongs. Bulychev is too intelligent to miss the meaning of events which accompany his slow agony. He understands all the intrigues of his familiars around the inheritance he is going to leave, he has no illusions about quacks, unscrupulous monks, fake "saints," and cowardly partners with whom he is surrounded, and while declining physically he is gaining in comprehension and feels remorse: as an individual, he has a tremendous lust for life, he has inner strength, and it would have suited him better to be with the people than with the exploiters and capitalists. His death coincides with the beginning of the Revolution of 1917.

Boris Zakhava interpreted *Bulychev* in the Vakhtangov Theater in 1932 as a critique of the old order, not from the outside, i.e., from the position of a revolutionary, but from the inside, through the eyes of a man who himself is a part of the world he actually despises and whose collapse he almost welcomes. Zakhava refused to put emphasis on the struggle around the inheritance as the vehicle of the plot, and concentrated on a gallery of comic or repellent figures opposed to the main protagonist. The Communist critics wanted Bulychev to be "exposed and branded as a representative of bourgeoisie" but Zakhava had the courage to reject the suggestions of "vulgar sociologism" and, with the help of Gorky, turned the play into a mild grotesque.

Shchukin interpreted Bulychev as a man full of mischief and innate creative vigor, which explained why he hated parasites, hoarders, and hypocrites. Bulychev's eccentricity is a disguised protest against his environment, and Shchukin showed it through subtle touches. Bulychev's sister, Mother Superior of a convent, is angry with him because he does not give her money, and she suddenly throws her staff at him. After her exit, Bulychev takes the staff, tries to break or bend it, and finally makes a movement as if it were a billiard cue, pretending to hit an imaginary ball.

Bulychev became one of the best productions of the Vakhtangov Theater, and was taken up by theaters throughout the country, including the Moscow Art (under Sakhnovsky's direction). *Dostigayev and the Others,* a sequel to *Bulychev,* concerning political intrigues of his partner in the period between the overthrow of tsarism and the bolshevik victory, was less successful: it lacked the sweep and the satirical bite of the first play.

Gorky's old dramas were usually interpreted in traditional forms of nineteenth-century realism, and although they became an organic part of national repertory, they hardly offered Soviet directors outstanding scenic material, with the exception of *The Lower Depths, Vassa Zheleznova,* and *Bulychev and the Others.* As for the number of performances, the plays by Gorky almost matched those of Ostrovsky. In 1939 thirty plays by Ostrovsky led in the RSSR with 12,913 performances.

VI

Of all the theaters of the twenties, the Kamerny had the longest life, but it was bought at the price of sacrifice and compromise. With his usual cunning, Tairov allotted a place of honor in his repertory to Soviet plays and alternated them with performances in which he gave free rein to his artistic inventiveness. This made the whole career of the theater very uneven and tortuous, but all the stratagems did not save it from dangerous straits. What helped Tairov in his staging of Soviet dramas was the heroic and romantic character he gave to such plays as Vishnevsky's *Optimistic Tragedy* which the Communists considered one of his best achievements. He was less successful with *Men of Might* by Dem-

yan Bedny, a well-established Party poet. This was a parody of
Russia's legendary past staged as a colored print by Tairov, but
it came at the wrong moment: in 1936 patriotism and rehabilita-
tion of national history became an official trend, and *Men of
Might* provoked a scandal as a "blunder, calumny, and ideological mistake," denounced in all Party papers. Tairov quickly produced Gorky's *Children of the Sun* in order to show his political
loyalty, but the Arts Committee did not find it sufficient and
took its own measures to cure the Kamerny of its defects: it
merged the company with that of the Realistic Theater led by
Okhlopkov (1937). At that moment Okhlopkov dreamt of heroic,
almost naturalistic, performances with large crowds, and his
Kochubey by Alexander Perventsev, instead of being an eighteenth-century historic drama, became a contemporary show. A
rift between him and Tairov, and his group and the rest of the
Kamerny company made things insufferable, and the newcomers
had to leave in 1939. During the next year the Kamerny scored
a big success with *Madame Bovary,* interpreted by Koonen as
the tragedy of a noble, idealistic woman trying to escape her
bourgeois environment. Tairov built the stage as a central place
for Emma Bovary, surrounded by "cells of triviality" for all the
other protagonists. The conflict between the poetic soul and the
rut of middle-class banality was understood by the critics as an
attack against capitalism.

At the end of the thirties when the war against "formalists
and decadents" in the theater was waged by all governmental
agencies and the Party press, Tairov resuscitated his "theory of
structural realism" which once served him as an argument against
the "proletarians" campaign of 1930-1931. In a rather confused
manner he affirmed the dependence of the inner structure of a
play and the dynamics of a character on the structure of reality,
i.e., on the composition of society, and claimed that all his search
was inspired by these dialectics. He tried to stress the kinship of
"structural realism" with "socialist realism" but Communist
critics refused to admit it. In any case, Tairov's readiness to "meet
Marxism halfway," as some reviewers remarked, put him in the
category of repentant sinner. In the era of trials and terror, political recantation was followed by "artistic penance." Okhlopkov,

Zakhava, and many others publicly recognized their former mistakes and repudiated "estheticism, individualism, formalism, and other bourgeois deviations."

War curtailed the Kamerny's activities, the theater was evacuated, produced a few patriotic plays and, upon its return to Moscow, gave a remarkable interpretation in 1946 of Chekhov's *The Sea Gull*. The joke in Moscow was that the sea gull became Tairov's "swan song." He made it a concert presentation with strong symbolic overtones, with black velvet drapes as main setting, and the actors wearing black (some reviewers spoke of the funereal mood of the evening). He used dialogues between Trigorin and Treplev for discussion of naturalism and other trends in the theater, and Treplev's search for new forms sounded very much like an attack on the drabness of socialist realism. But in the same 1946, when Zhdanov and the Party Central Committee condemned all formalism and experimentation in literature and the arts, Tairov tried to make pitiful statements about his own position, quoting Gorky and pretending to follow the Communist line in his own productions. His theater, however, became the target of vicious criticism and was liquidated in 1949. Tairov died in 1950.

A much more tragic fate befell Meyerhold, this last Mohican of the glorious twenties.

Since the beginning of the thirties Meyerhold's position in the Party was shattered. Many of his influential friends, such as Rykov and Tomsky, were accused of Trotskyism or of "ideological errors," while Bukharin was ousted from the Central Committee. Official agencies, such as the Repertory Committee in 1932 and the All-Union Committee of the Arts, never missed the opportunity to accuse Meyerhold of "formalism," and between 1932 and 1934 sharply reproached him for his "inimical attitude toward socialist realism."

Occasionally he still offered some brilliant performances, but his theater showed signs of decline; there was an inner rift in his company, disappointed by the arrogance of the Master and the powerful influence exercised by Raikh, his wife, on all theatrical issues. By the middle of the thirties a whole group of actors left Meyerhold's theater; quite a few of them quoted his contradictory attitudes as the main reason for their defection. There is

no doubt that during these years Meyerhold vainly attempted
some reconciliation of his theories with the reality of Soviet life.
He continued to aim at "a synthetic spectacle using a great variety
of means, just like Wagner, merging music, light, and rhythmic
movement." But he also began to talk about the necessity "to
bring beauty to our country." It is true that he spoke of "esthetic
constructivism" and pointed at Ford's automobiles as examples
of functional beauty, but he also made statements which could be
explained only by his aversion to the revival of theatrical realism.
"In our present conditions," he declared, "we have to renounce
our old slogan 'down with loveliness.' Construction should be
beautiful." Although he did produce Vishnevsky's *The Final
Decisive . . .*, with machine guns and revolver shots and all sorts
of military properties, he publicly opposed plays dealing with
civil war and the first years of the Revolution, and interpreted
the attitude of the audiences in these words: "How happy we are
that it is all over." He found agitational plays in which *"raisonneurs* made theoretical speeches" antiartistic and obnoxious. In
his opinion, the Soviet stage needed more smiles and variety,
more light, music, and uplifting art. His production of *Krechinsky's Wedding* in 1933, with Iliinsky portraying the swindled as
a magician and an agent of foreign capital, was conceived in this
spirit. But as usual, Meyerhold's public statements did not fully
correspond to his theatrical experiments. In search of "actuality,"
he produced in 1932 *Introduction* by Yuri Gherman, another
illustration of European decline. This half drama, half parody was
presented in a pointedly exaggerated manner, its two protagonists
being Kelberg, a talented engineer who is compelled to manu-
facture toilet paper, and Nunbach, another victim of the capitalist
order reduced to selling pornographic post cards. This vision of
pre-Hitler Germany ends with Kelberg departing for the USSR,
and Nunbach committing suicide after having kissed the bust of
Goethe. Critics did not approve of this play because it failed to
show "the progressive forces." It seemed, however, at this point,
that whatever Meyerhold did was bound to provoke hostile reviews in the official press. In 1934 his production of Dumas' *La
Dame aux camélias* was a sensational success with the public. For
once he hardly touched the text and concentrated on re-creating
the atmosphere of the France of 1840. The drama of Marguerite

Gautier, the tubercular courtesan who yields to sentimental love, was interpreted by Raikh in a slightly cold, almost contrived manner, but she did succeed in creating a poetic, chaste image, in accord with the style of the whole production, which was elegant, brilliant, and superficial. Communist critics attacked it as "glorification of bourgeois mentality," as "emotional trash," and "antidemocratic sortie of ideological enemies."

In 1935 Meyerhold returned to the opera and showed Tchaikovsky's *Queen of Spades* in Leningrad (and the next year in Moscow). Like the Dumas drama, it belonged to his last artistic attainments. He presented the story of Hermann's gambling passion and Liza's unhappy love as a grim tragedy with mystical overtones, and introduced into it some elements from "The Bronze Horseman," the famous and magnificent poem about Pyotr the Great as the symbol of historical necessity opposed to the fate of a lonely individual. Instead of following the old libretto and setting the action in the time of Yekaterina, he unfolded it against the severe landscape of Nikolay I's St. Petersburg, concentrating on pictorial settings and bringing in Pushkin's text. It was an impressive spectacle of great artistic unity, and it was a great success with the public.

Yet Meyerhold's general situation was deteriorating steadily. In January 1936 *Pravda*, the central organ of the Party, came out with an article against *Katerina Izmailova*, an opera by Shostakovich based on a story by Leskov, *The Lady Macbeth of Mtsensk District*, calling it "nonsense" and attacking violently other composers for not writing scores in the style of socialist realism. This condemnation came at a time when Soviet music included such composers as Prokofiev, Khachaturian, Kabalevsky, Myaskovsky, Shebalin (accused of having written music for Meyerhold's productions), Shaporin, Dzerzhinsky, Krein, and Khrennikov, and when numerous first-rate performers were being trained in excellent schools. The development of Russian music was very high in the thirties, but it showed too much kinship with Western modernism and too much advanced experimentation. The article in *Pravda* was the signal for a final assault on the "vestiges of formalism" in all fields of art, and was followed by others on ballet and painting. This meant that the Government had decided to liquidate the heretics and to impose uniformity ruthlessly. Political purge and incredible trials were eliminating Stalin's enemies. A similar kind of purge was taking care of "hostile elements" in literature, theater, music, and painting. In fact, the witch hunt was extended to all realms of creative activity.

Although Meyerhold was publicly dubbed "the head of formalism in the theater," some Party officials made an attempt to win him over to the side of the angels, and even succeeded in making him deliver a speech in which he recognized his errors and spoke of true realism as being his artistic aim. But this momentary "repentance" did not help him. The plays he was about to produce (by Seifullina and by Ostrovsky) were banned by the authorities after the dress rehearsal. Credits for his theater were stopped. Attacks by the press against him increased in violence. He was denounced as an enemy of realism, a "class alien" director who spread slander against the Soviet way of life, a politically dangerous individual. By this time (December 1937) other theaters had already capitulated, having recognized their past mistakes and promising complete obedience to the official line. But Meyerhold kept silent, and in January 1938, the Committee on the Arts ordered the closing of his theater. The fact that a few days later Kerzhentsev, Chairman of the Committee and the author of the article that accused Meyerhold of all sorts of crimes, was fired and his aides arrested, could hardly reassure Russia's great director who found himself unemployed, completely isolated, and branded as an enemy of the regime. At this tragic moment of his life, the only friendly gesture came from Stanislavsky, his former adversary. The old director had the courage to offer Meyerhold a position in the Moscow Art Theater Studios, but Stanislavsky died in the same year, 1938.

It is not known what Meyerhold did until June 1939, when he appeared at the All-Union Convention of theater directors. This gathering was arranged as a public manifestation of submission and artistic recantation. Andrey Vyshinsky, the Attorney General of the USSR and the prosecutor at the trials of the Bolshevik old guard, made the keynote speech as Party delegate. But Meyerhold also made a speech and it stunned the convention. He rejected the silly accusations of his enemies, and asked whether a master had no right to experiment and to check his creative ideas. He affirmed that what was going on in the theater was "frightful

and pitiful," and identified it with socialist realism. "This has
nothing to do with art, "exlaimed Meyerhold, "and without art
there is no theater." When one reads the full text of Meyerhold's
speech, published by Yuri Yelaghin in his *Taming of the Arts,* one
is greatly impressed by the courage and bitter sarcasm with which
Meyerhold hit murderous uniformity and official intolerance in
the arts. The conclusion of his bold and sensational statements
was that stupidity and pettiness were "eliminating art in Soviet
Russia." Three days later he was arrested and disappeared into
some Arctic concentration camp. Whether he died in exile or
committed suicide after having been liberated during the war is
still a matter of conjecture. Soon after his arrest, Zinaida Raikh
was found assassinated in her apartment, her throat cut, her face
disfigured, and knife wounds all over her body. Police reports
attributed the murder to an unknown tramp.

VII

The conservative, reactionary trend in arts promoted by the
Party under the slogans of "down with formalism" and "long
live socialist realism," reached its peak in 1936. It was enhanced
by administrative measures: between 1936 and 1939 numerous
writers and artists were arrested, exiled, or executed. During
these years such writers as Pilnyak, Babel, Mandelstam, Kirshon, together with a score of literary and dramatic critics, were
sent to concentration camps or executed by firing squads. The
period of the triumph of socialist realism and artistic uniformity
lasted until Stalin's death in 1953. It was interrupted in 1941
by the patriotic war against Germany which provided some re-
spite, but was resumed with increased intensity in 1946.

The gigantic efforts of total war, the terrible destruction
wrought by the German invaders, the ordeal of suffering and
starvation to which millions of Russians were subjected, disrupted
normal life and forced a number of theaters to close their doors.
Many Moscow and Leningrad theaters were evacuated to the
Urals or Central Asia, and even upon their return it took them a
long time to resume their activities. On the other hand, special
brigades of actors were formed to bring performances to the
army, and particularly to the fighters on the front. Quite naturally

the selection of plays and the manner in which they were staged depended upon material conditions which demanded the utmost economy of means and excluded any elaborate *mise en scène*. By 1944 there were twenty-five regular theaters on various segments of the front, organized either as independent units or as branches of existing enterprises. The total number of theatrical brigades was 3,685, and their companies were comprised of 42,000 men and women. They gave a total of 1,350,000 performances for the army and air forces.

The functioning of theaters in the rear, including those evacuated from Moscow, Leningrad, Kiev, and other cities, was hazardous and was assured only through sacrifice and devotion of actors and directors, and the response of the public.

For instance, in besieged and bombed Leningrad thousands of spectators wrapped in furs, blankets, and mufflers jammed the unheated halls and applauded *Emilia Galeotti* by Lessing, *La Dame aux camélias* by Dumas, and *Othello* by Shakespeare, or Soviet dramas such as *The Tempering of Steel*, adapted from Nikolay Ostrovsky's best-seller, *The Keys of Berlin,* by Gus and Finn, a chronicle of the Seven Years War when the Russians defeated the troops of Frederick the Great and occupied the German capital. The opera house was crammed, particularly when *Eugene Oneghin, Queen of Spades, Traviata,* or the ballet *Esmeralda* were offered. And the radio broadcast scenes from *Hamlet, Romeo and Juliet,* and contemporary plays by Soviet dramatists. One can only imagine what price the actors and producers had to pay to secure the operation of their institutions in the besieged city, hit by epidemics and starvation. At the same time, they served the front: in the first year of war Leningrad actors, singers, and musicians gave twenty-five thousand performances for the army, navy, and air force.

Of course, in the deep rear material conditions were better, but even in the cities far removed from the line of fire, theaters had many difficulties. Indirectly, the lack of settings and properties favored certain simplicity of staging which assumed at times the character of the abstract or even symbolist *mise en scène*. There is no doubt that war permitted directors such as Okhlopkov, Akimov, Zakhava, and Zavadsky to do things they would not have dared to try in Moscow under the eye of central authorities.

Besides, the latter loosened their controls over the arts because they were engaged in a mortal struggle for existence.

From the first months of the war, the repertory of most theaters comprised new plays reflecting the tragic events, patriotic dramas written before 1941, and some popular classics (including some thirty plays by Ostrovsky).

At the beginning, war plays were hastily put together and lacked any literary quality. The same defect of journalistic primitivism and rhetorical artificiality marred most of the dramas and comedies between 1941 and 1945, and this included such plays as *War* by Victor Stavsky, *The Navy Officer* by Alexander Kron, *The Men of Stalingrad* by Yuri Chepurin (which had some merit as a documentary chronicle), *The Victors* by Boris Chirskov, *The Illustrious Family* by Boris Romachov, *The Blue Kerchief* by Valentin Katayev, and *Soldier Wives* by Nikolay Virta (the latter three about life in the rear).

Only four plays stand out in all these productions: *The Front* by Alexander Korneychuk, *The Russians* by Konstantin Simonov, *The Invasion* by Leonid Leonov (all three published in 1942) and *Lyonushka,* also by Leonov (1943).

The success of *The Front* was due to the fact that it dealt frankly with the problem of Russia's initial reverses. Korneychuk portrayed two generations of Soviet commanders. The older one, Ivan Gorlov, formed in revolutionary battles of the twenties, brings to the modern war his dated military conceptions; he is surrounded by conservatives and complacent mediocrities. His younger opponent, Ognyov, is an innovator who understands that new tactics and new technology are needed today. His fight against Gorlov has vital importance for the future of the Red Army. Assisted by the head of the Army's Political Department and by members of Gorlov's family, Ognyov succeeds in replacing the old commander, whose errors have caused military disasters.

The Moscow Art Theater staged *The Front* with utter simplicity, showing a forest where the Army Headquarters was located in the first act, and a snowy Russian landscape with a black German tank in the last. Moskvin interpreted Gorlov as an honest old soldier unable to cope with a complex and changed situation, and Livanov presented an intelligent and well-trained Ognyov is a strategist of the new school. Avoiding any exaggerations, the theater dealt with *The Front* in strictly realistic colors. The Maly Theater also treated the play as a realistic one, but Tsarev made Ognyov a rebel, while Ivan Gorlov was interpreted by Shamin as an ignorant, pretentious, and ridiculous individual. State Academic Drama Theater, Vakhtangov's and many others throughout the country, however, presented Korneychuk's piece as a political revelation, and staged it as a meeting or debate addressed to the audience, using big strokes, grotesque in the portrayal of negative characters, and schematic, almost symbolic, images. It was a tremendous success with the public and remained a significant document of the period.

While *The Front* was openly political and sociological, *The Russians* by Konstantin Simonov, a poet, contains many lyrical elements projected against the grim reality of destruction and sacrifice. It presents war in two aspects: a town in the south of Russia, occupied by the Germans, with the usual chronicle of treason, torture, fear, and underground activity; and a Red detachment in the outskirts, commanded by Safonov. All the protagonists of the play are simple ordinary people. They are ready to die but, as Safonov puts it, "with sense." This means that they want to resist till the last ditch, and hold in control all their personal feelings. Safonov loves Valia, a nineteen-year-old girl who is to make a third reconnaissance trip to the occupied city, but he does not hesitate to assign her this dangerous mission. And the medical attendant Globa, a cynic and a rake, does not hesitate to cover Valia with his body when the Germans open fire on her and to save her at the price of his own life. They are unassuming, warm-hearted, and honest, and they represent the Russian people. Written almost as a comedy, with many light humorous touches (such as the journalist who does not know how to fire a gun, but marches at the head of a group of soldiers lest he be accused of cowardice), *The Russians* had an intimate quality which made millions of spectators laugh and cry. Diky, in Vakhtangov's theater, incorporated into the play Simonov's poems, "The Roads of Smolensk Region," and "Wait for Me" in which an army man begs his beloved to remain faithful to him and to protect him by the magic force of her love. Both poems enjoyed extraordinary popularity during the war. Nikolay Gorchakov, Stanislavsky's pupil, produced the play in the Moscow

Drama Theater as a highly pathetic drama, enhancing all the climactic moments. In the opening scene he showed the occupied town at night, illuminated by raging fires and projectiles, while the boots of German patrols, shouts, and shots resound in the night. These noises are merged with the music of Shostakovich's Seventh Symphony. The Moscow Art Theater showed a bird's-eye view of the occupied town which rendered the atmosphere of fear and anxiety. Dobronravov interpreted Safonov as a shy, unsophisticated man who rose to commander from his humble position as a cab driver, and who does not dare to confess his love to Valia. And Gribov had Globa sing a licentious song before embarking on the expedition which will cost him his life. The Moscow Art Theater toned down the pathos of the play in order to stress sacrifice and patriotism as natural manifestations of Russian organic heroism.

Encouraged by the success of *The Russians,* Simonov turned his poem "Wait for Me" into a drama, but his new play was rather mediocre.

Leonov's plays, as usual, were based on inner psychological conflicts. Talanov, the hero of *The Invasion,* comes to his native town after his release from prison and concentration camp as an embittered foe of the regime. But the German occupation provokes a deep change in him. The lone wolf, as he calls himself, becomes concerned with other people and with his country. The former criminal fights the invaders and, caught by them, pretends to be Kolesnikov, the chief of a guerilla band the invaders are vainly trying to destroy. Talanov deliberately chooses death in order to protect Kolesnikov and his men, and he dies at peace with his conscience. His mother identifies him as Kolesnikov, thus accepting and blessing his sacrifice. The gradual "conversion" of Talanov and the dramatic situations which formed the plot of *Invasion,* made it a tense, breathtaking play.

At the Theater of the Moscow Soviet, Zavadsky carefully studied all the details of his production and emphasized the tragic elements of Talanov's growth into a hero. The Maly Theater, where Solovyov appeared as Talanov, *Invasion* was treated as a strictly realistic piece. At the Leningrad State Academic Drama Theater, Kozich decided that Leonov did not show sufficiently the role of the Party in the struggle against the invaders and therefore pushed the figure of Talanov into the background while giving particular relief to Kolesnikov, the leader of the partisans and a Party man. This distortion of the play was foreshadowing the trend that prevailed in the late forties: all the merit of repelling Hitler had to be ascribed to the Party members and to the "leadership of Stalin."

Lyonushka, Leonov's second play, depicted the love of a Russian girl for a flier who was badly burnt when his plane was shot down by the German. He is hidden in the partisans' camp in the heart of a forest, and Lyonushka does everything to instill life and hope into her dying lover. The scenes in the camp, the songs and dances staged for the flier, have a strong national and symbolic flavor, and this is probably why *Lyonushka,* despite its obvious patriotic spirit, was not too popular with theatrical directors: they were afraid of being accused of formalistic tendencies and ideological deviations if they presented the play as it ought to be, namely, in nonrealistic terms. Nevertheless, it is a very interesting and complex drama.

VIII

At the end of the war many observers (including the author of this book) expected a liberalization of the regime and a more tolerant attitude toward the arts. Their hopes, however, were frustrated and, instead of loosening, Party controls were tightened in a most intransigent way. All compromises of the war years were canceled, and the period which began in 1946 became one of the worst in the history of Russian literature and theater. The signal for the general offensive was given by the resolution of the Central Committee of the All Union Communist Party of August 14, 1946, which condemned the prominent writers, Akhmatova and Zoshchenko, and two Leningrad monthlies for their political and ideological deviations. Andrey Zhdanov, a member of the Politbureau, spelled out the policy of the government in his comments. He quoted Lenin's words: "Literature must become Party literature. Down with non-Party literati, down with literary supermen. Literary work must become a part of all proletarian endeavor." "The aim of literature," continued Zhdanov, "is to help the State to educate the youth . . . and its purpose is to portray the Soviet Man and his qualities in full force and completeness . . . in performing this task it must protect itself against the poisonous miasmas of Western bourgeois art. Soviet literature is the most advanced, progressive, and revolutionary literature of the world, and Soviet writers have to attack the degenerated decadent bourgeois culture." And since formalism was proclaimed the typical outgrowth of capitalist art, two practical conclusions were drawn from these premises: formalism, experimentation, and kowtowing to Western culture or cosmopolitism are the most insidious enemies, and the struggle against them is a civic duty.

In no time the offensive, which assumed strong nationalistic and, at times, anti-Semitic overtones, was in full swing. Literary critics, playwrights, painters, and musicians were called to order, each in due turn. Party officials demanded "popular, simple, realistic art, suitable to the masses, as the only art befitting the great epoch of Socialism which is already looking forward to Communism." Socialist realism now meant an assertion of Russia's superiority in all fields combined with vitriolic attacks on European and American civilizations, and a cheerful, optimistic exaltation of Soviet positive heroes. In all novels and plays, the authors had to maintain "ideological integrity," in other words, strict conformity to official instructions. In the theater the latter were contained in a special resolution of the Central Committee (August 26, 1946) entitled "About the repertory of drama theaters and measures of its improvement": "Dramatic literature and the theaters must reflect in plays and performances the life of Soviet society in its incessant surge forward, and contribute fully to further development of the best sides of Soviet Man's character which have been shown so patently during the Great Fatherland War. Playwrights and directors must make Soviet youth spirited, optimistic, devoted to their country, believing in the victory of our cause, unafraid of obstacles and capable of overcoming any difficulty. The Soviet theater must also show that such qualities belong, not to a few elect ones or to heroes, but to many millions of Soviet people." This program was crowned by the following statement: "The Soviet theater owes all its successes, all its achievements, to the Communist

Party and its wise, truly Marxian solution of problems." A few years later (in 1954) the monumental *History Of Soviet Russian Theater* stated in the preface: "Soviet culture stands against the disgusting man-hating bourgeois 'culture' of imperialist America and capitalist countries of Western Europe which is used by new war-mongers as a weapon of ideological aggression."

The playwrights, obeying the command, produced between 1947 and 1949 a series of anti-American plays, among them *The Russian Question* and *The Foreign Shadow* by Simonov, *The Ill-Starred Haberdasher* by Anatoly Surov, *I Want to go Home* by Serghei Mikhalkov, *The Voice of America* by Lavrenyov, and scores of other potboilers in which tycoons, spies, Congressmen, diversonists, and corrupted journalists were opposed by Russian pure hearts and Revolutionary heroes. Plays dealing with the home front were no better. Vishnevsky in his *Unforgettable 1919* extolled Stalin's role in the defense of Petrograd against the Whites sustained by Churchill, and distorted history in order to glorify the Party. Serghei Mikhalkov in *Ilya Golovin* (1949) told the story of a composer (very similar to Prokofiev) who did not pay enough attention to the criticism of his symphonies by the Party press. Of course, those very symphonies, to the composers's dismay, were praised by American broadcasters. At the end, Golovin meets law-abiding Soviet citizens, recognizes his formalistic intoxication, turns for inspiration to the masses, and begins writing popular, national scores in the style of socialist realism. These kinds of plays were manufactured by the dozen, and by 1952 even Communist critics became appalled by their monotony and lack of taste and thought. Some of the plays sounded like parodies. In order to be "realistic," the author of the industrial play, *The White Van* filled a whole dialogue with quotations from a textbook on oil wells. In another play, Vanya, an agronomist, is passionately in love with Tanya, a *kolkhoz* girl and marries her, but soon leaves her because she has reactionary ideas about the method of growing potatoes. What made dramatists write such idiotic things was the fear of repressions and the desire for conformity. Censors and critics did everything to develop this mood. The playwright Afanassy Salynsky confessed in 1953: "Next to me at my desk sits an 'inner censor' and he ties down my thoughts and my tongue; he says, 'This is permitted, this is not permitted.' And on top of that, officials of repertory committee have also a word to say."

In his play *New Times*, G. Mdivani showed a chairman of a *kolkhoz* who has no special agricultural training and who understands his lack of preparation when confronted with new technology. Local censors felt that such a dangerous play should be banned: many chairmen, they argued, are actually in the same shoes, and they would resent being exposed in the theater.

By the way, a story by Valentin Ovechkin was criticized because he made the second Party secretary more intelligent than the first one and thus shattered the faith in Party justice. And Pogodin tells us that he concluded his play, *The Battle of the Lances* with a scene where a committee meets for "a distribution of rewards and punishments" because he "was afraid that without it the play would not pass."

In 1953, even Malenkov had to own that the results of the policy adopted in 1946 were rather poor and, together with leading Communist critics, attributed this to the reluctance of playwrights to present conflicts. For a couple of years, there was a heated discussion about the problem of conflicts in Soviet repertory: many dramatists felt that it was safer not to talk about contradictions and clashes, and they produced flat and pointless but highly optimistic plays which resembled "wine without alcohol," according to a daring reviewer.

The spectators reacted to this dull and contrived repertory by deserting the theaters when contemporary Soviet plays were presented. At the same time, all the other shows were crammed, and throughout the country theaters were attracting huge and appreciative audiences. In 1952, the current joke in Moscow was: "You will find good Soviet theater at the cemetery, and the cemetery at the Soviet theater." In 1951, Soviet plays made up 55 per cent of the whole repertory, and they dropped to 41 per cent in 1952. But these figures did not reflect the number of performances. For instance, in the Moscow Art Theater only 86 out of 467 performances were of contemporary Soviet plays; in the Maly, 128 out of 523; and in Vakhtangov's classics numbered three times as many performances as the "topical" Soviet plays. Some second-rate comedies had more success with the public than political or "industrial" plays highly publicized in the Communist press. Already by 1952 *Pravda* stated in an article which deplored the situation in the theaters: "The reason for dramatic poverty is that the playwrights do not base their words on deep conflicts. If one had to judge our life by those plays, one would come to the conclusion that everything is ideal, marvelous, that we have no conflicts. The playwrights think that it is prohibited to criticize the negative aspects of our reality."

Stalin's death in 1953 brought about a radical change. For some three or four years a "thaw" set in in literature, theater, and music. Writers and critics who had been banished or executed were now rehabilitated. After fifteen years of forced silence, periodicals could mention the name of Meyerhold. Comedies and dramas turned to personal problems of love and family, and satirical plays exposed different defects and shortcomings of Soviet society. In the Ukraine, by 1956, 60 per cent of contemporary repertory was light comedy like such hits as *Without Making Names* by V. Minko, who laughed at Soviet bureaucrats behaving like typical bourgeoisie. In Leningrad seven theaters staged forty new plays, of which only twelve were devoted to the contemporary Soviet reality. At the same time, plays by Barrie, Priestley, Sauvageon, Osborne, and other Western authors had most successful runs. Family and love dramas and comedies by native playwrights continued to be box office hits even though few of them had true literary merit. Theatergoers liked *Alone* by Serghey Aleshin, *Best Wishes* and *Eternally Alive* by Victor Rozov, *Anna Berezko's Love* by Pistolenko, *The Wheel of Fortune* by brothers Tur, *Svetlana* by Lavrentiev. All of them dealt with problems of unrequited love, marriage, divorce, women left alone by husbands who had found new passion. There was a considerable expansion of subject matter, resulting in a greater variety of plays offered by the leading theaters. The authors showed more independence in dealing with industrialization and social and political work.

A good example of the new climate was provided by two plays by Pogodin, one of the favorite playwrights, equally accepted by the general public and by the critics. In *The Three Who Went to Unploughed Lands,* he depicted as a difficult and often ungrateful task the crusade of the youth for the colonization of the steppes in the southeast of Russia, acclaimed by he Party officials and patronized by Khrushchev, and did not spare dark color in portraying young opportunists, climbers, or outright knaves. The customary presentation of the "positive hero" with a halo of Communist saintliness was replaced by a more sober and realistic characterization. *Petrarch's Sonnet,* another play by Pogodin (1956) shifted from social to personal issues. Its hero, Sukhodolov, the elderly head of a big industrial project in Siberia, falls in love with Maya, a young and charming librarian. Sukhodolov is aware of the difference in age between himself and his beloved, and does not want anything from her; he is satisfied with a platonic relationship. The letters he writes her, opening his heart are stolen and copied by Maya's nosey friend and the whole affair becomes a public scandal. Sukhodolov's wife leaves him, and the Party calls him to order. But Sukhodolov denies its right to meddle with his privacy and determine his intimate feelings. His dialogue with the secretary of the local organization is a passionate defense of Petrarchian love and of great emotions which are as important as great plants or dams. Thousands of spectators listened enraptured to such heretical opinions.

No less important was the comeback of Mayakovsky's *The Bedbug,* produced by several directors in the manner of Meyerhold after a twenty-five year ban. Particularly significant was the staging by Valentin Pluchek in the Theater of Satire, with mildly constructivist settings, and in the style of utter grotesquerie. Another interesting production of Mayakovsky was directed by Yutkevich. Several directors, such as Akimov, who returned to the Comedy Theater, Okhlopkov (in his *Hamlet*), Zavadsky, and others, made attempts at experimentation in the spirit of the twenties, and although their performances were isolated phenomena, they indicated what the direction of the Russian theater might have been if it acquired full freedom of expression. The success of certain "small forms" such as the one-man performances by the satirist Arkady Raikin, also showed the interest of theatergoers in parody and the grotesque liberated from the shackles of socialist realism.

In 1956, the "thaw" reached its highest point. It coincided with a boom in theater business and also in film production. Crippled by the war, this industry again flourished, and films made by old and new directors, such as Dovzhenko, Romm,

Chukhray, and others, matched to a certain extent the great creations of the thirties made by Eisenstein and Pudovkin.

The Soviet press of 1956 gave interesting figures about the place occupied by legitimate theaters in the USSR (theaters of the armed services, of trade unions, and amateurs were included in these statistics). In addition to the 335 regular drama and comedy theaters, there were 32 with permanent opera and ballet companies, 20 for operetta, and 101 children's and young people's theaters. Most of these enterprises were perfectly equipped, well organized and possessed their own buildings, workshops, settings, and costumes; their audiences counted by the dozens of millions. The Moscow Art Theater still maintained the moral and material leadership. Every night 2,300 spectators filled its two halls; its company numbered 148 actors, and its budget was made 80 per cent by ticket sales and 20 per cent by State subsidy. Regular actors performed from eleven to twenty-two times a month, and twenty-seven plays formed the main "stock repertory" of the theater.

The political situation on the morrow of the Hungarian Revolution of 1956 brought about "cold winds," according to a euphemistic expression of a Soviet journalist. It looked as if the Communist leaders became frightened by the growing signs of intellectual and artistic independence and decided to curb the movement toward greater freedom in the arts. In 1957 and 1958 there was a definite feeling that the clock was being turned back. The official press started a campaign against "revisionism" and opened a discussion on socialist realism which was again presented as "the most progressive and ideologically sound theory."

In its message to the Third Congress of Soviet Writers in May 1959, the Central Committee of the Party reiterated its old tenets: "Soviet writers must inspire people in their struggle for Communism, must educate them according to Communist principles, must develop in them high moral virtues and intransigent rejection of bourgeois ideology and morals. . . . Writers must become passionate propagandists of the Seven-Year Plan and bring cheerfulness, vigor and energy into the heart of man." Other public speeches and articles confirmed that the same guiding principles were applied to the theater and art.

Although the social command was couched in old terms and

the Party did not seem to renounce its controls or its pressure on the artist, there was a difference in tone and a shift in emphasis of most plays produced between 1958 and 1961. On the whole, we find more diversity in plot, more humanity in the treatment of emotions, more independence and objectivity in description of the bright and the dark sides of Communist reality. Of course, the road to be taken by the Russian theater is officially prescribed by the Kremlin, and the Party never misses the opportunity to stress its educational aims. But in the late fifties less intransigence was shown by the censorship and there were certain timid innovations in staging. The plays of that period did not offer anything spectacular, and it is no wonder that none of them has been taken up by the theaters in America or the non-Communist countries of Europe, but they presented a certain local interest. More lively than the stereotypes of the Stalin era were such plays as *The Irkutsk Story* by Alexey Arbuzov, who introduced a kind of Greek chorus into a contemporary drama (produced by Okhlopkov); *Unequal Battle* by Victor Rozov, emphasizing the sharp conflict of two generations; *Farewell to White Nights* by Vera Panova, an excellent writer who depicted the love life of Soviet youth; and light comedies by Anatoly Sofronov and Alexander Volodin.

It is true that "formalism" and "estheticism" continue to be catchwords to denigrate any "deviation from realism." The Russian theater still has a long way to go before it acquires a tenth of the freedom and variety it possessed in the twenties. But its march forward is an irreversible process, and we would like to believe that its future will be worthy of its glorious past.

INDEX

(Russian names in this book have been transliterated according to a definite system. However, where a deviation from the rule has already become established in general American usage, such as for example Tchaikovsky or Chaliapin, the more familiar spelling has been adopted.)

ABOUT THE AUTHOR

Born in Novgorod-Seversk, Russia, Marc Slonim was educated
at the University of Petrograd (Russia) and at the University
of Florence (Italy). In 1941 he came to the United States. Active
as a literary critic for many years, he has served as editor of
several Russian periodicals. Since 1949 Mr. Slonim has been a
contributor to the Book Review Section of *The New York Times*,
and he is well known for his articles about literature, which have
been published in both American and European journals. He
has taught for many years and has been visiting professor at a
number of European and American colleges and universities.
Since 1943, he has been a member of the faculty of Sarah Law-
rence College, where he teaches courses in comparative literature.

Mr. Slonim is the author of *The Epic of Russian Literature
From Its Origins Through Tolstoy* (1950); *Modern Russian
Literature From Chekhov to the Present* (1953); *Three Loves
of Dostoevsky* (1955); *An Outline of Russian Literature* (1958);
and other books. He is also the editor of *Modern Italian Short
Stories* (1954); and, in collaboration with George Reavey, he
edited and translated *Soviet Literature: An Anthology* (1934).
Translations of his work have been published in French, Italian,
Spanish, Greek, Japanese, Chinese, and other languages.

This book was set in

Baskerville and Solemnis types by

V and M Typographers.

It was printed and bound by

The Haddon Craftsmen.

Design is by Larry Kamp